TEACHER'S GU

CONNECTED MATHEMATI

Growing, Growing, Growing

Exponential Functions

Glenda Lappan, Elizabeth Difanis Phillips,
James T. Fey, Susan N. Friel

PEARSON

Boston, Massachusetts • Chandler, Arizona • Glenview, Illinois • Hoboken, New Jersey

Connected Mathematics™ was developed at Michigan State University with financial support from the Michigan State University Office of the Provost, Computing and Technology, and the College of Natural Science.

This material is based upon work supported by the National Science Foundation under Grant No. MDR 9150217 and Grant No. ESI 9986372. Opinions expressed are those of the authors and not necessarily those of the Foundation.

As with prior editions of this work, the authors and administration of Michigan State University preserve a tradition of devoting royalties from this publication to support activities sponsored by the MSU Mathematics Education Enrichment Fund.

Acknowledgments appear on page 290, which constitutes an extension of this copyright page.

PEARSON

13-digit ISBN 978-0-13-327664-0
10-digit ISBN 0-13-327664-3
5 6 7 8 9 10 V001 17 16

Authors

A Team of Experts

Glenda Lappan is a University Distinguished Professor in the Program in Mathematics Education (PRIME) and the Department of Mathematics at Michigan State University. Her research and development interests are in the connected areas of students' learning of mathematics and mathematics teachers' professional growth and change related to the development and enactment of K–12 curriculum materials.

Elizabeth Difanis Phillips is a Senior Academic Specialist in the Program in Mathematics Education (PRIME) and the Department of Mathematics at Michigan State University. She is interested in teaching and learning mathematics for both teachers and students. These interests have led to curriculum and professional development projects at the middle school and high school levels, as well as projects related to the teaching and learning of algebra across the grades.

James T. Fey is a Professor Emeritus at the University of Maryland. His consistent professional interest has been development and research focused on curriculum materials that engage middle and high school students in problem-based collaborative investigations of mathematical ideas and their applications.

Susan N. Friel is a Professor of Mathematics Education in the School of Education at the University of North Carolina at Chapel Hill. Her research interests focus on statistics education for middle-grade students and, more broadly, on teachers' professional development and growth in teaching mathematics K–8.

With... Yvonne Grant and Jacqueline Stewart
Yvonne Grant teaches mathematics at Portland Middle School in Portland, Michigan. Jacqueline Stewart is a recently retired high school teacher of mathematics at Okemos High School in Okemos, Michigan. Both Yvonne and Jacqueline have worked on all aspects of the development, implementation, and professional development of the CMP curriculum from its beginnings in 1991.

Development Team

CMP3 Authors

Glenda Lappan, University Distinguished Professor, Michigan State University
Elizabeth Difanis Phillips, Senior Academic Specialist, Michigan State University
James T. Fey, Professor Emeritus, University of Maryland
Susan N. Friel, Professor, University of North Carolina – Chapel Hill

With...

Yvonne Grant, Portland Middle School, Michigan
Jacqueline Stewart, Mathematics Consultant, Mason, Michigan

In Memory of... William M. Fitzgerald, Professor (Deceased), Michigan State University, who made substantial contributions to conceptualizing and creating CMP1.

Administrative Assistant

Michigan State University
Judith Martus Miller

Support Staff

Michigan State University
Undergraduate Assistants:
Bradley Robert Corlett, Carly Fleming,
Erin Lucian, Scooter Nowak

Development Assistants

Michigan State University
Graduate Research Assistants:
Richard "Abe" Edwards, Nic Gilbertson,
Funda Gonulates, Aladar Horvath,
Eun Mi Kim, Kevin Lawrence, Jennifer Nimtz,
Joanne Philhower, Sasha Wang

Assessment Team

Maine

Falmouth Public Schools
Falmouth Middle School: Shawn Towle

Michigan

Ann Arbor Public Schools
Tappan Middle School:
Anne Marie Nicoll-Turner

Portland Public Schools
Portland Middle School:
Holly DeRosia, Yvonne Grant

Traverse City Area Public Schools
Traverse City East Middle School:
Jane Porath, Mary Beth Schmitt

Traverse City West Middle School:
Jennifer Rundio, Karrie Tufts

Ohio

Clark-Shawnee Local Schools
Rockway Middle School: Jim Mamer

Content Consultants

Michigan State University
Peter Lappan, Professor Emeritus,
Department of Mathematics

Normandale Community College
Christopher Danielson, Instructor,
Department of Mathematics & Statistics

University of North Carolina – Wilmington
Dargan Frierson, Jr., Professor,
Department of Mathematics & Statistics

Student Activities

Michigan State University
Brin Keller, Associate Professor,
Department of Mathematics

Consultants

Indiana
Purdue University
Mary Bouck, Mathematics Consultant

Michigan
Oakland Schools
Valerie Mills, Mathematics Education Supervisor

Mathematics Education Consultants:
Geraldine Devine, Dana Gosen

Ellen Bacon, Independent Mathematics Consultant

New York
University of Rochester
Jeffrey Choppin, Associate Professor

Ohio
University of Toledo
Debra Johanning, Associate Professor

Pennsylvania
University of Pittsburgh
Margaret Smith, Professor

Texas
University of Texas at Austin
Emma Trevino, Supervisor of Mathematics Programs, The Dana Center

Mathematics for All Consulting
Carmen Whitman, Mathematics Consultant

Reviewers

Michigan
Ionia Public Schools
Kathy Dole, Director of Curriculum and Instruction

Grand Valley State University
Lisa Kasmer, Assistant Professor

Portland Public Schools
Teri Keusch, Classroom Teacher

Minnesota
Hopkins School District 270
Michele Luke, Mathematics Coordinator

Field Test Sites for CMP3

Michigan
Ann Arbor Public Schools
Tappan Middle School: Anne Marie Nicoll-Turner*

Portland Public Schools
Portland Middle School: Mark Braun, Angela Buckland, Holly DeRosia, Holly Feldpausch, Angela Foote, Yvonne Grant*, Kristin Roberts, Angie Stump, Tammi Wardwell

Traverse City Area Public Schools
Traverse City East Middle School: Ivanka Baic Berkshire, Brenda Dunscombe, Tracie Herzberg, Deb Larimer, Jan Palkowski, Rebecca Perreault, Jane Porath*, Robert Sagan, Mary Beth Schmitt*

Traverse City West Middle School: Pamela Alfieri, Jennifer Rundio, Maria Taplin, Karrie Tufts*

Maine
Falmouth Public Schools
Falmouth Middle School: Sally Bennett, Chris Driscoll, Sara Jones, Shawn Towle*

Minnesota
Minneapolis Public Schools
Jefferson Community School: Leif Carlson*, Katrina Hayek Munsisoumang*

Ohio
Clark-Shawnee Local Schools
Reid School: Joanne Gilley
Rockway Middle School: Jim Mamer*
Possum School: Tami Thomas

*Indicates a Field Test Site Coordinator

Look for these icons that point to enhanced content in *Teacher Place* Video Interactive Content

Contents

Growing, Growing, Growing

Exponential Functions

Unit Planning

Unit Overview

Unit Description

This Unit continues the discussion of functions by examining exponential functions. Models of exponential growth and decay are numerous such as growth or decay of populations—from bacteria, amoebas, radioactive material and money, to mammals (including people). Doubling, tripling, halving, and so on, are all intuitive situations for students to help them make sense of exponential functions.

The growth pattern in exponential functions is multiplicative. That is, for each additive change in the independent variable, there is a multiplicative change in the dependent variable. For example, in Problem 1.1, students look at the number of ballots created by repeatedly cutting in half a sheet of paper. As the number of cuts increases by one, the number of ballots increases by a factor of two. This factor is called the growth factor.

Investigation 1 continues to look at doubling, tripling, and quadrupling patterns. It ends by contrasting linear and exponential growth factors. Investigation 2 introduces the *y*-intercept, or initial value, which it is sometimes called in exponential growth situations. Investigation 3 introduces growth rates that are not whole numbers and leads to growth rates, usually expressed as percents. Investigation 4 introduces growth factors that are less than one, but greater than zero. These are exponential decay situations. In Investigation 5, patterns with exponents are explored.

The Unit ends by looking at the effects of growth factors and *y*-intercepts on graphs of exponential functions. Since exponential growth patterns can grow rapidly, students may encounter answers on their calculators expressed in scientific notation. Therefore, scientific notation is introduced in Investigation 1 and used throughout the Unit.

Summary of Investigations

Investigation 1: **Exponential Growth**

In Investigation 1, students explore situations that involve repeated doubling, tripling, and quadrupling. Students are introduced to one of the essential features of many exponential patterns: rapid growth. They make and study tables and graphs for exponential situations, describe the patterns they see, and write equations for them, looking for a general form of an exponential equation. They also compare and contrast linear and exponential patterns of growth. For example, in Investigation 1, Plan 1 places 1 ruba on the first square of a chessboard, 2 rubas on the second square, 4 rubas on the third square, etc. Plan 4 places 20 rubas on the first square, 25 rubas on the second, 30 rubas on the third, etc. The relationship between the number of the square on the chessboard and the number of rubas on Plan 1 is an exponential function, and the relationship for Plan 4 is a linear function. The *growth factor* for Plan 1 is 2 and the *constant rate of change* for Plan 4 is 5. Comparing multiplicative growth patterns (exponential functions) with additive growth patterns (linear functions) reinforces understanding of each function.

Investigation 2: Examining Growth Patterns

Investigation 2 focuses on exponential relationships with *y*-intercepts greater than 1. The standard form of an exponential equation is $y = a(b^x)$. When $x = 0$, the equation becomes $y = a$ since $b^0 = 1$. Thus *a*, the coefficient of the exponential term, generally indicates the initial value of the exponentially growing quantity. The growth factor is *b*. As the value of *x* increases by 1, the value of *y* increases by a factor of *b*. By contrast, a linear function is represented by the equation, $y = mx + b$, where *m* is the constant rate of change (or slope) and *b* is the *y*-intercept. Students explore situations given in context, tables, graphs, and equations and determine whether the situation represents an exponential function by identifying the growth factor. They use the growth factor and *y*-intercept to write an equation.

Investigation 3: Growth Factors and Growth Rates

In Investigation 3, students study fractional growth factors greater than 1. They relate these growth factors to growth rates. Some growth patterns such as investments are often expressed as percents. This means that to find the growth rate, the percent increase is calculated and added to the initial, or previous, value. The growth factor is determined by dividing the next value by the previous value. For example, if \$100 is invested at 6% annual interest rate. The value of the account at the start of the 1st year is 100 + 100(.06) or 100(1.06). The *growth factor* in this case is 1.06 while the *growth rate* is 6%, or 0.06. Students also explore how the growth rate and the initial value affect the growth pattern.

Investigation 4: Exponential Decay

Investigation 4 introduces students to exponential decay—patterns of change that exhibit successive, nonconstant decreases rather than increases. These decreasing relationships are generated by repeated multiplication by factors between 0 and 1, called decay factors. Strategies for finding decay factors, the initial population, and for representing decay patterns are similar to those used for exponential growth patterns. Exponential decay patterns are also represented by the equation $y = a(b^x)$; *a* is the *y*-intercept and *b* is the growth factor, which is greater than zero and less than 1.

Investigation 5: Patterns With Exponents

This Investigation develops rules for operating with exponents. Students examine patterns in a powers table for b^x for any *b* and $x = 1, 2, 3, 4, 5, 6, 7, 8, 9$. They look for relationships among numbers written in exponential form. This leads to the rules for operating on numerical expressions with exponents. Fractional exponents are introduced by looking at graphs of populations and asking questions about the population when $x = \frac{1}{2}, \frac{5}{3}$, and so on. *n*th roots are used to interpret and evaluate expressions with rational exponents. From these explorations, students observe that the rules for integral exponents apply to rational exponents. The rules for exponents are used to write and interpret equivalent expressions including some expressed in scientific notation. In the last problem, students use graphing calculators to study the effects of the values of *a* and *b* on the graph of $y = a(b^x)$.

Unit Vocabulary

- exponential form
- exponent
- base
- standard form
- scientific notation
- exponential growth
- growth factor
- exponential functions
- compound growth
- growth rate
- decay factor
- exponential decay
- rate of decay
- nth root

Planning Charts

Investigations & Assessments	Pacing	Materials	Resources
1 Exponential Growth	2 days	**Labsheet 1.1:** Number of Ballots (accessibility) **Labsheet 1ACE:** Exercise 3 (accessibility) **Labsheet 1.2:** Montarek Chessboard (accessibility) **Labsheet 1.3:** Different Reward Plans (accessibility) **Labsheet 1ACE:** Exercises 17–23 (accessibility) **Labsheet 1ACE** Exercise 51 paper, posterboard, transparencies, counters	**Teaching Aid 1.1** Number of Ballots
Mathematical Reflections	½ day		

continued on next page

Planning Charts *continued*

Investigations & Assessments	Pacing	Materials	Resources
2 Examining Growth Patterns	2 days	**Labsheet 2ACE** Exercise 2 **Labsheet 2ACE:** Exercise 3 (accessibility) **Labsheet 2ACE:** Exercise 4 (accessibility) **Labsheet 2ACE** Exercise 33 **Labsheet 2ACE** Exercise 8 **Labsheet 2ACE** Exercise 13 **Labsheet 2ACE:** Exercise 14 (accessibility) **Labsheet 2ACE** Exercises 25–28 **Labsheet 2ACE:** Exercise 33 (accessibility) graphing calculators, graph paper, transparencies	**Teaching Aid 2.1** Water Hyacinth Growth **Teaching Aid 2.2** Mold Experiment **Teaching Aid 2.3** Garter Snake Population Growth
Mathematical Reflections	½ day		
Assessment: Check Up	½ day		• Check Up • Spanish Check Up
3 Growth Factors and Growth Rates	3 days	**Labsheet 3ACE:** Exercise 1 (accessibility) **Labsheet 3.2** Stamp Value Tables **Labsheet 3ACE** Exercise 8 **Labsheet 3ACE** Exercise 9 **Labsheet 3.3** College Funds Table • Centimeter Grid Paper poster board, graphing calculators, graph paper	**Teaching Aid 3.1** Rabbit Population Table
Mathematical Reflections	½ day		
Assessment: Partner Quiz	½ day		• Partner Quiz • Spanish Partner Quiz

continued on next page

Planning Charts *continued*

Investigations & Assessments	Pacing	Materials	Resources
4 Exponential Decay	3 days	**Labsheet 4.1** Ballot Areas Table **Labsheet 4ACE** Exercise 1 **Labsheet 4ACE:** Exercise 3 (accessibility) **Labsheet 4.2** Medicine Table **Labsheet 4.3** Water Cooling Table **Labsheet 4ACE** Exercise 15 **Labsheet 4ACE** Exercise 16 • Inch Grid Paper • Quarter-Inch Grid Paper 8-inch square of grid paper for demo, inch grid paper or quarter-inch grid paper for students, scissors, very hot water, cups for holding hot liquid, watches or clocks with second hand, CBLs, graphing calculators, graph paper, thermometer for measuring room temperature	**Teaching Aid 4.2A** Breakdown of Medicine **Teaching Aid 4.2B** Areas Versus Medicine
Mathematical Reflections	½ day		
5 Patterns With Exponents	6½ days	**Labsheet 5.1A** Table of Positive Powers **Labsheet 5.1B** Table of Negative Powers **Labsheet 5.1C:** Patterns in the Ones Digits (accessibility) **Labsheet 5.2** Rules for Exponents • Labsheet 5.5A (accessibility) • Labsheet 5.5B (accessibility) **Labsheet 5ACE:** Exercise 15 (accessibility)	**Teaching Aid 5.1A** Completed Table of Positive Powers **Teaching Aid 5.1B** Completed Table of Negative Powers • Teaching Aid 5.3
Mathematical Reflections	½ day		

continued on next page

Planning Charts *continued*

Investigations & Assessments	Pacing	Materials	Resources
Looking Back	½ day		
Assessment: Unit Project	Optional 1 day		
Assessment: Self-Assessment	Take Home		• Self-Assessment • Notebook Checklist • Spanish Self-Assessment • Spanish Notebook Checklist
Assessment: Unit Test	1 day		• Unit Test • Spanish Unit Test • Unit Test Correlation
Total	22½ days	**Materials for All Investigations:** calculators; student notebooks; colored pens, pencils, or markers	

Block Pacing (Scheduling for 90-minute class periods)

Investigation	Block Pacing
1 Exponential Growth	**2 days**
Problem 1.1	½ day
Problem 1.2	½ day
Problem 1.3	½ day
Mathematical Reflections	½ day
2 Examining Growth Patterns	**2 days**
Problem 2.1	½ day
Problem 2.2	½ day
Problem 2.3	½ day
Mathematical Reflections	½ day

Investigation	Block Pacing
3 Growth Factors and Growth Rates	**2 days**
Problem 3.1	½ day
Problem 3.2	½ day
Problem 3.3	½ day
Mathematical Reflections	½ day
4 Exponential Decay	**2 days**
Problem 4.1	½ day
Problem 4.2	½ day
Problem 4.3	½ day
Mathematical Reflections	½ day
5 Patterns With Exponents	**4 days**
Problem 5.1	1 day
Problem 5.2	1 day
Problem 5.3	½ day
Problem 5.4	½ day
Problem 5.5	1 day
Mathematical Reflections	½ day

Parent Letter

- Parent Letter (English)
- Parent Letter (Spanish)

Goals and Standards

Goals

Exponential Functions Explore problem situations in which two or more variables have an exponential relationship to each other

- Identify situations that can be modeled with an exponential function
- Identify the pattern of change (growth/decay factor) between two variables that represent an exponential function in a situation, table, graph, or equation
- Represent an exponential function with a table, graph, or equation
- Make connections among the patterns of change in a table, graph, and equation of an exponential function
- Compare the growth/decay rate and growth/decay factor for an exponential function and recognize the role each plays in an exponential situation
- Identify the growth/decay factor and initial value in problem situations, tables, graphs, and equations that represent exponential functions
- Determine whether an exponential function represents a growth (increasing) or decay (decreasing) pattern, from an equation, table, or graph that represents an exponential function
- Determine the values of the independent and dependent variables from a table, graph, or equation of an exponential function
- Use an exponential equation to describe the graph and table of an exponential function
- Predict the *y*-intercept from an equation, graph, or table that represents an exponential function
- Interpret the information that the *y*-intercept of an exponential function represents
- Determine the effects of the growth (decay) factor and initial value for an exponential function on a graph of the function
- Solve problems about exponential growth and decay from a variety of different subject areas, including science and business, using an equation, table, or graph
- Observe that one exponential equation can model different contexts
- Compare exponential and linear functions

Equivalence Develop understanding of equivalent exponential expressions

- Write and interpret exponential expressions that represent the dependent variable in an exponential function
- Develop the rules for operating with rational exponents and explain why they work
- Write, interpret, and operate with numerical expressions in scientific notation
- Write and interpret equivalent expressions using the rules for exponents and operations
- Solve problems that involve exponents, including scientific notation

Standards

Common Core Content Standards

8.EE.A.1 Know and apply the properties of integer exponents to generate equivalent numerical expressions. *Investigation 5*

8.EE.A.2 Use square root and cube root symbols to represent solutions to equations of the form $x^2 = p$ and $x^3 = p$, where p is a positive rational number. Evaluate square roots of small perfect squares and cube roots of small perfect cubes. Know that $\sqrt{2}$ is irrational. *Investigation 5*

8.EE.A.3 Use numbers expressed in the form of a single digit times an integer power of 10 to estimate very large or very small quantities, and to express how many times as much one is than the other. For example, estimate the population of the United States as 3×10^8 and the population of the world as 7×10^9, and determine that the world population is more than 20 times larger. *Investigations 1 and 2*

8.EE.A.4 Perform operations with numbers expressed in scientific notation, including problems where both decimal and scientific notation are used. Use scientific notation and choose units of appropriate size for measurements of very large or very small quantities (e.g., use millimeters per year for seafloor spreading). Interpret scientific notation that has been generated by technology. *Investigations 1 and 5*

8.F.A.1 Understand that a function is a rule that assigns to each input exactly one output. The graph of a function is the set of ordered pairs consisting of an input and the corresponding output. *Investigations 1, 2, and 5*

8.F.A.2 Compare properties of two functions each represented in a different way (algebraically, graphically, numerically in tables, or by verbal descriptions). For example, given a linear function represented by a table of values and a linear function represented by an algebraic expression, determine which function has the greater rate of change. *Investigation 1*

8.F.A.3 Interpret the equation $y = mx + b$ as defining a linear function, whose graph is a straight line; give examples of functions that are not linear. For example, the function $A = s^2$ giving the area of a square as a function of its side length is not linear because its graph contains the points (1, 1), (2, 4) and (3, 9), which are not on a straight line. Understand that a function is a rule that assigns to each input exactly one output. The graph of a function is the set of ordered pairs consisting of an input and the corresponding output. *Investigations 1 and 5*

8.F.B.4 Construct a function to model a linear relationship between two quantities. Determine the rate of change and initial value of the function from a description of a relationship or from two (x, y) values, including reading these from a table or from a graph. Interpret the rate of change and initial value of a linear function in terms of the situation it models, and in terms of its graph or a table of values. *Investigation 1*

8.F.B.5 Describe qualitatively the functional relationship between two quantities by analyzing a graph (e.g., where the function is increasing or decreasing, linear or nonlinear). Sketch a graph that exhibits the qualitative features of a function that has been described verbally. *Investigations 1 and 2*

A-SSE.A.1.a Interpret parts of an expression, such as terms, factors, and coefficients. *Investigations 1, 3, 4, and 5*

A-SSE.A.1.b Interpret complicated expressions by viewing one or more of their parts as a single entity. *Investigations 3 and 4*

A-SSE.A.1.c Use the properties of exponents to transform expressions for exponential functions. *Investigation 5*

N-RN.A.1 Explain how the definition of the meaning of rational exponents follows from extending the properties of integer exponents to those values, allowing for a notation for radicals in terms of rational exponents. *Investigation 5*

N-RN.A.2 Rewrite expressions involving radicals and rational exponents using the properties of exponents. *Investigation 5*

A-CED.A.1 Create equations that describe numbers or relationships. Create equations and inequalities in one variable and use them to solve problems. *Investigations 1 and 2*

A-CED.A.2 Create equations in two or more variables to represent relationships between quantities; graph equations on coordinate axes with labels and scales. *Investigations 1, 2, 3, and 4*

A-REI.D.10 Understand that the graph of an equation in two variables is the set of all its solutions plotted in the coordinate plane, often forming a curve. *Investigations 1, 2, 3, and 4*

F-IF.B.4 For a function that models a relationship between two quantities, interpret key features of graphs and tables in terms of the quantities, and sketch graphs showing key features given a verbal description of the relationship. *Investigations 1, 2, 3, and 4*

F-.IF.B.6 Calculate and interpret the average rate of change of a function (presented symbolically or as a table) over a specified interval. Estimate the rate of change from a graph. *Investigations 2, 3, 4, and 5*

F-IF.C.7.e Graph exponential and logarithmic functions, showing intercepts and end behavior, and trigonometric functions, showing period, midline and amplitude. *Investigations 1, 2, 3, 4, and 5*

F-IF.C.8b Use the properties of exponents to interpret expressions for exponential functions. *Investigations 3 and 4*

F-IF.C.9 Compare properties of two functions each represented in a different way. *Investigations 1*

F-BF.A.1a Determine an explicit expression, a recursive process, or steps for calculation from a context. *Investigations 1, 2, 3, and 4*

F-BF.A.1b Combine standard function types using arithmetic operations. *Investigation 4*

F-LE.A.1.a Prove that linear functions grow by equal differences over equal intervals; and that exponential functions grow by equal factors over equal intervals. *Investigations 1, 3, and 4*

F-LE.A.1C Recognize situations in which a quantity grows or decays by a constant percent rate per unit interval relative to another. *Investigations 3 and 4*

F-LE.A.2 Construct linear and exponential functions, including arithmetic and geometric sequences, given a graph, a description of a relationship, or two input-output pairs (including reading these from a table). *Investigations 1, 2, 3, and 4*

F-LE.A.3 Observe using graphs and tables that a quantity increasing exponentially eventually exceeds a quantity increasing linearly, quadratically, or as a polynomial function. *Investigation 1*

F-LE.B.5 Interpret the parameters in a linear or exponential function in terms of a context. *Investigations 1, 2, 3, 4, and 5*

Facilitating the Mathematical Practices

Students in Connected Mathematics classrooms display evidence of multiple Standards for Mathematical Practice every day. Here are just a few examples of when you might observe students demonstrating the Standards for Mathematical Practice during this Unit.

Practice 1: Make sense of problems and persevere in solving them.
Students are engaged every day in solving problems and, over time, learn to persevere in solving them. To be effective, the problems embody critical concepts and skills and have the potential to engage students in making sense of mathematics. Students build understanding by reflecting, connecting, and communicating. These student-centered problem situations engage students in articulating the "knowns" in a problem situation and determining a logical solution pathway. The student-student and student-teacher dialogues help students not only to make sense of the problems, but also to persevere in finding appropriate strategies to solve them. The suggested questions in the Teacher Guides provide the metacognitive scaffolding to help students monitor and refine their problem-solving strategies.

Practice 2: Reason abstractly and quantitatively.
After students find the number of years it would take to double the value of the stamp collection in Problem 3.2, they learn about the "Rule of 72" in the *Did You Know*. The Rule of 72 gives an approximation for how long it will take to double an investment. Students use this rule to check their answer in Problem 3.2. Students see the usefulness of this rule in making rough approximations to help make sense of a situation that involves compound growth.

Practice 3: Construct viable arguments and critique the reasoning of others.
In Problem 1.2, students check their reasoning for the relationship between the number of rubas and the chessboard square. In Problem 1.1, the relationship between the number of ballots and the number of cuts is $T = 2^n$. Using this relationship, they check the equation $r = \frac{1}{2}2^n$, where r is the number of rubas on square n, against the table they have made. Working backward with the equation, they find that the y-intercept is $\frac{1}{2}$ and that $r = \frac{1}{2}2^n$ is equivalent to $r = 2^{n-1}$. In Problem 4.1, students conjecture from the shape of the graph that the relationship between cuts and the area of the ballot is inverse variation, but because the graph has a y-intercept, it can not be inverse variation after all.

Practice 4: Model with mathematics.
Throughout Investigations 1–4, students use exponential equations to model growth and decay in various real-world contexts. Some of the situations for growth of money, plant growth, population growth, and growth in value. Students use information about the growth factor, initial value, or other values to find a model and make predictions. They do the same for decay where they learn about cooling and the breakdown of medicine.

Practice 5: Use appropriate tools strategically.

In Investigation 1, students learn how to use calculators and interpret numbers displayed in scientific notation. In Investigation 4, they can use a graphing calculator to enter an exponential equation and scroll through a table or trace a graph. By adjusting the calculator settings, they can get more precise answers. Also, students can use a graphing calculator to make a STAT plots of their data to see if the relationship is exponential. In Problem 5.5, they use graphing calculators to compare the graphs of families of exponential functions and to solve problems involving scientific notation.

Practice 6: Attend to precision.

In Problem 1.2, students are introduced to scientific notation. In Problem 5.4, they learn how to perform operations with numbers in scientific notation using the rules of exponents. One aspect of calculations with very large and very small numbers is our inability to write the numbers or the results out precisely. This raises questions about precision. How precise do we need to be with very large or very small numbers? What determines the level of precision in our results? The answers to these questions depend on the precision of the tools used to take measurements and calculations. Students learn that calculators are limited by their memory and storage of digits in a number. Once that capacity is used, rounding occurs.

Practice 7: Look for and make use of structure.

In Problem 1.3, students compare linear growth to exponential growth. In the Problem, they learn that linear growth is additive and exponential growth is multiplicative. In Problem 2.1, they check characteristics of exponential growth and notice that it is a function, i.e., one input produces a single out put in an exponential equation. Students collect data to determine the pattern of change in the temperature of the water in a cup in Problem 4.3. They start by boiling water and recording the temperature every 5 minutes. Then they fit a graph to the data and use an equation to find an approximate decay factor. This process is similar to the one they used in determining bridge strength in the *Thinking With Mathematical Models*. In Problem 5.1, students make use of common prime factorizations to establish the equivalence of various exponential expressions for a number.

Practice 8: Look for and express regularity in repeated reasoning.

In the Investigations 1–4, students complete tables and look for number patterns. In Investigation 1, they begin with the ballot problem and notice that with every cut, the number of ballots doubles. In Problem 2.1, students work with plant growth patterns. Here they reason from a description of growth to an equation. They learn to deal with an initial value in their exponential growth situation, i.e., $a = 1{,}000(2^n)$ where a is the area of the lake that is covered and n is the number of months that have passed. They continue the process using fractional growth rates in Investigations 3 and 4 to explore percent increases and decreases.

Students identify and record their personal experiences with the Standards for Mathematical Practice during the *Mathematical Reflections* at the end of each Investigation.

Mathematics Background

Relationships of Variables

One of the central goals of algebra is describing and reasoning about relationships among quantitative variables. That goal has been addressed in many Connected Mathematics Units, as shown in the table below.

Unit	Algebra Topic
Gr6 U4 *Covering and Surrounding*	Connections among dimensions, perimeters, areas, and volumes of various figures
Gr6 U7 *Variables and Patterns*	General techniques for representing quantitative relationships with words, pictures, tables, graphs, and symbols
Gr7 U1 *Shapes and Designs*	Connections among sides and angles in regular polygons
Gr7 U5 *Moving Straight Ahead,*	An important family of quantitative relationships: linear functions that illustrate constant, additive rates of change
Gr8 U1 *Thinking With Mathematical Models*	Linear patterns of change and how those patterns contrast with inverse patterns of change
Gr8 U3 *Growing, Growing, Growing*	A family of useful nonlinear relationships: exponential functions, which model exponential growth and exponential decay

This algebra Unit, *Growing, Growing, Growing,* focuses students' attention on exponential functions. Studies of biological populations, from bacteria and amoebas to mammals (including humans), often reveal exponential patterns of growth. Such populations may increase over time and at increasing rates of growth. Graphs of the (time, population) data curve upward. This same pattern of growth at increasing rates is seen when money is invested in accounts paying compound interest, or when growth of amoeba is tracked.

continued on next page

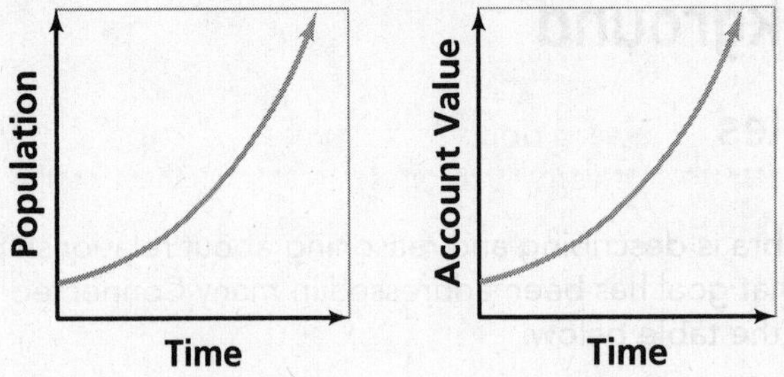

In a later Unit, *Frogs, Fleas, and Painted Cubes,* students will study quadratic functions.

The basic goals in *Growing, Growing, Growing* are for students to learn to recognize situations, data patterns, and graphs that are modeled with exponential functions and to use verbal descriptions, tables, graphs, and equations to answer questions about exponential patterns. This Unit is designed to introduce the topic of exponential functions and to give students a sound, intuitive foundation on which to build later.

Exponential Functions

An exponential pattern of change can often be recognized in a verbal description of a situation or in the pattern of change in a table of (x, y) values.

Application

Suppose you offer one of your classes a reward for days on which everyone works diligently for the entire class period. At the start of the year, you put 1 cent in a party fund. You promise that on the first good-work day, you will contribute 2 cents; on the second good-work day, you will contribute 4 cents; and on each succeeding good-work day, you will double the reward of the previous good-work day.

Class Party Fund

Good-Work Day	Reward (cents)
0 (start)	1
1	2
2	4
3	8
4	16
5	32
6	64
7	128
8	256

Growth Factor and Exponential Functions

For each good-work day, the monetary reward doubles. In the table, you multiply the previous reward by 2 to get the new reward. If the *x*-values increase by 1 unit, this constant factor can also be obtained by dividing each successive *y*-value by the previous *y*-value: $\frac{2}{1} = 2$, $\frac{4}{2} = 2$, and so on. This ratio is called the growth factor of the pattern. The constant growth factor is the key feature in identifying exponential functions.

The exponential growth in rewards for good-work days in the example can be represented in a graph. The increasing rate of growth is reflected in the upward curve of the plotted points.

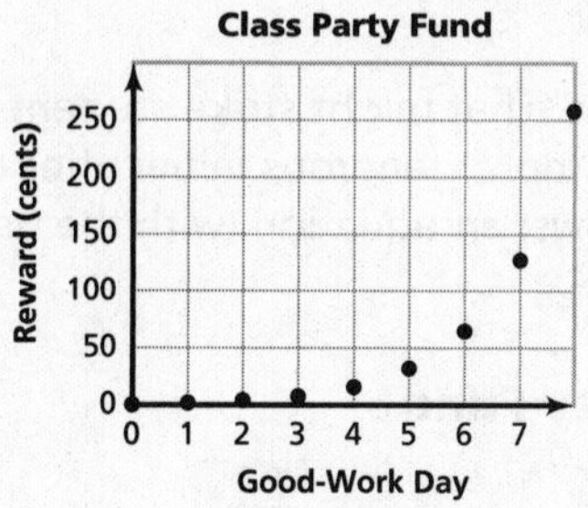

Examining the growth pattern in the class reward leads to an equation that represents the relationship between the variables in an exponential function.

Calculating the Reward

Day	Calculation	Reward (cents)
0	1	1
1	$1 \times 2 = 2^1$	2
2	$1 \times 2 \times 2 = 2^2$	4
3	$1 \times 2 \times 2 \times 2 = 2^3$	8
⋮	⋮	⋮
6	$1 \times 2 \times 2 \times 2 \times 2 \times 2 \times 2 = 2^6$	64
⋮	⋮	⋮
n	$1 \times 2 \times 2 \times \ldots \times 2 = 2^n$	2^n

This growth pattern can be summarized in symbolic form using exponents.

Summary

The reward on the tenth good-work day can be expressed as $1 \times 2 \times 2 \times 2 \times 2 \times 2 \times 2 \times 2 \times 2 \times 2 \times 2 = 2^{10}$.

continued on next page

On the *n*th good-work day, the reward *r* will be $r = 2^n$. Because the independent variable in this pattern appears as an exponent, the growth pattern is called an exponential function, or sometimes just an exponential. The growth factor is the base, 2. The exponent *n* tells the number of times the 2 is a factor.

y-intercept or Initial Value

The class party fund began with only 1 cent, which means the *y*-intercept was (0, 1). The following example illustrates a *y*-intercept that is not equal to 1. Since exponential functions are often used to model situations that involve population growth over time, the *y*-intercept is also called the *initial value.*

Application

The class party fund began with only 1 cent. That might strike students as a tiny seed for the fund, so suppose you made a more generous initial offer of 5 cents. The table for this new reward scheme follows; an equation (with the usual variable names, *x* and *y*) to represent it is $y = 5(2^x)$.

Class Party Fund

Good-Work Day	Reward (cents)
0 (start)	5
1	10
2	20
3	40
4	80
5	160
6	320

Note that the growth factor is still 2. In the table the reward on any given good-work day is twice that of the previous day. The reward is 5 times the reward for the same day in the original scheme, and the new starting amount is reflected in the equation by multiplying the original reward by 5.

The equation for the new plan is $y = 5(2^x)$. In the standard form for exponential equations, $y = a(b^x)$, *a* is the *y*-intercept, and *b* is the growth factor. Its graph on the next page.

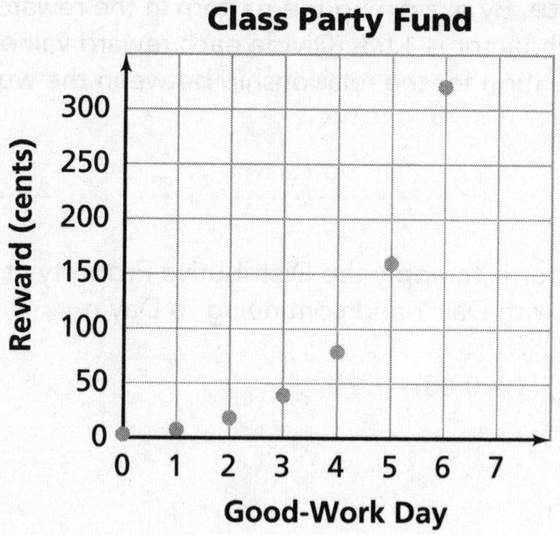

Note that students sometimes refer to the y-intercept (or initial value) as the "starting point." For exponential situations, they use the starting point and the growth factor to generate a table by multiplying the previous term by a constant factor. For a linear situation, they use the starting point (y-intercept) and the constant rate of change to generate a table by adding a constant amount to the previous term.

Growth Rates

A growth rate is different from, but related to, a growth factor. The following discussion will illustrate the connection between the two concepts.

Application

Suppose you offer students 5 cents for the first good-work day and then increase the reward by 8% for each succeeding good-work day. The table below shows the calculations required to find the reward for each day.

Calculating the Reward

Good-Work Day	Calculation	Reward (cents)
0 (start)	5	5
1	$5 + 0.08 \times 5$	5.4
2	$5.4 + 0.08 \times 5.4$	5.832
3	$5.832 + 0.08 \times 5.832$	6.29856
4	$6.29856 + 0.08 \times 6.29856$	6.8024448
⋮	⋮	⋮
n		$5(1.08)^n$

continued on next page

The 8% increase is the **growth rate**. By examining the pattern in the reward column, you can see that the growth factor is 1.08. (Divide each reward value by the previous reward value.) The equation for the relationship between the work day n and reward r is $r = 5(1.08)^n$.

Another way to find the growth factor is to apply the Distributive Property at each stage of the calculation, beginning with Day 1 and continuing to Day n.

Day 1: $5 + (0.08 \times 5) = 5(1 + 0.08)$

$= 5 \times (1.08)$

Day 2: $(5 \times 1.08) + (0.08 \times (5 \times 1.08)) = (5 \times 1.08)(1 + 0.08)$

$= (5 \times 1.08)(1.08)$

$= 5 \times (1.08)^2$

Day n: $5 \times (1.08)^n$

In general, a growth rate of r is associated with a growth factor of $(1 + r)$. Similarly, if the growth factor is f, then the growth rate is $(f - 1)$. Growth rates are often expressed as percents.

Exponential Decay

Exponential Functions also describe patterns in which the value of a dependent variable decreases as time passes. In this case, the constant multiplicative factor is referred to as the **decay factor**. Decay factors work just like growth factors, only they result in decreasing relationships because they are between 0 and 1.

Application

Suppose another teacher offers a different incentive for good-work days. At the start of the school year, the teacher puts $50 in a class party fund. For each day the class does not work diligently, she cuts the party fund in half. As the days pass, the class party fund will decrease in the pattern shown in the following table.

Class Party Fund

Bad-Work Day	Reward
0 (start)	$50.00
1	$25.00
2	$12.50
3	$6.25
4	$3.13
5	$1.56
6	$0.78
7	$0.39
8	$0.20

Notice that, although half the amount is removed at each stage, the amount removed each time decreases.

The exponential decay pattern is also represented in the graph below. The plotted points begin at (0, 50) and drop from left to right.

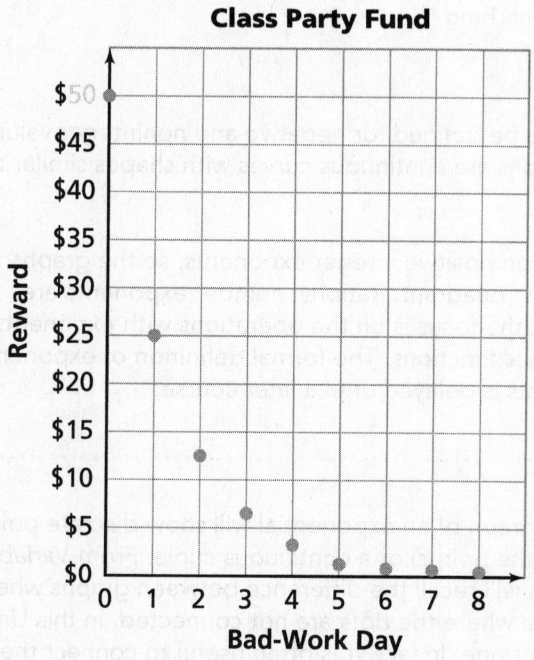

The decay factor for this exponential decay pattern is $\frac{1}{2}$. The amount in the party fund f after n bad-work days is given by the equation $f = 50\left(\frac{1}{2}^n\right)$. This exponential function is similar to that for exponential growth except that the repeating factor, the base, is a positive number less than 1. It is also called an *exponential decay function.*

Graphs of Exponential Functions

The basic patterns of exponential growth and exponential decay involve change from one point in time to the next by some constant factor.

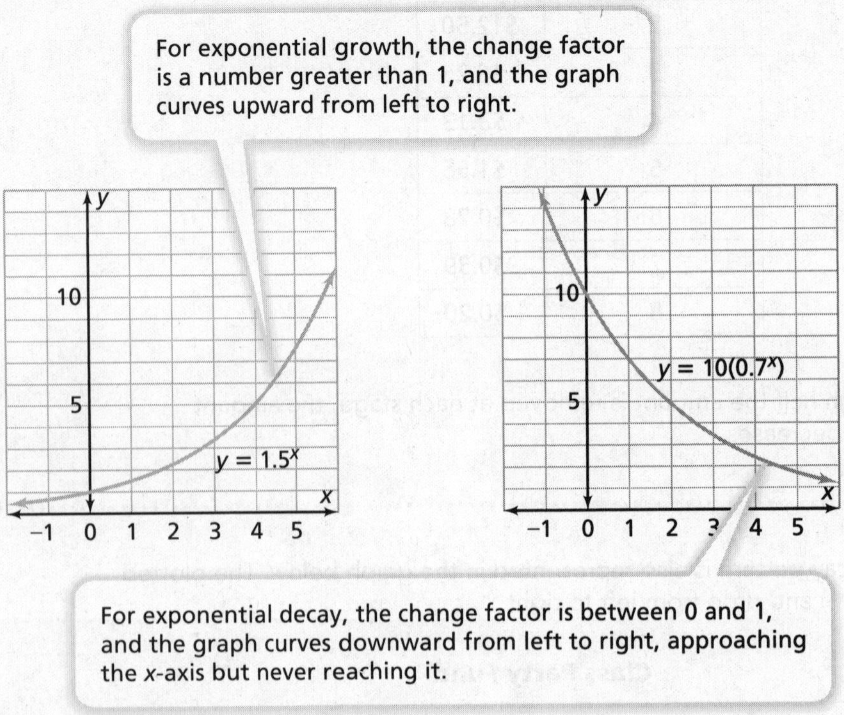
For exponential growth, the change factor is a number greater than 1, and the graph curves upward from left to right.
y
10
5
y = 1.5^x
x
−1 0 1 2 3 4 5
y
10
5
y = 10(0.7^x)
x
−1 0 1 2 3 4 5
For exponential decay, the change factor is between 0 and 1, and the graph curves downward from left to right, approaching the x-axis but never reaching it.

Exponential relationships can also be defined for negative and noninteger values of the exponent. The related graphs are continuous curves with shapes similar to those shown.

The focus of this Unit is primarily on positive integer exponents, so the graphs will generally be limited to the first quadrant. Rational number exponents are introduced in Investigation 5, but the focus is on the operations with exponents rather than their role in exponential functions. The formal definition of exponential functions for noninteger exponents is delayed until a later course.

Depending on the situation, the graph of an exponential will show discrete points (with or without a curve through the points) or a continuous curve. From *Variables and Patterns* in grade 6, students will recall the difference between graphs where the dots are connected and those where the dots are not connected. In this Unit, that distinction is not an important one. In fact, it is often useful to connect the dots to highlight a pattern. In such a case, though, it is important to remember that the points corresponding to noninteger values of x may not arise from the data of the problem at hand.

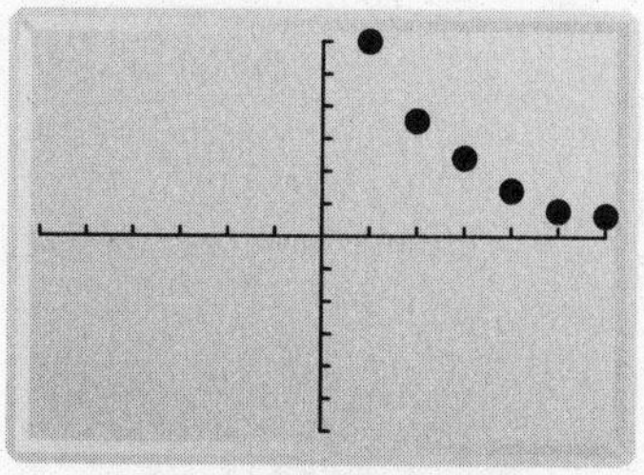

Graph of plotted points

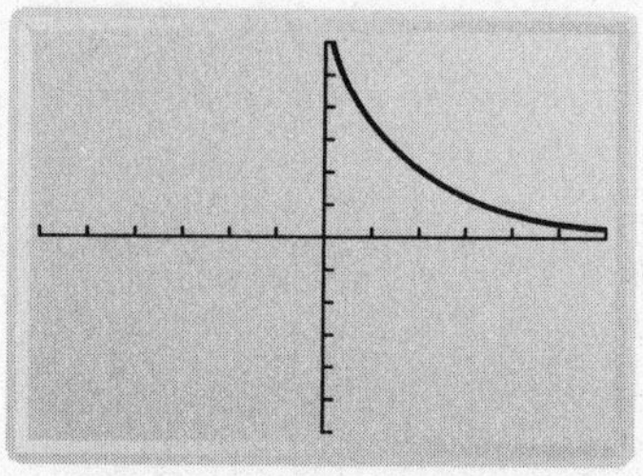

Graph of related equation

It is illuminating to occasionally ask students what information the continuous graphs produced by graphing calculators communicate at noninteger points. For example, in many contexts where time is the independent variable, the corresponding *y*-values have quite natural interpretations.

Equations for Exponential Functions

In general, the equation $y = a(b^x)$ represents the relationship in an exponential function; *a* and *b* are positive. The *y*-intercept (or initial value) is *a* and the growth factor is *b*. If *b* is greater than 1, the function is increasing and represents an exponential growth pattern. If *b* is less than 1, the function is decreasing and represents an exponential decay pattern. If *b* is equal to 1, then the equation $y = a(b^x)$ does not represent an exponential function. It is a linear function with a graph that is a horizontal (slope 0). Visit Teacher Place at Mathdashboard.com/cmp3 to see the image gallery.

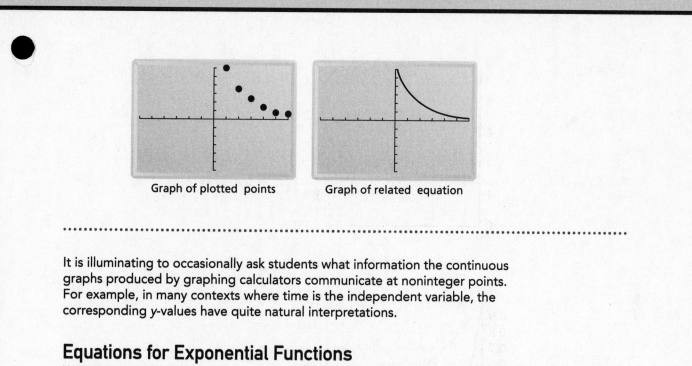

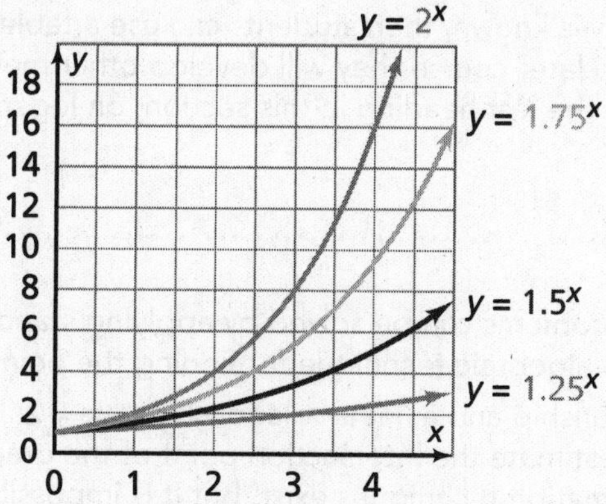

Exponential Growth: 1 < b

continued on next page

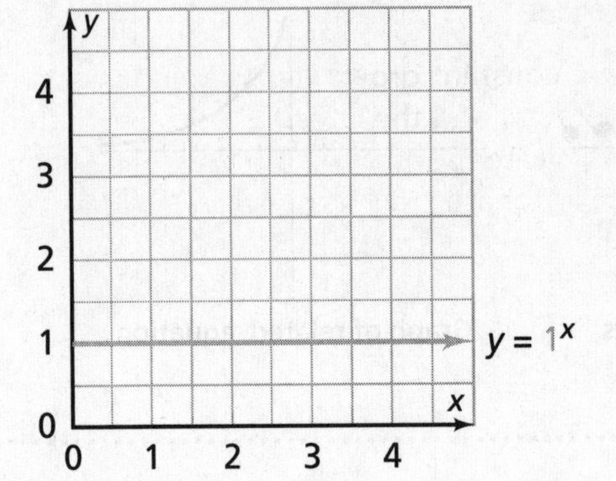

Constant Function: $b = 1$

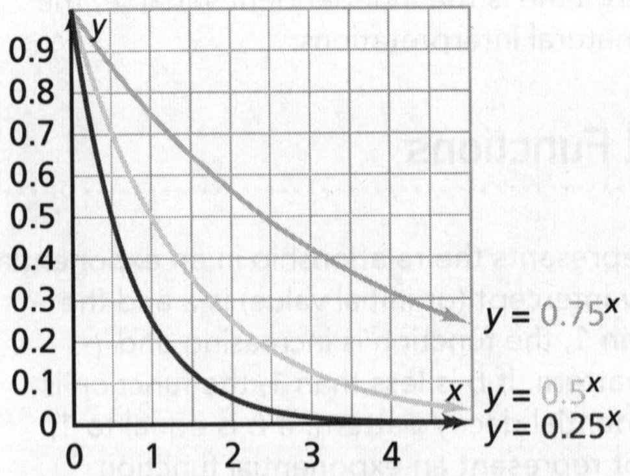

Exponential Decay: $0 < b < 1$

Students can use tables or graphs to find the value of y if x is known. They can also evaluate the expression $y = a(b^x)$. If y is known, then students can use a table or graph to estimate the value of x. In a later course they will develop other methods for finding x, called logarithms. (See the last heading in this section, on logarithms, for more information.)

It is interesting to note that not all problems can be solved by applying standard algorithms. For example, there is no algebraic technique for finding the point of intersection of an exponential relationship and a linear relationship. $y = \frac{1}{2}(2^x)$ and $y = 5x + 15$. The best we can do is estimate the intersection point of the graphs of the equations. Sophisticated estimation techniques exist, but it is impossible to solve such a problem directly.

Tables for Recursive, or Iterative, Processes

Students usually generate each value in their tables by working with the previous value. Either they add a constant to the previous value (in the case of linear relationships) or they multiply the previous value by a constant (in the case of exponential relationships). This process of generating a value from a previous value is called *recursion*, or *iteration*.

Exponential and Linear Functions

It is important to distinguish between a constant growth factor (multiplicative), as just illustrated in an exponential function, and the constant additive pattern in linear functions. The animation here illustrates successive iterations for linear and exponential growth. Visit Teacher Place at mathdashboard.com/cmp3 to see the complete animation.

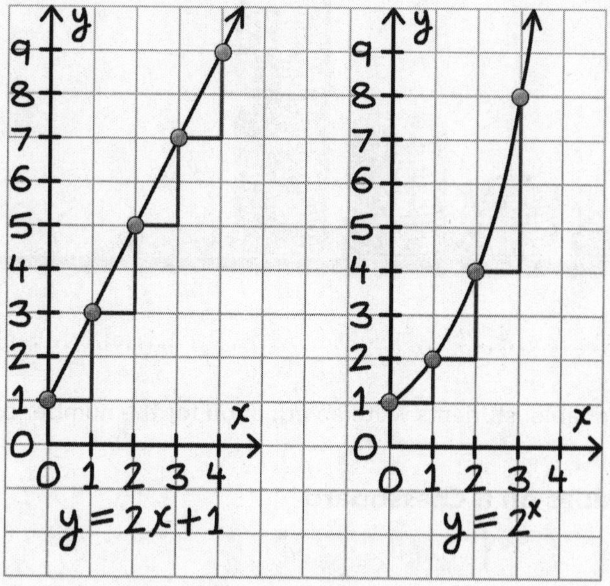

An exponential function represented by the equation $y = a(b^x)$ may increase slowly at first but grows at an increasing rate because its growth is multiplicative. The growth factor is *b*. The *y*-intercept of the linear function is *b* and the *y*-intercept of the exponential functions is *a*.

Equivalence

In *Growing, Growing, Growing,* equivalence occurs naturally as students generate two or more symbolic expressions for the dependent variable in an exponential function. Students use patterns from the table, graph, or verbal descriptions to justify the equivalence.

In Investigation 5, after the rules for operation with exponents are developed, students use properties of exponents and operations to demonstrate that two expressions are equivalent.

For example, in the first Investigation of this Unit, students may end up writing two different, but equivalent, exponential equations for this situation.

continued on next page

Application

A king places 1 ruba on the first square of a chessboard, 2 rubas on the second square, 4 on the third square, 8 on the fourth square, and so on, until he has covered all 64 squares. Each square has twice as many rubas as the previous square.

By examining the patterns in a table, students write an equation for the number of rubas *r* on square *n*.

Rubas on a Chessboard

Square Number	Number of Rubas
1	1
2	2
3	4
4	8
5	16

Some students will note that the number of rubas on a given square *n* is a product of $(n - 1)$ 2's and write $r = 2^{n-1}$.

Other students will reverse the pattern and find the number of rubas on "square 0," by dividing the number of rubas on square 1 by 2. This gives them the *y*-intercept, $\frac{1}{2}$. (Square 0 has no meaning in this context, but many students find it useful to use the *y*-intercept as a starting point when they write an equation.) They then note that the number of rubas on square *n* is half the product of *n* 2's, so they write $r = \frac{1}{2}(2^n)$.

It is important for students to recognize that the two forms, $r = 2^{n-1}$ and $r = \frac{1}{2}(2^n)$, are equivalent. They can verify the equivalence by generating tables or graphs.

Once students have developed the rules for operations with exponents, they can use them to work with exponentials having any value of the growth factor b. (In the chessboard example, $b = 2$.)

A general argument why b^{x-1} is equivalent to $\frac{1}{b}(b^x)$.

- *The equation $y = b^{x-1}$ is equivalent to $y = b^x \times b^{-1}$.*
- *Because $b^{-1} = \frac{1}{b}$, this is equivalent to $y = (b^x)\frac{1}{b} = \frac{1}{b}(b^x)$.*

Rules of Exponents

Students begin to develop understanding of the rules of exponents by examining patterns in the table of powers for the first 10 whole numbers. Visit Teacher Place at mathdashboard.com/cmp3 to see the complete animation.

$(b^m)^n = b^{mn} = (b^n)^m$ — *Power of a power*

$(b^m)(b^n) = b^{m+n}$ — *Product of two Powers with Same Base*

$\frac{a^m}{a^n}$ a^{m-n} — *Quotient of two powers*

$(a^m)(b^m) = (ab)^m$ — *Power of a product*

The rules for integral exponents are extended to include rational exponents by first noticing that in the graph of $y = 4^x$, the value of y is 2 when $x = \frac{1}{2}$. This means that $\sqrt{4} = 4^{\frac{1}{2}}$.

In an interesting optional labsheet, students discover that the ones digits for the powers repeat in cycles of 1, 2, or 4. They apply this observation to predict ones digits of powers and to estimate the value of exponential expressions.

Scientific Notation

Since exponential growth patterns can grow quite fast, students may encounter scientific notation on their calculators. Therefore, scientific notation is introduced in Investigation 1 and then used throughout the Unit. The ACE exercises in every Investigation also continue to reinforce the skills need to work with scientific notation.

Example
If you enter $(25{,}000{,}000{,}000{,}000)^2$, you might get a calculator screen that uses shorthand to indicate the value.

6.25E 26

This notation represents 6.25×10^{26}.

Sometimes if the numbers are very large or very small, you might get an approximation.

Example
Using a calculator to find the standard form for 2^{40} might give you this screen.

1.099511628E 12

Writing this number in standard form gives you 1099511628000. This is an approximation, because 2^{40} does not end in a 0. It ends in a 2, 4, 6, or 8.

Students use exponential notation and the rules of exponents to solve problems with scientific notation.

Logarithms

Understanding logarithms is not a goal of this Unit, and hence logarithms are not mentioned in the student book. However, there are several questions in the Unit that push students to think about the ideas behind logarithms.

In Problem 1.1, students examine a situation in which a sheet of paper is cut in half. The resulting two pieces are stacked and the stack is cut in half. Then the resulting four pieces are stacked, and the stack is again cut in half, and so on.

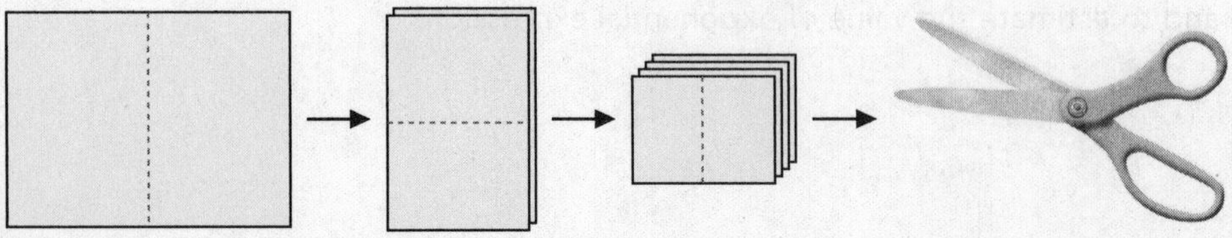

Students write the equation $y = 2^x$ to describe the relationship between the number of cuts x and the number of pieces of paper y. In one question, they are asked how many cuts it would take to create at least 500 pieces of paper. The answer is the solution to $500 = 2^x$.

Students will and should estimate the solution by using a guess-and-check method or by generating a calculator table or graph. In high school, they will learn to use logarithms to solve such an equation exactly.

A logarithmic function is the inverse of an exponential function, just as division is the inverse of multiplication. Taking a base 2 logarithm will undo raising 2 to a power, in the same way that dividing by 2 will undo multiplying by 2. So, taking $\log_2$ of both sides of $500 = 2x$ we get $\log_2 500 = x$. You can rewrite this equation as $x = \log_2 500$.

Some calculators can compute logarithms using any base (here the base is 2). Most scientific calculators are limited to the bases 10 and e. In that case, finding a logarithm for base 2 requires several steps.

Example

$500 = 2^x$

$\log_{10}(500) = \log_{10}(2^x)$

$\log_{10}(500) = x\log_{10}(2)$ (by the rules of exponents)

So, $x = \dfrac{\log_{10} 500}{\log_{10} 2}$.

Remember that all of this is far beyond what we ask students to do in this Unit. Logarithms will be addressed in later mathematics courses.

Using Graphing Calculators

Connected Mathematics was developed with the belief that calculators should be available and that students should learn when their use is appropriate. For this reason, we do not designate specific exercises as "calculator exercises."

Students will need access to graphing calculators for most of their work in this Unit. Ideally, the calculators should be able to display a function table. It is also helpful if you have an overhead display model of the calculator. Extensive exploration of exponential patterns with the assistance of graphing calculators, along with frequent class discussions to share observations and formulate explanations, will add a great deal to the effectiveness of this Unit.

continued on next page

The instructions here are written for the TI-83 graphing calculator. If your students use a different calculator, consult the manual for instruction on these various procedures.

Performing Recursive Multiplication

Because the essence of an exponential relationship is recursive multiplication, there are efficient calculator algorithms to shorten the process. Here is the output from a calculator that begins with 5 and repeatedly multiplies by 2.

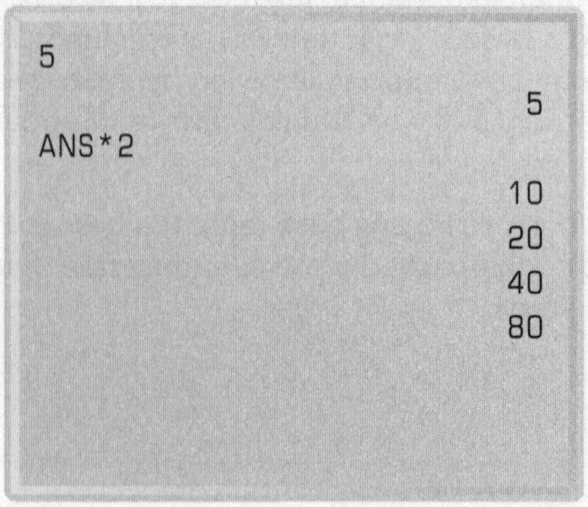

To accomplish this, press 5 and ENTER. To enter the formula ANS×2, press 2nd (-) × 2. Then, by repeatedly pressing ENTER you will generate a list of values, each of which is twice the previous value.

Entering Exponents

When entering equations in which the exponent consists of more than one character, such as $r = 2^{n-1}$, the entire exponent must be enclosed in parentheses. For instance, the right side of this equation would be entered as 2^(X – 1). This is because the calculator follows the correct order of operations. If you entered 2^X – 1 instead, the calculator would first find 2^X and then subtract 1.

Converting Decimals to Fractions

There are occasions in *Growing, Growing, Growing* when it is convenient to work with fractions rather than with decimals to see a pattern in the data. To convert a displayed decimal to a fraction, press MATH. Select choice 1 to convert the decimal to a simple fraction and then press ENTER.

Displaying a Function Table

Once an equation has been entered, you can display a table of (*x*, *y*) pairs that satisfy the equation. The values in the table can be displayed in decimal increments by changing the settings in the TABLE SETUP menu. Press 2nd WINDOW to access the menu and enter a new value for △TBL.

```
TABLE SETUP
  TblStart=0
  ΔTBL=1
Indpnt: Auto Ask
Depend: Auto Ask
```

Then press 2nd GRAPH to display the table. Below is a table for the equation $y = 1.4^x$.

X	Y1	
0	1	
.1	1.0342	
.2	1.0696	
.3	1.1062	
.4	1.1441	
.5	1.1832	
.6	1.2237	

X=0

Entering Data

Data given as (*x*, *y*) pairs can be entered into the calculator and plotted. To enter a list of (*x*, *y*) data pairs, press STAT and then press ENTER to select the Edit mode. Then enter the pairs into L1 and L2 columns: Enter the first number and press ENTER, use the arrow keys to change columns, enter the second number and press ENTER, then use the arrow keys to return to the L1 column.

1.099511628E 12

L1	L2	L3 1
0	100	----
1	180	
2	325	
3	580	
4	1050	
----	----	
----	----	

L1 (1)=0

continued on next page

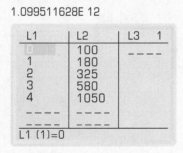

Plotting the Points

To plot the data you have entered, use the commands in the STAT PLOT menu. Display the STAT PLOT menu, which looks like the following screen, by pressing `2nd` `Y=`.

```
STAT PLOTS
1: Plot1...off
    ∠∙ L1  L2   ▫
2: Plot2...off
    ∠∙ L1  L2   ▫
3: Plot3...off
    ∠∙ L1  L2   ▫
4: PlotsOff
```

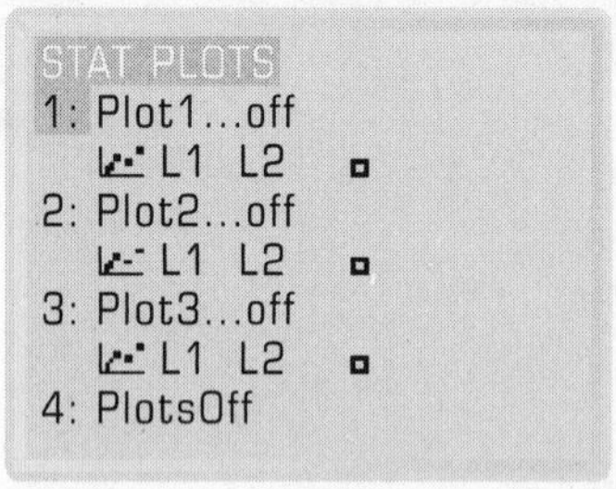

Press `ENTER` to select PLOT1. Use the arrow keys and `ENTER` to move around the screen and highlight the elements shown (ON, icon of discrete points, L1, L2, and open circle for mark).

```
Plot1 Plot2 Plot3
On Off
Type: ▨ ∠ ⊞
      ⊞ ⊡ ∠
Xlist: L1
Ylist: L2
Mark: ▣ +
```

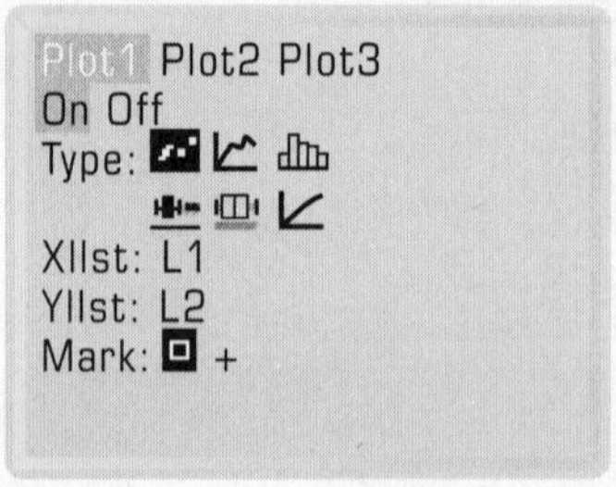

Next, press `WINDOW` which will display a screen similar to the one below. To accommodate the data you have for input, adjust the window settings by entering values and pressing `ENTER`.

```
WINDOW
 Xmin=0
 Xmax=5
 Xscl=1
 Ymin=0
 Ymax=1100
 Yscl=100
 Xres=1
```

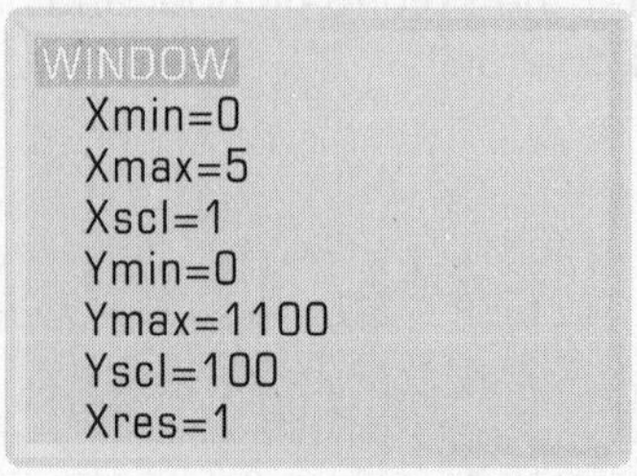

Press GRAPH.

1.099511628E 12

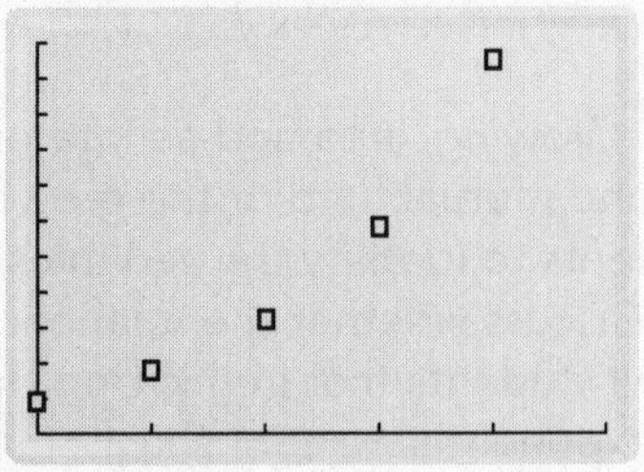

Exploring Sums of Sequences

The sum of a geometric sequence is a bit beyond what we hope to accomplish in this Unit, but students can use their calculators to derive sums of sequences fairly easily.

The following screen shows how to find the sum of terms in the sequence $2n$ for $n = 0$ to $n = 10$. The calculation involves two operations. The SUM operation gives the sum of all elements in a list. This operation is found in the LIST MATH menu, which is accessed by pressing 2nd STAT, selecting MATH, and choosing option 5, sum. (The SEQ operation defines a sequence. This operation is found in the LIST OPS menu. It is accessed by pressing 2nd STAT, selecting OPS, and choosing option 5, SEQ.)

```
sum(seq (2^X, X, 0, 10, 1))
                       2047
```

Unit Introduction

Using the Unit Opener

One way to introduce *Growing, Growing, Growing,* is to find an interesting graph of exponential growth—the return of a bond mutual fund or the growth of the world's population, for example. Ask students to identify the variables and to describe the relationship between them. Discuss whether the relationship is linear and how students can tell that it is not. Tell students that in this Unit they will study relationships like these, which are called exponential relationships.

Refer students to the three questions posed on the opening page of the Student Edition. The questions are designed to start students thinking about nonlinear relations between variables. Invite students to share personal experiences they have had with any of these situations. Then explain that all of these examples involve a similar type of pattern called exponential change.

Each question is posed again in the Investigations, after the students have learned the mathematical concepts required to answer it. Ask your students to keep these questions in mind as they work through the Investigations and to think about how they might use the ideas they are learning to help them determine the answers.

Using the Mathematical Highlights

The Mathematical Highlights page in the Student Edition provides information to students, parents, and other family members. It gives students a preview of the mathematics and some of the overarching questions that they should ask themselves while studying *Growing, Growing, Growing.*

As they work through the Unit, students can refer back to the Mathematical Highlights page to review what they have learned and to preview what is still to come. This page also tells students' families what mathematical ideas and activities will be covered as the class works through *Growing, Growing, Growing.*

Unit Project

Introduction

As a final assessment in *Growing, Growing, Growing*, you may assign the Unit Project, Half-Life. In this optional project, students investigate the phenomenon of radioactive decay. They simulate the decay of a substance, collect, and analyze data, and look for patterns.

Sample results and answers to the questions are given in the Assessment Resources section.

Assigning

The optional Unit Project, the Half-Life project, gives students an opportunity to apply what they have learned about exponential relationships to a real-world situation, radioactive decay. We recommend that students work on the project with a partner. Each pair will need 100 cubes (wooden, plastic, or sugar) to conduct the simulation. If it is not possible to have students mark on the cubes, supply them with stickers that can be removed later. Students can also use number cubes and choose one number to represent the marked side. The cubes can be shared.

Some teachers launch the project at the start of Investigation 4 and use the last several minutes of class each day for a few groups to experiment and collect data. By the end of Investigation 4, all groups have their data. A class period is then used for groups to finish the project. Sample results and answers to the questions are in *Half-Life Sample*.

Grading

Suggested Scoring Rubric

This rubric for scoring the project employs a scale that runs from 0 to 4, with a 4+ for work that goes beyond what has been asked for in some unique way. You may use the rubric as presented here or modify it to fit your district's requirements for evaluating and reporting students' work and understanding.

4+ Exemplary Response

- Complete, with clear, coherent explanations
- Shows understanding of the mathematical concepts and procedures
- Satisfies all essential conditions of the problem and goes beyond what is asked for in some unique way

4 Complete Response

- Complete, with clear, coherent explanations
- Shows understanding of the mathematical concepts and procedures
- Satisfies all essential conditions of the problem

3 Reasonably Complete Response

- Reasonably complete; may lack detail in explanations
- Shows understanding of most of the mathematical concepts and procedures
- Satisfies most of the essential conditions of the problem

2 Partial Response

- Gives response; explanation may be unclear or lack detail
- Shows some understanding of some of the mathematical concepts and procedures
- Satisfies some essential conditions of the problem

1 Inadequate Response

- Incomplete; explanation is insufficient or not understandable
- Shows little understanding of the mathematical concepts and procedures
- Fails to address essential conditions of problem

0 No Attempt

- Irrelevant response
- Does not attempt a solution
- Does not address conditions of the problem

Sample Student Work

Half-Life Sample

- Half-Life Sample

Notes

Looking Ahead

When the water hyacinth was introduced to Lake Victoria, it spread quickly over the lake's surface. At one point, the plant covered 769 square miles, and its area doubled every 15 days. **What** equation models this growth?

When Sam was in seventh grade, his aunt gave him a stamp worth $2,500. The value of the stamp increased by 6% each year for several years in a row. **What** was the value of Sam's stamp after four years?

What pattern of change would you expect to find in the temperature of a hot drink as time passes? **What** would a graph of the *(time, drink temperature)* data look like?

Notes

One of the most important uses of algebra is to model patterns of change. You are already familiar with linear patterns of change or linear functions. Linear patterns have constant differences and straight-line graphs. In a linear function, the y-value increases by a constant amount each time the x-value increases by 1.

In this Unit, you will study exponential patterns of change for exponential functions. Exponential growth patterns are fascinating because, although the values may change gradually at first, they eventually increase very rapidly. Patterns that decrease, or decay, exponentially may decrease quickly at first, but eventually they decrease very slowly.

Notes

Mathematical Highlights

Exponential Functions

In *Growing, Growing, Growing,* you will explore Exponential Functions, one of the most important types of nonlinear relationships.

The Investigations in this Unit will help you learn how to:

- Identify situations in which a quantity grows or decays exponentially
- Recognize the connections between the growth patterns in tables, graphs, and equations that represent exponential functions
- Construct equations to express the relationship between the variables in an exponential function in data tables, graphs, and problem situations
- Compare exponential and linear functions
- Develop and use rules for working with exponents, including scientific notation, to write and interpret equivalent expressions
- Solve problems about exponential growth and decay from a variety of different areas, including science and business

ASK YOURSELF

As you work on the Problems in this Unit, ask yourself questions about situations that involve nonlinear relationships such as:

How can I recognize whether the relationship between the variables is an exponential function?

What is the growth or decay factor?

What equation models the data in the table, graph, or problem situation?

What can I learn about this situation by studying a table or graph of the exponential function?

How can I answer questions about the problem situation by studying a table, graph, or equation that represents the exponential function?

Notes

Common Core State Standards

Mathematical Practices and Habits of Mind

UNIT | STUDENT PAGE

In the *Connected Mathematics* curriculum you will develop an understanding of important mathematical ideas by solving problems and reflecting on the mathematics involved. Every day, you will use "habits of mind" to make sense of problems and apply what you learn to new situations. Some of these habits are described by the *Common Core State Standards for Mathematical Practices* (MP).

MP1 Make sense of problems and persevere in solving them.

When using mathematics to solve a problem, it helps to think carefully about

- data and other facts you are given and what additional information you need to solve the problem;
- strategies you have used to solve similar problems and whether you could solve a related simpler problem first;
- how you could express the problem with equations, diagrams, or graphs;
- whether your answer makes sense.

MP2 Reason abstractly and quantitatively.

When you are asked to solve a problem, it often helps to

- focus first on the key mathematical ideas;
- check that your answer makes sense in the problem setting;
- use what you know about the problem setting to guide your mathematical reasoning.

MP3 Construct viable arguments and critique the reasoning of others.

When you are asked to explain why a conjecture is correct, you can

- show some examples that fit the claim and explain why they fit;
- show how a new result follows logically from known facts and principles.

When you believe a mathematical claim is incorrect, you can

- show one or more counterexamples—cases that don't fit the claim;
- find steps in the argument that do not follow logically from prior claims.

Notes

MP4 Model with mathematics.

When you are asked to solve problems, it often helps to

- think carefully about the numbers or geometric shapes that are the most important factors in the problem, then ask yourself how those factors are related to each other;
- express data and relationships in the problem with tables, graphs, diagrams, or equations, and check your result to see if it makes sense.

MP5 Use appropriate tools strategically.

When working on mathematical questions, you should always

- decide which tools are most helpful for solving the problem and why;
- try a different tool when you get stuck.

MP6 Attend to precision.

In every mathematical exploration or problem-solving task, it is important to

- think carefully about the required accuracy of results; is a number estimate or geometric sketch good enough, or is a precise value or drawing needed?
- report your discoveries with clear and correct mathematical language that can be understood by those to whom you are speaking or writing.

MP7 Look for and make use of structure.

In mathematical explorations and problem solving, it is often helpful to

- look for patterns that show how data points, numbers, or geometric shapes are related to each other;
- use patterns to make predictions.

MP8 Look for and express regularity in repeated reasoning.

When results of a repeated calculation show a pattern, it helps to

- express that pattern as a general rule that can be used in similar cases;
- look for shortcuts that will make the calculation simpler in other cases.

You will use all of the Mathematical Practices in this Unit. Sometimes, when you look at a Problem, it is obvious which practice is most helpful. At other times, you will decide on a practice to use during class explorations and discussions. After completing each Problem, ask yourself:

- What mathematics have I learned by solving this Problem?
- What Mathematical Practices were helpful in learning this mathematics?

Notes

Notes

Unit Project

Half-Life

Most things around you are composed of atoms that are stable. However, the atoms that make up *radioactive* substances are unstable. They break down in a process known as *radioactive decay*. From their decay, they emit radiation. At high levels, radiation can be dangerous.

Rates of decay vary from substance to substance. The term *half-life* describes the time it takes for half of the atoms in a radioactive sample to change into other more stable atoms. For example, the half-life of carbon-11 is 20 minutes. This means that 2,000 carbon-11 atoms are reduced to 1,000 carbon-11 atoms and 1,000 boron-11 atoms in 20 minutes. After 40 minutes, the carbon-11 atoms are reduced to 500 carbon-11 atoms and 1,500 boron-11 atoms.

Half-lives vary from a fraction of a second to billions of years. For example, the half-life of polonium-214 is 0.00016 seconds. The half-life of rubidium-87 is 49 billion years.

In this experiment, you will model the decay of a radioactive substance known as iodine-124. About $\frac{1}{6}$ of the atoms in a sample of iodine-124 decay each day. This experiment will help you determine the half-life of this substance.

Follow these steps to conduct your experiment:

- Use 100 cubes to represent 100 iodine-124 atoms. Mark one face of each cube.
- For the first day, place all 100 cubes in a container, shake the container, and pour the cubes onto the table.
- The cubes for which the mark is facing up represent atoms that have decayed. Remove these cubes, and record the number of cubes that remain.
- For the next day, place the remaining cubes in the container, shake the container, and pour the cubes onto the table.
- Repeat the last two steps until one cube or no cubes remain.

Notes

When you complete your experiment, answer the following questions.

1. a. In your experiment, how many days did it take to reduce the 100 iodine-124 atoms to 50 atoms? In other words, how many times did you have to roll the cubes until about 50 cubes remained?

   b. How many days did it take to reduce 50 iodine-124 atoms to 25 atoms?

   c. Based on your answers to parts (a) and (b), what is the half-life of iodine-124?

2. a. In a sample of real iodine-124, $\frac{1}{6}$ of the atoms decay after 1 day. What fraction of the atoms remain after 1 day?

   b. Suppose a sample contains 100 iodine-124 atoms. Use your answer from part (a) to write an equation for the number of atoms n remaining in the sample after d days.

   c. Use your equation to find the half-life of iodine-124.

   d. How does the half-life you found based on your equation compare to the half-life you found from your experiment?

3. a. Make up a problem involving a radioactive substance with a different rate of decay that can be modeled by an experiment involving cubes or other common objects. Describe the situation and your experiment.

   b. Conduct your experiment and record your results.

   c. Use your results to predict the half-life of your substance.

   d. Use what you know about the rate of decay to write an equation that models the decay of your substance.

   e. Use your equation to find the half-life of your substance.

Write a report that summarizes your findings about decay rates and half-lives. Your report should include tables and graphs justifying your answers to the questions above.

Notes

Investigation 1

PLANNING

Exponential Growth

Investigation Overview

Investigation Description

In Investigation 1, students explore situations that involve repeated doubling, tripling, and quadrupling. Students are introduced to one of the essential features of many exponential patterns: rapid growth. They make and study tables and graphs for exponential situations, describe the patterns they see, and write equations for them, looking for a general form of an exponential equation. They also compare and contrast linear and exponential patterns of growth.

For example, in Investigation 1, Plan 1 places 1 ruba on the first square of a checkerboard, 2 rubas on the second square, 4 rubas on the third square, etc. Plan 4 places 20 rubas on the first square, 25 rubas on the second, 30 rubas on the third, etc. The relationship between the number of the square on the checkerboard and the number of rubas on Plan 1 is an exponential function and the relationship for Plan 4 is a linear function. The *growth factor* for Plan 1 is 2 and the *constant rate of change* for Plan 4 is 5. Comparing multiplicative growth patterns (exponential functions) with additive growth patterns (linear functions) reinforces understanding of each function.

Investigation Vocabulary

- base
- exponent
- exponential form
- exponential functions
- exponential growth
- growth factor
- scientific notation
- standard form

Mathematics Background

- Exponential Functions
- Growth Factor and Exponential Functions

Planning Chart

Content	ACE	Pacing	Materials	Resources
Problem 1.1	1–3, 22–41	½ day	**Labsheet 1.1:** Number of Ballots (accessibility) **Labsheet 1ACE:** Exercise 3 (accessibility) paper, poster board, transparencies	**Teaching Aid 1.1** Number of Ballots
Problem 1.2	4–12, 42–43, 50	½ day	**Labsheet 1.2:** Montarek Chessboard (accessibility) counters	
Problem 1.3	13–21, 44–49, 51–52	1 day	**Labsheet 1.3:** Different Reward Plans (accessibility) **Labsheet 1ACE:** Exercises 17–21 (accessibility) **Labsheet 1ACE** Exercise 51 counters	
Mathematical Reflections		½ day		

Goals and Standards

Goals

Exponential Functions Explore problem situations in which two or more variables have an exponential relationship to each other

- Identify situations that can be modeled with an exponential function
- Identify the pattern of change (growth factor) between two variables that represent an exponential function in a situation, table, graph, or equation
- Represent an exponential function with a table, graph, or equation
- Make connections among the patterns of change in a table, graph, and equation of an exponential function
- Compare the growth rate and growth factor for an exponential function and recognize the role each plays in an exponential situation
- Identify the growth factor and initial value in problem situations, tables, graphs, and equations that represent exponential functions
- Determine whether an exponential function represents a growth (increasing) or decay (decreasing) pattern, from an equation, table, or graph that represents an exponential function
- Determine the value of the independent and dependent value from a table, graph, or equation of an exponential function
- Use an exponential equation to describe the graph and table of an exponential function
- Predict the *y*-intercept from an equation, graph, or table that represents an exponential function
- Interpret the information that the *y*-intercept of an exponential function represents
- Determine the effects of the growth factor and initial value for an exponential function on a graph of the function
- Solve problems about exponential growth and decay from a variety of different subject areas, including science and business, using an equation, table, or graph
- Observe that one exponential equation can model different contexts
- Compare exponential and linear functions

Equivalence Develop understanding of equivalent exponential expressions

- Write and interpret exponential expressions that represent the dependent variable in an exponential function
- Develop the rules for operating with rational exponents and explain why they work
- Write and interpret numerical expressions in scientific notation

- Judge the reasonableness of large and small numbers determined by calculators
- Write and interpret equivalent expressions using the rules for exponents and operations
- Solve problems that involve exponents, including scientific notation

Mathematical Reflections

Look for evidence of student understanding of the goals for this Investigation in their responses to the questions in *Mathematical Reflections*. The goals addressed by each question are indicated below.

1. Describe an exponential growth pattern. Include key properties such as growth factors.

   Goals

   - Identify situations that can be modeled with an exponential function
   - Identify the pattern of change (growth factor) between two variables that represent an exponential function in a situation, table, graph, or equation
   - Represent an exponential function with a table, graph, or equation
   - Make connections among the patterns of change in a table, graph, and equation of an exponential function
   - Determine the value of the independent and dependent value from a table, graph, or equation of an exponential function
   - Write and interpret numerical expressions in scientific notation

2. How are exponential functions similar to and different from the linear functions you worked with in earlier units?

   Goals

   - Compare exponential and linear functions
   - Make connections among the patterns of change in a table, graph, and equation of an exponential function
   - Solve problems about exponential growth and decay from a variety of different subject areas, including science and business, using an equation, table, or graph

Standards

Common Core Content Standards

8.EE.A.3 Use numbers expressed in the form of a single digit times an integer power of 10 to estimate very large or very small quantities, and to express how many times as much one is than the other. For example, estimate the population of the United States as 3×10^8 and the population of the world as 7×10^9, and determine that the world population is more than 20 times larger. *Problems 2 and 3*

8.EE.A.4 Perform operations with numbers expressed in scientific notation, including problems where both decimal and scientific notation are used. Use scientific notation and choose units of appropriate size for measurements of very large or very small quantities (e.g., use millimeters per year for seafloor spreading). Interpret scientific notation that has been generated by technology. *Problem 2*

8.F.A.1 Understand that a function is a rule that assigns to each input exactly one output. The graph of a function is the set of ordered pairs consisting of an input and the corresponding output. *Problems 1, 2, and 3*

8.F.A.2 Compare properties of two functions each represented in a different way (algebraically, graphically, numerically in tables, or by verbal descriptions). For example, given a linear function represented by a table of values and a linear function represented by an algebraic expression, determine which function has the greater rate of change. *Problems 2 and 3*

8.F.A.3 Interpret the equation $y = mx + b$ as defining a linear function, whose graph is a straight line; give examples of functions that are not linear. For example, the function $A = s^2$ giving the area of a square as a function of its side length is not linear because its graph contains the points (1,1), (2,4) and (3,9), which are not on a straight line. Understand that a function is a rule that assigns to each input exactly one output. The graph of a function is the set of ordered pairs consisting of an input and the corresponding output. *Problems 1 and 3*

8.F.B.4 Construct a function to model a linear relationship between two quantities. Determine the rate of change and initial value of the function from a description of a relationship or from two (x, y) values, including reading these from a table or from a graph. Interpret the rate of change and initial value of a linear function in terms of the situation it models, and in terms of its graph or a table of values. *Problem 3*

8.F.B.5 Describe qualitatively the functional relationship between two quantities by analyzing a graph (e.g., where the function is increasing or decreasing, linear or nonlinear). Sketch a graph that exhibits the qualitative features of a function that has been described verbally. *Problems 2 and 3*

A-SSE.A.1.a Interpret parts of an expression, such as terms, factors, and coefficients. *Problem 3*

A-CED.A.1 Create equations that describe numbers or relationships. Create equations and inequalities in one variable and use them to solve problems. *Problem 1*

A-CED.A.2 Create equations in two or more variables to represent relationships between quantities; graph equations on coordinate axes with labels and scales. *Problems 1, 2, and 3*

A-REI.D.10 Understand that the graph of an equation in two variables is the set of all its solutions plotted in the coordinate plane, often forming a curve. *Problems 1, 2, and 3*

F-IF.B.4 For a function that models a relationship between two quantities, interpret key features of graphs and tables in terms of the quantities, and sketch graphs showing key features given a verbal description of the relationship. *Problems 1, 2, and 3*

F-IF.C.7e Graph exponential and logarithmic functions, showing intercepts and end behavior, and trigonometric functions, showing period, midline, and amplitude. *Problems 1, 2, and 3*

F-IF.C.9 Compare properties of two functions each represented in a different way. *Problem 3*

F-BF.A.1a Determine an explicit expression, a recursive process, or steps for calculation from a context. *Problems 1, 2, and 3*

F-LE.A.1.a. Prove that linear functions grow by equal differences over equal intervals; and that exponential functions grow by equal factors over equal intervals. *Problems 2 and 3*

F-LE.A.2 Construct linear and exponential functions, including arithmetic and geometric sequences, given a graph, a description of a relationship, or two input-output pairs (including reading these from a table). *Problems 2 and 3*

F-LE.A.3 Observe using graphs and tables that a quantity increasing exponentially eventually exceeds a quantity increasing linearly, quadratically, or as a polynomial function. *Problem 3*

F-LE.B.5 Interpret the parameters in a linear or exponential function in terms of a context. *Problems 2 and 3*

F-IF.C.7.e Graph exponential and logarithmic functions, showing intercepts and end behavior, and trigonometric functions, showing period, midline and amplitude. *Problem 3*

Facilitating the Mathematical Practices

Students in *Connected Mathematics* classrooms display evidence of multiple Common Core Common Core Standards for Mathematical Practice every day. Here are just a few examples where of when you might observe students demonstrating the Standards for Mathematical Practice during this Investigation.

Practice 1: **Make sense of problems and persevere in solving them.**

Students are engaged every day in solving problems and, over time, learn to persevere in solving them. To be effective, the problems embody critical concepts and skills and have the potential to engage students in making sense of mathematics. Students build understanding by reflecting, connecting, and communicating. These student-centered problem situations engage students in articulating the "knowns" in a problem situation and determining a logical solution pathway. The student-student and student-teacher dialogues help students to not just make sense of the problems, but also to persevere in finding appropriate strategies to solve them. The suggested questions in the Teacher Guides provide the metacognitive scaffolding to help students monitor and refine their problem-solving strategies.

Practice 3: Construct viable arguments and critique the reasoning of others.

In Problem 1.2, students check their reasoning for the relationship between the number of rubas and the chessboard square. In Problem 1.1, the relationship between the number of ballots and the number of cuts is $T = 2^n$. Using this relationship, they check the equation $r = \frac{1}{2}2^n$, where r is the number of rubas on square n, against the table they have made. Working backwards with the equation, they find that the y-intercept is $\frac{1}{2}$ and that $r = \frac{1}{2}2^n$ is equivalent to $r = 2^{n-1}$.

Practice 5: Use appropriate tools strategically.

In Problems 1.1, 1.2, and 1.3, students learn how to use calculators and interpret numbers displayed in scientific notation.

Practice 6: Attend to precision.

In Problem 1.2, students are introduced to scientific notation. One aspect of calculations with very large and very small numbers is our inability to write the numbers or the results out precisely. This raises questions about precision. How precise do we need to be with very large or very small numbers? What determines the level of precision in our results? The answers to these questions depend on the precision of the tools used to take measurements and calculations. Students learn that calculators are limited by their memory and storage of digits in a number. Once that capacity is used, rounding occurs.

Practice 7: Look for and make use of structure.

In Problem 1.3, students compare linear growth to exponential growth. In the Problem, they learn that linear growth is additive and exponential growth is multiplicative.

Students identify and record their personal experiences with the Standards for Mathematical Practice during the *Mathematical Reflections* at the end of the Investigation.

PROBLEM 1.1

Making Ballots

Introducing Exponential Functions

Problem Overview

Focus Question What are the variables in this situation and how are they related?

Problem Description

In earlier Units, students studied linear functions. This Problem introduces a nonlinear function called an exponential function. Students investigate the growth in the number of ballots created by repeatedly cutting a piece of paper in half. By examining the table, they see that, as the number of cuts increases by one, the number of ballots doubles or increases by a factor of 2. They also create a graph and write an equation to represent the doubling pattern.

Problem Implementation

Students should work in groups of two to four.

Materials

- **Labsheet 1.1:** Number of Ballots (accessibility)
- **Labsheet 1ACE:** Exercise 3 (accessibility)
- **Teaching Aid 1.1:** Number of Ballots

paper
poster board (optional)
transparencies (optional)

Vocabulary

There are no new glossary terms introduced in this Problem.

Mathematics Background

- Exponential Functions
- Growth Factor and Exponential Functions

At a Glance and Lesson Plan

- At a Glance: Problem 1.1 Growing, Growing, Growing
- Lesson Plan: Problem 1.1 Growing, Growing, Growing

Launch

Launch Video

This animation shows ballot growth that arises from cutting a piece of paper in half and then in half again, and so on. Use this animation to help students understand the context of the Problem.

After showing the video, ask the Suggested Questions in Presenting the Challenge. Visit Teacher Place at mathdashboard.com/cmp3 to see the complete video.

Connecting to Prior Knowledge

Suggested Questions

Remind students that in *Thinking With Mathematical Models* they looked at two kinds of functions, linear functions and inverse variation.

- Give an example of each function. What are the variables? What is the pattern of change for each function? Describe the graphs. (For linear functions, students might give $d = t \times r$ for the relationship between distance, time, and rate, where d and t are the two variables. For example, $d = 5t$. As t increases, d increases by a constant amount. In the example, d increases by 5 for each one unit increase in t. Students might use these same variables but fix d to represent an inverse variation. $100 = r \times t$. As r increases, t decreases. The graph of a linear function is a straight line and the graph of inverse variation is a curve.)

Presenting the Challenge

Describe Chen's ballot-making task or show the Launch Video. You might ask students to jot down predictions for the number of ballots that would result from three, four, or even ten cuts.

Suggested Questions

Gather a few suggestions, but let students sort the answers out as they work on the Problem.

- How can you predict the number of ballots after 8 cuts? (Various answers. Try it for a few cuts and make a conjecture about the number pattern. Or keep cutting 8 times and count the ballots.)

- How can you predict how many cuts to make if we need 128 ballots? (Various answers. Using the conjecture, continue the pattern until it reaches 128. Or keep cutting until you get 128 ballots.)

Later, they can compare their predictions to their results from the activity. Hand out **Labsheet 1.1: Number of Ballots** (accessibility).

Explore

Providing for Individual Needs

Have students cut and stack paper for the first two or three cuts. This helps them see and understand the relationship between the number of cuts and the number of ballots created.

Suggested Questions

Encourage students to look for the multiplicative pattern in the table by asking questions like these:

- How did you find each of the entries in your table? (For the first three entries, I found the entries by counting ballots, but after that, I used the doubling pattern.)
- What is the relationship between this number of ballots and the previous number of ballots? (It is twice the previous number.)
- Explain that relationship in terms of the number of cuts. (When the number of cuts increases by 1, the number of ballots doubles.)

As students work on Question C, look for interesting strategies to share during the Summarize. Students might be using exponential notation rather than listing all the factors of 2 that are needed for each cut. Some will begin to reason using the general relationship between cuts and number of ballots.

You may want to distribute poster board for some groups to record their answers to share during the Summarize.

Planning for the Summary

What evidence will you use in the summary to clarify and deepen understanding of the Focus Question?

What will you do if you do not have evidence?

Summarize

Orchestrating the Discussion

Suggested Questions

As groups share their answers to the Problem, you may want to ask questions like these:

- In Question A, how do your results compare to the predictions you made earlier? (Answers will vary and depend on the prediction.)
- For Question B, how is the number of ballots after each cut related to the number of ballots before the cut? (The number of ballots doubles with each successive cut.)
- What does the graph look like? How could you predict this from the table? (The graph is nearly flat at the start and then it curves and rises steeply. In the table, the numbers are small at first, so doubling is not a very big change. Once the numbers are large, doubling makes a big difference.)
- Is this a linear function? Explain. (Students should be able to start talking about additive growth for linear functions and multiplicative growth for exponential functions. They may use words like *add a constant* or the *same number* for a linear function, and *multiply by* or *double* for an exponential function.)
- In Question C, part (1), how many ballots are made after 20 cuts? After 40 cuts? Describe how you found your answers. ($2^{20} = 1{,}048{,}576$. $2^{40} = 1{,}099{,}511{,}627{,}776$. For 20 cuts, I multiplied the number for 10 cuts by itself, which would represent 10 more doublings. For 40 cuts, I multiplied the number for 20 cuts by itself, which would represent 20 more doublings.)
- Question C, part (2) asked you to work in reverse to predict the number of cuts needed to make enough ballots for 500 students. Describe your method. (Students generally find it more difficult to work in reverse, especially because no exact power of 2 is equal to 500. Because 8 cuts gives 256 ballots and 9 cuts gives 512 ballots, 9 cuts are needed to guarantee at least 500 ballots.)

Ask about the pattern in the number of ballots and how it relates to the number of cuts shown in the table. Then lead the class in a discussion of exponents.

Display the **Labsheet 1.1: Number of Ballots** and ask:

- How did you get the number of ballots for 5 cuts? (Most students will say they started with 1 cut and 2 ballots and then multiplied the number of ballots by 2 for each cut until they reached 5 cuts.)

Add a third column to the table and illustrate each calculation, showing each factor of 2. Stop after showing the calculation for 5 cuts.

Number of Cuts	Number of Ballots	Calculation
1	2	2
2	4	2×2
3	8	$2 \times 2 \times 2$
4	16	$2 \times 2 \times 2 \times 2$
5	32	$2 \times 2 \times 2 \times 2 \times 2$
6	64	
7	128	
8	256	
9	512	
10	1,024	

- How many times is 2 used as a factor to find the number of ballots after 1 cut? After 2 cuts? After 3 cuts? After 4 cuts? After 5 cuts? (once; twice; three times; four times; five times)
- How many factors of 2 will be used to find the number of ballots after 6 cuts? After 10 cuts? After 30 cuts? (six; ten; thirty)

Explain to students that they can use exponents rather than writing the factor of 2 over and over again. Display this equation:

$$2 \times 2 \times 2 \times 2 \times 2 \times 2 \times 2 \times 2 \times 2 \times 2 = 2^{10}$$

Make sure students see that there are 10 factors of 2 on the left side of the equation and a raised number 10 on the right side. Point to the expression 2^{10}. Explain that the number 2 is the base, the number 10 is the exponent, and the expression 2^{10} is in exponential form.

Explain that 1,024 is the standard form of 2^{10}. Exponential notation was first introduced in *Prime Time*.

These review questions on exponential notation lead into the next Problem. In the Launch for Problem 1.2, they are used to introduce scientific notation.

- How many ballots are there after 0 cuts? (one ballot)
- How could we show this in our table? (Add a row at the top that has 0 in the Number of Cuts column and 1 in the Number of Ballots column from dividing 2 by 2.)

Reflecting on Student Learning

Use the following questions to assess student understanding at the end of the lesson.

- What evidence do I have that students understand the Focus Question?
  - Where did my students get stuck?
  - What strategies did they use?
  - What breakthroughs did my students have today?
- How will I use this to plan for tomorrow? For the next time I teach this lesson?
- Where will I have the opportunity to reinforce these ideas as I continue through this Unit? The next Unit?

ACE Assignment Guide

- **Applications:** 1–3
- **Connections:** 22–41

Labsheet 1ACE: Exercise 3 (accessibility) contains a larger version of the table in the Student Edition and graph paper. You can give this labsheet to students to help them organize their data. This can allow students to remain focused on the mathematics of the Exercise.

PROBLEM 1.2

Requesting a Reward

Representing Exponential Functions

Problem Overview

Focus Question In what ways are the relationships represented on a chessboard and in ballot-cutting situations similar? Different?

Problem Description

Students investigate an exponential situation set in the fictitious ancient kingdom of Montarek. One coin is placed on the first square of a chessboard, two on the second square, four on the third square, and so on. Students explore and compare patterns of change for these exponential functions. This plan is similar to the one in Problem 1.1 with a growth factor of 2, but the y-intercept is not 1.

Students might write the equation $y = 2^{x-1}$ or $\frac{1}{2}(2^x)$, where y is the number of rubas and x is the number of squares. The two expressions for the number of rubas are equivalent. Students can show they are equivalent since they both represent the same patterns in the table. Also, they both have the same graph. By going backwards in the table, students find that $\frac{1}{2}$ is the y-intercept.

Exponential notation is reviewed and scientific notation is introduced at the beginning of the Problem. Since exponential growth patterns can grow quickly, answers on the calculator may be displayed in scientific notation if the calculation is very large or very small. Skill and interpretation of scientific notation is reinforced throughout the Unit.

Problem Implementation

Students should work in groups of two to four.

Materials

- **Labsheet 1.2:** Montarek Chessboard (accessibility)

counters (optional; 65 per group)

Vocabulary

- base
- exponent
- exponential form
- scientific notation
- standard form

Mathematics Background

- Exponential Functions
- Growth Factor and Exponential Functions

At a Glance and Lesson Plan

- At a Glance: Problem 1.2 Growing, Growing, Growing
- Lesson Plan: Problem 1.2 Growing, Growing, Growing

Launch

Launch Video

Begin the lesson with Connecting to Prior Knowledge. Then, show this animation about the story of the king and the peasant from the Introduction in the Student Edition. You can use this animation to engage students with the idea of exponential growth patterns and the massive payoffs on the last squares.

After showing the video, continue with Presenting the Challenge. Visit Teacher Place at mathdashboard.com/cmp3 to see the complete video.

Connecting to Prior Knowledge

The terms *exponential form, exponent, base,* and *standard form* are introduced in the opening paragraph of Problem 1.2. If you did not discuss these terms in the summary of Problem 1.1, do so now. These should be a review since they were first introduced in the 6th grade in *Prime Time.*

Suggested Questions

- **Write each expression in exponential form.**

  $2 \times 2 \times 2$

  (2^3)

  $5 \times 5 \times 5 \times 5$

  (5^4)

  $1.5 \times 1.5 \times 1.5 \times 1.5 \times 1.5 \times 1.5 \times 1.5$

  (1.5^7)

- **Write each expression in standard form.**

  2^7

  (128)

  3^3

  (27)

  4.2^3

  (74.088)

- Most calculators have a ^ or y^x key for evaluating exponents. Use your calculator to find the standard form for each expression.

  2^{15}

  To use a calculator, press "2", then the ^ or y^x key, and "15." Then press = or ENTER.

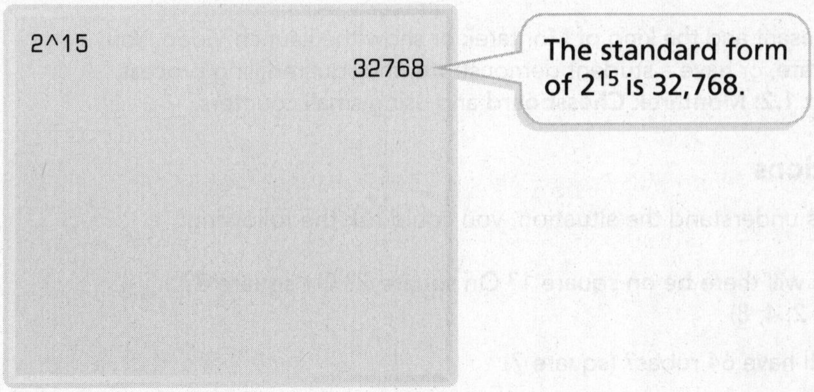
2^15
32768
The standard form of 2^15 is 32,768.

  (32,768)

  3^{10}

  (59,049)

  1.5^{20}

  ($\approx$ 3,325.26)

- Explain how the meanings of 5^2, 2^5, and 5×2 differ. (5^2 has two factors of 5; 2^5 has five factors of 2; and 5×2 has one factor of 5 and one factor of 2. Also, $5^2 = 25$, $2^5 = 32$, and $5 \times 2 = 10$.)

To introduce scientific notation, use the example in the book about the number of ballots after 40 cuts. Students might write $2 \times 2 \times 2 \times 2 \ldots \times 2$ (forty times). If they use a calculator, they get $1.099511628 \times 10^{12}$.

- Write $1.099511628 \times 10^{12}$ in standard form. (1,099,511,628,800)

Note: The exact answer is not given by this scientific notation on a calculator. A calculator can only show a fixed number of digits. We know that if we start with 1 and repeatedly multiply by 2, the number will never end in 0. That is, we know that the power of 2 ends in 2, 4, 8, and 6—never 0.

- Write each expression in scientific notation.

  6,234,890,001

  (6.234890001×10^9)

  20,000,033,339,999

  ($2.000033339999 \times 10^{13}$)

Scientific notation is introduced so that students can interpret calculations that might arise on their calculators. It is revisited in Investigation 5.

Presenting the Challenge

Tell the story of the peasant and the king of Montarek or show the Launch Video. You may want to demonstrate, or have a student demonstrate, the square-filling process by displaying **Labsheet 1.2: Montarek Chessboard** and using small counters.

Suggested Questions

To check that students understand the situation, you could ask the following:

- How many rubas will there be on square 1? On square 2? On square 3? On square 4? (1; 2; 4; 8)
- Which square will have 64 rubas? (square 7)

Pose the following questions, and record all student responses. Later, students can compare their predictions to their findings.

- Make a prediction as to how many rubas you think will be placed on the last square of the chessboard. (Answers will vary. Actual: $2^{63} \approx 9.223372 \times 10^{18}$)
- If a Montarek ruba is worth 1 cent, do you think the peasant's plan is a good deal for her? (Answers will vary. Students will not know the actual answer at this point. This is part of their challenge. Their answers will be mostly based on opinion. Many will think this is not a good deal, since it looks like we are just dealing with pennies.

Explore

Providing for Individual Needs

Encourage students to place counters on a chessboard or **Labsheet 1.2: Montarek Chessboard** (accessibility) for at least the first five or six squares.

Students should quickly recognize the doubling pattern.

Suggested Questions

To help students who do not recognize the pattern immediately, ask:

- How did the number of rubas increase from square 1 to square 2? From square 2 to square 3? From square 3 to square 4? (Some students might suggest adding 1, then 2, then 4, and so on, rather than multiplying by 2 for the pattern. If so, encourage them to think of another way to explain the growth.)

From Question A, part (2), you may want to have one or two groups display their graphs in the Summarize.

Students may need help with writing the equation for exponential growth. They may recognize that it is similar to the last problem and write $r = 2^n$. If this happens, ask them to check a few values. Students generally come up with either $r = 2^{n-1}$ or $r = \frac{1}{2}(2^n)$. These equations are equivalent and will be discussed in the Summarize.

To guide students to find the equation $r = 2^{n-1}$, ask the following questions:

- How many rubas are on square 4? (8)
- How can you write this as a power of 2? (2^3)

  Note: Students will be formally introduced to the term "power" in Investigation 5. If they have difficulty with this term now, you may want to add, "in other words, 8 equals 2 to what exponent?"
- How many rubas are on square 5? (16)
- How can you write this as a power of 2? (2^4)
- How many rubas are on square 4? (8)
- How many rubas are on square 6? (32)
- How can you write this as a power of 2? (2^5)
- In all these cases, how is the exponent related to the number of the square? (It is 1 less.)
- How can you write the number of rubas on the *n*th square as a power of 2? (2^{n-1})
- So what is the equation? ($r = 2^{n-1}$)

Encourage students to check their equations for another value in the table, such as $n = 9$ or $n = 10$, to make sure the equation works.

If students are making sense of the problem, ask:

- How many rubas will be on square 64? (Answers will vary. Actual: $2^{63} \approx 9.223372 \times 10^{18}$)

The number of rubas on the chessboard escalates quickly. This is good time to use or reinforce expressing large numbers using scientific notation. Some students may need help in interpreting or writing numbers in scientific notation.

Planning for the Summary

What evidence will you use in the summary to clarify and deepen understanding of the Focus Question?

What will you do if you do not have evidence?

Summarize

Orchestrating the Discussion

Have some students share their graphs. Ask students to describe the graph.

Suggested Questions

- Choose points in the table and ask: Where are these points on the graph? (Answers will vary and depend on the coordinates you choose. For example, if you choose (5, 16), the point will be close to the middle of the *x*-axis and a not far up the *y*-axis. If you choose (10, 512), the point will be at the far right of the *x*-axis and in the top right-hand corner of the graph.)
- Choose points on the graph and ask: Where are these points in the table? (Answers will vary and depend on the points you choose. For example, if you choose the point at the bottom left-hand corner of the graph, that coordinate will be on the first line of the table. If you choose the point at the top right-hand corner of the graph, that coordinate will be on the last line of the table.)
- How does the growth pattern show up in the graph? (For any two consecutive values of the independent variable, the coordinate points are only one unit apart on the *x*-axis. On the *y*-axis, the higher point is two times higher then the previous point. Draw the horizontal and vertical segments between the two consecutive points to illustrate this relationship between the "rise" and "run.")

For Question A, part (3), there are three ways students may come up with equations for the relationship between the number of the square n and the number of rubas r on the square.

METHOD 1 Students recognize that the number of times 2 is used as a factor is 1 less than the number of the square. This is because we start with 1 ruba on square 1; on square 2, we place 1×2 rubas; on square 3, we place $1 \times 2 \times 2$ rubas, and so on. The number of rubas on the *n*th square is the product of $(n - 1)$2s, which is 2^{n-1}. The equation is then $r = 2^{n-1}$. Students will get this same equation if they write the exponential forms and notice that there are 2^1 rubas on square 2, 2^2 rubas on square 3, 2^3 rubas on square 4, and so on. From this form, it is apparent that the exponent is always 1 less than the number of the square.

METHOD 2 Students go back one step in the table to find the *y*-intercept—that is, the number of rubas on "square 0." Moving up the rubas column, each value is half the value below it. Because there is 1 ruba on square 1, there would be $\frac{1}{2}$ of a ruba on square 0. Students use this as a starting point and double the rubas for each successive square. This gives the equation $r = \frac{1}{2}(2^n)$.

Square Number	Number of Rubas
0	$\frac{1}{2}$
1	$\frac{1}{2} \times 2 = 1$
2	$\frac{1}{2} \times 2 \times 2 = 2$
3	$\frac{1}{2} \times 2 \times 2 \times 2 = 4$
4	$\frac{1}{2} \times 2 \times 2 \times 2 \times 2 = 8$
5	$\frac{1}{2} \times 2 \times 2 \times 2 \times 2 \times 2 = 16$
⋮	⋮
n	$\frac{1}{2} \times 2 \times 2... \times 2 = \frac{1}{2}(2^n)$

METHOD 3 Another way students might come up with the equation $r = \frac{1}{2}(2^n)$ is by comparing the ruba table to the ballot table from Problem 1.1. The number of rubas on square *n* is half the number of ballots after *n* cuts. Because there are 2^n ballots after *n* cuts, there are $\frac{1}{2}(2^n)$ rubas on square *n*.

The use of the *y*-intercept as a starting point begins in Grade 7 in *Moving Straight Ahead*, and the *y*-intercept becomes a strong reference point for many students as they study new functions. The *y*-intercept for exponential relationships is discussed in the next Investigation. In Investigation 5, students prove these two expressions are equivalent using the rules of exponents.

This is an appropriate time to discuss the fact that $2^0 = 1$.

- What do we get when we substitute 1 for n in the equation $r = 2^{n-1}$? ($r = 2^{1-1} = 2^0$)
- You know that this value, 2^0, is the number of rubas on square 1. How many rubas are on that square? (1)
- So, what is 2^0 equal to? (1)

You might tell students that a^0 for any nonzero number is 1. Students will explore why this is true in Problem 5.2.

Discuss the answers to Question C, Part (2). Ask students how they found the first square that had at least one million rubas. Students may have repeatedly multiplied by 2, keeping track of the number of 2s, until the product exceeded one million, and then counted the number of 2s and subtracted 1. Or, they may have evaluated 2^n for increasingly large values of n until the result was over one million, and then subtracted 1 from the last value of n.

Discuss the questions you posed in the Launch and compare the answers to students' predictions. The numbers are much easier to work with if students write them in scientific notation.

- How many rubas will be on the last square? (about 9.2×10^{18})
- How did you find that number? (by finding 2^{63} or by multiplying 63 factors of 2)
- If each ruba is worth 1 cent, what is the value of the rubas on the last square in dollars? (about 9.2×10^{16})
- How did you find this answer? (To change 9.2×10^{18} cents to dollars, you need to divide by 100, or 10^2. This gives 9.2×10^{16}.)
- Is this plan a good deal for the peasant? (Yes!)

To emphasize how much money 9.2×10^{16} dollars is, you might write the approximate value in standard form: \$92,000,000,000,000,000. Tell students this number is read, "ninety-two quadrillion."

End by asking students to compare the ballot-cutting situation to the chessboard situation.

- In what ways are the chessboard and ballot-cutting situations similar? (They are both doubling patterns. They are both exponential growth functions with the same base.)
- In what ways are the two situations different? (They have different y-intercepts. The functions have different initial values.)
- Compare the relationships in Problems 1.1 and 1.2 to linear functions. (Neither relationship represents a linear function. As the number of cuts or number of squares increases by 1, the number of ballots and number of rubas is doubling. The ballots or rubas are not increasing by adding a constant number.)

Reflecting on Student Learning

Use the following questions to assess student understanding at the end of the lesson.

- What evidence do I have that students understand the Focus Question?
  - Where did my students get stuck?
  - What strategies did they use?
  - What breakthroughs did my students have today?
- How will I use this to plan for tomorrow? For the next time I teach this lesson?
- Where will I have the opportunity to reinforce these ideas as I continue through this Unit? The next Unit?

ACE Assignment Guide

- **Applications:** 4–12
- **Connections:** 42–43
- **Extensions:** 50

PROBLEM

1.3 Making a New Offer

Growth Factors

Problem Overview

Focus Question How does the growth pattern for an exponential function show up in a table, graph, or equation that represents the function and how does it compare to the growth pattern in a linear function?

Problem Description

Students consider two variations on Plan 1 from the previous problem. In Plan 2, the number of coins is tripled on each square. In Plan 3, the number is quadrupled. Students make tables and graphs for the variations, describe patterns, write equations for them, and look for a general form for exponential equations. The term *growth factor* is introduced and students investigate how it shows up in a table, graph, and equation. Students use an equation for an exponential function to generate a table of values for an exponential function. Plan 4 has a linear growth pattern, which provides an opportunity to compare a linear function to an exponential function.

Problem Implementation

Students should work in groups of two to four.

Materials

- **Labsheet 1.3:** Different Reward Plans (accessibility)
- **Labsheet 1ACE:** Exercises 17–21 (accessibility)
- **Labsheet 1ACE:** Exercise 51

counters (optional; 65 per group)

Vocabulary

- exponential functions
- exponential growth
- growth factor

Mathematics Background

- Exponential Functions
- Growth Factor and Exponential Functions

At a Glance and Lesson Plan

- At a Glance: Problem 1.3 Growing, Growing, Growing
- Lesson Plan: Problem 1.3 Growing, Growing, Growing

Launch

Connecting to Prior Knowledge

The introduction to this problem discusses the terms *exponential growth*, *exponential function*, and *growth factor.* Use the situations in Problems 1.1 and 1.2 to illustrate these terms. If you did not compare these functions to linear functions in the prior two problems, do so now.

Suggested Questions

- What are the growth factors for the situations in Problems 1.1 and 1.2? (In both the ballot situation and the ruba-reward situation, the growth factor is 2.)

Presenting the Challenge

Tell the class about the next chapter in the peasant's saga. Both the king and the queen have offered new plans. Have students examine the graph and the equation.

Suggested Questions

Check that students understand the new plans.

- How many squares are on the board for each new plan? (16 for the king's Plan 2 and 12 for the queen's Plan 3; there are 64 squares for Plan 1.)
- For each plan, how many rubas are placed on the first square? (Plan 2: 1 ruba; Plan 3: 1 ruba; Plan 4: 20 rubas)
- What is the rule for placing rubas on each successive square? (Plan 2: triple on the next square; Plan 3: quadruple on the next square; Plan 4: add 5 for the next square)

- Which plan do you think is the best for the king? For the peasant? (Answers will vary. Record their answers and come back to these in the Summarize.)

Distribute **Labsheet 1.3: Different Reward Plans** (accessibility) to students who you think will benefit from writing on the tables as they work through the Problem.

Explore

Providing for Individual Needs

When finding the equation for Plan 2, some students will write $r = 3^{n-1}$. Others will be more comfortable finding the *y*-intercept and using it as a starting point, giving them the equation $r = \frac{1}{3}(3^n)$.

Note: Refer to the discussion of Method 2 in the Summarize below.

For Question B, students can graph the data by hand or enter the data pairs into their graphing calculators to make a plot. See **Mathematical Background: Using the Graphing Calculator**. Students may need help choosing suitable scales for the axes. Some students may use the equation to graph Plan 3.

You may want to have one or two pairs display their graphs. Have at least one group display all three graphs on the same set of axes.

Going Further

Ask students to find and compare the total reward for the three plans. Suggest that they use their calculators to find the totals.

Students will find that the total reward for Plan 2 is less than the number on individual squares in the later stages of Plan 1. In fact, the total reward for Plan 2 is 21,523,360 rubas, less than the number of rubas on square 26 of Plan 1. The total reward for Plan 3 is 5,592,405 rubas. The totals show that Plan 1 is best for the peasant and Plan 3 is best for the king.

- For Plan 1, look at how the total number of rubas on the board changes with each square. What pattern do you see? (doubling pattern minus 1)
- Do you find similar patterns for Plans 2 and 3? Explain. (Answers may vary. The patterns are not the same. That is, the sums are not obviously connected to powers of 3 and 4.)

If students keep a running total, they may see that for Plan 1, the sum for the first *n* squares is 2^{n-1}. Each sum is 1 less than a power of 2.

Students may think of $r = 2^{n-1}$ as an exponential function. It is not an exponential function since it does not exhibit the multiplicative patterns for exponential functions. That is, there is no growth factor.

Square Number	Rubas	Total Rubas
1	1	1
2	2	3
3	4	7
4	8	15
5	16	31
6	32	63
7	64	127
8	128	255
9	256	511
10	512	1,023
n	2^{n-1} or $\frac{1}{2}(2^n)$	$2^n - 1$

Note: Similar patterns hold for sums of powers of 3 and 4. The sum of the first n powers of 3, $3^0 + 3^1 + 3^2 + \ldots + 3^{n-1}$, is $\frac{1}{2}\left(3^n - 1\right)$, and the sum of the first n powers of 4, $4^0 + 4^1 + 4^2 + \ldots + 4^{n-1}$, is $\frac{1}{3}\left(4^n - 1\right)$. In this Problem, we are summing the sequence 3^0 to 3^{n-1} and 4^0 to 4^{n-1}, not 3^n and 4^n, so this formula has to be adjusted to accommodate this shift. These sums are the sum of a geometric sequence, which are discussed in *Function Junctions*.

Planning for the Summary

What evidence will you use in the summary to clarify and deepen understanding of the Focus Question?

What will you do if you do not have evidence?

Summarize

Orchestrating the Discussion

Begin by asking for another show of hands about which plan is best for the peasant and which is best for the king. Then discuss the answers to the Problem.

In Question A, students should understand that the growth pattern for each plan is exponential because the number of rubas for any square is a fixed number times the number on the previous square. For Plan 2, the fixed number, or growth factor, is 3, and for Plan 3, it is 4.

Students will eventually be comparing the four plans. A large visual record of essential information about each plan will facilitate making comparisons. Display **Labsheet 1.3: Different Reward Plans.** This might be a way to work with students to start a class chart and graph for the plans. In the chart, include the number of squares on the board, the equation, and the number of rubas on the last square.

Students can enter information on the class chart as they find it.

This is how the chart might look at the end of Problem 1.3 for the first three plans:

Reward Plans

Plan	Squares	Equation	Rubas on Last Square
Plan 1	64	$r = 2^{n-1}$	9.2×10^{18}
Plan 2	16	$r = 3^{n-1}$	14,348,907
Plan 3	12	$r = 4^{n-1}$	4,194,304

Ask students to compare the graphs. Discuss how the growth patterns show up in the tables and graphs. Be sure students identify the growth factor for each plan and can describe how this number affects the table, graph, and equation.

This is an opportunity to discuss the standard form of an exponential equation, $y = a(b^x)$. The equation $r = \frac{1}{4}(4^n)$ is in standard form, while the equation $r = 4^{n-1}$ is not. If you have not yet discussed equations in standard form, do so now. Students need not master this form here, but they should begin thinking about it and about how they can check that the two forms of the equation are equivalent.

Suggested Questions

- What are the growth factors for the relationships in Plans 1, 2, and 3? (2, 3, and 4)
- How does the growth factor show up in the table for each relationship? (It is the constant factor that is used to generate the next entry.)
- How does the growth factor show up in the equation for each relationship? (It is the base of the exponential expression, or the value of b in the equation $y = a(b^x)$.)
- How does the growth factor affect the shape of the graph? (It causes the graph to increase slowly at first and then zoom upward.)
- In the last problem, you saw that $2^0 = 1$. Do 3^0 and 4^0 also equal 1? Explain. (Yes; the equation $r = 3^{n-1}$ is the number of rubas on square n for Plan 2. When $n = 1$, $r = 3^{1-1} = 3^0$. We know this is equal to 1 because there is 1 ruba on square 1. Using the same argument for Plan 3 gives $4^0 = 1$.)
- Is the growth pattern in Plan 4 an exponential function? (No; it is a linear function.)

- Compare the growth patterns for linear and exponential functions. (When linear functions are graphed, they produce a straight line. When exponential functions are graphed, they produce a curve that starts out almost flat and then curves upward steeply.)

You could pose the Going Further questions from the Explore for homework or discuss them as a class. You could also end the Summarize with ACE Exercise 16.

Reflecting on Student Learning

Use the following questions to assess student understanding at the end of the lesson.

- What evidence do I have that students understand the Focus Question?
  - Where did my students get stuck?
  - What strategies did they use?
  - What breakthroughs did my students have today?
- How will I use this to plan for tomorrow? For the next time I teach this lesson?
- Where will I have the opportunity to reinforce these ideas as I continue through this Unit? The next Unit?

ACE Assignment Guide

- **Applications:** 13–21
- **Connections:** 44–48
- **Extensions:** 49, 51–52

Labsheet 1ACE: Exercises 17–21 (accessibility) contains the tables for Exercises 17–21. You can give this labsheet to students who you think may benefit from writing on the tables as they work out their solutions.
Labsheet 1ACE: Exercise 51 contains a larger version of the table in the Student Edition.

Mathematical Reflections

Possible Answers to Mathematical Reflections

1. One key property of exponential growth patterns is that each time you increase the value of the independent variable by 1, you multiply the value of the dependent variable by the same constant number, the growth factor. Another key property of exponential growth patterns is that the numbers begin to grow very quickly. The graphs of exponential growth patterns are increasing curves. You can use either the table or graph to find the values of the variables, and you can use the equation to compute the value of the dependent variable, given a value of the independent variable. Since values of the dependent variable can grow so quickly, it is convenient to write them in scientific notation.
2. With exponential growth patterns, you multiply the y-value by a constant each time the x-value increases by 1. With linear growth patterns, you add or subtract a constant to the y-value each time the x-value increases by 1. Also, the graphs of linear patterns are straight lines, while graphs of exponential growth patterns are curves. The problems that can be modeled by each function are quite different. You need to check if the growth pattern is additive or multiplicative. You can use the problem context or the table, graph, or equation to decide which function is needed to solve the problem.

Possible Answers to Mathematical Practices Reflections

Students may have demonstrated all of the eight Common Core Standards for Mathematical Practice during this Investigation. During the class discussion, have students provide additional Practices that the Problem cited involved and identify the use of other Mathematical Practices in the Investigation.

One student observation is provided in the Student Edition. Here is another sample student response.

We compared the growth patterns in linear and exponential functions in Problem 1.3. In a linear function, as the independent variable increases by one, the dependent variable changes by adding a constant number. In an exponential function, as the independent variable increases by one, the dependent variable changes by multiplying by a constant number.

MP7: Look for and make use of structure.

STUDENT PAGE

Investigation 1

Exponential Growth

In this Investigation, you will explore *exponential growth*. You will cut paper in half over and over to experience exponential growth. You will read a story about the land of Montarek. That story shows how exponential growth can be used. Finally, you will explore exponential patterns and compare them to linear growth patterns with tables, graphs, and equations.

1.1 Making Ballots

Introducing Exponential Functions

Chen is the secretary of the Student Government Association. He is making ballots for a meeting. Chen starts by cutting a sheet of paper in half. Then, he stacks the two pieces and cuts them in half again. With four pieces now, he stacks them and cuts them in half. By repeating this process, he makes smaller and smaller paper ballots.

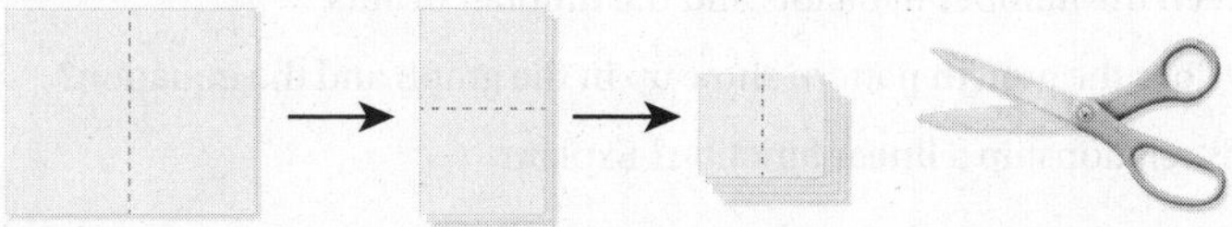

Common Core State Standards

8.F.A.2 Compare properties of two functions each represented in a different way (algebraically, graphically, numerically in tables, or by verbal descriptions).

8.F.A.3 Interpret the equation $y = mx + b$ as defining a linear function, whose graph is a straight line; give examples of functions that are not linear.

8.EE.A.3 Use numbers expressed in the form of a single digit times an integer power of 10 to estimate very large or very small quantities, and to express how many times as much one is than the other.

Also 8.EE.A.4, A-CED.A.1, A-CED.A.2, A-REI.B.3, F-IF.C.7, F-IF.C.7a, F-IF.C.7e, F-IF.C.9, F-BF.A.1, F-BF.A.1a, F-LE.A.1, F-LE.A.1a, F-LE.A.3, F-LE.B.5

Notes

After each cut, Chen counts the ballots and records the results in a table.

Number of Cuts	Number of Ballots
1	2
2	4
3	
4	
5	

He wants to predict the number of ballots after any number of cuts.

Describe the pattern of change. How many ballots are there after *n* cuts?

Problem 1.1

A **1.** Make a table to show the number of ballots after each of the first 5 cuts.

2. Look for a pattern in the way the number of ballots changes with each cut. Use your observations to extend your table to show the number of ballots for up to 10 cuts.

B **1.** Graph the data and write an equation that represents the relationship between the number of ballots and the number of cuts.

2. How does the growth pattern show up in the graph and the equation?

3. Is this relationship a linear function? Explain.

C **1.** Suppose Chen could make 20 cuts. How many ballots would he have? How many ballots would he have if he could make 40 cuts?

2. How many cuts would it take to make 500 ballots?

ACE Homework starts on page 14.

Notes

1.2 Requesting a Reward
Representing Exponential Functions

When you found the number of ballots after 10, 20, and 40 cuts, you may have multiplied long strings of 2s. Instead of writing long product strings of the same factor, you can use **exponential form,** such as 2^5. You can write $2 \times 2 \times 2 \times 2 \times 2$ as 2^5, which is read "2 to the fifth power."

In the expression 2^5, 5 is the **exponent** and 2 is the **base.** When you evaluate 2^5, you get $2^5 = 2 \times 2 \times 2 \times 2 \times 2 = 32$. Since there are two ways to write 2^5, we call 32 the **standard form** and $2 \times 2 \times 2 \times 2 \times 2$ the **expanded form** of 2^5.

Stella used her calculator in Problem 1.1 to compute the number of ballots after 40 cuts. Calculators use shorthand for displaying very large numbers.

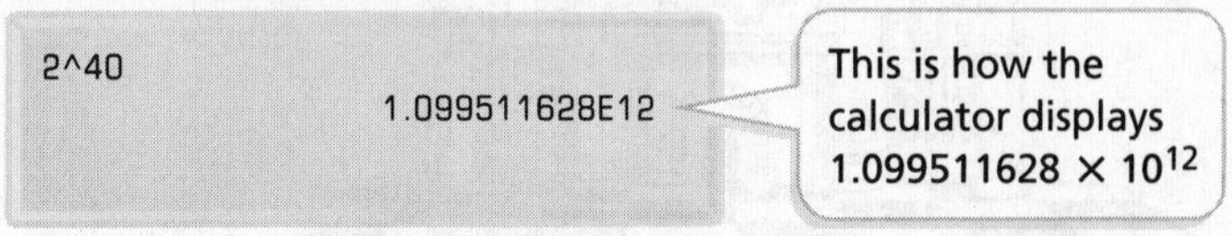
2^40
1.099511628E12
This is how the calculator displays $1.099511628 \times 10^{12}$

The number $1.099511628 \times 10^{12}$ is written in **scientific notation.**

This notation can be expanded as follows:

$$\begin{aligned} 1.099511628 \times 10^{12} &= 1.099511628 \times 1{,}000{,}000{,}000{,}000 \\ &= 1{,}099{,}511{,}628{,}000 \end{aligned}$$

The number 1,099,511,628,000 is the standard form for the number $1.099511628 \times 10^{12}$ written in scientific notation.

The calculator above has approximated 2^{40} as accurately as it can with the number of digits it can store. A number written in scientific notation must be in the form:

(a number greater than or equal to 1 but less than 10) × (a power of 10)

Notes

As you explore the king's dilemma below, you can use scientific notation to express large numbers.

One day in the ancient kingdom of Montarek, a peasant saved the life of the king's daughter. The king was so grateful he told the peasant she could have any reward she desired. The peasant, the kingdom's chess champion, made an unusual request:

Plan 1—The Peasant's Plan

"I would like you to place 1 ruba on the first square of my chessboard, 2 rubas on the second square, 4 on the third square, 8 on the fourth square, and so on. Continue this pattern until you have covered all 64 squares. Each square should have twice as many rubas as the previous square."

The king replied, "Rubas are the least valuable coin in the kingdom. Surely you can think of a better reward." But the peasant insisted, so the king agreed to her request.

- Did the peasant make a wise choice? Explain.

Notes

STUDENT PAGE

Problem 1.2

A 1. Make a table showing the number of rubas the king will place on squares 1 through 10 of the chessboard.

2. Graph the points (*number of the square, number of rubas*) for squares 1 to 10.

3. Write an equation for the relationship between the number of the square n and the number of rubas r.

B 1. How does the number of rubas change from one square to the next?

2. How does the pattern of change you observed in the table show up in the graph? How does it show up in the equation?

C 1. Which square will have 2^{30} rubas? Explain.

2. What is the first square on which the king will place at least one million rubas? How many rubas will be on this square?

3. Larissa uses a calculator to compute the number of rubas on a square. When is the first time the answer is displayed in scientific notation?

D Compare the growth pattern to the growth pattern in Problem 1.1.

ACE Homework starts on page 14.

1.3 Making a New Offer
Growth Factors

The patterns of change in the number of ballots in Problem 1.1 and in the number of rubas in Problem 1.2 show **exponential growth.** In each case, you can find the value for any cut or square by multiplying the previous value by a fixed number. This fixed number is called the **growth factor.** These relationships are called **exponential functions.** The number of the cut or square is the *independent variable.* The number of pieces of paper or rubas on the square is the *dependent variable.*

- What are the growth factors for Problems 1.1 and 1.2?

Notes

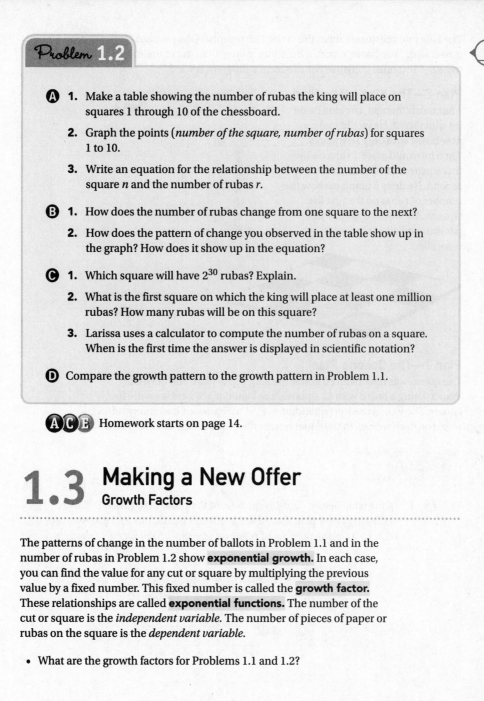

The king told the queen about the reward he promised the peasant. The queen said, "You have promised her more money than the entire royal treasury! You must convince her to accept a different reward."

Plan 2—The King's New Plan

After much thought, the king came up with Plan 2. He would make a new board with only 16 squares. Then he would place 1 ruba on the first square and 3 rubas on the second. He drew a graph to show the number of rubas on the first five squares. He would continue this pattern until all 16 squares were filled.

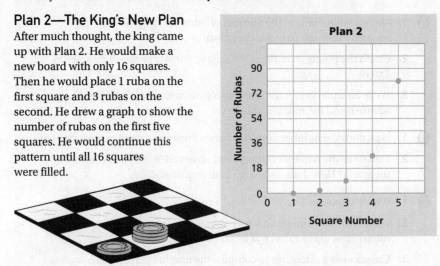

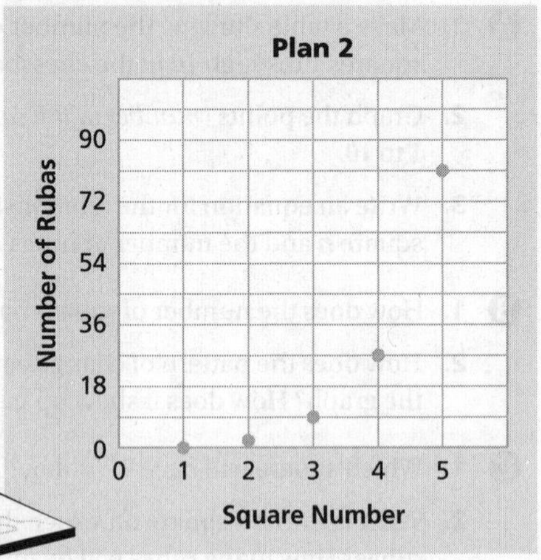

Plan 3—The Queen's Plan

The queen was unconvinced about the king's new plan. She devised Plan 3. Using a board with 12 squares, she would place 1 ruba on the first square. She would use the equation $r = 4^{n-1}$ to figure out how many rubas to put on each square. In the equation, r is the number of rubas on square n.

Problem 1.3

A 1. In the table below, Plan 1 is the reward the peasant requested. Plan 2 is the king's new plan. Plan 3 is the queen's plan. Copy and extend the table to show the number of rubas on squares 1 to 10 for each plan.

Reward Plans

Square Number	Number of Rubas		
	Plan 1	Plan 2	Plan 3
1	1	1	1
2	2	3	4
3	4	■	■
4	■	■	■

Notes

Problem 1.3 continued

2. a. What are the independent and dependent variables in each plan?

   b. How are the patterns of change in the number of rubas under Plans 2 and 3 similar to Plan 1? How are they different from Plan 1?

3. Do the growth patterns for Plans 2 and 3 represent exponential functions? If so, what is the growth factor for each? Explain.

B 1. Write an equation for the relationship between the number of the square n and the number of rubas r for Plan 2.

2. Make a graph of Plan 3 for $n = 1$ to 10. How does your graph compare to the graphs for Plans 1 and 2?

3. How is the growth factor represented in the equations and graphs for Plans 2 and 3?

C The king's financial advisor said that either Plan 2 or Plan 3 would devastate the royal treasury. She proposed a fourth plan.

Plan 4—The Financial Advisor's Plan

The advisor proposed Plan 4. The king would put 20 rubas on the first square, 25 on the second, 30 on the third, and so on. He would increase the number of rubas by 5 for each square. He would continue this pattern until all 64 squares are covered.

1. Compare the growth pattern of Plan 4 to Plans 1, 2, and 3. Is the pattern in Plan 4 an exponential function? Explain.

2. Write an equation that represents the relationship in Plan 4.

D For each plan, how many rubas are on the final square? List them from least to greatest.

ACE Homework starts on page 14.

Notes

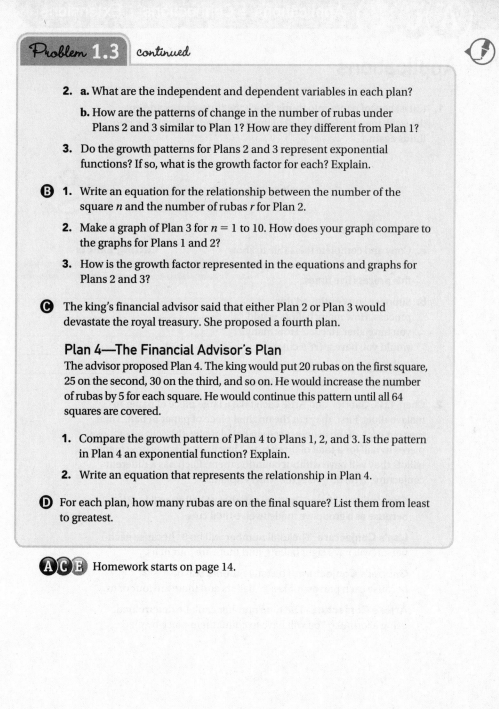

Applications | Connections | Extensions

Applications

1. Cut a sheet of paper into thirds. Stack the three pieces and cut the stack into thirds. Stack all of the pieces and cut the stack into thirds again.

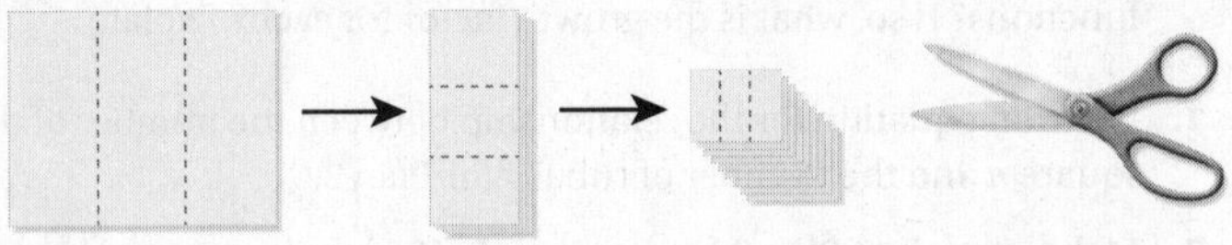

a. Copy and complete this table to show the number of ballots after repeating this process five times.

b. Suppose you continued this process. How many ballots would you have after 10 cuts? How many would you have after n cuts?

c. How many cuts would it take to make at least one million ballots?

Cutting Ballots

Cutting Processes	Number of Ballots
1	3
2	■
3	■
4	■
5	■

2. Chen, Lisa, Gabriel, and Artie each take a large piece of paper to make ballots. First, they cut the original piece of paper in half. Then, they cut each of those new pieces in half. Finally, they cut all of those pieces in half for a total of three cuts. They want to know how many ballots they will have without counting them. Each has a different conjecture. Who do you agree with? Explain.

Chen's Conjecture The total number of ballots will be 2^{12} because as a group we made twelve total cuts.

Lisa's Conjecture The total number will be 8^4 because each person will have eight ballots, and there are four of us.

Gabriel's Conjecture The total number will be 4×2^3 because each person makes 2^3 ballots and there are four of us.

Artie's Conjecture The total number can't be determined using a formula. You will have to count them piece by piece.

Notes

3. Angie is studying her family's history. She discovers records of ancestors 12 generations back. She wonders how many ancestors she has from the past 12 generations. She starts to make a diagram to help her figure this out. The diagram soon becomes very complex.

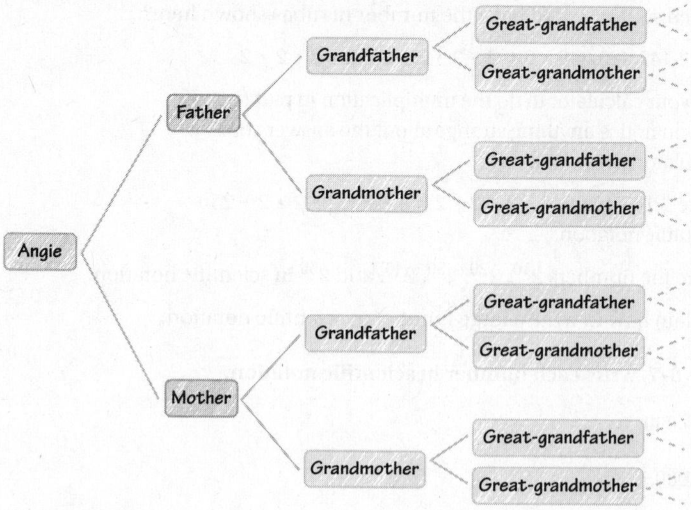

a. Make a table and a graph showing the number of ancestors in each of the 12 generations.

b. Write an equation for the number of ancestors a in a given generation n.

c. What is the total number of ancestors in all 12 generations?

Notes

4. Sarah was working on Problem 1.2. She found that there will be 2,147,483,648 rubas on square 32.

   a. How many rubas will be on square 33? How many will be on square 34? How many will be on square 35?

   b. Which square would have the number of rubas shown here?

   $$2{,}147{,}483{,}648 \cdot 2 \cdot 2 \cdot 2 \cdot 2 \cdot 2 \cdot 2 \cdot 2 \cdot 2 \cdot 2$$

   c. Use your calculator to do the multiplication in part (b). Do you notice anything strange about the answer your calculator gives? Explain.

   d. Write $2{,}147{,}483{,}648 \cdot 2 \cdot 2 \cdot 2 \cdot 2 \cdot 2 \cdot 2 \cdot 2 \cdot 2 \cdot 2$ in scientific notation.

   e. Write the numbers 2^{10}, 2^{20}, 2^{30}, 2^{40}, and 2^{50} in scientific notation.

   f. Explain how to write a large number in scientific notation.

For Exercises 5–7, write each number in scientific notation.

5. 100,000,000

6. 29,678,900,522

7. 11,950,500,000,000

For Exercises 8–10, write each number in standard form.

8. 6.43999001×10^8

9. 8.89234×10^5

10. $3.4348567000 \times 10^{10}$

11. What is the largest whole-number value of n that your calculator will display in standard notation?

    a. 3^n

    b. π^n

    c. 12^n

    d. 237^n

Notes

12. What is the smallest value of n that your calculator will display in scientific notation?

a. 10^n

b. 100^n

c. $1000n^n$

13. Many single-celled organisms reproduce by dividing into two identical cells.

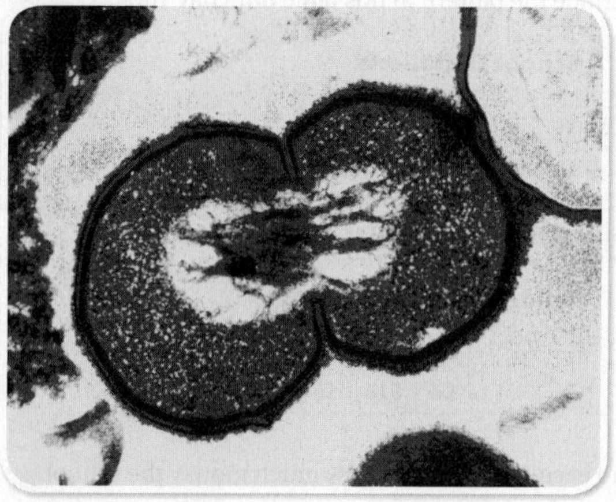

Suppose an amoeba (uh MEE buh) splits into two amoebas every half hour.

a. A biologist starts an experiment with one amoeba. Make a table showing the number of amoebas she would have at the end of each hour over an 8-hour period.

b. Write an equation for the number of amoebas a after t hours. Which variable is the independent variable? Dependent variable?

c. How many hours will it take for the number of amoebas to reach one million?

d. Make a graph of the data (*time, amoebas*) from part (a).

e. What similarities do you notice in the pattern of change for the number of amoebas and the patterns of change for other situations in this Investigation? What differences do you notice?

Notes

14. Zak's uncle wants to donate money to Zak's school. He suggests three possible plans. Look for a pattern in each plan.

Plan 1 He will continue the pattern in this table until day 12.

School Donations

Day	1	2	3	4
Donation	$1	$2	$4	$8

Plan 2 He will continue the pattern in this table until day 10.

School Donations

Day	1	2	3	4
Donation	$1	$3	$9	$27

Plan 3 He will continue the pattern in this table until day 7.

School Donations

Day	1	2	3	4
Donation	$1	$4	$16	$64

a. Copy and extend each table to show how much money the school would receive each day.

b. For each plan, write an equation for the relationship between the day number n and the number of dollars donated d.

c. Are any of the relationships in Plans 1, 2, or 3 exponential functions? Explain.

d. Which plan would give the school the greatest total amount of money?

Notes

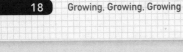

15. Carmelita is planning to swim in a charity swim-a-thon. Several relatives said they would sponsor her.

> I will give you $1 if you swim 1 lap, $3 if you swim 2 laps, $5 if you swim 3 laps, $7 if you swim 4 laps, and so on.—**Grandmother**

> I will give you $1 if you swim 1 lap, $3 if you swim 2 laps, $9 if you swim 3 laps, $27 if you swim 4 laps, and so on.—**Father**

> I will give you $2 if you swim 1 lap, $3.50 if you swim 2 laps, $5 if you swim 3 laps, $6.50 if you swim 4 laps, and so on.—**Aunt Josie**

> I will give you $1 if you swim 1 lap, $2 if you swim 2 laps, $4 if you swim 3 laps, $8 if you swim 4 laps, and so on.—**Uncle Sebastian**

> WOW! Thanks everyone for your support!—**Carmelita**

a. Decide whether each donation pattern is an *exponential function*, *linear function*, or *neither*.

b. For each relative, write an equation for the total donation d if Carmelita swims n laps. Which variable is the independent variable? Dependent variable?

c. For each plan, tell how much money Carmelita will raise if she swims 20 laps.

Notes

16. The graphs below represent the equations $y = 2^x$ and $y = 2x + 1$.

Graph 1

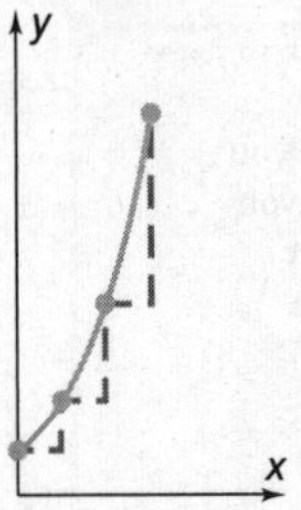

Graph 2

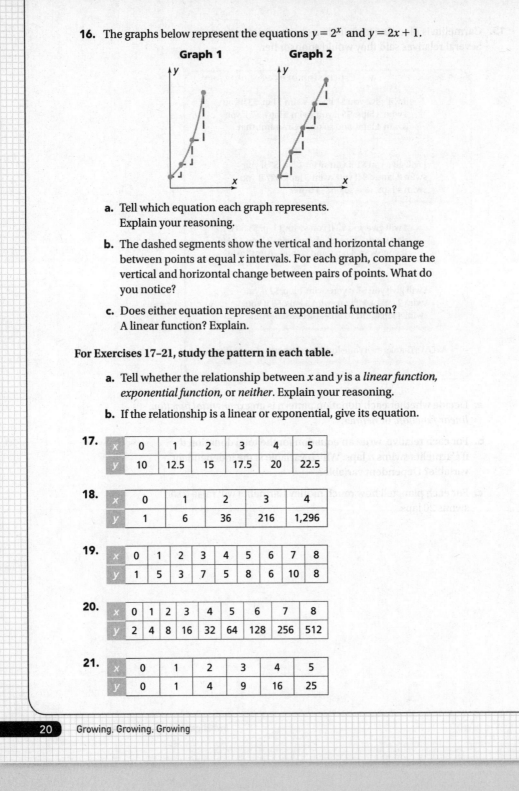

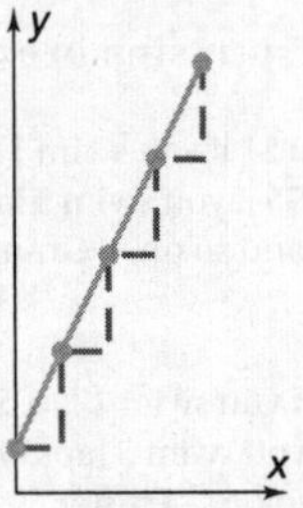

a. Tell which equation each graph represents. Explain your reasoning.

b. The dashed segments show the vertical and horizontal change between points at equal x intervals. For each graph, compare the vertical and horizontal change between pairs of points. What do you notice?

c. Does either equation represent an exponential function? A linear function? Explain.

For Exercises 17–21, study the pattern in each table.

a. Tell whether the relationship between x and y is a *linear function, exponential function,* or *neither*. Explain your reasoning.

b. If the relationship is a linear or exponential, give its equation.

17.

x	0	1	2	3	4	5
y	10	12.5	15	17.5	20	22.5

18.

x	0	1	2	3	4
y	1	6	36	216	1,296

19.

x	0	1	2	3	4	5	6	7	8
y	1	5	3	7	5	8	6	10	8

20.

x	0	1	2	3	4	5	6	7	8
y	2	4	8	16	32	64	128	256	512

21.

x	0	1	2	3	4	5
y	0	1	4	9	16	25

Notes

Connections

For Exercises 22–24, write each expression in exponential form.

22. $2 \times 2 \times 2 \times 2$

23. $10 \cdot 10 \cdot 10 \cdot 10 \cdot 10 \cdot 10 \cdot 10$

24. $2.5 \times 2.5 \times 2.5 \times 2.5 \times 2.5$

For Exercises 25–27, write each expression in standard form.

25. 2^{10} **26.** 10^2 **27.** 3^9

28. You know that $5^2 = 25$. How can you use this fact to evaluate 5^4?

29. The standard form for 5^{10} is 9,765,625. How can you use this fact to evaluate 5^{11}?

30. Multiple Choice Which expression is equal to one million?

A. 10^6 **B.** 6^{10} **C.** 100^2 **D.** 2^{100}

31. Use exponents to write an expression for one billion (1,000,000,000).

For Exercises 32–34, decide whether each number is more or less than one million *without using a calculator* or multiplying. Explain how you found your answer. Use a calculator to check your answer.

32. 9^6 **33.** 3^{10} **34.** 11^6

For Exercises 35–40, write the number in exponential form using 2, 3, 4, or 5 for the base.

35. 125 **36.** 64 **37.** 81

38. 3,125 **39.** 1,024 **40.** 4,096

41. Refer to Problem 1.1. Suppose 250 sheets of paper is 1 inch high.

a. How high would the stack of ballots be after 20 cuts? After 30 cuts?

b. How many cuts would it take to make a stack 1 foot high?

c. The average distance from Earth to the moon is about 240,000 miles. Which (if any) of the stacks in part (a) would reach the moon?

Notes

42. In Problem 1.2, suppose a Montarek ruba has the value of a modern U.S. penny. What are the dollar values of the rubas on squares 10, 20, 30, 40, 50, and 60?

43. A ruba has the same thickness as a modern U.S. penny (about 0.06 inch). Suppose the king had been able to reward the peasant by using Plan 1 (doubling the number of rubas in each square). What would be the height of the stack of rubas on square 64?

44. One of the king's advisors suggested another plan. Put 100 rubas on the first square of a chessboard, 125 on the second square, 150 on the third square, and so on, increasing the number of rubas by 25 for each square.

a. Write an equation for the numbers of rubas r on square n. Explain the meanings of the numbers and variables in your equation.

b. Describe the graph of this plan.

c. What is the total number of rubas on the first 10 squares? The first 20 squares?

For Exercises 45–47, find the slope and *y*-intercept of the graph of each equation.

45. $y = 3x - 10$ **46.** $y = 1.5 - 5.6x$ **47.** $y = 15 + \frac{2}{5}x$

48. Write an equation whose line is less steep than the line represented by $y = 15 + \frac{2}{5}x$.

Notes

Extensions

49. Consider the two equations below.

Equation 1	**Equation 2**
$r = 3^n - 1$	$r = 3^{n-1}$

a. For each equation, find r when n is 2.

b. For each equation, find r when n is 10.

c. Explain why the equations give different values of r for the same value of n.

d. Do either of these equations represent an exponential function? Explain why.

50. The table below represents the number of ballots made by repeatedly cutting a sheet of paper in half.

Cutting Ballots

Number of Cuts	Number of Ballots
1	2
2	4
3	8
4	16

a. Write an equation for the pattern in the table.

b. Use your equation and the table to determine the value of 2^0.

c. What do you think b^0 should equal for any number b? For example, do you think 6^0 and 23^0 should equal? Explain.

Notes

51. The king tried to figure out the total number of rubas the peasant would receive under Plan 1. He noticed an interesting pattern.

a. Extend and complete this table for the first 10 squares.

Reward Plan 1

Square	Number of Rubas on Square	Total Number of Rubas
1	1	1
2	2	3
3	4	7
4	■	■

b. Describe the pattern of growth in the total number of rubas as the number of the square increases. Do either of these relationships represent an exponential function? Explain.

c. Write an equation for the relationship between the number of the square n and the total number of rubas on the board t.

d. When the total number of rubas reaches 1,000,000, how many squares will have rubas?

e. Suppose the king had been able to give the peasant the reward she requested. How many rubas would she have received?

52. Refer to Plans 1–4 in Problem 1.3.

a. Which plan should the king choose? Explain.

b. Which plan should the peasant choose? Explain.

c. Write an ending to the story of the king and the peasant.

Notes

Mathematical Reflections 1

In this Investigation, you explored situations in which the relationship between the two variables represented exponential functions. You saw how you could recognize patterns of exponential growth in tables, graphs, and equations.

Think about your answers to these questions. Discuss your ideas with other students and your teacher. Then write a summary of your findings in your notebook.

1. **Describe** an exponential growth pattern. Include key properties such as growth factors.
2. **How** are exponential functions similar to and different from the linear functions you worked with in earlier Units?

STUDENT PAGE

Notes

Common Core Mathematical Practices

As you worked on the Problems in this Investigation, you used prior knowledge to make sense of them. You also applied Mathematical Practices to solve the Problems. Think back over your work, the ways you thought about the Problems, and how you used Mathematical Practices.

Tori described her thoughts in the following way:

We wrote the equation, $r = \frac{1}{2}2^n$ to represent the relationship between the number of rubas, r on square n in Problem 1.2. As the number of squares increase by 1, the number of rubas doubles.

We went backwards in the table to find the number of rubas on square 0. To find the number of rubas on square 0, we divided the number of rubas on square 1 by 2. One divided by two is $\frac{1}{2}$. $\frac{1}{2}$ is the y-intercept.

If you start with square 0, you get the number of rubas on the next square by multiplying the number of rubas on square 0 by 2. This process is repeated for the next square, etc.

So, on square n, you multiply $\frac{1}{2}$ by 2, n times. $\frac{1}{2} \times 2 \times 2 \times ... \times 2$ or $\frac{1}{2}(2^n)$.

Common Core Standards for Mathematical Practice

MP3 Construct viable arguments and critique the reasoning of others

- What other Mathematical Practices can you identify in Tori's reasoning?
- Describe a Mathematical Practice that you and your classmates used to solve a different Problem in this Investigation.

Notes

Examining Growth Patterns

Investigation Overview

Investigation Description

Investigation 2 focuses on exponential relationships with *y*-intercepts greater than 1. The standard form of an exponential equation is $y = a(b^x)$. When $x = 0$, the equation becomes $y = a$ since $b^0 = 1$. Thus *a*, the coefficient of the exponential term, generally indicates the initial value of the exponentially growing quantity. The growth factor is *b*. As the value of *x* increases by 1, the value of *y* increases by a factor of *b*.

By contrast a linear function is represented by the equation, $y = mx + b$ where *m* is the constant rate of change (or slope) and *b* is the *y*-intercept.

Students explore situations given in context, tables, graphs, and equations and determine whether the situation represents an exponential function by identifying the growth factor in each representation. They use the growth factor and *y*-intercept to write an equation.

Investigation Vocabulary

There are no new glossary terms introduced in this Investigation.

Mathematics Background

- Growth Factor and Exponential Functions
- *y*-Intercept or Initial Value

Planning Chart

Content	ACE	Pacing	Materials	Resources
Problem 2.1	1–4, 15–23, 33–35	1 day	**Labsheet 2ACE** Exercise 2 **Labsheet 2ACE:** Exercise 3 (accessibility) **Labsheet 2ACE:** Exercise 4 (accessibility) **Labsheet 2ACE:** Exercise 33 (accessibility) graphing calculators graph paper transparencies	**Teaching Aid 2.1** Water Hyacinth Growth
Problem 2.2	5–8, 24, 29	½ day	**Labsheet 2ACE** Exercise 8 graphing calculators	**Teaching Aid 2.2** Mold Experiment
Problem 2.3	9–14, 25–28, 30–32	½ day	**Labsheet 2ACE** Exercise 13 **Labsheet 2ACE:** Exercise 14 (accessibility) **Labsheet 2ACE** Exercises 25–28 graphing calculators	**Teaching Aid 2.3** Garter Snake Population Growth
Mathematical Reflections		½ day		
Assessment: Check Up		½ day		• Check Up

Goals and Standards

Goals

Exponential Functions Explore problem situations in which two or more variables have an exponential relationship to each other

- Identify situations that can be modeled with an exponential function
- Identify the pattern of change (growth factor) between two variables that represent an exponential function in a situation, table, graph, or equation
- Represent an exponential function with a table, graph, or equation
- Make connections among the patterns of change in a table, graph, and equation of an exponential function
- Compare the growth rate and growth factor for an exponential function and recognize the role each plays in an exponential situation
- Identify the growth factor and initial value in problem situations, tables, graphs, and equations that represent exponential functions
- Determine whether an exponential function represents a growth (increasing) or decay (decreasing) pattern, from an equation, table, or graph that represents an exponential function
- Determine the value of the independent and dependent value from a table, graph, or equation of an exponential function
- Use an exponential equation to describe the graph and table of an exponential function
- Predict the *y*-intercept from an equation, graph, or table that represents an exponential function
- Interpret the information that the *y*-intercept of an exponential function represents
- Determine the effects of the growth factor and initial value for an exponential function on a graph of the function
- Solve problems about exponential growth and decay from a variety of different subject areas, including science and business, using an equation, table, or graph
- Observe that one exponential equation can model different contexts
- Compare exponential and linear functions

Mathematical Reflections

Look for evidence of student understanding of the goals for this Investigation in their responses to the questions in *Mathematical Reflections*. The goals addressed by each question are indicated below.

1. How can you use a table, a graph, and an equation that represent an exponential function to find the *y*-intercept and growth factor for the function? Explain.

Goals

- Identify the growth factor and initial value in problem situations, tables, graphs and equations that represent exponential functions
- Represent an exponential function with a table, graph, or equation
- Make connections among the patterns of change in a table, graph, and equation of an exponential function
- Determine the value of the independent and dependent value from a table, graph, or equation of an exponential function
- Use an exponential equation to describe the graph and table of an exponential function
- Solve problems about exponential growth and decay from a variety of different subject areas, including science and business, using an equation, table or graph

2. How can you use the *y*-intercept and growth factor to write an equation that represents an exponential function? Explain.

Goals

- Identify the growth factor and initial value in problem situations, tables, graphs and equations that represent exponential functions
- Identify situations that can be modeled with an exponential function
- Solve problems about exponential growth and decay from a variety of different subject areas, including science and business, using an equation, table or graph

3. How would your answers to Questions 1 and 2 change for a linear function?

Goals

- Compare exponential and linear functions
- Identify the growth factor and initial value in problem situations, tables, graphs and equations that represent exponential functions

Standards

Common Core Content Standards

8.EE.A.3 Use numbers expressed in the form of a single digit times an integer power of 10 to estimate very large or very small quantities, and to express how many times as much one is than the other. For example, estimate the population of the United States as 3×10^8 and the population of the world as 7×10^9, and determine that the world population is more than 20 times larger. *Problem 1*

8.F.A.1 Understand that a function is a rule that assigns to each input exactly one output. The graph of a function is the set of ordered pairs consisting of an input and the corresponding output. *Problems 1, 2, and 3*

8.F.B.5 Describe qualitatively the functional relationship between two quantities by analyzing a graph (e.g., where the function is increasing or decreasing, linear or nonlinear). Sketch a graph that exhibits the qualitative features of a function that has been described verbally. *Problems 1, 2, and 3*

A-SSE.A.1.a Interpret parts of an expression, such as terms, factors, and coefficients. *Problem 2*

A-CED.A.2 Create equations in two or more variables to represent relationships between quantities; graph equations on coordinate axes with labels and scales. *Problems 1, 2, and 3*

A-REI.D.10 Understand that the graph of an equation in two variables is the set of all its solutions plotted in the coordinate plane, often forming a curve. *Problems 1, 2, and 3*

F-IF.B.4 For a function that models a relationship between two quantities, interpret key features of graphs and tables in terms of the quantities, and sketch graphs showing key features given a verbal description of the relationship. *Problems 1, 2, and 3*

F-BF.A.1a Determine an explicit expression, a recursive process, or steps for calculation from a context. *Problems 1, 2, and 3*

F-LE.A.2 Construct linear and exponential functions, including arithmetic and geometric sequences, given a graph, a description of a relationship, or two input-output pairs (including reading these from a table). *Problems 1 and 3*

F-LE.B.5 Interpret the parameters in a linear or exponential function in terms of a context. *Problems 1, 2, and 3*

F-IF.C.7.e. Graph exponential and logarithmic functions, showing intercepts and end behavior, and trigonometric functions, showing period, midline and amplitude. *Problems 1 and 3*

Facilitating the Mathematical Practices

Students in *Connected Mathematics* classrooms display evidence of multiple Common Core Common Core Standards for Mathematical Practice every day. Here are just a few examples where of when you might observe students demonstrating the Standards for Mathematical Practice during this Investigation.

Practice 1: Make sense of problems and persevere in solving them.

Students are engaged every day in solving problems and, over time, learn to persevere in solving them. To be effective, the problems embody critical concepts and skills and have the potential to engage students in making sense of mathematics. Students build understanding by reflecting, connecting, and communicating. These student-centered problem situations engage students in articulating the "knowns" in a problem situation and determining a logical solution pathway. The student-student and student-teacher dialogues help students to not just make sense of the problems, but also to persevere in finding appropriate strategies to solve them. The suggested questions in the Teacher Guides provide the metacognitive scaffolding to help students monitor and refine their problem-solving strategies.

Practice 7: Look for and make use of structure.

In Problem 2.1, they check characteristics of exponential growth and notice that it is a function, i.e., one input produces a single out put in an exponential equation. Students identify and record their personal experiences with the Standards for Mathematical Practice during the *Mathematical Reflections* at the end of the Investigation.

Practice 8: Look for and express regularity in repeated reasoning.

In Problem 2.1, students work with plant growth patterns. Here they reason from a description of growth to an equation. They learn to deal with an initial value in their exponential growth situation, i.e., $a = 1{,}000(2^n)$ where a is the area of the lake that is covered and n is the number of months that have passed.

Students identify and record their personal experiences with the Standards for Mathematical Practice during the *Mathematical Reflections* at the end of the Investigation.

PROBLEM
2.1

Killer Plant Strikes Lake Victoria

y-Intercepts Other Than 1

Problem Overview

Focus Question What information do you need to write an equation that represents an exponential function?

Problem Description

Students read about a real situation in which a non-native plant spread rapidly and began to cover Lake Victoria in Africa. They then solve a Problem about a similar situation. In the Problem, the area of the plant doubles each month, and the starting value is greater than 1.

Students create and look for patterns in a table, graph, and equation representing the growth pattern. They compare this doubling situation to the doubling situations in Investigation 1 and find that the y-intercept is 1,000, not 1. The growth factor and the shape of the graph are the same as in Problems 1.1 and 1.2.

Problem Implementation

Students should work in groups of two to four.

Materials

- **Labsheet 2ACE:** Exercise 2 (accessibility)
- **Labsheet 2ACE:** Exercise 3 (accessibility)
- **Labsheet 2ACE:** Exercise 4 (accessibility)
- **Labsheet 2ACE:** Exercise 33 (accessibility)
- **Teaching Aid 2.1:** Water Hyacinth Growth

graph paper
transparencies (optional)

Using Technology

Graphing calculators can be used to create graphs and tables, and to test equations.

Vocabulary

There are no new glossary terms introduced in this Problem.

Mathematics Background

- Growth Factor and Exponential Functions
- *y*-Intercept or Initial Value

At a Glance and Lesson Plan

- At a Glance: Problem 2.1 Growing, Growing, Growing
- Lesson Plan: Problem 2.1 Growing, Growing, Growing

Launch

Launch Video

This animation shows the situation in Ghost Lake from the water plant growth in the Problem. You can use this animation during the Presenting the Challenge after discussing Lake Victoria.

After showing the video, continue with the rest of Presenting the Challenge. Visit Teacher Place at mathdashboard.com/cmp3 to see the complete video.

Connecting to Prior Knowledge

If the two forms of the equation for Problem 1.2 did not arise in Investigation 1, begin by discussing the situation and the questions in the introduction to the Investigation.

Investigation 1 presented two forms of the equation for the queen's reward plan, so the ideas in the introduction should not be completely new to students.

Suggested Questions

- In Problem 1.2, some students came up with two equations for the situation, $r = 2^{n-1}$ and others wrote $r = \frac{1}{2}(2^n)$. Are both equations correct? Explain. (Both equations are correct. We can check by comparing tables or graphs.)
- What is the value of r if $n = 1$? ($\left(\frac{1}{2}(2^n)\right) = \frac{1}{2}(2^1) = 1$, so $2^{n-1} = 2^0 = 1$)

- What is the *y*-intercept for this relationship? (The *y*-intercept is $\frac{1}{2}$. This is clearer from the form $r = \frac{1}{2}(2^n)$. Some students will use the fact that $2^0 = 1$ to find $\frac{1}{2}(2^0) = \frac{1}{2}$. Others will work backward and use the fact that, each time *n* decreases by 1, *r* is halved. Because the value of *r* for $n = 1$ is 1, the value of *r* for $n = 0$ must be $\frac{1}{2}$.)

Make sure students have a way of checking that the forms are equivalent, perhaps by generating a table or a graph. You may need to remind students of the meaning of *y*-intercept. Just as with linear equations, the *y*-intercept is the *y*-value when $x = 0$ (or in this case, the *r* value when $n = 0$).

Point out that the *y*-intercept has no meaning in this situation. It would be the number of rubas on square 0, which does not make sense.

Presenting the Challenge

Tell the real story about the water hyacinths taking over Lake Victoria.

Suggested Questions

- The article says the plant doubles in size every 5 to 15 days. Does this mean the growth factor is 2? (It depends on what you consider to be a "unit" of time. Say, the plant area doubles every 10 days. The growth factor is the number the *y*-value is multiplied by each time the *x*-value increases by 1 unit, for example, 1 day, 1 month, or 1 year. If you considered a 10-day period to be 1 unit of time, then the growth factor would be 2.)
- Are there similar situations in our state? (Answers will vary. In the states that border the Great Lakes, there is concern that the Asian Carp will invade the lakes and consume the local fish population. As of 2013, there is much discussion as to how to contain the carp.)

Now back to Lake Victoria. Tell students to consider the area of 769 square miles to be the initial value, or the value at time 0. Have students help you make a table to show the growth pattern.

Water Hyacinth Growth

Days	Area Covered (sq. mi)
0	769
10	1,578
20	3,156
30	6,312
40	12,624
50	25,248

Now tell the class that Ghost Lake has a problem similar to the one on Lake Victoria. Discuss the first paragraph of Problem 2.1, which gives the details, or show the Launch Video.

- Is the area of the plant growing exponentially? How do you know? (Yes it is. The Problem says the area covered by the plant is doubling every month.)
- How is this problem similar to the problems you solved in Investigation 1? (A quantity is being multiplied by a constant factor at each stage. For this situation, the growth factor is 2, as it was in the ballot-cutting problem and in Reward Plan 1.)
- How is this problem different from previous problems? (The initial value is 1,000 when the independent variable, in this case time, is 0. In the ballot-cutting problem, the initial value is 1 when the independent variable, the number of cuts, is 0. In the reward problems, the initial value is 1 when the independent variable, the number for the square, is 1.)

Explain that we want to represent the growth of the plant starting today, when the area is 1,000 square feet.

- The initial value, 1,000 square feet, is the *y*-intercept for this relationship. Can anybody explain why? (It is the value when the time is 0, before any months have passed.)

Explore

Providing for Individual Needs

If students are having trouble writing an equation, suggest that they make a table for the first few months.

Suggested Questions

- What is the starting value, or *y*-intercept? (1,000)
- What is the growth factor? (2)
- What information do you need to write an equation? (You need the initial starting amount and the growth factor.)

If students are still having difficulty, refer them to the equation $r = \frac{1}{2}(2^n)$ for Reward Plan 1, which was discussed before the Problem.

- What does the $\frac{1}{2}$ in the ruba equation represent? (the *y*-intercept)
- What does the 2 in the ruba equation represent? (the growth factor)
- How could you write an equation in a similar form for the Ghost Lake plant growth? (Use 1,000 instead of $\frac{1}{2}$ for the *y*-intercept. Use 2 for the growth factor.)

Suggest that students test their equation for a couple of months' values to make sure it works. Some students may also need prompting to choose appropriate scales for the *y*-axis of the graph.

You might distribute large sheets of paper for students to display their equations and graphs for the Summarize.

Going Further

- Find the daily growth factor for the Lake Victoria situation if the area doubles every 10 days. (It is approximately 1.072. Students can get close by guessing and checking.)

Planning for the Summary

What evidence will you use in the summary to clarify and deepen understanding of the Focus Question?
What will you do if you do not have evidence?

▼ Summarize

Orchestrating the Discussion

Call on a couple of students to display their equations and to explain what the numbers and variables mean.

Suggested Questions

- Does it make sense to connect the dots on the graph? (Yes; since time is continuous.)
- How would the equation change if the initial area covered was 1,500 square feet? (The equation would be $a = 1{,}500(2^n)$, where n is the number of months.)
- How would the equation change if the area covered tripled every month? (The equation would be $a = 1{,}000(3^n)$, where n is the number of months.)
- Use your equation to find the area of the lake that is covered with the plant after 11 months. (177,147,000 ft^2)
- How did you find the number of months it will take the plant to completely cover the lake? (Some students will use a table, some will use the graph, and some will guess and check, using the equation and their calculator.)

If you did not assign the Going Further in the Explore, you can use it as a final question in the Summarize.

Reflecting on Student Learning

Use the following questions to assess student understanding at the end of the lesson.

- What evidence do I have that students understand the Focus Question?
  - Where did my students get stuck?
  - What strategies did they use?
  - What breakthroughs did my students have today?
- How will I use this to plan for tomorrow? For the next time I teach this lesson?
- Where will I have the opportunity to reinforce these ideas as I continue through this Unit? The next Unit?

ACE Assignment Guide

- **Applications:** 1–4
- **Connections:** 15–23
- **Extensions:** 33–35

Distribute **Labsheet 2ACE: Exercise 2** (accessibility). You can give **Labsheet 2ACE: Exercise 3** (accessibility), **Labsheet 2ACE: Exercise 4** (accessibility), and **Labsheet 2ACE: Exercise 33** (accessibility) to students who you think may benefit from writing or drawing on these tables as they work out their solutions.

PROBLEM
2.2 Growing Mold
Interpreting Equations for Exponential Functions

Problem Overview

Focus Question How is the growth factor and initial population for an exponential function represented in an equation that represents the function?

Problem Description

Exponential data for the growth of mold is presented in the form of an equation that represents an exponential function. Students find and interpret the y-intercept and growth factor for the function from the equation. They also use the equation to answer questions about the situation.

Problem Implementation

Students should work in groups of two to four.

Materials

- **Labsheet 2ACE:** Exercise 8
- **Teaching Aid 2.2:** Mold Experiment

Note: You might wish to have your class conduct an experiment in which they grow mold, collect data on the mold's growth, and then analyze that data. See **Teaching Aid 2.2: Mold Experiment**.

If the class begins the mold-growing experiment at the start of Problem 2.2, they should have enough data by the end of the Unit to analyze the pattern of growth in the mold.

Using Technology

Graphing calculators can be used to create graphs, tables, and test equations.

Vocabulary

There are no new glossary terms introduced in this Problem.

Mathematics Background

- Growth Factor and Exponential Functions
- *y*-Intercept or Initial Value

At a Glance and Lesson Plan

- At a Glance: Problem 2.2 Growing, Growing, Growing
- Lesson Plan: Problem 2.2 Growing, Growing, Growing

Launch

Connecting to Prior Knowledge

In the last Problem, students looked at a situation and found that it represented an exponential relationship. They found the *y*-intercept, which was not 0, and the growth rate from the context and used this information to write an equation. They then used the equation to predict when the lake would be covered by the invasive water plant.

Presenting the Challenge

In this Problem, students are given an equation for an exponential function. They will use it to study how mold grows on bread and use it to determine the initial population and the growth factor.

Discuss with your students the information in the student edition about moldy food. Having a piece of moldy bread or cheese on display makes a great attention grabber.

Suggested Questions

- How much mold is there at the end of day 1? At the end of day 2? At the end of day 3? (Since this question is part of the Problem, collect some conjectures. 1,500 mm^2; 4,500 mm^2; 13,500 mm^2.)
- Do you see any similarities between the pattern of change in this situation and the patterns of change in some of the Problems in the last Investigation and in Problem 2.1? Explain. (The area covered by the mold increases by repeated multiplication. This is similar to the patterns seen in many of the reward plans from Investigation 1 and to the pattern of plant growth in Problem 2.1. It is also similar to Problem 2.1 in that both Problems have an initial value greater than 1 and both involve an area being covered by something—either a plant or mold.)

Explore

Providing for Individual Needs

This problem is similar to Problem 2.1, but it describes an exponential relationship with an equation, rather than with a verbal description.

When students evaluate the equation for a specific *d* value, make sure they raise only the base to the exponent, and not both the base and the initial value. For example, when computing $50(3^5)$, watch for students who find 50×3 and then raise the product, 150, to the exponent of 5. This is not correct.

Remind students to follow the Order of Operations: Evaluate exponents first and then multiply. Most graphing calculators use the correct order of operations.

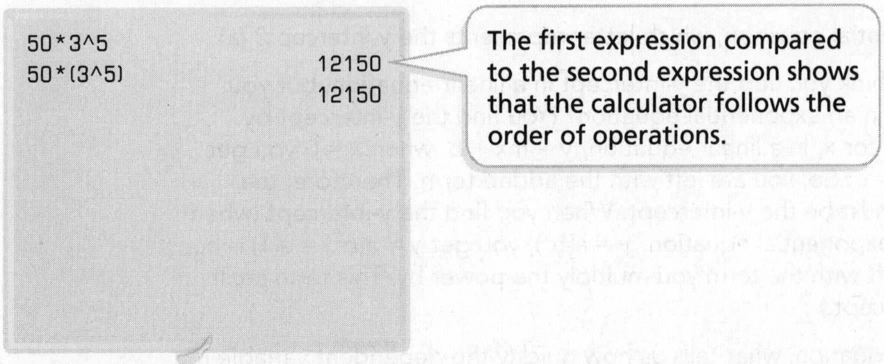

50*3^5
12150
50*(3^5)
12150
The first expression compared to the second expression shows that the calculator follows the order of operations.

Planning for the Summary

What evidence will you use in the summary to clarify and deepen understanding of the Focus Question?

What will you do if you do not have evidence?

Summarize

Orchestrating the Discussion

To initiate a discussion, use the following.

Suggested Questions

- How does the mold grow from one day to the next? (It triples from one day to the next.)
- Is the mold growth similar to other growth situations you have studied? Explain. (Yes; Plan 2 tripled in Problem 1.2.)

- What does each part of your equation tell you about the growth of the mold? (The constant, 50, tells how much mold you start with measured by mm^2. The base, 3, tells you the growth pattern. The exponent, d, is where you insert the amount of time that it grows over.)
- Suppose you started with 25 mm^2 of mold and it grew in the same way that it did in the Problem. How would the equation change? How would the graph change? (The constant would be 25, not 50 in the equation. The graph would have a y-intercept at 25, not 50. The equation would be $m = 25(3^d)$)

Discuss the standard form for an exponential equation introduced in Question E: $y = a(b^x)$. Help students see how this equation is similar to and different from the slope-intercept form of a linear equation.

- In the linear equation, $y = mx + b$, which letter represents the y-intercept? (b)
- In the exponential equation, which letter represents the y-intercept? (a)
- Why do you think you add the y-intercept in a linear equation, but you multiply by it in an exponential equation? (You find the y-intercept by substituting 0 for x. In a linear equation, $y = mx + b$, when $x = 0$ you get $y = m(0) + b = b$. So, you are left with the added term. Therefore, the added term must be the y-intercept. When you find the y-intercept (when $x = 0$) for an exponential equation, $y = a(b^x)$, you get $y = a(b^0) = a(1) = a$. So, you are left with the term you multiply the power by. This term must be the y-intercept.)
- In the linear equation, what tells us how quickly the dependent variable is changing as the value of the independent variable increases in increments of 1? (the slope, m)
- In the exponential equation, what tells us how quickly the dependent variable is changing as the value of the independent variable increases in increments of 1? (the base, b)
- What other similarities and differences do you notice between linear and exponential equations?

Check for Understanding

Repeat the last set of questions with specific examples such as these:

$y = -3x + 4$

$y = 1.5x$

$y = 3^x$

$y = 10(5^x)$

Reflecting on Student Learning

Use the following questions to assess student understanding at the end of the lesson.

- What evidence do I have that students understand the Focus Question?
  - Where did my students get stuck?
  - What strategies did they use?
  - What breakthroughs did my students have today?
- How will I use this to plan for tomorrow? For the next time I teach this lesson?
- Where will I have the opportunity to reinforce these ideas as I continue through this Unit? The next Unit?

ACE Assignment Guide

- **Applications:** 5–8
- **Connections:** 24, 29
- **Labsheet 2ACE:** Exercise 8 contains the table from the Student Edition.

PROBLEM

2.3

Studying Snake Populations

Interpreting Graphs of Exponential Functions

Problem Overview

Focus Question How is the growth factor and initial population for an exponential function represented in a graph that represents the function?

Problem Description

Students are given a graph from a real-world exponential growth relationship for a snake population. This is the first time that they find and interpret the *y*-intercept and growth factor from a graph of an exponential function. They use this information to write an equation that represents the relationship and then use the equation to answer questions about the relationship.

Problem Implementation

Students should work in groups of two to four.

Materials

- **Labsheet 2ACE:** Exercise 13 (accessibility)
- **Labsheet 2ACE:** Exercise 14 (accessibility)
- **Labsheet 2ACE:** Exercises 25–28
- **Teaching Aid 2.3:** Garter Snake Population Growth

Using Technology

Graphing calculators can be used to create graphs, tables, and test equations.

Vocabulary

There are no new glossary terms introduced in this Problem.

Mathematics Background

- Growth Factor and Exponential Functions
- *y*-Intercept or Initial Value

At a Glance and Lesson Plan

- At a Glance: Problem 2.3 Growing, Growing, Growing
- Lesson Plan: Problem 2.3 Growing, Growing, Growing

Launch

Connecting to Prior Knowledge

In the last two Problems, students looked at exponential functions that were represented with a verbal description of a real-world problem and with an equation for the growth of a mold. In this Problem, students are given a graph of an exponential function. They will use the graph to determine the growth factor and the *y*-intercept and use this information to write an equation.

Presenting the Challenge

Display the graph of the snake population using **Teaching Aid 2.3: Garter Snake Population Growth**. Briefly describe the Problem. Then challenge the students to find an equation that represents the graph of the exponential function and to use the equation to make predictions about the population of the snake.

Explore

Providing for Individual Needs

It is difficult to read the *y*-intercept from the graph. To guide student thinking, ask the following:

Suggested Questions

- Which points are easy to read? ((2, 25), (3, 125) and (4, 625))
- What is the growth pattern for these 3 years? (The growth factor is 5.)
- If we assume this same growth pattern for years 0 to *n*, what is the population in year 1? What is the population in year 0? (Students may need to put the data in a table and then reason backward to reach year 1, then year 0. Dividing 25 by 5, the population in year 1 is 5. Dividing 5 by 5, the population in year 0 is 1.)
- What is the *y*-intercept? (0, 1)

Students should now be able to write the equation $p = 1(5^n)$, or just $p = 5^n$. Look for other ways students may arrive at the equation. Some students may write the equation in a different form. (See Summarize for Problem 2.3.)

Planning for the Summary

What evidence will you use in the summary to clarify and deepen understanding of the Focus Question?

What will you do if you do not have evidence?

Summarize

Orchestrating the Discussion

Ask the class to share the ways they found their equations. Some students may have used (2, 25) as a starting point and written $p = 25(5^{n-2})$. This is also correct. You can ask students to check a few points to verify that the two equations are equivalent. You can come back to these two equations after students learn the properties of exponents in Investigation 5. Then, they will be able to show the equivalence symbolically: $25(5^{n-2}) = 5^2 \cdot 5^{n-2} = 5^{2+n} = 5^n$.

Some classes have had interesting discussions around the *y*-intercept, (0,1). Students are curious about how one snake at the start can produce 5 snakes by the end of year one. Some students conjecture that the snake must have been pregnant at the start.

Check for Understanding

On a large sheet of paper, have each group or pair of students write an exponential equation for the growth of a population and describe the variables. As each group holds up its poster, ask the rest of the class:

- What is the growth factor?
- What is the initial population?
- How large is the population after 4 years?
- How long will it take the population to reach a certain number?

After a couple of presentations, say:

- Compare the growth of this population to some of the previous examples we have seen.

Reflecting on Student Learning

Use the following questions to assess student understanding at the end of the lesson.

- What evidence do I have that students understand the Focus Question?
  - Where did my students get stuck?
  - What strategies did they use?
  - What breakthroughs did my students have today?
- How will I use this to plan for tomorrow? For the next time I teach this lesson?
- Where will I have the opportunity to reinforce these ideas as I continue through this Unit? The next Unit?

ACE Assignment Guide

- **Applications:** 9–14
- **Connections:** 25–28, 30–32

Labsheet 2ACE: Exercise 13 (accessibility), **Labsheet 2ACE: Exercise 14** (accessibility), and **Labsheet 2ACE: Exercises 25–28** (accessibility) contain the graphs for the corresponding Exercises in the Student Edition. You can give these Labsheets to students who you think may benefit from writing or drawing on these graphs as they work out their solutions.

Mathematical Reflections

Possible Answers to Mathematical Reflections

1. Using the table, the y-intercept is the point where $x = 0$. If the y-intercept is not given in the table, you can use the growth factor to find it. To find the growth factor, divide a y-value by the previous y-value. Then, start with a y-value and divide by this growth factor, moving backward in the table until you find the y-value for the point with x-coordinate 0. Using the equation $y = a(b^x)$, the y-intercept is a and the growth factor is b. Using the graph, the y-intercept is the point where the graph crosses the y-axis. The growth factor can be found by taking two points on the graph with x-values 1 unit apart, such as (2, 4) and (3, 8) and then dividing the second y-value by the first y-value.

2. In the graph of $y = a(b^x)$, the b is how much one y-value is multiplied by to get the next y-value. A greater value of b will increase the rate of growth, resulting in a steeper graph at each x-value. The growth factor is b and the y-intercept (the value when $x = 0$) is a.

   If a is the y-intercept and b is the growth factor, then these values can be substituted in place of a and b in the equation $y = a(b^x)$.

Note: some students may observe that the *y*-intercept occurs when $x = 0$. This means that if $x = 0$, then $y = a(b^0)$. This means that $b^0 = 1$. Exponents were discussed in Grade 6, but students may not remember that a number raised to the 0 power is 1. Exponents are revisited in Investigation 5.

3. The process is similar. For linear functions, the *y*-intercept occurs at the point (0, *b*) on the graph or the entry (0, *b*) in a table or *b* in the equation, $y = mx + b$. The rate of change or slope of the line is *m* in the equation. It is also the ratio of $\frac{y^2 - y^1}{x^2 - x^1}$. In a table, it is also the difference between two consecutive values of *y* that correspond to $x_n - x_{n-1}$. The *y*-intercept *b* and the rate of change *m* can be used to write an equation for a linear function in the form $y = mx + b$. Note that using the slash notation without using parentheses changes the meaning, as $y_2 - y_1/x_2 - x_1 = y_2 - \frac{y_1}{x_2} - x_1$, which is not the correct ratio.

Possible Answers to Mathematical Practices Reflections

Students may have demonstrated all of the eight Common Core Standards for Mathematical Practice during this Investigation. During the class discussion, have students provide additional Practices that the Problem cited involved and identify the use of other Mathematical Practices in the Investigation.

One student observation is provided in the Student Edition. Here is another sample student response.

We found it difficult to find the y-intercept from the graph in Problem 2.3 since the first part of the graph look like it was a straight line. We knew the growth rate was 5, so we found a few points on the graph that were easy to read and put them in a table. We used the points (2, 25), (3, 125) and (4, 625). We then reasoned backward to find the value of y that corresponded to x = 0. We divided 25 by 5. The population in year 1 is 5. Then we divided 5 by 5. The population in year 0 is 1. This is the y-intercept. We thought it was strange that there was one snake at the start and then the population grew. The snake must have been pregnant.

MP1: Make sense of problems and persevere in solving them.

Investigation 2

Examining Growth Patterns

STUDENT PAGE

In Investigation 1, you learned to recognize exponential growth patterns. Now you are ready to take a closer look at the tables, graphs, and equations that represent exponential functions. You will explore this question:

- How do the starting value and growth factor show up in the table, graph, and equation that represent an exponential function?

For example, students at West Junior High wrote two equations to represent the reward in Plan 1 of Problem 1.2. Some students wrote $r = 2^{n-1}$ and others wrote $r = \frac{1}{2}\left(2^n\right)$. In both equations, r represents the number of rubas on square n.

- Are both equations correct? Explain.
- What is the value of r in both equations if $n = 1$? Does this make sense?
- What is the y-intercept for the graph of these equations?
- Do you think there is any value for n that will result in more than one value for r?

Common Core State Standards

8.F.A.1 Understand that a function is a rule that assigns to each input exactly one output. The graph of a function is the set of ordered pairs consisting of an input and the corresponding output.

8.F.B.5 Describe qualitatively the functional relationship between two quantities by analyzing a graph. Sketch a graph that exhibits the qualitative features of a function that has been described verbally.

Also N-Q.A.1, N-Q.A.2, A-SSE.A.1, A-SSE.A.1a, A-CED.A.1, A-CED.A.2, F-IF.C.7e, F-BF.A.1, F-BF.A.1a, F-LE.A.1, F-LE.A.1a, F-LE.A.2, F-LE.B.5

Notes

2.1 Killer Plant Strikes Lake Victoria

y-Intercepts Other Than 1

Exponential functions occur in many real-life situations. For example, consider this story:

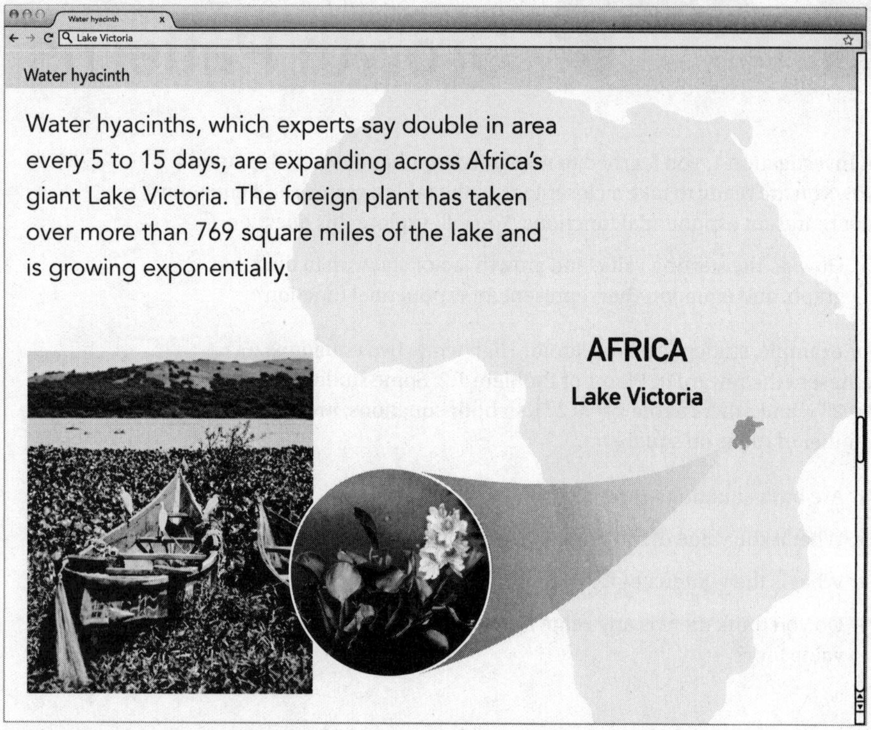

Water hyacinth
Lake Victoria
Water hyacinth
Water hyacinths, which experts say double in area every 5 to 15 days, are expanding across Africa's giant Lake Victoria. The foreign plant has taken over more than 769 square miles of the lake and is growing exponentially.
AFRICA
Lake Victoria

Little progress has been made to reverse the effects of the water hyacinths. Plants like the water hyacinth that grow and spread rapidly can affect native plants and fish. This in turn can affect the livelihood of fishermen. It can also impede rescue operations in case of a water disaster. To understand how such plants grow, you will look at a similar situation.

Notes

Problem 2.1

Ghost Lake is a popular site for fishermen, campers, and boaters. In recent years, a certain water plant has been growing on the lake at an alarming rate. The surface area of Ghost Lake is 25,000,000 square feet. At present, the plant covers 1,000 square feet of the lake. The Department of Natural Resources estimates that the area covered by the water plant is doubling every month.

A 1. Write an equation that represents the growth pattern of the plant.

2. Explain what information the variables and numbers in your equation represent.

3. Compare this equation to the equations in Investigation 1.

B 1. Make a graph of the equation.

2. How does this graph compare to the graphs of the exponential functions in Investigation 1?

3. Recall that a function is a relationship between two variables where, for each value of the independent variable, there is exactly one corresponding value of the dependent variable. Is the plant growth relationship a function? Justify your answer using a table, graph, or equation.

C 1. How much of the lake's surface will be covered at the end of a year by the plant?

2. How many months will it take for the plant to completely cover the surface of the lake?

ACE Homework starts on page 32.

2.2 Growing Mold

Interpreting Equations for Exponential Functions

Mold can spread rapidly. For example, the area covered by mold on a loaf of bread that is left out in warm weather grows exponentially.

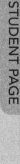

STUDENT PAGE

Notes

Problem 2.2

Students at Magnolia Middle School conducted an experiment. They put a mixture of chicken bouillon (BOOL yahn), gelatin, and water in a shallow pan. Then they left it out to mold. Each day, the students recorded the area of the mold in square millimeters.

The students wrote the equation $m = 50(3^d)$ to model the growth of the mold. In this equation, m is the area of the mold in square millimeters after d days.

A For each part, answer the question and explain your reasoning.

1. What is the area of the mold at the start of the experiment?
2. What is the growth factor?
3. What is the area of the mold after 5 days?
4. On which day will the area of the mold reach 6,400 mm^2?

B An equation that represents an exponential function can be written in the form $y = a(b^x)$ where a and b are constant values.

1. What is the value of b in the mold equation? What does this value represent? Does this make sense in this situation? Explain.
2. What is the value of a in the mold equation? What does this value represent?

ACE Homework starts on page 32.

2.3 Studying Snake Populations

Interpreting Graphs of Exponential Functions

Garter snakes were introduced to a new area 4 years ago. The population is growing exponentially. The relationship between the number of snakes and the year is modeled with an exponential function.

Notes

Problem 2.3

A The graph shows the growth of the garter snake population.

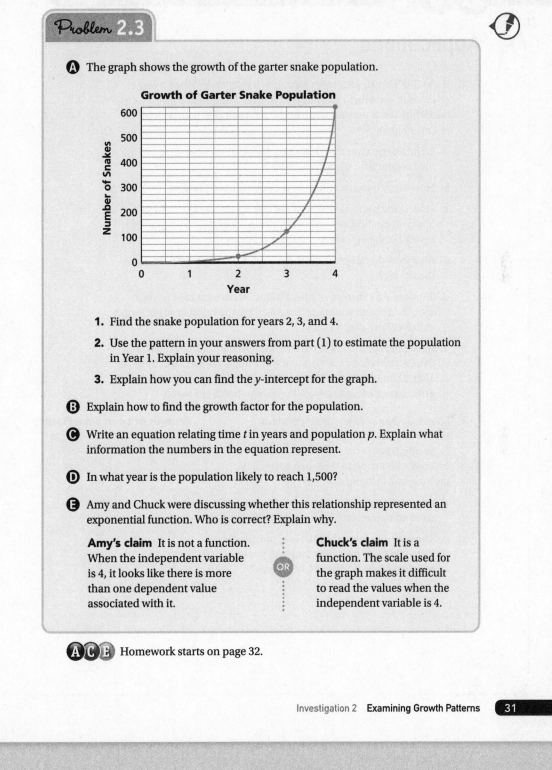

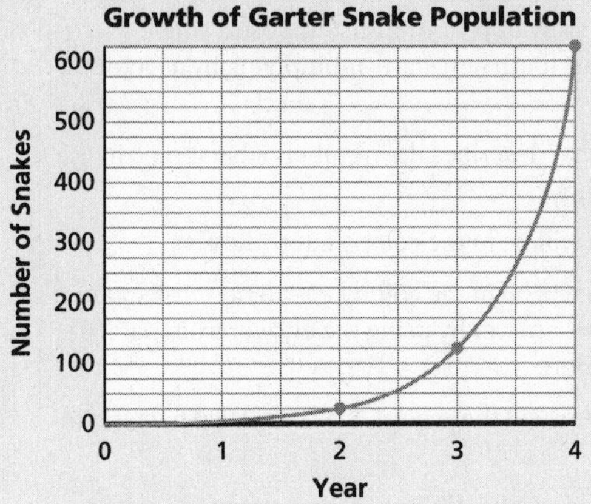

1. Find the snake population for years 2, 3, and 4.
2. Use the pattern in your answers from part (1) to estimate the population in Year 1. Explain your reasoning.
3. Explain how you can find the y-intercept for the graph.

B Explain how to find the growth factor for the population.

C Write an equation relating time t in years and population p. Explain what information the numbers in the equation represent.

D In what year is the population likely to reach 1,500?

E Amy and Chuck were discussing whether this relationship represented an exponential function. Who is correct? Explain why.

Amy's claim It is not a function. When the independent variable is 4, it looks like there is more than one dependent value associated with it.

OR

Chuck's claim It is a function. The scale used for the graph makes it difficult to read the values when the independent variable is 4.

ACE Homework starts on page 32.

STUDENT PAGE

Notes

Applications | Connections | Extensions

Applications

1. If you don't brush your teeth regularly, it won't take long for large colonies of bacteria to grow in your mouth. Suppose a single bacterium lands on your tooth and starts multiplying by a factor of 4 every hour.

   a. Write an equation that describes the number of bacteria b in the new colony after n hours.

   b. How many bacteria will be in the colony after 7 hours?

   c. How many bacteria will be in the colony after 8 hours? Explain how you can find this answer by using the answer from part (b) instead of the equation.

   d. After how many hours will there be at least 1,000,000 bacteria in the colony?

   e. Suppose that, instead of 1 bacterium, 50 bacteria land in your mouth. Write an equation that describes the number of bacteria b in this colony after n hours.

   f. Under the conditions of part (e), there will be 3,276,800 bacteria in this new colony after 8 hours. How many bacteria will there be after 9 hours and after 10 hours? Explain how you can find these answers without going back to the equation from part (e).

2. Loon Lake has a "killer plant" problem similar to Ghost Lake in Problem 2.1. Currently, 5,000 square feet of the lake is covered with the plant. The area covered is growing by a factor of 1.5 each year.

   a. Copy and complete the table to show the area covered by the plant for the next 5 years.

   b. The surface area of the lake is approximately 200,000 square feet. How long will it take before the lake is completely covered?

Growth of Loon Lake Plant

Year	Area Covered (sq. ft)
0	5,000
1	■
2	■
3	■
4	■
5	■

Notes

3. Leaping Liang just signed a contract with a women's basketball team. The contract guarantees her $20,000 the first year, $40,000 the second year, $80,000 the third year, $160,000 the fourth year, and so on, for 10 years.

   a. Make a table showing Liang's salary for each year of this contract.

   b. What is the total amount Liang will earn over the 10 years?

   c. Does the relationship between the number of years and salary represent an exponential function? Explain.

   d. Write an equation for Liang's salary s for any year n of her contract.

4. As a biology project, Talisha is studying the growth of a beetle population. She starts her experiment with 5 beetles. The next month she counts 15 beetles.

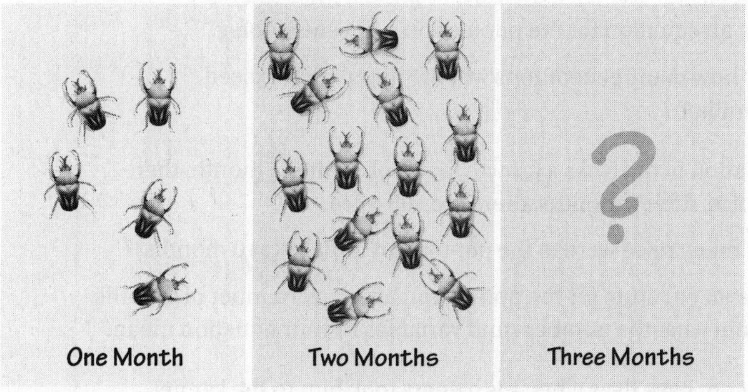

   a. Suppose the beetle population is growing linearly. How many beetles can Talisha expect to find after 2, 3, and 4 months?

   b. Suppose the beetle population is growing exponentially. How many beetles can Talisha expect to find after 2, 3, and 4 months?

   c. Write an equation for the number of beetles b after m months if the beetle population is growing linearly. Explain what information the variables and numbers represent.

   d. Write an equation for the number of beetles b after m months if the beetle population is growing exponentially. Explain what information the variables and numbers represent.

   e. How long will it take the beetle population to reach 200 if it is growing linearly?

   f. How long will it take the beetle population to reach 200 if it is growing exponentially?

Notes

5. Fruit flies are often used in genetic experiments because they reproduce very quickly. In 12 days, a pair of fruit flies can mature and produce a new generation. The table below shows the number of fruit flies in three generations of a laboratory colony.

Growth of Fruit-Fly Population

Generations	0	1	2	3
Number of Fruit Flies	2	120	7,200	432,000

   a. Does this data represent an exponential function? If so, what is the growth factor for this fruit-fly population? Explain how you found your answers.

   b. Suppose this growth pattern continues. How many fruit flies will be in the fifth generation?

   c. Write an equation for the population p of generation g.

   d. After how many generations will the population exceed one million?

6. A population of mice has a growth factor of 3. After 1 month, there are 36 mice. After 2 months, there are 108 mice.

   a. How many mice were in the population initially (at 0 months)?

   b. Write an equation for the population after any number of months. Explain what the numbers and variables in your equation mean.

7. Fido did not have fleas when his owners took him to the kennel. The number of fleas on Fido after he returned from the kennel grew according to the equation $f = 8(3^n)$, where f is the number of fleas and n is the number of weeks since he returned from the kennel. (Fido left the kennel at week 0.)

   a. How many fleas did Fido pick up at the kennel?

   b. Is the relationship represented by the equation an exponential function? If so, what is the growth factor for the number of fleas?

   c. How many fleas will Fido have after 10 weeks if they are untreated?

Notes

8. Consider the equation $y = 150(2^x)$.

a. Make a table of x and y-values for whole-number x-values from 0 to 5.

b. What do the numbers 150 and 2 in the equation tell you about the relationship between the variables x and y?

For Exercises 9–12, find the growth factor and the y-intercept of the equation's graph.

9. $y = 300(3^x)$

10. $y = 300(3)^x$

11. $y = 6{,}500(2)^x$

12. $y = 2(7)^x$

13. The following graph represents the population growth of a certain kind of lizard.

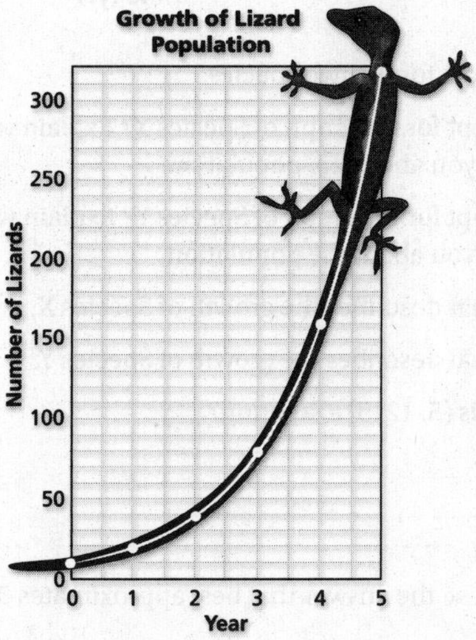

a. What information does the point (2, 40) on the graph tell you?

b. What information does the point (1, 20) on the graph tell you?

c. When will the population exceed 100 lizards?

d. Explain how you can use the graph to find the growth factor for the population.

STUDENT PAGE

Notes

14. The following graphs show the population growth for two species. Each graph represents an exponential function.

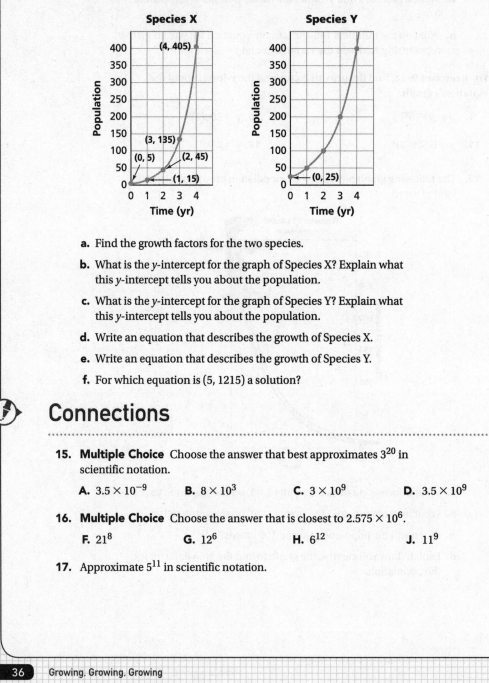

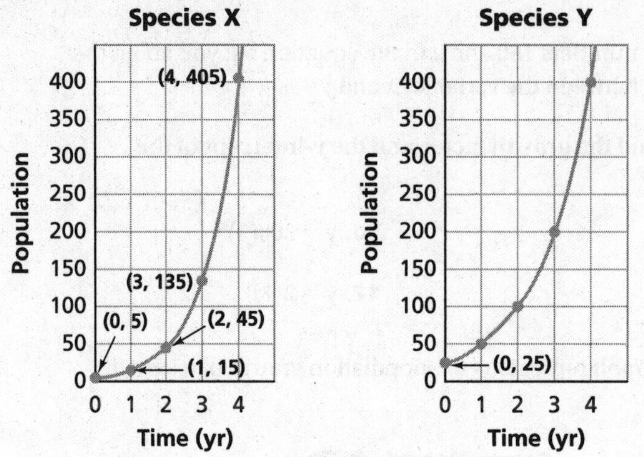

a. Find the growth factors for the two species.

b. What is the y-intercept for the graph of Species X? Explain what this y-intercept tells you about the population.

c. What is the y-intercept for the graph of Species Y? Explain what this y-intercept tells you about the population.

d. Write an equation that describes the growth of Species X.

e. Write an equation that describes the growth of Species Y.

f. For which equation is (5, 1215) a solution?

Connections

15. Multiple Choice Choose the answer that best approximates 3^{20} in scientific notation.

A. 3.5×10^{-9} **B.** 8×10^3 **C.** 3×10^9 **D.** 3.5×10^9

16. Multiple Choice Choose the answer that is closest to 2.575×10^6.

F. 21^8 **G.** 12^6 **H.** 6^{12} **J.** 11^9

17. Approximate 5^{11} in scientific notation.

Notes

For Exercises 18–20, decide whether each number is less than or greater than one million without using a calculator. Explain.

18. 3^6 **19.** 9^5 **20.** 12^6

For Exercises 21–23, write the prime factorization of each number using exponents. Recall the prime factorization of 54 is $3 \times 3 \times 3 \times 2$. This can be written using exponents as $3^3 \times 2$.

21. 45 **22.** 144 **23.** 2,024

24. Consider the two equations below.

Equation 1	**Equation 2**
$y = 10 - 5x$	$y = (10)5^x$

a. What is the *y*-intercept of each equation?

b. For each equation, explain how you could use a table to find how the *y*-values change as the *x*-values increase. Describe the change.

c. Explain how you could use the equations to find how the *y*-values change as the *x*-values increase.

d. For each equation, explain how you could use a graph to find how the *y*-values change as the *x*-values increase.

For Exercises 25–28, write an equation for each line. Identify the slope and *y*-intercept.

25.

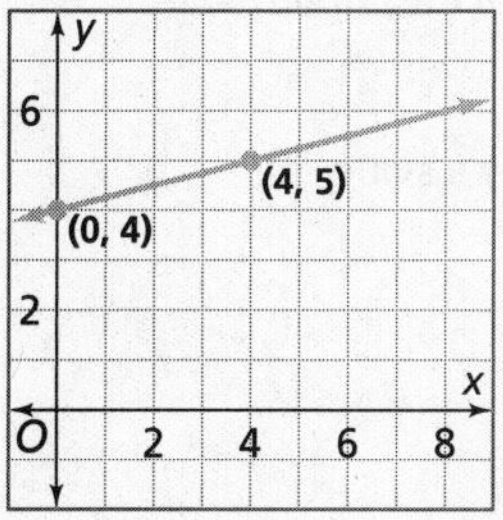

26.

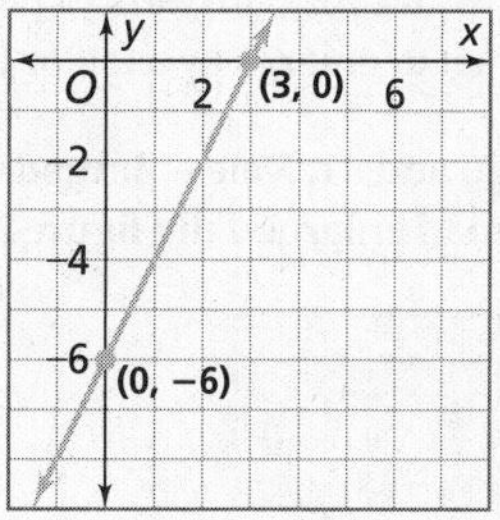

27.

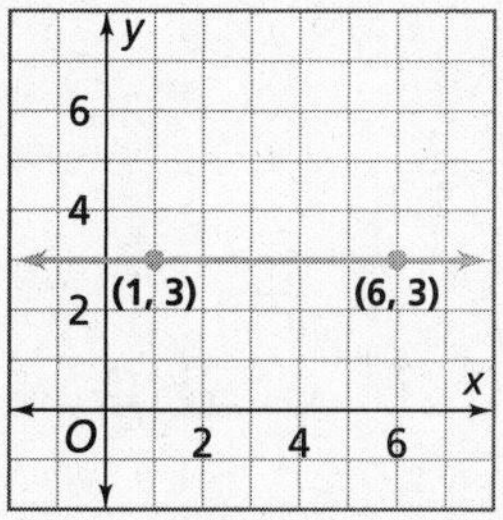

28.

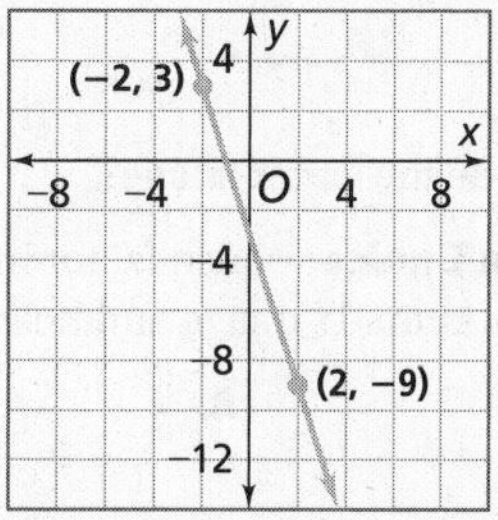

STUDENT PAGE

Notes

29. Maria enlarges a 2-cm-by-3-cm rectangle by a factor of 2 to get a 4-cm-by-6-cm rectangle. She then enlarges the 4-cm-by-6-cm rectangle by a factor of 2. She continues this process, enlarging each new rectangle by a factor of 2.

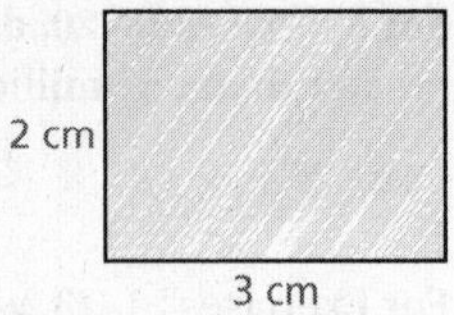

a. Copy and complete the table to show the dimensions, perimeter, and area of the rectangle after each enlargement.

Rectangle Changes

Enlargement	Dimensions (cm)	Perimeter (cm)	Area (cm^2)
0 (original)	2 by 3	■	■
1	4 by 6	■	■
2	■	■	■
3	■	■	■
4	■	■	■
5	■	■	■

b. Is the pattern of growth for the perimeter linear, exponential, or neither? Explain.

c. Does the pattern of growth for the area represent a linear function, exponential function, or neither? Explain.

d. Write an equation for the perimeter P after n enlargements.

e. Write an equation for the area A after n enlargements.

f. How would your answers to parts (a)–(e) change if the copier were set to enlarge by a factor of 3?

For Exercises 30 and 31, Kele enlarged the figure below by a scale factor of 2. Ahmad enlarged the figure 250%.

30. Who made the larger image?

31. Multiple Choice Which factor would give an image between Ahmad's image and Kele's image in size?

A. $\frac{2}{5}$ **B.** $\frac{3}{5}$ **C.** $\frac{9}{4}$ **D.** $\frac{10}{4}$

Notes

32. Companies sometimes describe part-time jobs by comparing them to full-time jobs. For example, a job that requires working half the number of hours of a full-time job is described as a $\frac{1}{2}$-time job or a 50%-time job. ACME, Inc. has three part-time job openings.

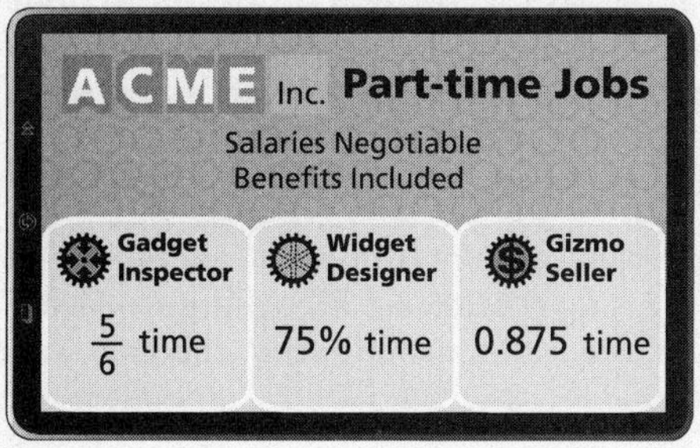
ACME Inc. Part-time Jobs
Salaries Negotiable
Benefits Included
Gadget Inspector
5/6 time
Widget Designer
75% time
Gizmo Seller
0.875 time

Order these jobs from the most time to the least time.

Extensions

33. **a.** Make a table and a graph for the equation $y = 1^x$.

b. How are the patterns in the table and the graph of $y = 1^x$ similar to patterns you have observed for other exponential and linear functions? How are they different?

34. If you know that a graph represents an exponential function, you can find the equation for the function from two points on its graph. Find the equation of the exponential function whose graph passes through each pair of points. Explain.

a. (1, 6) and (2, 12) **b.** (2, 90) and (3, 270)

35. Leaping Liang plays basketball. A team promised her \$1 million a year for the next 25 years. The same team offered Dribbling Dinara \$1 the first year, \$2 the second year, \$4 the third year, \$8 the fourth year, and so on, for 25 years.

a. Suppose Liang and Dinara each accept the offers and play for 20 years. At the end of 20 years, who receives more money?

b. Tell which player will receive more after 21 years, 22 years, 23 years, and 25 years.

c. Do either of the two plans represent an exponential function? Explain.

Notes

Mathematical Reflections 2

In this Investigation, you studied quantities that grew exponentially. These patterns of growth represent exponential functions. You looked at how the values changed from one stage to the next, and you wrote equations to represent the relationship and used them to find the value of a quantity at any stage of growth.

You also graphed coordinate pairs from exponential functions and saw that there is a single output for each input. You sketched graphs from situations described in the Problems and analyzed graphs.

Think about your answers to these questions. Discuss your ideas with other students and your teacher. Then write a summary of your findings in your notebook.

1. **How** can you use a table, a graph, and an equation that represent an exponential function to find the y-intercept and growth factor for the function? Explain.
2. **How** can you use the y-intercept and growth factor to write an equation that represents an exponential function? Explain.
3. **How** would you change your answers to Questions 1 and 2 for a linear function?

Notes

Common Core Mathematical Practices

As you worked on the Problems in this Investigation, you used prior knowledge to make sense of them. You also applied Mathematical Practices to solve the Problems. Think back over your work, the ways you thought about the Problems, and how you used Mathematical Practices.

Jayden described his thoughts in the following way:

We noticed differences between the equations for the growth patterns. In Problem 2.1, the water plant on Ghost Lake equation had an additional factor before the base.

Equations in Investigation 1 were of the form $y =$ some number raised to an exponent. Examples are $y = 2^n$ and $y = 3^{n-1}$. These equations did not have a number in front of the bases, 2 and 3.

In Problem 2.1, there is a number in front of the 2^n. The equation is $a = 1{,}000(2^n)$. In this situation, we start tracking growth at $n = 0$ rather than $n = 1$. So, these graphs have a meaningful y-intercept.

Common Core Standards for Mathematical Practice

MP8 Look for and express regularity in repeated reasoning

- What other Mathematical Practices can you identify in Jayden's reasoning?
- Describe a Mathematical Practice that you and your classmates used to solve a different Problem in this Investigation.

Notes

Investigation 3

PLANNING

Growth Factors and Growth Rates

Investigation Overview

Investigation Description

In this Investigation, students study nonwhole-number growth factors other than 1 and relate these growth factors to growth rates. Some growth patterns, such as investments, are often expressed as percents. This means that to find the growth rate, you calculate the percent increase and add it to the initial or previous value. Then you determine the growth factor from one value to the next. For example, if you invest \$100 at a 6% annual interest rate, the value of the account at the start of the first year is 100 + 100(0.06), or 100(1.06). The growth factor in this case is 1.06, while the growth rate is 6%, or 0.06. Students also explore how the growth rate and the initial value affect the growth pattern.

Investigation Vocabulary

- compound growth
- growth rate

Mathematics Background

- Exponential Functions
- Growth Factor and Exponential Functions
- *y*-intercept or Initial Value
- Growth Rates
- Graphs of Exponential Functions
- Equations for Exponential Functions
- Recursive, or Iterative, Processes
- Equivalence
- Logarithms
- Using Graphing Calculators

Planning Chart

Content	ACE	Pacing	Materials	Resources
Problem 3.1	1–8, 24–30	1 day	**Labsheet 3ACE:** Exercise 1 (accessibility) **Labsheet 3ACE** Exercise 8 poster board	**Teaching Aid 3.1** Rabbit Population Table
Problem 3.2	9–20, 31–32, 40–45	1 day	**Labsheet 3.2** Stamp Value Tables **Labsheet 3ACE** Exercise 9 graphing calculators, graph paper	
Problem 3.3	21–23, 33–39, 46–47	1 day	**Labsheet 3.3** College Funds Table • Centimeter Grid Paper graphing calculators, graph paper	
Mathematical Reflections		½ day		
Assessment: Partner Quiz		1 day		• Partner Quiz

Goals and Standards

Goals

Exponential Functions Explore problem situations in which two or more variables have an exponential relationship to each other

- Identify situations that can be modeled with an exponential function
- Identify the pattern of change (growth/decay factor) between two variables that represent an exponential function in a situation, table, graph, or equation
- Represent an exponential function with a table, graph, or equation
- Make connections among the patterns of change in a table, graph, and equation of an exponential function
- Compare the growth/decay rate and growth/decay factor for an exponential function and recognize the role each plays in an exponential situation
- Identify the growth factor and initial value in problem situations, tables, graphs, and equations that represent exponential functions
- Determine whether an exponential function represents a growth (increasing) or decay (decreasing) pattern, from an equation, table, or graph that represents an exponential function
- Determine the values of the independent and dependent variables from a table, graph, or equation of an exponential function
- Use an exponential equation to describe the graph and table of an exponential function
- Predict the y-intercept from an equation, graph, or table that represents an exponential function
- Interpret the information that the y-intercept of an exponential function represents
- Determine the effects of the growth/decay factor and initial value for an exponential function on a graph of the function
- Solve problems about exponential growth and decay from a variety of different subject areas, including science and business, using an equation, table, or graph
- Observe that one exponential equation can model different contexts
- Compare exponential and linear functions

Equivalence Develop understanding of equivalent exponential expressions

- Write and interpret exponential expressions that represent the dependent variable in an exponential function
- Develop the rules for operating with rational exponents and explain why they work
- Write, interpret, and operate with numerical expressions in scientific notation
- Write and interpret equivalent expressions using the rules for exponents and operations
- Solve problems that involve exponents, including scientific notation

Mathematical Reflections

Look for evidence of student understanding of the goals for this Investigation in their responses to the questions in *Mathematical Reflections*. The goals addressed by each question are indicated below.

1. Suppose you know the initial value for a population and the yearly growth rate.

a. How can you determine the population several years from now?

b. How is a growth rate related to the growth factor for the population?

c. How can you use this information to write an equation that models the situation?

Goals

- Identify the pattern of change (growth/decay factor) between two variables that represent an exponential function in a situation, table, graph, or equation
- Represent an exponential function with a table, graph, or equation
- Make connections among the patterns of change in a table, graph, and equation of an exponential function
- Compare the growth/decay rate and growth/decay factor for an exponential function and recognize the role each plays in an exponential situation
- Determine the values of the independent and dependent variables from a table, graph, or equation of an exponential function
- Determine the effects of the growth/decay factor and initial value for an exponential function on a graph of the function
- Write and interpret exponential expressions that represent the dependent variable in an exponential function
- Solve problems that involve exponents, including scientific notation

2. Suppose you know the initial value for a population and the yearly growth factor.

a. How can you determine the population several years from now?

b. How can you determine the yearly growth rate?

Goals

- Represent an exponential function with a table, graph, or equation
- Make connections among the patterns of change in a table, graph, and equation of an exponential function
- Compare the growth/decay rate and growth/decay factor for an exponential function and recognize the role each plays in an exponential situation
- Determine the values of the independent and dependent variables from a table, graph, or equation of an exponential function
- Determine the effects of the growth/decay factor and initial value for an exponential function on a graph of the function
- Write and interpret exponential expressions that represent the dependent variable in an exponential function
- Solve problems that involve exponents, including scientific notation

3. Suppose you know the equation that represents the exponential relationship between the population *p* and the number of years *n*. How can you determine the doubling time for the population?

Goal

- Solve problems about exponential growth and decay from a variety of different subject areas, including science and business, using an equation, table, or graph

Standards

Common Core Content Standards

8.F.A.1 Understand that a function is a rule that assigns to each input exactly one output. The graph of a function is the set of ordered pairs consisting of an input and the corresponding output. *Problem 3*

8.F.A.2 Compare properties of two functions each represented in a different way (algebraically, graphically, numerically in tables, or by verbal descriptions). *Problems 2 and 3*

8.F.A.3 Interpret the equation $y = mx + b$ as defining a linear function, whose graph is a straight line; give examples of functions that are not linear. *Problems 1, 2, and 3*

8.F.B.5 Describe qualitatively the functional relationship between two quantities by analyzing a graph (e.g., where the function is increasing or decreasing, linear or nonlinear). Sketch a graph that exhibits the qualitative features of a function that has been described verbally. *Problems 1 and 3*

A-SSE.A.1a Interpret parts of an expression, such as terms, factors, and coefficients. *Problem 1*

A-SSE.A.1b Interpret complicated expressions by viewing one or more of their parts as a single entity. *Problems 2 and 3*

A-CED.A.2 Create equations in two or more variables to represent relationships between quantities; graph equations on coordinate axes with labels and scales. *Problems 1, 2, and 3*

A-REI.D.10 Understand that the graph of an equation in two variables is the set of all its solutions plotted in the coordinate plane, often forming a curve (which could be a line). *Problems 1, 2, and 3*

F-IF.B.4 For a function that models a relationship between two quantities, interpret key features of graphs and tables in terms of the quantities, and sketch graphs showing key features given a verbal description of the relationship. *Problems 1, 2, and 3*

F-IF.B.6 Calculate and interpret the average rate of change of a function (presented symbolically or as a table) over a specified interval. Estimate the rate of change from a graph. *Problem 1*

F-IF.C.7e Graph exponential and logarithmic functions, showing intercepts and end behavior, and trigonometric functions, showing period, midline, and amplitude. *Problem 3*

F-IF.C.8b Use the properties of exponents to interpret expressions for exponential functions. *Problem 2*

F-BF.A.1a Determine an explicit expression, a recursive process, or steps for calculation from a context. *Problems 1, 2, and 3*

F-LE.A.1a Prove that linear functions grow by equal differences over equal intervals, and that exponential functions grow by equal factors over equal intervals. *Problems 1 and 2*

F-LE.A.1c Recognize situations in which a quantity grows or decays by a constant percent rate per unit interval relative to another. *Problems 1 and 2*

F-LE.A.2 Construct linear and exponential functions, including arithmetic and geometric sequences, given a graph, a description of a relationship, or two input-output pairs (include reading these from a table). *Problems 1 and 2*

F-LE.B.5 Interpret the parameters in a linear or exponential function in terms of a context. *Problems 1, 2, and 3*

Facilitating the Mathematical Practices

Students in *Connected Mathematics* classrooms display evidence of multiple Common Core Standards for Mathematical Practice every day. Here are just a few examples of when you might observe students demonstrating the Standards for Mathematical Practice during this Investigation.

Practice 1: **Make sense of problems and persevere in solving them.**

Students are engaged every day in solving problems and, over time, learn to persevere in solving them. To be effective, the problems embody critical concepts and skills and have the potential to engage students in making sense of mathematics. Students build understanding by reflecting, connecting, and communicating. These student-centered problem situations engage students in articulating the "knowns" in a problem situation and determining a logical solution pathway. The student–student and student–teacher dialogues help students not only to make sense of the problems, but also to persevere in finding appropriate strategies to solve them. The suggested questions in the Teacher Guides provide the metacognitive scaffolding to help students monitor and refine their problem-solving strategies.

Practice 2: **Reason abstractly and quantitatively.**

After students find the number of years it would take to double the value of the stamp collection in Problem 3.2, they learn about the "Rule of 72" in the *Did You Know?* The Rule of 72 gives an approximation for how long it will take to double an investment. Students use this rule to check their answer in Problem 3.2. Students see the usefulness of this rule in making rough approximations to help make sense of a situation that involves compound growth.

Practice 4: **Model with mathematics.**

Throughout the Investigation, students use exponential equations to model growth in various real-world contexts: growth in rabbit populations, an increase in value in a stamp collection, and the balances in college funds. Students use information about the growth factor, initial value, or other values to find a model and make predictions.

Practice 5: **Use appropriate tools strategically.**

Students can choose to enter exponential equations on a graphing calculator and scroll through a table or trace a graph. They can adjust the calculator settings to get a more precise answer. Students can also use a graphing calculator to make a STAT plot of data.

Students identify and record their personal experiences with the Standards for Mathematical Practice during the *Mathematical Reflections* at the end of the Investigation.

PROBLEM

3.1 Reproducing Rabbits

Fractional Growth Patterns

Problem Overview

Focus Question How is the growth factor in this Problem similar to that in the previous Problems? How is it different?

Problem Description

This Problem is set in the context of a historical account of a rapidly multiplying rabbit population in Australia. Rabbits are not native to Australia. In the Problems students have studied in this Unit so far, the exponential growth factor was a whole number, either given in the Problem story or evident from the pattern in the data.

When the growth factor is not a whole number—as it is in this Problem—the pattern is not as obvious, and it will be important to explore ratios of successive terms. However, the strategy for finding the growth factor is the same as in previous Problems—divide successive y-values.

The language of decimals and percents is commonly used in situations involving fractional growth factors to describe both the growth factor and its effects.

In Question A, students use population data given in table form to write an equation to model population growth. Question B gives an equation for the growth of another rabbit population. Students use the equation to find the growth factor and initial population. The growth factors in these situations are not whole numbers. Students also find the doubling time for each population.

Problem Implementation

Students should work in groups of two to four.

Ask some groups of students to make a graph of the data to present during the Summarize. You may wish to have them present their graphs on poster board.

You might want to assign ACE Exercises 24–26 with Problem 3.1 to give students a chance to think about percents again before Problem 3.2, which uses percents.

Materials

- **Labsheet 3ACE:** Exercise 1 (accessibility)
- **Labsheet 3ACE:** Exercise 8
- **Teaching Aid 3.1:** Rabbit Population Table

poster board

Using Technology

During the Launch or Summarize, you may want to use a graphing calculator to demonstrate how to make a STAT plot of the data. (See **Using Graphing Calculators** in the Mathematics Background for a description of how to enter data pairs and make a plot.) Making a STAT plot is a visual way to ascertain the exponential nature of the pattern. If time permits, let students enter the data into their calculators. For these data, window settings of x-values from 0 to 5 with a scale of 1 and y-values from 0 to 1,100 with a scale of 100 work well.

Vocabulary

There are no new glossary terms introduced in this Problem.

Mathematics Background

- Exponential Functions
- Growth Factor and Exponential Functions
- y-intercept or Initial Value
- Growth Rates
- Graphs of Exponential Functions
- Equations for Exponential Functions
- Recursive, or Iterative, Processes
- Equivalence
- Logarithms
- Using Graphing Calculators

At a Glance and Lesson Plan

- At a Glance: Problem 3.1 Growing, Growing, Growing
- Lesson Plan: Problem 3.1 Growing, Growing, Growing

Launch

Connecting to Prior Knowledge

Students have looked at exponential relationships represented in a context, table, graph, or equation. In all of these situations, the growth factor has been a whole number. Ask students:

Suggested Questions

- Could the growth factor be a nonwhole number? Explain. (Gather some explanations.)

Presenting the Challenge

Discuss with students the story of the rabbits that English settlers introduced to Australia. Direct students' attention to the table of data in the student edition, or display the table using **Teaching Aid 3.1: Rabbit Population Table**. You might tell students that one pair of rabbits can increase in 18 months to 184 rabbits, so it is difficult to completely eliminate them. Ask:

Suggested Questions

- Does the relationship between time and rabbit population appear to be linear, exponential, or neither?

Because the growth factor is not a whole number, the exponential nature of the relationship may not be immediately apparent to students. If they guess that the relationship is linear, ask:

- By how much did the rabbit population increase in each year shown? (by 80, 145, 258, and then 467 rabbits)
- Is that a constant rate of change? (No.)
- Why is this pattern exponential? (Collect a few answers.)

The relationship is, in fact, exponential. However, unlike the other exponential relationships they have studied, the growth factor is not a whole number. Students will determine the growth factor as they work on the Problem. Present the challenge to find an equation that models the data.

Explore

Providing for Individual Needs

To find the overall growth factor, students will need to find the growth factor for consecutive years and decide on a typical, or average, value.

As you circulate, you might ask students questions to guide them in finding the year-to-year growth factors and in determining an overall growth factor.

Suggested Questions

- How can you determine the growth factor from one year to the next? (Divide the number of rabbits in any year by the number in the preceding year. In other words, find the ratio of one year's population to the previous year's population.)
- What is the growth factor from the initial year (year 0) to year 1? (180 ÷ 100, or 1.80)
- What is the growth factor from year 1 to year 2? (325 ÷ 180, or about 1.81)
- Why do you think these ratios are not equal? (The data are experimental. Factors such as food availability and weather conditions would affect the growth of the population from year to year.)
- How can you find an overall growth factor for these data? (Students might suggest using the mean, median, or mode of the year-to-year growth factors. Or, they might simply approximate the growth factor at 1.80. Any of these methods is viable.)

To answer part (4) of Question A, students are likely to use a guess-and-check approach or to extend the table. Students can also enter the equation $y = 100(1.8)^x$ on a graphing calculator and scroll through a table or trace a graph. They can adjust the calculator settings to get a more precise answer.

For Question B, you might suggest that some students make a table for the first 4 years to help them make sense of the equation. Ask students about their understanding of the "doubling time."

- How can you find the doubling time for the population? (Using a table or graph, choose a population value and then find the population value that is twice the value you chose. The difference in the time values for these two population values is the doubling time.)

Planning for the Summary

What evidence will you use in the summary to clarify and deepen understanding of the Focus Question?

What will you do if you do not have evidence?

Summarize

Orchestrating the Discussion

Ask:

Suggested Questions

- When you look at a table of population data like this one, how can you determine whether the data represent a linear relationship? How can you determine whether the data represent an exponential relationship? (Students should be able to explain that if the time values increase by a constant amount, then the relationship is linear if the difference between successive population values is constant, and the relationship is exponential if the ratio of successive population values is constant. This is a review, but these ideas are fundamental. Students need many opportunities to think about and articulate their understanding of linear and exponential patterns.)
- How did you determine the growth factor for these data? (Find the ratio of one year's population to the previous year's population.)

Because this is the first time students have encountered an exponential equation with a base that is not a whole number, you might talk with them about this explicitly. Although this may seem counterintuitive to students at first, there is no reason that the base should be a whole number.

Quickly sketch the graph relating to the equation $p = 100(1.8)^n$ or ask the class to describe 3 or 4 important points and have them make the sketch.

Tell students you want to figure out how long it took the rabbit population to double from 100 to 200.

- Find the point corresponding to a population of 200.

Growth of a Rabbit Population

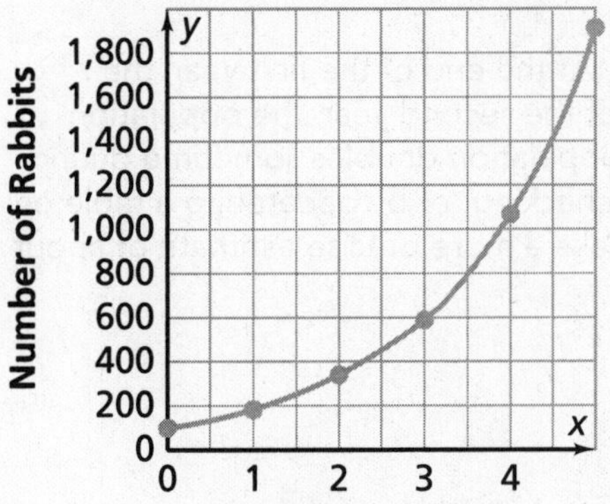

- About how many years did it take for the initial population to double? (From the graph or the table, students can see that it took between 1 and 2 years for the population to double. Discuss how students could find a more exact time. For example, the graph shows that the doubling occurred closer to year 1 than to year 2. Students can use their calculators to check the population for time values such as 1.1 and 1.2 to find a time value that gives a population close to 200.)
- Pick another point. How many years does it take the population to double from this point? (between 1 and 2 more years)

The doubling time is the same no matter the starting population. (**Note:** This can be shown algebraically. If s is the starting population, then the doubling time is the value of t in the equation $2s = s(1.8)^t$. Dividing each side by s (since $s \neq 0$) gives $2 = (1.8)^t$. From this second, simplified equation, it is clear that the initial population is not important.)

Students revisit doubling time in Question B. They do not need to do algebraic calculations to find the doubling time. Students can use a table or graph or guess and check. Doubling time is not an essential idea at this stage, but many students find it interesting. It also provides an opportunity to make sense of exponential functions. In a later high school course, students will use logarithms to solve for t in equations like the one in Question B.

Ask students to evaluate the accuracy of the exponential model in making long-range predictions.

- In part (3) of Question A, what was your estimate for the number of rabbits in the population after 50 years? (about 5.8×10^{14} rabbits)
- Does this seem realistic? (This is nearly 600 trillion rabbits, which seems highly unlikely. This question raises the point that mathematical models are often not reliable for long-range predictions.)

Check for Understanding

- Suppose the growth factor for a population of cats is 1.7 per year and the starting population is 50 cats. What is an equation for the population growth? ($p = 50(1.7)^t$)
- When will the population double? (At the end of the first year, the population will be 85. At the end of the second year, the population will be about 145. Therefore, the population doubles sometime during the second year. By guessing and checking, or by generating a table on their calculators, students could make a more precise estimate of about 1.3 years.)

Reflecting on Student Learning

Use the following questions to assess student understanding at the end of the lesson.

- What evidence do I have that students understand the Focus Question?
  - Where did my students get stuck?
  - What strategies did they use?
  - What breakthroughs did my students have today?
- How will I use this to plan for tomorrow? For the next time I teach this lesson?
- Where will I have the opportunity to reinforce these ideas as I continue through this Unit? The next Unit?

ACE Assignment Guide

- **Applications:** 1–8
- **Connections:** 24–30

You may wish to provide students with **Labsheet 3ACE: Exercise 8** (accessibility). It contains larger versions of the tables as well as the questions found in the Student Edition. You can give this labsheet to students to help them organize their answers. This can allow students to remain focused on the mathematics of the Exercise while saving time.

To provide additional support for students when they are working on the ACE Exercises, you may choose to give hints, partially fill in tables, and emphasize key words. See **Labsheet 3ACE: Exercise 1** (accessibility) for an example of how to do this.

PROBLEM

3.2 Investing for the Future

Growth Rates

Problem Overview

Focus Question How are the growth factor and growth rate for an exponential function related? When might you use each in an exponential growth pattern?

Problem Description

Many exponential situations present the growth rate as a percent. Students look at the rise in value of a stamp for 6% and 4% annual rates of growth. They use these rates to find the growth factors, which are 1.06 and 1.04, respectively.

For example, if you invest $100 at 6% annual interest rate, the value of the account at the start of the first year is 100 + 100(.06), or 100(1.06). The *growth factor* in this case is 1.06 while the *growth rate* is 6%, or 0.06. Students also explore how the growth rate and the initial value affect the growth pattern. Students examine patterns of change due to compound growth and connect growth rate (or percent change) and growth factor. That is, students find the growth factor given the growth rate and vice versa.

Problem Implementation

Students should work in groups of two to four.

Comment: You might change the stamp to something that is more interesting to your students—an antique car, gold coin, etc.

You may want to have one or two groups of students prepare their responses for sharing during the Summarize discussion of the Problem.

Materials

- **Labsheet 3.2:** Stamp Value Tables (one per group)
- **Labsheet 3ACE:** Exercise 9

graphing calculators
graph paper

Vocabulary

- growth rate

Mathematics Background

- Exponential Functions
- Growth Factor and Exponential Functions
- *y*-intercept or Initial Value
- Growth Rates
- Graphs of Exponential Functions
- Equations for Exponential Functions
- Recursive, or Iterative, Processes
- Equivalence
- Logarithms
- Using Graphing Calculators

At a Glance and Lesson Plan

- At a Glance: Problem 3.2 Growing, Growing, Growing
- Lesson Plan: Problem 3.2 Growing, Growing, Growing

Launch

Launch Video

This animation shows the growth in value of Sam's rare stamp in the Problem. You can use this animation at the beginning of Presenting the Challenge to set the context for the Problem. Visit Teacher Place at mathdashboard.com/cmp3 to see the complete video.

Connecting to Prior Knowledge

Use the rabbit population situation in Problem 3.1 to introduce the concept of growth rate. Carefully model the calculation for students.

Suggested Questions

- In Problem 3.1, the initial rabbit population is 100, and the yearly growth factor is 1.8, so there are 180 rabbits at the end of year 1. What is the increase in the number of rabbits? (80 rabbits)

- What percent change in the original population does this represent? (% change $= \frac{\text{changes in population}}{\text{previous population}} = 80 \div 100 = 0.8$ or 80%)
- How can you use this percent change to calculate the approximate population at the end of year 2? ($180 \times 0.80 = 144$. Add this increase to 180; $180 + 144 = 324$.)
- How can you write this as one calculation? (Because $180 + 0.80 \times 180 = 180(1 + 0.80)$, you can write this as 180(1.8). Note that 1.8 is the growth factor.)

Tell students that the percent change is called the *growth rate*. Explain that some exponential growth situations give the growth rate instead of the growth factor. (**Note:** In Problems 3.2 and 3.3, the percent change is an increase. In the next Investigation, students solve Problems in which the percent change is a decrease.)

Presenting the Challenge

Show the Launch Video to set the context of the Problem. Discuss the story of Sam's stamp. You may find it helpful to display for the class the calculations of the increase in the value of the stamp after each of the first 2 years. This will help students to clarify their understanding of percent change. You can also take this opportunity to introduce the term *compound growth*. (Problem 3.3 formally introduces this term.)

Suggested Questions

- When you calculate the increase for the second year, do you base it on the original \$2,500 value or on the value at the end of the first year? (You base it on the value at the end of the first year; the change is from one year to the next year.)
- Why is the increase in value in the second year greater than the increase in value in the first year? (It is greater because the 6% increase is applied to the increased value of \$2,650 at the end of year 1, not to the original value of \$2,500.)

Help the class to understand that this idea is the reason this pattern of change is called compound growth.

- In this Problem, you will make tables to find the growth factor for the value of the stamp between successive years. How would you find the growth factor for the values between two years? (Divide the value in one year by the value in the previous year.)
- Will you get the same factor between any two successive years? (Yes; if the growth is exponential. Students may reply that they don't have enough information to answer this question. Some may say yes, the factor will be constant because the percent increase is constant.)

  Note: Students will confirm this information during the Explore.

Explore

Providing for Individual Needs

Hand out **Labsheet 3.2: Stamp Value Tables**. As you circulate, be sure each student is calculating the value of the stamp and the growth factor correctly.

Some students may need help in generating the table using the percent increase. Use questions similar to those given at the start of the Launch.

This is a good review of the use of percents.

Planning for the Summary

What evidence will you use in the summary to clarify and deepen understanding of the Focus Question?

What will you do if you do not have evidence?

Summarize

Orchestrating the Discussion

Have groups of students share their strategies for determining the values in the tables and their answers to the questions. Display their data for the class.

The class can generate the data by performing repeated multiplication by hand or with a calculator. (See **Using Graphing Calculators** in the Mathematics Background for a description of how to use a calculator to perform recursive multiplication.)

Suggested Questions

Relate the growth factor to the percent increase.

- What is the growth factor from year 1 to year 2? (1.06)
- What is the growth factor from year 2 to year 3? (1.06)
- What is the growth factor from year 4 to year 5? (1.06)

Write each growth factor on the table between the appropriate years. Students should be comfortable dividing the value for one year by the value for the previous year to find the growth factor. You want them to understand that if the pattern in the table is exponential, this ratio, or growth factor, will be the same (or approximately the same) for any two successive years. In other words, the growth factor will be constant.

- How is this relationship similar to others you have investigated in this Unit? (You multiply each value by the growth factor to get the next value.)
- If the growth factor is constant for consecutive values of x (or years, in this case), what kind of relationship is this? (exponential)

You could make a quick sketch of the graph to show that it has an exponential shape. Plot additional points to make the exponential pattern clear.

The intent of Question B is to provide more help to students to see how the concepts of percent increase and growth factor are related. Extend the Question by asking:

- What is the growth factor for a yearly increase of 7%? (1.07)
- What is the growth factor for a yearly increase of 70%? (1.70 or 1.7)
- If you know the growth rate, or percent increase, how can you find the growth factor? Why? (Write the growth rate as a decimal, and then add 1. To see why, look at an example: If the growth rate is 7%, then to get from the amount A one year to the amount the following year, you calculate $A + A \times 0.07$. Using the Distributive Property, this is $A(1.07)$, so the growth factor is 1.07.)
- If you know the growth factor, how can you find the growth rate? Why? (Subtract 1 from the growth factor, and then write the result as a percent. To see why, look at an example: If the growth factor is 1.07, then to get from the amount A one year to the amount the following year, you calculate $A(1.07)$. This is the same as $A(1 + 0.07)$, or $A +$ (7% of A). The increase is (7% of A), so the percent increase, or growth rate, is 7%.)

Use Questions C and D to assess students' understanding of the relationship between growth rate and growth factor. In part 1(a) of Question C, the growth rate is 0. It may be intuitive to students that there is no growth factor. So the growth factor is 1. Multiplying by 1 does not change the value and hence the growth rate is 0%. Reversing this reasoning shows that a growth factor of 1 is associated with a growth rate of 0% in part 1(d) of Question D.

Some students may be interested in the Rule of 72 in the *Did You Know?* box before Problem 3.3. Make sure students understand that this rule does not give exact answers. However, it is very useful for making estimates and is often used in practice, particularly for growth rates between 2% and 14%. For growth rates over 20%, the estimate errs significantly on the small side.

Explain that the Rule of 72 can be used in other contexts as well.

- The world population is currently about 6.4 billion, and the growth rate is 3%. If this rate continues, about how many years will it take the population to double? (Using the Rule of 72, it will take $72 \div 3 \approx 24$years.)
- Do you think this rate of growth could continue indefinitely? (Answers will vary. It is unlikely that this growth rate could continue indefinitely.)

Reflecting on Student Learning

Use the following questions to assess student understanding at the end of the lesson.

- What evidence do I have that students understand the Focus Question?
  - Where did my students get stuck?
  - What strategies did they use?
  - What breakthroughs did my students have today?
- How will I use this to plan for tomorrow? For the next time I teach this lesson?
- Where will I have the opportunity to reinforce these ideas as I continue through this Unit? The next Unit?

ACE Assignment Guide

- **Applications:** 9–20
- **Connections:** 31–32
- **Extensions:** 40–45

You may wish to provide students with **Labsheet 3ACE: Exercise 9** that contains a larger version of the table as well as the questions found in the Student Edition. You can give this labsheet to students to help them organize their answers.

PROBLEM

3.3 Making a Difference

Connecting Growth Rate and Growth Factor

Problem Overview

Focus Question How does the initial population affect the growth patterns in an exponential function?

Problem Description

Problems 3.2 and 3.3 work in conjunction to help students explore the ideas of compound growth and growth rate. In Problem 3.2, students focused on finding the growth factor in a situation involving compound growth. In this Problem, they use growth rates and different starting values to write equations for three different savings plans set up by a grandmother for her grandchildren.

Problem Implementation

Students should work in groups of two to four.

Materials

- **Labsheet 3.3:** College Funds Table (one per group)
- Centimeter Grid Paper

graphing calculators

graph paper

Vocabulary

- compound growth

Mathematics Background

- Exponential Functions
- Growth Factor and Exponential Functions
- *y*-intercept or Initial Value
- Growth Rates
- Graphs of Exponential Functions
- Equations for Exponential Functions
- Recursive, or Iterative, Processes
- Equivalence
- Logarithms
- Using Graphing Calculators

At a Glance and Lesson Plan

- At a Glance: Problem 3.3 Growing, Growing, Growing
- Lesson Plan: Problem 3.3 Growing, Growing, Growing

Launch

Launch Video

This animation shows the situation in the Problem of Cassie and Kaylee receiving graduation gifts. You can use this animation instead of telling the story to engage students with the idea of compound growth.

After showing the video, continue with the Suggested Questions. Visit Teacher Place at mathdashboard.com/cmp3 to see the complete video.

Connecting to Prior Knowledge

Review the idea of compound growth, or introduce it if you did not do so in Problem 3.2.

Presenting the Challenge

Tell the story about Mrs. Jones and her two granddaughters' college funds, or simply show the Launch Video.

Suggested Questions

Ask the class to predict the effects of the different initial values.

- The two funds have the same growth rate, but different starting values. How do you think this will affect the growth pattern? (Collect some suggestions. Some students may think the growth factor will change.)

Explore

Providing for Individual Needs

Hand out **Labsheet 3.3: College Funds Table**. Circulate as students work, and assess who is having difficulty with the concept of growth rate. Exploring this concept provides an opportunity for students to strengthen the understanding of exponential growth patterns and the equations that represent them.

Planning for the Summary

What evidence will you use in the summary to clarify and deepen understanding of the Focus Question?
What will you do if you do not have evidence?

Summarize

Orchestrating the Discussion

Discuss the Problem, paying particular attention to whether students understand how to use the given information to write an equation. By this time, students should be very familiar with exponential growth patterns in tables and should recognize that the ratio between any two successive values is a constant. They should also understand how the initial value affects the value over time and that the initial value has no effect on the rate of growth. The growth factor is determined only by the yearly rate of increase in value.

Suggested Questions

- When comparing the values of the investment over the 10 years, what differences did you notice? (Kaylee's investment seems to grow more quickly because she starts with more money.)

- Can you explain how to use the growth factor and the initial value to write an equation for an exponential relationship? (The value for any year is the initial value multiplied by the growth factor raised to a variable power that represents the number of years that have passed.
value = initial value(growth factor)^{year})

Discuss Question B. This gives you a chance to check students' understanding of the mathematics that underpin the equation.

Question C provides an opportunity to pull ideas together. Students should observe that the amount in the account with the higher interest rate will eventually surpass the amount in the account with the lower interest rate even though the initial value is greater for the account with the lower interest rate.

Check for Understanding

- For a growth factor of 1.10, what is the growth rate, or percent increase? (Because $1.10 = 1 + 0.10$, the growth rate is 10%. Be sure that students understand why this rule works.)
- Suppose you have a stamp collection worth \$880 and a stamp-collecting expert tells you the value will increase by about 3% per year. What equation will tell you the value after t years? What is the growth factor for this situation? (The equation is $v = 880(1.03)^t$. The growth factor is 1.03. Be sure that students understand how to figure this out.)
- What would be the equation if the initial value were \$1,760 and the projected increase were 1% per year? ($v = 1{,}760(1.01)^t$)

Reflecting on Student Learning

Use the following questions to assess student understanding at the end of the lesson.

- What evidence do I have that students understand the Focus Question?
  - Where did my students get stuck?
  - What strategies did they use?
  - What breakthroughs did my students have today?
- How will I use this to plan for tomorrow? For the next time I teach this lesson?
- Where will I have the opportunity to reinforce these ideas as I continue through this Unit? The next Unit?

ACE Assignment Guide

- **Applications:** 21–23
- **Connections:** 33–39
- **Extensions:** 46–47

You may wish to have students use centimeter grid paper for **ACE Exercise 33**.

Mathematical Reflections

Possible Answers to Mathematical Reflections

1. a. You can convert the growth rate to a growth factor by adding 100% to the growth rate and changing the result to a decimal. Then, you can use an equation of the form $p = a \times b^n$, where b is the growth factor, a is the size of the original population, and n is the number of years, or time. You can also compute the population from one time to the next by finding the percent increase and adding it to the previous value to get the next successive value. If the growth rate is 4% and the population after n years is P, then the value after $n + 1$ years is $P + 0.04P$ or $P(1.04)$.

   b. A growth rate is the percent growth. If you convert the growth rate to a decimal and add 1, you will get the growth factor. For example, a growth rate of 4% corresponds to a growth factor of 1.04.

   c. You can use the initial value a and growth factor b to substitute into the equation $y = a(b)^x$.

2. a. You can use the equation $p = a \times b^t$, where b is the growth factor and a is the size of the original population. You can also generate the population for each year recursively, by multiplying the population for each year by the growth factor to get the population for the next year.

   b. Figure out the percent change from one year to the next. If you convert the growth factor to a percent and subtract 100%, you will get the growth rate. For example, a growth factor of 1.04 corresponds to a growth rate of 4%.

3. You can model the population by the expression $p = a \cdot b^n$, where a is the initial population, b is the growth factor, and n is the number of years after the initial population. Because you are looking for the time when a is twice as great as it is now, you are solving the equation $2a = a \cdot b^n$ or $2 = b^n$. In other words, given b, you need to find n so that $b^n = 2$. As a side note, this doubling property is often referred to as the "Rule of 72." If you have a certain growth rate (say, 4%), then the amount of time it takes to double is about $72 \div 4$. You can use a table or graph to find n, when $b^n = 2$.

Possible Answers to Mathematical Practices Reflections

Students may have demonstrated all of the eight Common Core Standards for Mathematical Practice during this Investigation. During the class discussion, have students provide additional Practices that the Problem cited involved and identify the use of other Mathematical Practices in the Investigation.

One student observation is provided in the Student Edition. Here is another sample student response.

After we found the number of years it would take to double the value of the stamp collection, we read about the "Rule of 72" in the *Did You Know?* The Rule of 72 gives an approximation for how long it will take to double an investment. We used this rule to check our answer in Problem 3.2. It was very close. We think this rule could be useful for making rough approximations to help make sense of a situation that involves compound growth.

MP2: Reason abstractly and quantitatively.

Investigation 3

Growth Factors and Growth Rates

In Investigation 2, you studied exponential growth of plants, mold, and a snake population. You used a whole-number growth factor and the starting value to write an equation and make predictions. In this Investigation, you will study exponential growth with fractional growth factors.

3.1 Reproducing Rabbits

Fractional Growth Patterns

In 1859, English settlers introduced a small number of rabbits to Australia. The rabbits had no natural predators in Australia, so they reproduced rapidly and ate grasses intended for sheep and cattle.

Did You Know?

In the mid-1990s, there were more than 300 million rabbits in Australia. The damage they caused cost Australian agriculture $600 million per year. In 1995, a deadly rabbit disease was deliberately spread, reducing the rabbit population by about half. However, because rabbits are developing immunity to the disease, the effects of this measure may not last.

Common Core State Standards

8.F.A.2 Compare properties of two functions each represented in a different way (algebraically, graphically, numerically in tables, or by verbal descriptions).

Also 8.F.A.1, 8.F.A.3, 8.F.B.5, A-SSE.A.1a, A-SSE.A.1b, A-CED.A.2, F-IF.B.4, F-IF.B.6, F-IF.C.8b, F-BF.A.1a, F-LE.A.1a, F-LE.A.1c, F-LE.A.2, F-LE.B.5

Notes

Problem 3.1

Suppose biologists had counted the rabbits in Australia in the years after English settlers introduced them. The biologists might have collected data like those shown in the table.

A The table shows the rabbit population growing exponentially.

Growth of Rabbit Population

Time (yr)	Population
0	100
1	180
2	325
3	583
4	1,050

1. What is the growth factor? Explain how you found your answer.
2. Assume this growth pattern continued. Write an equation for the rabbit population p for any year n after the biologists first counted the rabbits. Explain what the numbers in your equation represent.
3. How many rabbits will there be after 10 years? How many will there be after 25 years? After 50 years?
4. In how many years will the rabbit population exceed one million?

B Suppose that, during a different time period, biologists could predict the rabbit population using the equation $p = 15(1.2)^n$, where p is the population in millions, and n is the number of years.

1. What is the growth factor?
2. What was the initial population?
3. In how many years will the initial population double?
4. What will the population be after 3 years? After how many more years will the population at 3 years double?
5. What will the population be after 10 years? After how many more years will the population at 10 years double?
6. How do the doubling times for parts (3)–(5) compare? Do you think the doubling time will be the same for this relationship no matter where you start the count? Explain your reasoning.

ACE Homework starts on page 48.

STUDENT PAGE

Notes

3.2 Investing for the Future

Growth Rates

The yearly growth factor for one of the rabbit populations in Problem 3.1 is about 1.8. Suppose the population data fit the equation $p = 100(1.8)^n$ exactly. Then its table would look like the one below.

Growth of Rabbit Population

n	p
0	100
1	100 × 1.8 = **180**
2	180 × 1.8 = 324
3	324 × 1.8 = **583.2**
4	583.2 × 1.8 = **1,049.76**

- Does it make sense to have a fractional part of a rabbit?
- What does this say about the reasonableness of the equation?

The *growth factor* 1.8 is the ratio of the population for a year divided by the population for the previous year. That is, the population for year $n + 1$ is 1.8 times the population for year n.

You can think of the growth factor in terms of a percent change. To find the percent change, compare the difference in population for two consecutive years, n and $n + 1$, with the population of year, n.

- From year 0 to year 1, the percent change is $\frac{180 - 100}{100} = \frac{80}{100} = 80\%$. The population of 100 rabbits in year 0 increased by 80%, resulting in $100 \times 80\% = 80$ additional rabbits.
- From year 1 to year 2, the percent change is $\frac{324 - 180}{180} = \frac{144}{180} = 80\%$. The population of 180 rabbits in year 1 increased by 80%, resulting in $180 \times 80\% = 144$ additional rabbits.

The percent increase is called the **growth rate.** In some growth situations, the growth rate is given instead of the growth factor. For example, changes in the value of investments are often expressed as percents.

- How are the growth rate 80% and the growth factor 1.8 related to each other?

Notes

Problem 3.2

When Sam was in seventh grade, his aunt gave him a stamp worth $2,500. Sam considered selling the stamp, but his aunt told him that, if he saved it, it would increase in value.

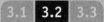

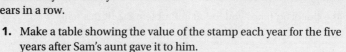

A Sam saved the stamp, and its value increased by 6% each year for several years in a row.

1. Make a table showing the value of the stamp each year for the five years after Sam's aunt gave it to him.
2. Look at the pattern of growth from one year to the next. Is the value growing exponentially? Explain.
3. Write an equation for the value v of Sam's stamp after n years.
4. How many years will it take to double the value?

B Suppose the value of the stamp increased 4% each year instead of 6%.

1. Make a table showing the value of the stamp each year for the five years after Sam's aunt gave it to him.
2. What is the growth factor from one year to the next?
3. Write an equation that represents the value of the stamp for any year.
4. How many years will it take to double the value?
5. How does the change in percent affect the graphs of the equations?

C 1. Find the growth factor associated with each growth rate.

a. 0% **b.** 15% **c.** 30%

d. 75% **e.** 100% **f.** 150%

2. How you can find the growth factor if you know the growth rate?

D 1. Find the growth rate associated with each growth factor.

a. 1.5 **b.** 1.25 **c.** 1.1 **d.** 1

2. How can you find the growth rate if you know the growth factor?

ACE Homework starts on page 48.

STUDENT PAGE

Notes

Did You Know?

Some investors use a rule of thumb called the "Rule of 72" to approximate how long it will take the value of an investment to double. To use this rule, simply divide 72 by the annual interest rate.

For example, an investment at an 8% interest rate will take approximately 72 ÷ 8, or 9, years to double. At a 10% interest rate, the value of an investment will double approximately every 7.2 years. This rule doesn't give you exact doubling times, only approximations.

- Do the doubling times you found in Problem 3.2 fit this rule?

3.3 Making a Difference

Connecting Growth Rate and Growth Factor

In Problem 3.2, the value of Sam's stamp increased by the same percent each year. However, each year, this percent was applied to the previous year's value. So, for example, the increase from year 1 to year 2 is 6% of $2,650, not 6% of the original $2,500. This type of change is called **compound growth.**

Notes

In this Problem, you will continue to explore compound growth. You will consider the effects of both the initial value and the growth factor on the value of an investment.

Problem 3.3

Mrs. Ramos started college funds for her two granddaughters. She gave $1,250 to Cassie and $2,500 to Kaylee. Mrs. Ramos invested each fund in a 10-year bond that pays 4% interest a year.

A **1.** Write an equation to show the relationship between the number of years and the amount of money in each fund.

2. Make a table to show the amount in each fund for 0 to 10 years.

3. Compare the graphs of each equation you wrote in part (1).

4. **a.** How does the initial value of the fund affect the yearly value increases?

b. How does the initial value affect the growth factor?

c. How does the initial value affect the final value?

B A year later, Mrs. Ramos started a fund for Cassie's cousin, Matt. Cassie made this calculation to predict the value of Matt's fund several years from now:

$$\text{Value} = \$2{,}000 \times 1.05 \times 1.05 \times 1.05 \times 1.05$$

1. What initial value, growth rate, growth factor, and number of years is Cassie assuming?

2. If the value continues to increase at this rate, how much would the fund be worth in one more year?

C Cassie's and Kaylee's other grandmother offers them a choice between college fund options.

Option 1		**Option 2**
$1,000 at 3% interest per year	OR	$800 at 6% per year

Which is the better option? Explain your reasoning.

ACE Homework starts on page 48.

STUDENT PAGE

Notes

Applications | Connections | Extensions

Applications

1. In parts of the United States, wolves are being reintroduced to wilderness areas where they had become extinct. Suppose 20 wolves are released in northern Michigan, and the yearly growth factor for this population is expected to be 1.2.

   a. Make a table showing the projected number of wolves at the end of each of the first 6 years.

   b. Write an equation that models the growth of the wolf population.

   c. How long will it take for the new wolf population to exceed 100?

2. This table shows the growth of the elk population in a state forest.

   a. The table shows that the elk population is growing exponentially. What is the growth factor? Explain how you found it.

Growth of Elk Population

Time (yr)	Population
0	30
1	57
2	108
3	206
4	391
5	743

   b. Suppose this growth pattern continues. How many elk will there be after 10 years? How many elk will there be after 15 years?

   c. Write an equation you could use to predict the elk population p for any year n after the elk were first counted.

   d. In how many years will the population exceed one million?

3. Suppose there are 100 trout in a lake and the yearly growth factor for the population is 1.5. How long will it take for the number of trout to double?

Notes

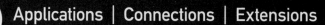

4. Suppose there are 500,000 squirrels in a forest and the growth factor for the population is 1.6 per year. Write an equation you could use to find the squirrel population p in n years.

5. **Multiple Choice** The equation $p = 200(1.1)^t$ models the exponential growth of a population. The variable p is the population in millions and t is the time in years. How long will it take this population to double?

A. 4 to 5 years **B.** 5 to 6 years **C.** 6 to 7 years **D.** 7 to 8 years

In Exercises 6 and 7, the equation models the exponential growth of a population, where p is the population in millions and t is the time in years. Tell how much time it would take the population to double.

6. $p = 135(1.7)^t$

7. $p = 1{,}000(1.2)^t$

8. **a.** Fill in the table for each equation.

$y = 50(2.2)^x$

x	0	1	2	3	4	5
y	■	■	■	■	■	■

$y = 350(1.7)^x$

x	0	1	2	3	4	5
y	■	■	■	■	■	■

b. What is the growth factor for each equation?

c. Predict whether the graphs of these equations will ever cross.

d. Estimate any points at which you think the graphs will cross.

9. Maya's grandfather opened a savings account for her when she was born. He opened the account with $100 and did not add or take out any money after that. The money in the account grows at a rate of 4% per year.

a. Make a table to show the amount in the account from the time Maya was born until she turned 10.

b. What is the growth factor for the account?

c. Write an equation for the value of the account after any number of years.

STUDENT PAGE

Notes

Find the growth rate associated with the given growth factor.

10. 1.4 **11.** 1.9 **12.** 1.75

Find the growth factor associated with the given growth rate.

13. 45% **14.** 90% **15.** 31%

16. Suppose the price of an item increases by 25% per year. What is the growth factor for the price from year to year?

17. Currently, 1,000 students attend Greenville Middle School. The school can accommodate 1,300 students. The school board estimates that the student population will grow by 5% per year for the next several years.

a. When will the population outgrow the present building?

b. Suppose the school limits its growth to 50 students per year. How many years will it take for the population to outgrow the school?

18. Suppose that, for several years, the number of radios sold in the United States increased by 3% each year.

a. Suppose one million radios sold in the first year of this time period. About how many radios sold in each of the next 6 years?

b. Suppose only 100,000 radios sold in the first year. About how many radios sold in each of the next 6 years?

19. Suppose a movie ticket costs about $7, and inflation causes ticket prices to increase by 4.5% a year for the next several years.

a. How much will a ticket cost 5 years from now?

b. How much will a ticket cost 10 years from now? 30 years from now?

c. How many years will it take for the cost of a ticket to exceed $26?

Notes

20. Find the growth rate (percent growth) for an exponential function represented by the equation $y = 30(2)^x$.

21. **Multiple Choice** Ms. Diaz wants to invest $500 in a savings bond. At which bank would her investment grow the most over 8 years?

A. Bank 1: 7% annual interest for 8 years

B. Bank 2: 2% annual interest for the first 4 years and 12% annual interest for the next four years

C. Bank 3: 12% annual interest for the first 4 years and 2% annual interest for the next four years

D. All three result in the same growth.

22. Oscar made the following calculation to predict the value of his baseball card collection several years from now:

$$\text{Value} = \$130 \times 1.07 \times 1.07 \times 1.07 \times 1.07 \times 1.07$$

a. What initial value, growth rate, growth factor, and number of years is Oscar assuming?

b. If the value continues to increase at this rate, how much would the collection be worth in three more years?

23. Carlos, Latanya, and Mila work in a biology laboratory. Each of them is responsible for a population of mice.

The growth factor for Carlos's population of mice is $\frac{3}{8}$.	The growth factor for Latanya's population of mice is 3.	The growth factor for Mila's population of mice is 125%.

a. Whose mice are reproducing fastest?

b. Whose mice are reproducing slowest?

STUDENT PAGE

Notes

Connections

Calculate each percent.

24. 120% of $3,000 **25.** 150% of $200 **26.** 133% of $2,500

For Exercises 27–30, tell whether the pattern represents exponential growth. Explain your reasoning. If the pattern is exponential, give the growth factor.

27. 1 1.1 1.21 1.331 1.4641 1.61051 1.771561

28. 3 5 $8\frac{1}{3}$ $13\frac{8}{9}$ $23\frac{4}{27}$

29. 3 $4\frac{2}{3}$ $6\frac{1}{3}$ 8 $9\frac{2}{3}$ $11\frac{1}{3}$

30. 2 6.4 20.5 66 210

31. A worker currently receives a yearly salary of $20,000.

a. Find the dollar values of a 3%, 4%, and 5% raise for this worker.

b. Find the worker's new annual salary for each raise in part (a).

c. Joanne says that she can find the new salary with a 3% raise in two ways:

Method 1		Method 2
Add $20,000 to (3% of $20,000).	OR	Find 103% of $20,000.

Explain why these two methods give the same result.

Notes

32. The graph shows the growth in the number of wireless subscribers in the United States from 1994 to 2009.

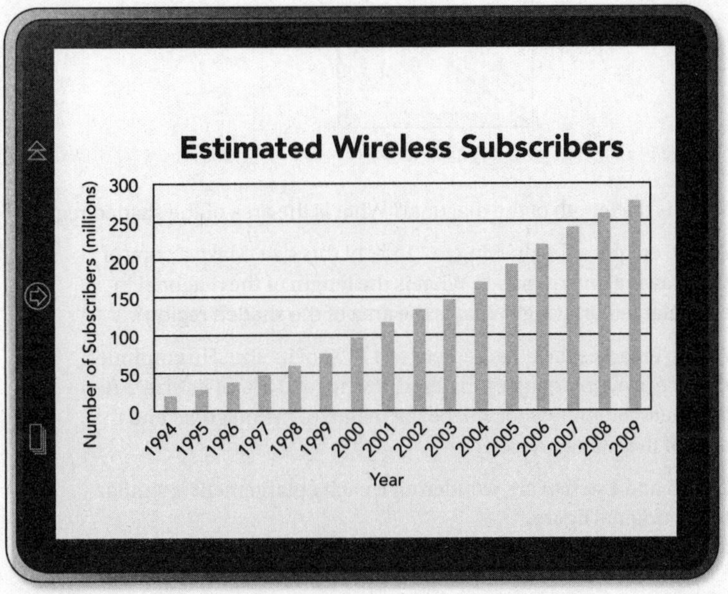

a. What do the bars in the graph represent?

b. What does the implied curve represent?

c. Describe the pattern of change in the total number of subscribers from 1994 to 2009. Could the pattern be modeled by an exponential function or a linear function? Explain.

d. The number of subscribers in 2010 was 300,520,098. In 2011, the number was 322,857,207. Do these numbers fit the pattern you described in part (c)? Explain.

e. If the U.S. population in 2010 was approximately 308 million, what might explain the number of subscriptions from 2011?

STUDENT PAGE

Notes

33. Refer to the drawing below.

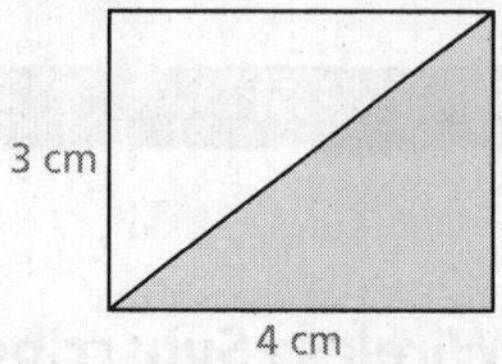

a. What is the length of the diagonal? What is the area of the shaded region?

b. Arturo enlarges the drawing to 110% of this size. Make a copy of the drawing on grid paper. What is the length of the diagonal in the enlarged drawing? What is the area of the shaded region?

c. Arturo enlarges the enlargement to 110% of its size. He continues this process, enlarging each new drawing to 110% of its size. After five enlargements, what will be the length of the diagonal and the area of the shaded region?

d. Arturo and Esteban are wondering if each enlargement is similar to the original figure.

Auturo's Conjecture

All the rectangles are similar because the ratio new width : new length is always 3 : 4. This ratio is the same as the ratio of the width to the length in the original figure.

Esteban's Conjecture

In part (a), the ratio diagonal length : area was different from the same ratio in part (b). Therefore, the figures are not similar.

Which conjecture do you think is correct? Explain. Why is the other conjecture incorrect?

34. Kwan cuts lawns every summer to make money. One customer offers to give her a 3% raise next summer and a 4% raise the summer after that.

Kwan says she would prefer to get a 4% raise next summer and a 3% raise the summer after that. She claims she will earn more money this way. Is she correct? Explain.

Notes

35. After graduating from high school, Kim accepts a job with a package delivery service, earning $9 per hour.

a. How much will Kim earn in a year if she works 40 hours per week for 50 weeks and gets 2 weeks of paid vacation time?

b. Write an equation showing the relationship between the number of weeks Kim works w and the amount she earns a.

c. Kim writes the following equation: $9{,}000 = 360w$. What question is she trying to answer? What is the answer to that question?

d. Suppose Kim works for the company for 10 years, receiving a 3% raise each year. Make a table showing how her annual income grows over this time period.

e. When Kim was hired, her manager told her that instead of a 3% annual raise, she could choose to receive a $600 raise each year. How do the two raise plans compare over a 10-year period? Which plan do you think is better? Explain your answer.

36. Which represents faster growth, a growth factor of 2.5 or a growth rate of 25%?

37. Order these scale factors from least to greatest.

130% $\frac{3}{2}$ 2 1.475

38. Christopher made a drawing that measures $8\frac{1}{2}$ by 11 inches. He needs to reduce it so it will fit into a space that measures $7\frac{1}{2}$ by 10 inches. What scale factor should he use to get a similar drawing that is small enough to fit? (Do not worry about getting it to fit perfectly.)

39. a. Match each growth rate from List 1 with the equivalent growth factor in List 2 if possible.

List 1

20%, 120%, 50%, 200%, 400%, 2%

List 2

1.5, 5, 1.2, 2.2, 4, 2, 1.02

b. Order the growth rates from List 1 from least to greatest.

c. Order the growth factors from List 2 from least to greatest.

Notes

Extensions

40. In Russia, shortly after the breakup of the Soviet Union, the yearly growth factor for inflation was 26. What growth rate (percent increase) is associated with this growth factor? We call this percent increase the *inflation rate.*

41. In 2000, the population of the United States was about 282 million and was growing exponentially at a rate of about 1% per year.

a. At this growth rate, what will the population of the United States be in the year 2020?

b. At this rate, how long will it take the population to double?

c. The population in 2010 was about 308 million. How accurate was the growth rate?

42. Use the table to answer parts (a)–(d).

a. One model of world population growth assumes the population grows exponentially. Based on the data in this table, what would be a reasonable growth factor for this model?

b. Use your growth factor from part (a) to write an equation for the growth of the population at 5-year intervals beginning in 1955.

c. Use your equation from part (b) to predict the year in which the population was double the 1955 population.

d. Use your equation to predict when the population will be double the 2010 population.

World Population Growth

Year	Population (billions)
1955	2.76
1960	3.02
1965	3.33
1970	3.69
1975	4.07
1980	4.43
1985	4.83
1990	5.26
1995	5.67
2000	6.07
2005	6.46
2010	6.84

Notes

For Exercises 43–45, write an equation that represents the exponential function in each situation.

43. A population is initially 300. After 1 year, the population is 361.

44. A population has a yearly growth factor of 1.2. After 3 years, the population is 1,000.

45. The growth rate for an investment is 3% per year. After 2 years, the value of the investment is $2,560.

46. Suppose your calculator did not have an exponent key. You could find 1.5^{12} by entering:

$1.5 \times 1.5 \times 1.5 \times 1.5 \times 1.5 \times 1.5 \times 1.5 \times 1.5 \times 1.5 \times 1.5 \times 1.5 \times 1.5$

a. How could you evaluate 1.5^{12} with fewer keystrokes?

b. What is the fewest times you could press [×] to evaluate 1.5^{12}?

47. Mr. Watson sold his boat for $10,000. He wants to invest the money.

Growth of $10,000 Investment at 4% Interest Compounded Quarterly

Time (mo)	Money in Account
0	$10,000
3	$10,100
6	$10,201
9	$10,303.01

a. How much money will Mr. Watson have after 1 year if he invests the $10,000 in an account that pays 4% interest per year?

b. Mr. Watson sees an advertisement for another type of savings account:

"4% interest per year compounded quarterly."

He asks the bank teller what "compounded quarterly" means. She explains that instead of giving him 4% of $10,000 at the end of one year, the bank will give him 1% at the end of each 3-month period (each quarter of a year).

If Mr. Watson invests his money at this bank, how much will be in his account at the end of one year?

c. Mr. Watson sees an advertisement for a different bank that offers 4% interest per year *compounded monthly*. (This means he will get $\frac{1}{12}$ of 4% interest every month.) How much money will he have at the end of the year if he invests his money at this bank?

d. Which account would have the most money at the end of one year? Explain.

STUDENT PAGE

Notes

Mathematical Reflections 3

In this Investigation, when you were given tables and descriptions of relationships, you explored exponential functions in which the growth factor was not a whole number. In some of these situations, the growth was described by giving the percent growth, or growth rate.

Think about these questions. Discuss your ideas with other students and your teacher. Then write a summary of your findings in your notebook.

1. Suppose you know the initial value for a population and the yearly growth rate.
   a. How can you determine the population several years from now?
   b. How is a growth rate related to the growth factor for the population?
   c. How can you use this information to write an equation that models the situation?
2. Suppose you know the initial value for a population and the yearly growth factor.
   a. How can you determine the population several years from now?
   b. How can you determine the yearly growth rate?
3. Suppose you know the equation that represents the exponential function relating the population p and the number of years n. How can you determine the doubling time for the population?

Notes

Common Core Mathematical Practices

As you worked on the Problems in this Investigation, you used prior knowledge to make sense of them. You also applied Mathematical Practices to solve the Problems. Think back over your work, the ways you thought about the Problems, and how you used Mathematical Practices.

Nick described his thoughts in the following way:

We thought that the growth of the rabbit population in Problem 3.1 represented an exponential function.

We compared the population from one year with the next year's population. We found that the ratio was not exactly, but was very close to, 1.8.

This data is experimental. Factors such as food availability and weather conditions could affect the growth of the population from year to year. So, we used 1.8 as an approximation of the growth rate.

Common Core Standards for Mathematical Practice
MP4 Model with mathematics

- What other Mathematical Practices can you identify in Nick's reasoning?
- Describe a Mathematical Practice that you and your classmates used to solve a different Problem in this Investigation.

Notes

Investigation 4

PLANNING

Exponential Decay

Investigation Overview

Investigation Description

This Investigation introduces students to exponential decay—patterns of change that exhibit successive, nonconstant decreases rather than increases. These decreasing relationships are generated by repeated multiplication by factors between 0 and 1, called *decay factors*. Strategies for finding decay factors and initial population and for representing decay patterns are similar to those used for exponential growth patterns. You can also represent exponential decay patterns by the equation $y = a(b)^x$, where a is the y-intercept and b is the decay factor, which is greater than 0 and less than 1.

In Problem 4.3, students collect and analyze data from an experiment that they conduct in class. Gathering the data will require an entire class period, but students almost certainly will not be able to analyze the data the same day. They will need time during the following class period to compile and analyze their data. To save time, you could have three students gather data during Problem 4.2 for the entire class to use the next day. If you decide the whole class should be involved in collecting data, then you can assign ACE Exercises for students to do between temperature readings. Alternatively, students could do these tasks at home and discuss their results in their groups the next day. Another option for collecting the data is to use a CBL (Computer-Based Laboratory).

Investigation Vocabulary

- decay factor
- exponential decay
- rate of decay

Mathematics Background

- Exponential Functions
- Growth Factor and Exponential Functions
- y-intercept or Initial Value
- Growth Rates
- Exponential Decay
- Graphs of Exponential Functions
- Equations for Exponential Functions
- Recursive, or Iterative, Processes
- Equivalence
- Scientific Notation
- Logarithms
- Using Graphing Calculators

Planning Chart

Content	ACE	Pacing	Materials	Resources
Problem 4.1	1–3, 19–22	1 day	**Labsheet 4.1** Ballot Areas Table **Labsheet 4ACE** Exercise 1 **Labsheet 4ACE:** Exercise 3 (accessibility) • Inch Grid Paper • Quarter-Inch Grid Paper 8-inch square of inch grid paper for demo, inch grid paper or quarter-inch grid paper for students, scissors	
Problem 4.2	4–7, 23–24, 25	1 day	**Labsheet 4.2** Medicine Table	**Teaching Aid 4.2A** Breakdown of Medicine **Teaching Aid 4.2B** Area Versus Medicine
Problem 4.3	8–18	1 day	**Labsheet 4.3** Water Cooling Table **Labsheet 4ACE** Exercise 15 **Labsheet 4ACE** Exercise 16 very hot water, cups for holding hot liquid, watches or clocks with second hand, CBLs, graphing calculators, graph paper, thermometer for measuring room temperature	
Mathematical Reflections		½ day		

Goals and Standards

Goals

Exponential Functions Explore problem situations in which two or more variables have an exponential relationship to each other

- Identify situations that can be modeled with an exponential function
- Identify the pattern of change (growth/decay factor) between two variables that represent an exponential function in a situation, table, graph, or equation
- Represent an exponential function with a table, graph, or equation
- Make connections among the patterns of change in a table, graph, and equation of an exponential function
- Compare the growth/decay rate and growth/decay factor for an exponential function and recognize the role each plays in an exponential situation
- Identify the growth/decay factor and initial value in problem situations, tables, graphs, and equations that represent exponential functions
- Determine whether an exponential function represents a growth (increasing) or decay (decreasing) pattern, from an equation, table, or graph that represents an exponential function
- Determine the values of the independent and dependent variables from a table, graph, or equation of an exponential function
- Use an exponential equation to describe the graph and table of an exponential function
- Predict the *y*-intercept from an equation, graph, or table that represents an exponential function
- Interpret the information that the *y*-intercept of an exponential function represents
- Determine the effects of the growth factor and initial value for an exponential function on a graph of the function
- Solve problems about exponential growth and decay from a variety of different subject areas, including science and business, using an equation, table, or graph
- Observe that one exponential equation can model different contexts
- Compare exponential and linear functions

Mathematical Reflections

Look for evidence of student understanding of the goals for this Investigation in their responses to the questions in *Mathematical Reflections*. The goals addressed by each question are indicated below.

1. How can you recognize an exponential decay pattern from the following?

a. a table of data

b. a graph

c. an equation

Goals

- Identify situations that can be modeled with an exponential function
- Identify the pattern of change (growth/decay factor) between two variables that represent an exponential function in a situation, table, graph, or equation
- Make connections among the patterns of change in a table, graph, and equation of an exponential function
- Identify the growth/decay factor and initial value in problem situations, tables, graphs, and equations that represent exponential functions
- Compare the growth/decay rate and growth/decay factor for an exponential function and recognize the role each plays in an exponential situation
- Represent an exponential function with a table, graph, or equation
- Use an exponential equation to describe the graph and table of an exponential function
- Predict the *y*-intercept from an equation, graph, or table that represents an exponential function
- Interpret the information that the *y*-intercept of an exponential function represents
- Write and interpret exponential expressions that represent the dependent variable in an exponential function

2. How are exponential growth functions and exponential decay functions similar? How are they different?

Goals

- Determine whether an exponential function represents a growth (increasing) or decay (decreasing) pattern, from an equation, table, or graph that represents an exponential function
- Determine the values of the independent and dependent variables from a table, graph, or equation of an exponential function
- Determine the effects of the growth/decay factor and initial value for an exponential function on a graph of the function

3. How are exponential decay functions and decreasing linear functions similar? How are they different?

Goals

- Compare exponential and linear functions
- Solve problems about exponential growth and decay from a variety of different subject areas, including science and business, using an equation, table, or graph

Standards

Common Core Content Standards

8.F.A.1 Understand that a function is a rule that assigns to each input exactly one output. The graph of a function is the set of ordered pairs consisting of an input and the corresponding output. *Problems 1 and 2*

8.F.A.2 Compare properties of two functions each represented in a different way (algebraically, graphically, numerically in tables, or by verbal descriptions). *Problems 1, 2, and 3*

8.F.A.3 Interpret the equation $y = mx + b$ as defining a linear function, whose graph is a straight line; give examples of functions that are not linear. *Problems 1, 2, and 3*

8.F.B.5 Describe qualitatively the functional relationship between two quantities by analyzing a graph (e.g., where the function is increasing or decreasing, linear or nonlinear). Sketch a graph that exhibits the qualitative features of a function that has been described verbally. *Problems 1, 2, and 3*

A-SSE.A.1a Interpret parts of an expression, such as terms, factors, and coefficients. *Problems 1 and 2*

A-SSE.A.1b Interpret complicated expressions by viewing one or more of their parts as a single entity. *Problem 2*

A-CED.A.2 Create equations in two or more variables to represent relationships between quantities; graph equations on coordinate axes with labels and scales. *Problems 1, 2, and 3*

A-REI.D.10 Understand that the graph of an equation in two variables is the set of all its solutions plotted in the coordinate plane, often forming a curve (which could be a line). *Problems 1, 2, and 3*

F-IF.B.4 For a function that models a relationship between two quantities, interpret key features of graphs and tables in terms of the quantities, and sketch graphs showing key features given a verbal description of the relationship. *Problems 1, 2, and 3*

F-IF.B.6 Calculate and interpret the average rate of change of a function (presented symbolically or as a table) over a specified interval. Estimate the rate of change from a graph. *Problems 1, 2, and 3*

F-IF.C.7e Graph exponential and logarithmic functions, showing intercepts and end behavior, and trigonometric functions, showing period, midline, and amplitude. *Problems 1, 2, and 3*

F-IF.C.9 Compare properties of two functions each represented in a different way (algebraically, graphically, numerically in tables, or by verbal descriptions). *Problem 2*

F-BF.A.1a Determine an explicit expression, a recursive process, or steps for calculation from a context. *Problems 1, 2, and 3*

F-BF.A.1b Combine standard function types using arithmetic operations. *Problem 3*

F-LE.A.1a Prove that linear functions grow by equal differences over equal intervals, and that exponential functions grow by equal factors over equal intervals. *Problems 1, 2, and 3*

F-LE.A.1c Recognize situations in which a quantity grows or decays by a constant percent rate per unit interval relative to another. *Problems 1 and 2*

F-LE.A.2 Construct linear and exponential functions, including arithmetic and geometric sequences, given a graph, a description of a relationship, or two input-output pairs (include reading these from a table). *Problems 1 and 2*

F-LE.B.5 Interpret the parameters in a linear or exponential function in terms of a context. *Problems 1, 2, and 3*

Facilitating the Mathematical Practices

Students in *Connected Mathematics* classrooms display evidence of multiple Common Core Standards for Mathematical Practice every day. Here are just a few examples of when you might observe students demonstrating the Standards for Mathematical Practice during this Investigation.

Practice 1: Make sense of problems and persevere in solving them.

Students are engaged every day in solving problems and, over time, learn to persevere in solving them. To be effective, the problems embody critical concepts and skills and have the potential to engage students in making sense of mathematics. Students build understanding by reflecting, connecting, and communicating. These student-centered problem situations engage students in articulating the "knowns" in a problem situation and determining a logical solution pathway. The student-student and student-teacher dialogues help students not only to make sense of the problems, but also to persevere in finding appropriate strategies to solve them. The suggested questions in the Teacher Guides provide the metacognitive scaffolding to help students monitor and refine their problem-solving strategies.

Practice 3: Model with mathematics.

In Problem 4.1, some students may claim that the relationship is an inverse variation based on the shape of the graph. Others may argue that this is not an inverse variation because inverse variation can never have a y-intercept, and this relationship does have a y-intercept. Some students might present a different argument to show that it is not an inverse relationship: The variables in an inverse variation have a "factor pair" relationship. That is, $xy =$ constant. This is not true for the relationship in this Problem.

Practice 7: Look for and make use of structure.

Students collect data to determine the pattern of change in the temperature of the water in a cup in Problem 4.3. They start with boiling water and record the temperature every 5 minutes. They then fit a graph to the data and use an equation to find an approximate decay factor. This process is very similar to the one they used in determining bridge strength in the *Thinking With Mathematical Models* Unit.

Students identify and record their personal experiences with the Standards for Mathematical Practice during the *Mathematical Reflections* at the end of the Investigation.

PROBLEM
4.1

Making Smaller Ballots
Introducing Exponential Decay

Problem Overview

Focus Question How does the pattern of change in this situation compare to the growth patterns you have studied in previous Problems? How does the difference show up in a table, graph, and equation?

Problem Description

Students revisit the paper-cutting activity of Investigation 1 with a new question in mind: How does the area of a ballot change with each successive cut? The initial area of the paper is 64 square inches. Students look at a table, an equation, and a graph for the data and compare them to exponential growth patterns in the previous three Investigations. Students find that the multiplicative rate is $\frac{1}{2}$ and that the area is decreasing by the factor $\frac{1}{2}$ after each cut. This pattern is similar to exponential growth patterns, but, in this case, as the independent variable increases, the dependent variable decreases.

When the multiplicative factor is less than 1 and greater than 0, the exponential pattern is called *exponential decay*. The factor the quantity is multiplied by at each stage is called the *decay factor*.

Problem Implementation

Students should work in pairs.

Materials

- **Labsheet 4.1:** Ballot Areas Table (one per pair)
- **Labsheet 4ACE:** Exercise 1
- **Labsheet 4ACE:** Exercise 3 (accessibility)
- Inch Grid Paper
- Quarter-Inch Grid Paper

8-inch square of inch grid paper for demo
inch grid paper or quarter-inch grid paper for students
scissors

Vocabulary

There are no new glossary terms introduced in this Problem.

Mathematics Background

- Exponential Functions
- Growth Factor and Exponential Functions
- *y*-intercept or Initial Value
- Growth Rates
- Exponential Decay
- Graphs of Exponential Functions
- Equations for Exponential Functions
- Recursive, or Iterative, Processes
- Equivalence
- Scientific Notation
- Logarithms
- Using Graphing Calculators

At a Glance and Lesson Plan

- At a Glance: Problem 4.1 Growing, Growing, Growing
- Lesson Plan: Problem 4.1 Growing, Growing, Growing

Launch

Connecting to Prior Knowledge

Remind students that in the ballot-cutting activity in Investigation 1, they looked at how the number of ballots changes with each cut. Explain that they are going to revisit that activity, but this time, they will look at how the area of a ballot changes with each cut. Demonstrate, starting with an 8-inch square of inch grid paper. **(Inch Grid Paper)**

Presenting the Challenge

Hold up your square of grid paper. Then ask the following questions.

Suggested Questions

- This sheet of paper has an area of 64 square inches. When you make the first cut, what happens to the area of a ballot? (It becomes half the original area, or 32 in.^{2}.)
- What will be the area of each ballot after the second cut? (16 in.^{2})
- What would a ballot look like if you made 10 cuts? (It would be very small.)
- Do you think it would be large enough for you to write your name on it? (No.)
- Will you ever have a ballot with an area of 0 square inches? (No; although the area will become smaller and smaller, it will theoretically never reach 0 square inches.)

Tell students that their task is to determine the pattern of change between the number of cuts and the area of the ballots. To save class time, hand out **Labsheet 4.1: Ballot Areas Table.**

Explore

Providing for Individual Needs

Distribute a sheet of **Inch Grid Paper** or **Quarter-Inch Grid Paper** and scissors to each group of students. Students will also need grid paper for their graphs. Have the class cut 8-inch squares from the grid paper. Each group should then cut their paper square into ballots as directed, complete the table, and answer Questions B–E. (Students need only actually cut the paper for the first two or three cuts.)

You may wish to provide students with **Labsheet 4.1: Ballot Areas Table** (accessibility) for Question A. The labsheet contains a larger version of the table in the Student Edition. You can give this labsheet to students to help them organize their answers. This can allow students to remain focused on the mathematics of the Question while saving time.

Have some students prepare their graphs to display for the Summarize.

Some students may write the expression as $64\left(\frac{1}{2}\right)^n$, while some might write $64(0.5)^n$. Be sure to bring these up during the Summarize and ask the class to show that the expressions are equivalent. In this case they may point out that $\frac{1}{2} = 0.5$. **Note:** In some CMP classes, students made the observation that the graph looks like the graph of an inverse variation relationship. If this occurs, ask them to show why it is or is not an inverse variation. ACE Exercise 2 provides sample student reasoning to show that it is not an inverse variation problem.

Planning for the Summary

What evidence will you use in the summary to clarify and deepen understanding of the Focus Question?

What will you do if you do not have evidence?

Summarize

Orchestrating the Discussion

Have students share what they discovered in the Problem. Ask them the following questions.

Suggested Questions

- What happens to the area of a ballot with each successive cut? (It is half the previous area, or the previous area divided by 2.)
- Does this pattern remain consistent as you make more cuts? (Yes.)
- Do the data in your table look like data from other situations you have encountered? (In some ways, no; the values are decreasing. In previous situations, the values increased. In other ways, yes; you can determine each value by multiplying the previous value by a constant number.)
- How can you determine the area of a ballot from the area of the previous ballot? (Multiply it by $\frac{1}{2}$, or 0.5.)
- Start at the beginning and generate the table using the constant factor $\frac{1}{2}$. If you know the area of the original ballot is 64 square inches, how do you get the area of a ballot after one cut? (Multiply 64 by $\frac{1}{2}$.)
- What is the area after two cuts? (16 in.^2)
- Suppose you could continue cutting. How could you find the area of a ballot after 50 cuts? (Multiply 64 by a string of 50 factors of $\frac{1}{2}$, or calculate $64\left(\frac{1}{2}\right)^{50}$.)
- What is the area of a ballot after *n* cuts? ($64\left(\frac{1}{2}\right)^n$ in.^2)
- Explain how you got your equation in Question C. (You can represent this situation using an exponential decay equation of the form $y = a(b)^x$. In this case, y is the area A of a ballot, x is the number of cuts n, a is the initial value, 64, and b is the decay factor, $\frac{1}{2}$.)
- What does the graph of this situation look like? How is the graph similar to and different from the graphs in the previous Problems? (Students should realize that the graph is not a straight line because this is not a linear relationship. It has a curved shape similar to a graph of exponential growth, but it is decreasing rather than increasing.)

Check for Understanding

Ask questions that connect the various representations of the relationship.

- Pick a pair of values from the table and ask students to explain what these values mean in terms of the context, the equation, and the graph.
- Have students explain how the variables and numbers in the equation relate to the context of the situation, the table, and the graph.
- Have students discuss how the pattern and features of the graph are related to the equation, situation, and table.

Then ask the following question:

- When will the area be about 0.01 square inches? Explain your reasoning. (after 12 cuts; because $64\left(\frac{1}{2}\right)^{12} = 0.015625$ and $64\left(\frac{1}{2}\right)^{13} = 0.0078125$)

Reflecting on Student Learning

Use the following questions to assess student understanding at the end of the lesson.

- What evidence do I have that students understand the Focus Question?
  - Where did my students get stuck?
  - What strategies did they use?
  - What breakthroughs did my students have today?
- How will I use this to plan for tomorrow? For the next time I teach this lesson?
- Where will I have the opportunity to reinforce these ideas as I continue through this Unit? The next Unit?

ACE Assignment Guide

- **Applications:** 1–3
- **Connections:** 19–22

You may wish to provide students with **Labsheet 4ACE: Exercise 1** that contains a larger version of the table in the Student Edition. You can give this labsheet to students to help them organize their answers.

To provide additional support for students when they are working on the ACE Exercises, you may choose to give hints, partially fill in tables, and emphasize key words. See **Labsheet 4ACE: Exercise 3** (accessibility) for an example of how to do this.

PROBLEM

4.2 Fighting Fleas

Representing Exponential Decay

Problem Overview

Focus Question How can you recognize an exponential decay function from a contextual setting, table, graph, and equation that represents the function?

Problem Description

This Problem focuses on the decreasing amount of active medicine in an animal's bloodstream in the hours following the initial dose. Question A gives a graph and a table for the decay pattern and asks students to find the decay factor and initial value. Students use this information to write an equation for the decay pattern and to compare the patterns in the amount of flea medicine to the pattern of area of the ballots in the previous Problem. Question B presents the decay of another flea medicine by giving the decay rate (or percent decrease) of the medicine. Again, students identify the decay factor and initial value and write an equation for the population decay.

Problem Implementation

Students should work in pairs. They can move into groups of four to discuss their findings.

Materials

- **Labsheet 4.2:** Medicine Table (one per pair)
- **Teaching Aid 4.2A:** Breakdown of Medicine
- **Teaching Aid 4.2B:** Area Versus Medicine

Vocabulary

- decay factor
- exponential decay
- rate of decay

Mathematics Background

- Exponential Functions
- Growth Factor and Exponential Functions
- y-intercept or Initial Value
- Growth Rates
- Exponential Decay
- Graphs of Exponential Functions
- Equations for Exponential Functions
- Recursive, or Iterative, Processes
- Equivalence
- Scientific Notation
- Logarithms
- Using Graphing Calculators

At a Glance and Lesson Plan

- At a Glance: Problem 4.2 Growing, Growing, Growing
- Lesson Plan: Problem 4.2 Growing, Growing, Growing

Launch

Launch Video

This animation shows a situation similar to the Introduction to the Problem of the breakdown of medicine in the bloodstream, which is exponential decay. You can show this video at the beginning of Presenting the Challenge to help students with the context of the Problem.

After showing the video, continue with Presenting the Challenge. Visit Teacher Place at mathdashboard.com/cmp3 to see the complete video.

Connecting to Prior Knowledge

You could start by writing an equation for the pattern in Problem 4.1, $A = 64\left(\frac{1}{2}\right)^n$. Then, introduce the terms *exponential decay* and *decay factor*.

Suggested Questions

- What are the similarities and differences between exponential decay patterns and exponential growth patterns? (In both exponential growth and exponential decay, you find each y-value by multiplying the previous y-value by a constant factor (assuming the x-values change by a constant amount).

  In exponential growth, the constant factor (the growth factor) is greater than 1. In exponential decay, the constant factor (the decay factor) is between 0 and 1.)
- What was the decay factor in the ballot-area situation in Problem 4.1? ($\frac{1}{2}$)

- How was this represented in the table? In the graph? In the equation? (In the table, you find each successive area by multiplying the previous area by the decay factor $\frac{1}{2}$. In the graph, you find each y-value by multiplying the previous y-value by the decay factor $\frac{1}{2}$. In the equation, the decay factor $\frac{1}{2}$ is the base of the exponential expression.)

Presenting the Challenge

Show the Launch Video to help students understand the context of medicine breaking down in the bloodstream over time. Talk with the class about the context of a flea medicine being administered to a dog and subsequently breaking down in the dog's blood. Display **Teaching Aid 4.2A: Breakdown of Medicine.**

Suggested Questions

- According to the table, how much medicine was in the dog's blood initially? (400 mg)
- How much active medicine remained after 1 hour? After 2 hours? (100 mg; 25 mg)
- How would you describe the pattern of decline in the amount of active medicine in the dog's blood? (The medicine breaks down quickly at first, and then more slowly.)

▼ Explore

Providing for Individual Needs

As you circulate, verify that students are finding a decay factor by dividing the milligrams of medicine remaining in the dog's blood in any hour by the milligrams remaining in the *previous* hour. Because the decay factor is less than 1, some students may be tempted to divide by the number for the next hour to get a number greater than 1.

Students may need help understanding the 20% decay rate in Question B. Hand out **Labsheet 4.2: Medicine Table** for students to use with Question B.

Planning for the Summary

What evidence will you use in the summary to clarify and deepen understanding of the Focus Question?

What will you do if you do not have evidence?

Summarize

Orchestrating the Discussion

Have students compare the equation they wrote in this Problem to the equation for ballot area in Problem 4.1. Ask the following questions.

Suggested Questions

- How do the equation for the ballot-area $A = 64\left(\frac{1}{2}\right)^n$ and the equation $m = 400\left(\frac{1}{4}\right)^h$ in this Problem compare? (In the first equation, the decay factor is $\frac{1}{2}$, or 0.5, and in the second, it is $\frac{1}{4}$, or 0.25. So, the area of a ballot is half the previous area, and the amount of active medicine in the blood each hour is $\frac{1}{4}$ the previous amount. The initial values are different. For the ballot Problem, the sheet of paper had an initial area of 64 in.^{2}. For this Problem, the initial dose of medicine was 400 mg.)

For Question B, you may wish to display **Teaching Aid 4.2B: Area Versus Medicine** to compare the graph of the data to the graph of the ballot data from Problem 4.1.

- How do these graphs compare? (Both graphs display data points in an exponential decay pattern. However, in the graph of the medicine in the dog's blood, the points are connected by a smooth curve. The ballot graph descends much more quickly and then levels out.)
- Why does it make sense to connect the points in the active-medicine graph but not in the ballot-area graph? (You can connect the points in the active-medicine graph because the amount of medicine in the blood changes continuously. In the ballot model, the area does not change between cuts, so only whole-number values for the number of cuts make sense. The active-medicine graph represents a continuous relationship between time and amount of active medicine in the blood; the ballot-area graph represents a discrete relationship between number of cuts and area of a ballot.)

Be sure to discuss the equation for the situation in Question B, focusing on the decay factor and its relationship to the decay rate. Students may find it confusing that because 20%, or $\frac{1}{5}$, of the active medicine is used each hour, 80%, or $\frac{4}{5}$, remains. However, this is the key to understanding the exponential decay nature of the situation.

- Is the decay factor greater than 1 or less than 1? (less than 1)
- If 20% of the medicine is used each hour, what percent remains active in the blood each hour? (80% of the amount at the start of the hour)
- What is the fractional equivalent of that percent? ($\frac{8}{10}$, or $\frac{4}{5}$)
- So, what is the decay factor in this situation? ($\frac{4}{5}$, or 0.8)

Reflecting on Student Learning

Use the following questions to assess student understanding at the end of the lesson.

- What evidence do I have that students understand the Focus Question?
  - Where did my students get stuck?
  - What strategies did they use?
  - What breakthroughs did my students have today?
- How will I use this to plan for tomorrow? For the next time I teach this lesson?
- Where will I have the opportunity to reinforce these ideas as I continue through this Unit? The next Unit?

ACE Assignment Guide

- **Applications:** 4–7
- **Connections:** 23–24
- **Extensions:** 25

PROBLEM 4.3

Cooling Water

Modeling Exponential Decay

Problem Overview

Focus Question How can you find the initial population and decay factor for an exponential decay relationship?

Problem Description

Students conduct an experiment to determine the rate at which a cup of water cools, a phenomenon that can be closely modeled by an exponential decay function.

Problem Implementation

Students should work in groups of four.

Suggestions for Conducting the Experiment

Suggestion 1

To save time, you could have three students gather data during Problem 4.2 for the entire class to use the next day. One student could read the water temperature, a second could watch the time, and a third could make the table. Everyone could then make a graph from the collected data, estimate the decay factor, and answer the questions.

Suggestion 2

If you decide the whole class should be involved in collecting data, then you can assign ACE Exercises for students to do between temperature readings. The trick is to keep them busy, but not so busy that they forget to record the temperature at the correct intervals. You might set a timer to go off at regular intervals, reminding groups to stop and record the temperature.

One thermometer for measuring the room temperature will suffice for the entire class.

Gathering the data will require an entire class period. Students will need time during the following class period to compile their data, find the differences between the water and room temperatures, and determine the decay factor for the cooling of the water. Alternatively, they could do these tasks at home and discuss their results in their groups the next day.

If the whole-class approach is taken, the data tables, graphs, and equations would make a good bulletin board display.

You might also try different kinds of containers—glass, porcelain, styrofoam, travel mug, etc.—to compare the different growth patterns.

Suggestion 3

A CBL (Computer-Based Laboratory) can be used to collect the temperature data. If you have one CBL, you could demonstrate this for the whole class. If you have several, you might let the groups use the CBLs themselves after you have given them instructions.

Graphing the Data

Students construct two graphs from the data they collect in this Problem. The graph of the (*time, water temperature*) data will appear exponential, but the value that it eventually approaches is not 0, as has been the case in the exponential decay relationships students have studied so far. Instead, the water temperature eventually approaches room temperature. To adjust the graph so it behaves like those for which students know how to write equations, the room temperature must be subtracted from each water temperature. In effect, this translates the graph down the *y*-axis so the graph approaches the *x*-axis rather than the room temperature.

Students will probably not completely understand this important technique through this one exposure. In later science classes, they will likely revisit this cooling experiment and be able to make more sense of it. At this time, it is enough to expect every student to construct the two graphs, to observe that they both appear to be exponential, and to notice how they are different. In addition, students need to understand why they are different: They are seeing the effect of subtracting a constant value from each data value.

Materials

- **Labsheet 4.3:** Water Cooling Table (one per group)
- **Labsheet 4ACE:** Exercise 15 (one per student)
- **Labsheet 4ACE:** Exercise 16 (one per student)

very hot water
cups for holding hot liquid (1 per group)
watches or clocks with second hand (1 per group)
graphing calculators
graph paper
thermometer for measuring room temperature
CBLs (1 per group, optional)

Vocabulary

There are no new glossary terms introduced in this Problem.

Mathematics Background

- Exponential Functions
- Growth Factor and Exponential Functions
- *y*-intercept or Initial Value
- Growth Rates
- Exponential Decay
- Graphs of Exponential Functions
- Equations for Exponential Functions
- Recursive, or Iterative, Processes
- Equivalence
- Scientific Notation
- Logarithms
- Using Graphing Calculators

At a Glance and Lesson Plan

- At a Glance: Problem 4.3 Growing, Growing, Growing
- Lesson Plan: Problem 4.3 Growing, Growing, Growing

Launch

Connecting to Prior Knowledge

You might ask students to discuss some of the real-world applications for exponential functions that they discussed in previous Problems or that they have encountered in their daily lives. Tell them that in this Problem they will study another real-world situation.

Presenting the Challenge

Introduce the experiment by discussing the questions in the opening paragraph. Describe how students should conduct the experiment, emphasizing that they will need to record both the water temperature and the room temperature. Students will later analyze the differences between these two temperature readings. Hand out **Labsheet 4.3: Water Cooling Table.**

Explore

Providing for Individual Needs

The main goal of this Problem is to give students a hands-on experience in gathering data that produce an exponential graph and to let them proceed as far as they can toward writing an equation. Students have learned from Investigations 1, 2, and 3 that they can recognize an exponential relationship by the presence of a constant growth or decay factor. There is no constant growth factor relating the data in Question A, but there is in Question B. To help students clarify this, you might ask the following questions.

Suggested Questions

- In Question A, in what way does the graph you have made look like or unlike other graphs of exponential decay relationships? (The shape is similar, but the graph does not end up approaching the x-axis. In fact, the lowest temperature will be room temperature, not 0 degrees.)
- Does the table for Question A indicate that you are working with an exponential decay relationship? (No; because there is no approximate common factor.)
- Does the table in Question B indicate you are working with an exponential decay relationship? Explain. (Yes; because there is an approximate common decay factor. Working with the difference in temperatures, instead of actual temperatures, means that the differences will decrease, getting closer to zero, a pattern typical of exponential decay relationships.)

Planning for the Summary

What evidence will you use in the summary to clarify and deepen understanding of the Focus Question?

What will you do if you do not have evidence?

Summarize

Orchestrating the Discussion

As a class, compare the collected data and the graphs for each group. Ask how students found the decay factor. In the table, display for the class the ratios, which will vary. For Question B, ask the following.

Suggested Questions

- In Question B, to write an equation in the form $y = a(b)^x$, you need the values of a and b. What is the value of a in this situation? (Answers will vary. The value of a should equal the starting difference in temperature of the water.)

- What information does *a* represent in this experiment? (It is the starting temperature difference, or the temperature difference at time 0.)
- How did you find the decay factor for the cooling water? (You find the decay factor by finding the ratios between successive temperature differences and averaging them.)
- How does the decay factor affect the equation? (It is the value of *b*, the base.
- What things might affect the cooling rate you found? (These things might affect the cooling rate: the room temperature, the shape and material of the cup, the accuracy of the temperature readings, and so on.)
- If you wanted to get different cooling rates, how could you vary the experiment? (You could vary the experiment by stirring the liquid, by using a different liquid, by using a different container, and so on.)

As a class, choose one group's decay factor and starting value. Use these values to write an equation and sketch its graph. Discuss the relationship of the graph of the equation to the graph of the group's experimental data. Students should notice that they are not identical. Review with the class the idea that mathematical models are a generalized view of the actual data.

Check for Understanding

- Using the class equation, about how long will it take for the water temperature to reach room temperature? (Answers to this question will vary. Theoretically, because this is an exponential relationship, the temperature will never reach room temperature. The graph of the (*time, temperature difference*) equation might help students understand this idea. In this graph, the temperature will have reached room temperature when the temperature difference reaches 0.)

Reflecting on Student Learning

Use the following questions to assess student understanding at the end of the lesson.

- What evidence do I have that students understand the Focus Question?
  - Where did my students get stuck?
  - What strategies did they use?
  - What breakthroughs did my students have today?
- How will I use this to plan for tomorrow? For the next time I teach this lesson?
- Where will I have the opportunity to reinforce these ideas as I continue through this Unit? The next Unit?

ACE Assignment Guide

- **Applications:** 8–18

You may wish to provide students with **Labsheet 4ACE: Exercise 15** and **Labsheet 4ACE: Exercise 16**, which contains a larger version of the table as well as the questions found in the Student Edition.

Mathematical Reflections

Possible Answers to Mathematical Reflections

1. a. In a table, if the *x*-values are evenly spaced, and there is a constant ratio between any *y*-value and the previous *y*-value, and that ratio is between 0 and 1, then the data show an exponential decay pattern.

b. In a graph, an exponential decay pattern appears as a curve that drops downward from left to right, eventually becoming almost horizontal.

c. Exponential decay patterns have equations of the form $y = a \cdot b^x$, with $a > 0$ and b between 0 and 1.

2. Exponential growth and decay both have equations of the form $y = a \cdot b^x$, where $a > 0$. For exponential growth, b is greater than 1. For exponential decay, b is between 0 and 1. A graph of exponential decay is decreasing, and a graph of exponential growth is increasing. In a table, both exponential growth and decay are indicated by a constant ratio between any *y*-value and the previous *y*-value (assuming the *x*-values increase by a constant amount). However, in a growth situation, the ratio is greater than 1. In a decay situation, the ratio is between 0 and 1.

3. In both exponential decay situations and decreasing linear relationships, *y* decreases as *x* increases. In a table, you can see this difference easily. If the difference between consecutive *y*-values is constant and decreasing, then the table exhibits a linear relationship. If the ratio of consecutive *y*-values is constant and between 0 and 1, then the table exhibits an exponential decay pattern. A graph of a linear function looks like a straight line and has an *x*-intercept, and a graph of an exponential function is curved and does not have an *x*-intercept (if it is of the form $y = a \cdot b^x$, where $a > 1$), although it may sometimes appear linear depending on the scale.

Possible Answers to Mathematical Practices Reflections

Students may have demonstrated all of the eight Common Core Standards for Mathematical Practice during this Investigation. During the class discussion, have students provide additional Practices that the Problem cited involved and identify the use of other Mathematical Practices in the Investigation.

One student observation is provided in the Student Edition. Here is another sample student response.

As we made the table and graph for the data in Problem 4.1, we thought that the relationship was an inverse variation, since the graph "swooped" down. Other groups made the same conjecture. But in the Summarize, Collin showed that this was not an inverse variation because inverse variation can never have a y-intercept, and this relationship does have a y-intercept. Another group used a different argument to show that it was not an inverse relationship. James claimed that the variables in an inverse variation have a "factor pair" relationship. That is, $xy =$ constant. This is not true for the relationship in this Problem.

MP3: Construct viable arguments and critique the reasoning of others.

Investigation 4

Exponential Decay

The exponential functions you have studied so far have all involved quantities that increase. In this Investigation, you will explore quantities that decrease, or decay, exponentially as time passes.

4.1 Making Smaller Ballots

Introducing Exponential Decay

In Problem 1.1, you read about the ballots Chen is making. Chen cuts a sheet of paper in half. He stacks the two pieces and cuts them in half. Chen then stacks the resulting four pieces and cuts them in half, and so on.

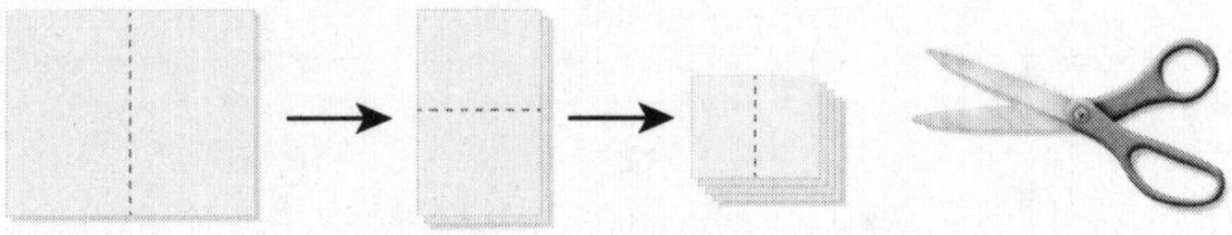

Common Core State Standards

8.F.A.2 Compare properties of two functions each represented in a different way (algebraically, graphically, numerically in tables, or by verbal descriptions).

8.F.A.3 Interpret the equation $y = mx + b$ as defining a linear function, whose graph is a straight line; give examples of functions that are not linear.

8.F.B.5 Describe qualitatively the functional relationship between two quantities by analyzing a graph . . . Sketch a graph that exhibits the qualitative features of a function that has been described verbally.

Also 8.F.A.1, A-SSE.A.1a, A-SSE.A.1b, A-CED.A.2, A-REI.D.10, F-IF.B.4, F-IF.B.6, F-IF.C.7e, F-BF.A.1a, F-LE.A.1a, F-LE.A.1c, F-LE.A.2, F-LE.B.5

Notes

You investigated the pattern in the number of ballots each cut made. In this Problem, you will look at the pattern in the areas of the ballots.

Problem 4.1

A The paper Chen starts with has an area of 64 square inches. Copy and complete the table to show the area of a ballot after each of the first 10 cuts.

Areas of Ballots

Number of Cuts	Area (in.^{2})
0	64
1	32
2	16
3	■
4	■
5	■
6	■
7	■
8	■
9	■
10	■

B How does the area of a ballot change with each cut?

C Write an equation for the area A of a ballot after any cut n.

D Make a graph of the data.

E **1.** How is the pattern of change in the area different from the exponential growth patterns you studied? How is it similar?

2. How is the pattern of change in the area different from linear patterns you studied? How is it similar?

ACE Homework starts on page 66.

STUDENT PAGE

Notes

4.2 Fighting Fleas
Representing Exponential Decay

Exponential patterns like the one in Problem 4.1, in which a quantity decreases at each stage by a constant factor, show **exponential decay.** The factor the quantity is multiplied by at each stage is called the **decay factor.** A decay factor is always greater than 0 and less than 1. In Problem 4.1, the decay factor is $\frac{1}{2}$.

- Are exponential decay patterns also exponential functions? Explain.

After an animal receives flea medicine, the medicine breaks down in the animal's bloodstream. With each hour, there is less medicine in the blood.

A dog receives a 400-milligram dose of flea medicine. The table and graph show the amount of medicine in the dog's bloodstream each hour for 6 hours after the dose.

Breakdown of Medicine

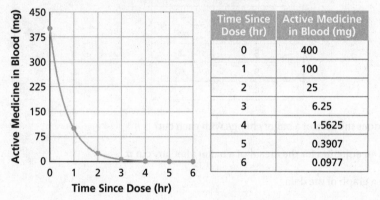

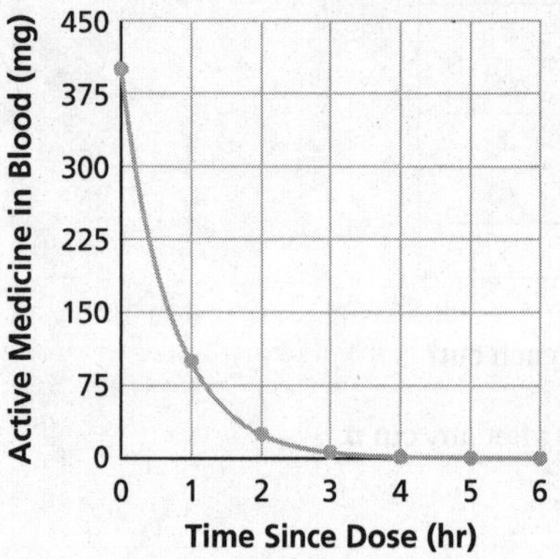

Time Since Dose (hr)	Active Medicine in Blood (mg)
0	400
1	100
2	25
3	6.25
4	1.5625
5	0.3907
6	0.0977

Notes

Problem 4.2

A Study the pattern of change in the graph and the table.

1. How does the amount of active medicine in the dog's blood change from one hour to the next?
2. Write an equation to model the relationship between the number of hours h since the dose is given and the milligrams of active medicine m.
3. How is the graph for this Problem similar to the graph you made in Problem 4.1? How is it different?
4. Does the relationship displayed in the table and graph represent an exponential function? Explain.

B 1. A different flea medicine breaks down at a rate of 20% per hour. This means that as each hour passes, 20% of the active medicine is used. This is the **rate of decay** of the medicine. The initial dose is 60 milligrams. Extend and complete this table to show the amount of active medicine in an animal's blood at the end of each hour for 6 hours.

Breakdown of Medicine

Time Since Dose (hr)	Active Medicine in Blood (mg)
0	60
1	■
2	■
⋮	⋮
6	■

2. Make a graph using the table you completed in part (1).
3. For the medicine in part (1), Janelle wrote the equation $m = 60(0.8)^h$ to show the amount of active medicine m after h hours. Compare the quantities of active medicine in your table to the quantities given by Janelle's equation. Explain any similarities or differences.
4. Dwayne was confused by the terms *decay rate* (or *rate of decay*) and *decay factor*. He said:

> Because the rate of decay is 20%, the decay factor should be 0.2, and the equation should be $m = 60(0.2)^h$.

Do you agree with him? Explain.

5. Steven recalled that when the growth rate is 80%, the growth factor is 1.8 or 180%. How is the relationship between growth rate and growth factor similar to the relationship between decay rate and decay factor?

ACE Homework starts on page 66.

STUDENT PAGE

Notes

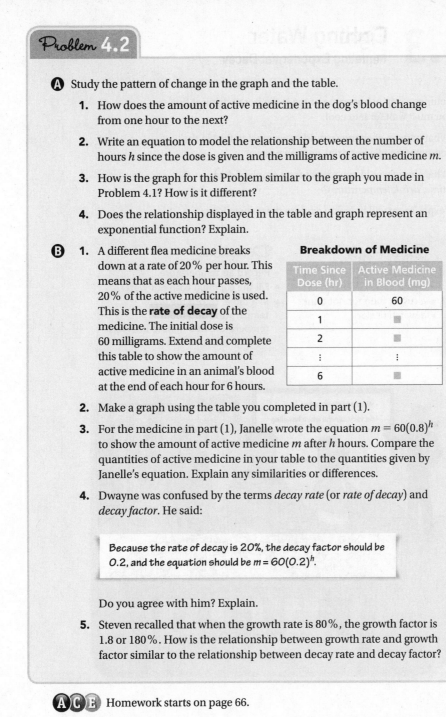

4.3 Cooling Water
Modeling Exponential Decay

Sometimes a cup of hot cocoa or tea is too hot to drink at first. So you must wait for it to cool.

- What pattern of change would you expect to find in the temperature of a hot drink as time passes?
- What shape would you expect for a graph of data (*time, drink temperature*)?

This experiment will help you explore these questions.

Equipment

- very hot water
- two thermometers
- a cup or mug for hot drinks
- a watch or clock

Directions

- Record air temperature.
- Fill the cup/mug with hot water.
- In a table, record the water temperature and room temperature at 5-minute intervals throughout your class period.

Notes

Problem 4.3

A **1.** Complete the table with data from your experiment.

Hot Water Cooling

Time (min)	Water Temperature	Room Temperature
0	■	■
5	■	■
10	■	■
■	■	■

Make a graph of your (*time, water temperature*) data.

2. Describe the pattern of change in the data. When did the water temperature change most rapidly? When did it change most slowly?

3. Is the relationship between time and water temperature an exponential decay relationship? Explain.

B **1.** Add a column to your table. In this column, record the difference between the water temperature and the air temperature for each time value.

2. Make a graph of the (*time, temperature difference*) data. Compare this graph with the graph you made in Question A.

3. Describe the pattern of change in the data. When did the temperature difference change most rapidly? Most slowly?

4. Estimate the decay factor for the relationship between temperature difference and time in this experiment.

5. Write an equation for the (*time, temperature difference*) data. Your equation should allow you to predict the temperature difference at the end of any 5-minute interval.

C **1.** What do you think the graph of the (*time, temperature difference*) data would look like if you had continued the experiment for several more hours?

2. What factors might affect the rate at which a cup of hot liquid cools?

3. What factors might introduce errors in the data you collect?

D Compare the graphs in Questions A and B with the graphs in Problems 4.1 and 4.2. What similarities and differences do you observe?

ACE Homework starts on page 66.

STUDENT PAGE

Notes

Applications | Connections | Extensions

Applications

1. Chen, from Problem 4.1, finds that his ballots are very small after only a few cuts. He decides to start with a larger sheet of paper. The new paper has an area of 324 in.^{2}. Copy and complete this table to show the area of each ballot after each of the first 10 cuts.

Areas of Ballots

Number of Cuts	Area (in.^{2})
0	324
1	162
2	81
3	■
4	■
5	■
6	■
7	■
8	■
9	■
10	■

a. Write an equation for the area A of a ballot after any cut n.

b. With the smaller sheet of paper, the area of a ballot is 1 in.^{2} after 6 cuts. Start with the larger sheet. How many cuts does it take to get ballots this small?

c. Chen wants to be able to make 12 cuts before getting ballots with an area of 1 in.^{2}. How large does his starting piece of paper need to be?

Notes

2. During the exploration of Problem 4.1, several groups of students in Mrs. Dole's class made a conjecture. They conjectured that the relationship between the number of cuts and the area of the ballot was an *inverse variation* relationship.

The class came up with two different arguments for why the relationship was not an inverse variation.

Argument 1

An inverse variation situation has a "factor-pair" relationship. Choose some constant number k. The two factors multiply to equal k, such as $yx = k$. For example, if the area of rectangle with length, l, and width, w, is 24,000 square feet, then $24{,}000 = lw$. This is an inverse variation.

In an exponential relationship, the values of the two variables x and y do not have this "factor-pair" relationship. For example, in Problem 4.1, the equation is $A = 64\left(\frac{1}{2}\right)^n$, but A and n do not multiply to get a constant number.

Argument 2

Any inverse variation will never have a y-intercept and this relationship does. Therefore, this relationship is not an inverse variation.

Which argument is correct? Explain why the students might have made this conjecture.

3. Latisha has a 24-inch string of licorice (LIK uh rish) to share with her friends. As each friend asks her for a piece, Latisha gives him or her half of what she has left. She doesn't eat any of the licorice herself.

a. Make a table showing the length of licorice Latisha has left each time she gives a piece away.

b. Make a graph of the data from part (a).

c. Suppose that, instead of half the licorice that is left each time, Latisha gives each friend 4 inches of licorice. Make a table and a graph for this situation.

d. Compare the tables and the graphs for the two situations. Explain the similarities and the differences.

STUDENT PAGE

Notes

4. Penicillin decays exponentially in the human body. Suppose you receive a 300-milligram dose of penicillin to combat strep throat. About 180 milligrams will remain active in your blood after 1 day.

   a. Assume the amount of penicillin active in your blood decreases exponentially. Make a table showing the amount of active penicillin in your blood for 7 days after a 300-milligram dose.

   b. Write an equation for the relationship between the number of days d since you took the penicillin and the amount of the medicine m remaining active in your blood.

   c. What is the equation for a 400-milligram dose?

For Exercises 5 and 6, tell whether the equation represents exponential decay or exponential growth. Explain your reasoning.

5. $y = 0.8(2.1)^x$

6. $y = 20(0.5)^x$

7. The graph below shows an exponential decay relationship.

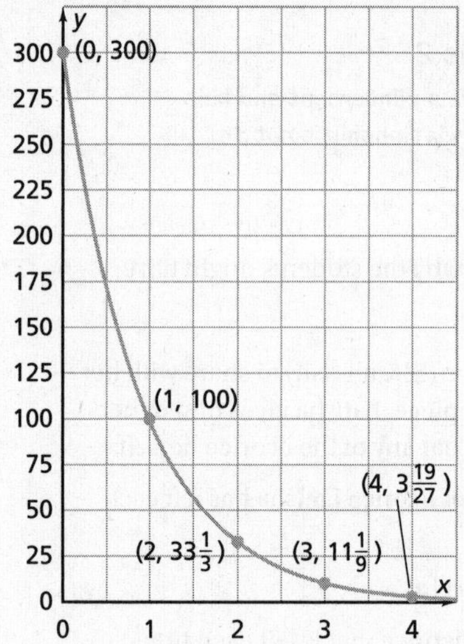

   a. Find the decay factor and the y-intercept.

   b. What is the equation for the graph?

Notes

For Exercises 8 and 9, use the table of values to determine the exponential decay equation. Then, find the decay factor and the decay rate.

8.

x	y
0	24
1	6
2	1.5
3	0.375
4	0.09375

9.

x	y
0	128
1	96
2	72
3	54

For Exercises 10–13, use Lara's conjecture below. Explain how you found your answer.

Lara's Conjecture

If you know the y-intercept and another point on the graph of an exponential function, then you can find all the other points.

10. The exponential decay graph has y-intercept $= 90$, and it passes through (2, 10). When $x = 1$, what is y?

11. The exponential decay graph has y-intercept $= 40$, and it passes through (2, 10). When $x = 4$, what is y?

12. The exponential decay graph has y-intercept $= 75$, and it passes through (2, 3). When $x = -2$, what is y?

13. The exponential decay graph has y-intercept $= 64$, and it passes through (3, 0.064). When $x = 2$, what is y?

Notes

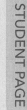

14. Karen shops at Aquino's Groceries. Her bill came to $50 before tax. She used two of the coupons shown below.

AQUINO'S GROCERIES
5%
off all purchases
can be used with other coupons (including this one)

Karen was expecting to save 10%, which is $5. The cashier rang up the two coupons. Karen was surprised when the total price rang up as $45.13 before tax. She was not sure why there was an extra $0.13 charge.

a. What would explain why the coupons did not take off 10% the way Karen expected?

b. Write an equation to represent the total amount Karen would spend based on the number of coupons she would use.

c. Karen had originally thought that if she used 10 coupons on her next trip to Aquino's Groceries she would save 50%. Her bill is still $50. How much would Karen actually spend?

d. How many coupons would you estimate it would take for Karen to get the $50 of groceries for free?

15. Hot coffee is poured into a cup and allowed to cool. The difference between coffee temperature and room temperature is recorded every minute for 10 minutes.

Cooling Coffee

Time (min)	0	1	2	3	4	5	6	7	8	9	10
Temperature Difference (°C)	80	72	65	58	52	47	43	38	34	31	28

a. Plot the data (*time, temperature difference*). Explain what the patterns in the table and the graph tell you about the rate at which the coffee cools.

b. Approximate the decay factor for this relationship.

c. Write an equation for the relationship between time and temperature difference.

d. About how long will it take the coffee to cool to room temperature? Explain.

Notes

16. The pizza in the ad for Mr. Costa's restaurant has a diameter of 5 inches.

a. What are the circumference and area of the pizza in the ad?

b. Mr. Costa reduces his ad to 90% of its original size. He then reduces the reduced ad to 90% of its size. He repeats this process five times. Extend and complete the table to show the diameter, circumference, and area of the pizza after each reduction.

Advertisement Pizza Sizes

Reduction Number	Diameter (in.)	Circumference (in.)	Area (in.^{2})
0	5	■	■
1	■	■	■

c. Write equations for the diameter, circumference, and area of the pizza after n reductions.

d. How would your equations change if Mr. Costa had used a reduction setting of 75%?

e. Express the decay factors from part (d) as fractions.

f. Mr. Costa claims that when he uses the 90% reduction setting on the copier, he is reducing the size of the drawing by 10%. Is Mr. Costa correct? Explain.

17. Answer parts (a) and (b) without using your calculator.

a. Which decay factor represents faster decay, 0.8 or 0.9?

b. Order the following from least to greatest:

0.9^4 $\quad 0.9^2$ $\quad 90\%$ $\quad \frac{2}{10}$ $\quad \frac{2}{9}$ $\quad 0.8^4$ $\quad 0.84$

18. Natasha and Michaela are trying to find growth factors for exponential functions. They claim that if the independent variable is increasing by 1, then you divide the two corresponding y values to find the growth factor. For example, if (x_1, y_1) and (x_2, y_2) are two consecutive entries in the table, then the growth factor is $y_2 \div y_1$.

a. Is their reasoning correct? Explain.

b. Would this method work to find the growth pattern for a linear function? Explain.

STUDENT PAGE

Notes

Connections

For Exercises 19–22, write each number in scientific notation.

19. There are about 33,400,000,000,000,000,000,000 molecules in 1 gram of water.

20. There are about 25,000,000,000,000 red blood cells in the human body.

21. Earth is about 93,000,000 miles (150,000,000 km) from the sun.

22. The Milky Way galaxy is approximately 100,000 light years in diameter. It contains about 300,000,000,000 stars.

23. Consider these equations:

$$y = 0.75^x \qquad y = 0.25^x \qquad y = -0.5x + 1$$

a. Sketch graphs of all three equations on one set of coordinate axes.

b. What points, if any, do the three graphs have in common?

c. In which graph does y decrease the fastest as x increases?

d. How can you use your graphs to figure out which of the equations is not an example of exponential decay?

e. How can you use the equations to figure out which is not an example of exponential decay?

24. A cricket is on the 0 point of a number line, hopping toward 1. She covers half the distance from her current location to 1 with each hop. So, she will be at $\frac{1}{2}$ after one hop, $\frac{3}{4}$ after two hops, and so on.

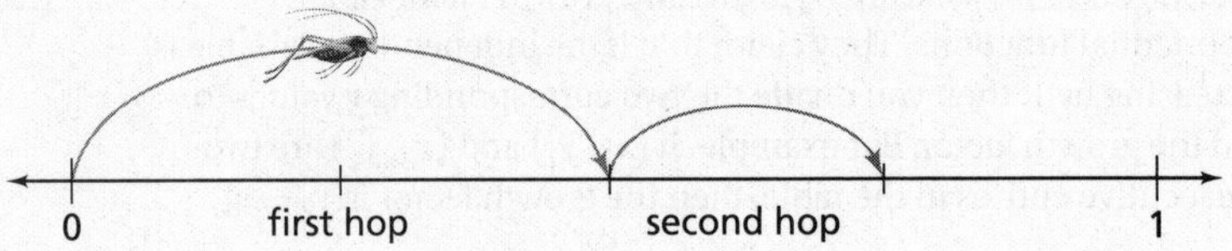

a. Make a table showing the cricket's location for the first 10 hops.

b. Where will the cricket be after n hops?

c. Will the cricket ever get to 1? Explain.

Notes

Extensions

25. Freshly cut lumber, known as *green lumber*, contains water. If green lumber is used to build a house, it may crack, shrink, and warp as it dries. To avoid these problems, lumber is dried in a kiln that circulates air to remove moisture from the wood.

GREEN LUMBER KILN

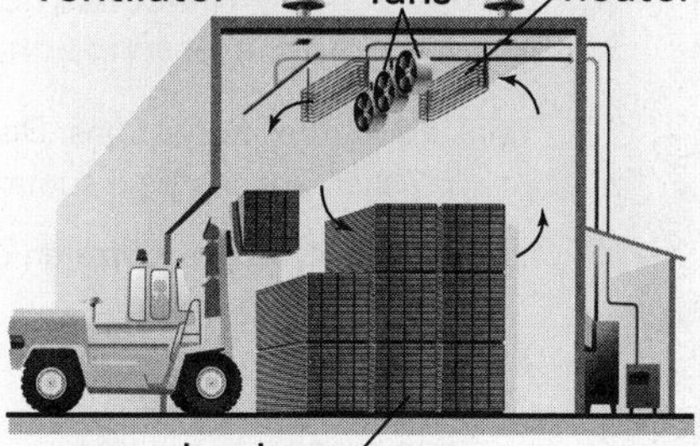

Suppose that, in 1 week, a kiln removes $\frac{1}{3}$ of the moisture from a stack of lumber.

a. What fraction of the moisture remains in the lumber after 5 weeks in a kiln?

b. What fraction of the moisture has been removed from the lumber after 5 weeks?

c. Write an equation for the fraction of moisture m remaining in the lumber after w weeks.

d. Write an equation for the fraction of moisture m that has been removed from the lumber after w weeks.

e. Graph your equations from parts (c) and (d) on the same set of axes. Describe how the graphs are related.

f. A different kiln removes $\frac{1}{4}$ of the moisture from a stack of lumber each week. Write equations for the fraction of moisture remaining and the fraction of moisture removed after w weeks.

g. Graph your two equations from part (f) on the same set of axes. Describe how the graphs are related. How do they compare to the graphs from part (e)?

h. Green lumber is about 40% water by weight. The moisture content of lumber used to build houses is typically 10% or less. For each of the two kilns described above, how long should lumber be dried before it is used to build a house?

STUDENT PAGE

Notes

Mathematical Reflections 4

In this Investigation, you explored situations in which a quantity decayed by a constant percent rate per unit interval and graphed them. You constructed exponential decay functions given a graph, a description, or a table.

Think about these questions. Discuss your ideas with other students and your teacher. Then write a summary of your findings in your notebook.

1. **How** can you recognize an exponential decay pattern from the following?
   a. a table of data
   b. a graph
   c. an equation
2. **How** are exponential growth functions and exponential decay functions similar? **How** are they different?
3. **How** are exponential decay functions and decreasing linear functions similar? **How** are they different?

Notes

Common Core Mathematical Practices

As you worked on the Problems in this Investigation, you used prior knowledge to make sense of them. You also applied Mathematical Practices to solve the Problems. Think back over your work, the ways you thought about the Problems, and how you used Mathematical Practices.

Sophie described her thoughts in the following way:

We collected data to determine the pattern of change in the temperature of the water in a cup in Problem 4.3. We started with boiling water and checked the temperature every 5 minutes. Then, we compared the water temperature to the room temperature and recorded the difference.

We then fit a graph to the data. We used the equation to find an approximate decay factor.

This process was very similar to the one we used in determining bridge strength in the Thinking with Mathematical Models Unit.

Common Core Standards for Mathematical Practice

MP7 Look for and make use of structure

- What other Mathematical Practices can you identify in Sophie's reasoning?
- Describe a Mathematical Practice that you and your classmates used to solve a different Problem in this Investigation.

STUDENT PAGE

Notes

Investigation 5

PLANNING

Patterns With Exponents

Investigation Overview

Investigation Description

This Investigation develops rules for operating with exponents. Students examine patterns in a powers table for b^x for b and $x = 1, 2, 3, 4, 5, 6, 7, 8, 9$. They look for relationships among numbers written in exponential form. This leads to the rules for operating on numerical expressions with exponents. Fractional exponents are introduced by looking at graphs of population and asking questions about the population when $x = \frac{1}{2}, \frac{5}{3}$, and so on. Students use *n*th roots to interpret and evaluate expressions with rational exponents.

From these explorations, students observe that the rules for integral exponents apply to rational exponents. The rules for exponents are used to write and interpret equivalent expressions including some expressed in scientific notation. In the last Problem, students use graphing calculators to study the effects of the values of a and b on the graph of $y = a(b^x)$.

Investigation Vocabulary

- *n*th root

Mathematics Background

- Exponential Functions
- Rules of Exponents
- Scientific Notation
- Using Graphing Calculators

Planning Chart

Content	ACE	Pacing	Materials	Resources
Problem 5.1	1, 67–69, 82–90	1½ days	**Labsheet 5.1A** Table of Positive Powers **Labsheet 5.1B** Table of Negative Powers **Labsheet 5.1C:** Patterns in the Ones Digits (accessibility)	**Teaching Aid 5.1A** Completed Table of Positive Powers **Teaching Aid 5.1B** Completed Table of Negative Powers
Problem 5.2	2–25, 70–71, 91	1½ days	**Labsheet 5.2** Rules for Exponents	
Problem 5.3	26–38, 72–74, 79–81, 92–93	1 day		• Teaching Aid 5.3
Problem 5.4	39–62, 75–76	1 day		
Problem 5.5	63–66, 77–78	1½ days	• Labsheet 5.5A (accessibility) • Labsheet 5.5B (accessibility) **Labsheet 5ACE:** Exercise 15 (accessibility)	
Mathematical Reflections		½ day		
Looking Back & Looking Ahead		½ day		
Unit Project		Optional		
Self-Assessment		Take home	• Self-Assessment	• Notebook Checklist • Spanish Self-Assessment
Assessment: Unit Test		1 day	• Unit Test	• Spanish Unit Test

Goals and Standards

Goals

Exponential Functions Explore problem situations in which two or more variables have an exponential relationship to each other

- Identify situations that can be modeled by an exponential function
- Identify the pattern of change (growth/decay factor) between two variables that represent an exponential function in a situation, table, graph, or equation
- Represent an exponential function with a table, graph, or equation
- Make connections among the patterns of change in a table, graph, and equation of an exponential function
- Compare the growth/decay rate and growth/decay factor for an exponential function and recognize the role each plays in an exponential situation
- Identify the growth/decay factor and initial value in problem situations, tables, graphs, and equations that represent exponential functions
- Determine whether an exponential function represents a growth (increasing) or decay (decreasing) pattern, from an equation, table, or graph that represents an exponential function
- Determine the values of the independent and dependent variables from a table, graph, or equation of an exponential function
- Use an exponential equation to describe the graph and table of an exponential function
- Predict the *y*-intercept from an equation, graph, or table that represents an exponential function
- Interpret the information that the *y*-intercept of an exponential function represents
- Determine the effects of the growth factor and initial value for an exponential function on a graph of the function
- Solve problems about exponential growth and decay from a variety of different subject areas, including science and business, using an equation, table, or graph
- Observe that one exponential equation can model different contexts
- Compare exponential and linear functions

Equivalence Develop understanding of equivalent exponential expressions

- Write and interpret exponential expressions that represent the dependent variable in an exponential function
- Develop the rules for operating with rational exponents and explain why they work
- Write, interpret, and operate with numerical expressions in scientific notation
- Write equivalent expressions using the rules for exponents and operations
- Solve problems that involve exponents, including scientific notation

Mathematical Reflections

Look for evidence of student understanding of the goals for this Investigation in their responses to the questions in *Mathematical Reflections*. The goals addressed by each question are indicated below.

1. a. Describe some of the rules for operating with exponents.

b. What is scientific notation? What are its practical applications?

Goals

- Develop the rules for operating with rational exponents and explain why they work
- Write and interpret equivalent expressions using the rules for exponents and operations
- Write, interpret, and operate with numerical expressions in scientific notation
- Solve problems that involve exponents, including scientific notation

2. Describe the effects of a and b on the graph of $y = a(b^x)$.

Goals

- Determine the effects of the growth factor and initial value for an exponential function on a graph of the function
- Write and interpret exponential expressions that represent the dependent variable in an exponential function

3. Compare exponential and linear functions. Include in your comparison information about their patterns of change, y-intercepts, whether the function is decreasing or increasing, and any other information you think is important.

Goal

- Compare exponential and linear functions

Standards

Common Core Content Standards

8.EE.A.1 Know and apply the properties of integer exponents to generate equivalent numerical expressions. *Problems 1, 2, 3, 4, and 5*

8.EE.A.2 Use square root and cube root symbols to represent solutions to equations of the form $x^2 = p$ and $x^3 = p$, where p is a positive rational number. Evaluate square roots of small perfect squares and cube roots of small perfect cubes. Know that $\sqrt{2}$ is irrational. *Problems 1, 2, 3, and 4*

8.EE.A.4 Perform operations with numbers expressed in scientific notation, including problems where both decimal and scientific notation are used. Use scientific notation and choose units of appropriate size for measurements of very large or very small quantities (e.g., use millimeters per year for seafloor spreading). Interpret scientific notation that has been generated by technology. *Problem 4*

8.F.A.3 Interpret the equation $y = mx + b$ as defining a linear function, whose graph is a straight line; give examples of functions that are not linear. *Problem 4*

A-SSE.A.1a Interpret parts of an expression, such as terms, factors, and coefficients. *Problems 1, 2, and 3*

A-SSE.A.2 Use the structure of an expression to identify ways to rewrite it. *Problems 2 and 3*
B. Write expressions in equivalent forms to solve problems.

A-SSE.B.3c Use the properties of exponents to transform expressions for exponential functions. *Problems 1, 2, and 3*

N-RN.A.1 Explain how the definition of the meaning of rational exponents follows from extending the properties of integer exponents to those values, allowing for a notation for radicals in terms of rational exponents. *Problem 3*

N-RN.A.2 Rewrite expressions involving radicals and rational exponents using the properties of exponents. *Problem 3*

F-IF.C.7e Graph exponential and logarithmic functions, showing intercepts and end behavior, and trigonometric functions, showing period, midline, and amplitude. *Problem 5*

F-IF.C.8b Use the properties of exponents to interpret expressions for exponential functions. *Problem 1*

F-LE.B.5 Interpret the parameters in a linear or exponential function in terms of a context. *Problem 2*

Facilitating the Mathematical Practices

Students in *Connected Mathematics* classrooms display evidence of multiple Common Core Standards for Mathematical Practice every day. Here are just a few examples of when you might observe students demonstrating the Standards for Mathematical Practice during this Investigation.

Practice 1: Make sense of problems and persevere in solving them.

Students are engaged every day in solving problems and, over time, learn to persevere in solving them. To be effective, the problems embody critical concepts and skills and have the potential to engage students in making sense of mathematics. Students build understanding by reflecting, connecting, and communicating. These student-centered problem situations engage students in articulating the "knowns" in a problem situation and determining a logical solution pathway. The student-student and student-teacher dialogues help students to not just make sense of the problems, but also to persevere in finding appropriate strategies to solve them. The suggested questions in the Teacher Guides provide the metacognitive scaffolding to help students monitor and refine their problem-solving strategies.

Practice 5: Use appropriate tools strategically.

Students use calculators to solve problems involving scientific notation in Problem 5.5. They use graphing calculators to compare graphs of families of exponential functions in Problem 5.5.

Practice 7: Look for and make use of structure.

In Problem 5.1, students make use of common prime factorizations to establish the equivalence of various exponential expressions for a number.

Students identify and record their personal experiences with the Standards for Mathematical Practice during the *Mathematical Reflections* at the end of the Investigation.

PROBLEM

5.1 Looking for Patterns Among Exponents

Problem Overview

Focus Question What patterns did you observe in the table of powers?

Problem Description

Students use the table of powers to find special relationships among numbers written in exponential form. This provides a chance to review exponential notation and extend their understanding of multiplicative structure of numbers. Students may notice that $4^2 = 2^4$ or $\left(2^2\right)^2 = (2 \times 2)(2 \times 2)$. This is an example of a general property of exponents: $(a^m)^n = a^{mn}$. Examining the product $2 \times 2 \times 2 \times 2$ suggests several equivalent expressions: $4^2 = 2^4 = 2\left(2^3\right)$.

Problem Implementation

Students should fill out the powers table in Question A on their own and then work in groups of two or three for Questions B and C.

Materials

- **Labsheet 5.1A:** Table of Positive Powers
- **Labsheet 5.1B:** Table of Negative Powers
- **Labsheet 5.1C:** Patterns in the Ones Digits (accessibility)
- **Teaching Aid 5.1A:** Completed Table of Positive Powers
- **Teaching Aid 5.1B:** Completed Table of Negative Powers

poster of Teaching Aid 5.1A: Completed Table of Positive Powers (optional)

Vocabulary

There are no new glossary terms introduced in this Problem.

Mathematics Background

- Rules of Exponents

At a Glance and Lesson Plan

- At a Glance: Problem 5.1 Growing, Growing, Growing
- Lesson Plan: Problem 5.1 Growing, Growing, Growing

Launch

Connecting to Prior Knowledge

In previous Problems, students used powers of numbers to express exponential relationships—for example, 2^n, 3^n, 1.5^n, etc. Sometimes they needed to operate with numbers expressed as powers—for example, $2^3 \times 5^2 = \blacksquare$.

Presenting the Challenge

Launch this Problem by writing the values of $y = 2^x$ for whole-number x-values from 1 to 8. Write both the exponential and standard form for 2^x in the y-column.

x	y
1	2^1 or 2
2	2^2 or 4
3	2^3 or 8
4	2^4 or 16
5	2^5 or 32
6	2^6 or 64
7	2^7 or 128
8	2^8 or 256

Have students look for patterns in the table. Collect their discoveries on a large sheet of paper. If students are ready, have them give reasons for why the patterns occur. You will come back to these patterns in the Explore and the Summarize.

Here are some patterns students may notice. (Some of these have already been mentioned.)

- The ones digits are all even.
- The ones digits repeat in cycles of 4.

Note: There are many interesting patterns among the ones digits of b^x. You can encourage students who finish early or are interested to find other patterns. See discussion at the end of the Summarize.

- If you divide the exponent by 4, the remainder tells you where the power is in a cycle.
- When you multiply two powers of 2, the exponent in the product is the sum of the exponents of the factors. For example, $2^3 \times 2^4 = 2^7$, as you can see in the table.

x	y
.	.
3	2^3 or 8
4	2^4 or 16
.	.
7	2^7 or 128

Suggested Questions

- Does 2^4 equal $2(2^2)$? Does 2^6 equal $2(2^3)$? Explain. (This is false, because when multiplying you should add the exponents. For the first example you only get 2^3 instead of 2^4, and for the second example you get 2^4 instead of 2^6.)

Next, introduce Problem 5.1. Make sure students understand how the table is organized. To save class time and help students organize their work, hand out **Labsheet 5.1A: Table of Positive Powers** and **Labsheet 5.1B: Table of Negative Powers**.

Students should fill out the table of powers in Question A on their own and then work in groups of two or three for Questions B and C.

Explore

Providing for Individual Needs

Students should have no trouble filling in the table. Encourage them to take some care in completing the table because they will use it as a reference in the next problem.

Students will find many interesting patterns. Here are some examples:

- Some numbers occur more than once in the powers chart. For example, 64 appears three times: $2^6 = 64$, $4^3 = 64$, $8^2 = 64$. So $\left(2^3\right)^2 = 2^6$.
- When you multiply powers of 2, the exponent of the product is the sum of the exponents of the factors. For example, $2^3 \times 2^4 = 2^{3+4} = 2^7$.
- $2^2 \times 3^2 = 6^2$ so $\left(2^2 \times 3^2\right) = (2 \times 3)^2$.
- The number of zeros in 10^n is n.

Going Further

Labsheet 5.1C: Patterns in the Ones Digits (accessibility) concerns the ones digits of the various powers in the expanded form of b^n. It can be assigned as classroom work or as homework for interested students.

- Look at the column of *y*-values in the table. What pattern do you see in how the ones digits of the standard form change? (Students should notice that the ones digits repeat in cycles of four: 2, 4, 8, and 6. If necessary, extend the table to convince students that this pattern continues.)
- Can you predict the ones digit for 2^{15}? What is it? (Yes; 8. Some students can continue the table or use their calculator to find 2^{15}. Hopefully, at least some students will use the pattern to reason as follows: The ones digits occur in cycles of four. The third complete cycle ends with 2^{12}, and the fourth cycle starts with 2^{13}. The number 2^{15} is the third number in this fourth cycle, so its ones digit is 8.)
- What can you predict as the ones digit for 2^{50}? (4. Students will not be able to find the ones digit of 2^{50} by using their calculators; the result will be displayed in scientific notation, and the ones digit will not be shown. Students will need to use the pattern previously described.)
- What are the *x*-value and values for the six missing digits that will make the following a true number sentence? $2^x =$ ■■■■■■6 ($x = 20$, which gives $2^{20} = 1{,}048{,}576$.)

If students are having trouble with using the patterns of the ones digits, ask the following questions.

- What are the lengths of the cycle of repeating ones digits? (The length of a cycle is 1, 2, or 4, depending on the base. For example, for the powers of 3, the ones digits 3, 9, 7, 1 repeat, so the cycle is of length 4.)
- Which bases have a cycle of length 4? (2, 3, 7, and 8)
- Which bases have a cycle of length 1? (1, 5, 6, and 10)
- Which bases have a cycle of length 2? (4 and 9)
- If you know the exponent, how can you use the pattern of the cycle to determine the ones digit of the power? For example, the ones digits for 2^n repeat in a cycle: 2, 4, 8, 6. How can you use this fact to find the ones digit of 2^{21}? (For powers of 2, the exponents 1, 5, 9, 13, 17, 21, and so on correspond to a ones digit of 2. Students may recognize that each of these numbers is one more than a multiple of 4. In other words, when you divide these numbers by 4 you get a remainder of 1. The exponents 2, 6, 10, 14, 18, and so on correspond to a ones digit of 4. Students may recognize that these numbers are 2 more than a multiple of 4. The exponents 3, 7, 11, 15, 19, and so on correspond to a ones digit of 8. These numbers are 3 more than a multiple of 4. Finally, the exponents 4, 8, 12, 16 and so on correspond to a ones digit of 6.)
- Predict the ones digits for 31^{10}, 12^{10}, 17^{21}, and 29^{10}. (Ones digits for these powers are 1, 4, 7, and 1.)

Students should reason that the ones digit of a power is determined by the ones digits of the base. For example, the ones digits for powers of 12 are the same as the ones digits for powers of 2, 22, and 92.The ones digits for powers of 17 are the same as the ones digits for powers of 7, 57, and 87.

If students struggle with this idea, ask the following.

- Suppose you look at the ones digits for powers of 12. You will find that they follow the same pattern as the ones digits for the powers of 2. Why do you think this is true? What affects the ones digit? (To get successive powers of 12, you multiply by 12, so the ones digit will be the same as the ones digit of 2 times the previous ones digit. For 12^1, the ones digit is 2; for 12^2, the ones digit is 4 because $2 \times 2 = 4$. For 12^3, the ones digit is 8 because $4 \times 2 = 8$; and for 12^4, the ones digit is 6 because $8 \times 2 = 16$. Then the ones digits start to repeat. A similar argument will work for all whole-number bases greater than 10.)
- Find the value of *a* that makes each number sentence true.

  $a^{12} = 531{,}441$

  $a^9 = 387{,}420{,}489$

  $a^6 = 11{,}390{,}625$

  ($a = 3$; $a = 9$; $a = 15$)

Remind students to use their knowledge about the patterns of the ones digit to narrow the choices. For example, for $a^{12} = 531{,}441$, *a* must be 1, 3, 7, or 9. Obviously, 1 is not a choice. And 9^{12} would be close to 10^{12}, which has 13 digits—much too large a number. The number 531,441 has only 6 digits. At this point, students should argue that 7^{12} is too large. They may use an argument similar to the following but with words, not symbols:

$72 \approx 50$, so $7^{12} = 7^2 \cdot 7^2 \cdot 7^2 \cdot 7^2 \cdot 7^2 \cdot 7^2 \approx 50 \cdot 50 \cdot 50 \cdot 50 \cdot 50 \cdot 50$, or $5 \cdot 5 \cdot 5 \cdot 5 \cdot 5 \cdot 5 \cdot 10 \cdot 10 \cdot 10 \cdot 10 \cdot 10 \cdot 10$, which equals $5^6 \cdot 10^6$.

You know that 10^6 has 7 digits, which is too large, so the answer is $3^{12} = 531{,}441$.

x	2^x	Pattern	Ones Digit
1	$2^1 = 2$		2
2	$2^2 = 4$		4
3	$2^3 = 8$		8
4	$2^4 = 16$	**End of first cycle. The exponent 4 is a multiple of 4.**	6
5	$2^5 = 32$	The exponent 5 has a remainder of 1 when divided by 4.	2
6	$2^6 = 64$	The exponent 6 has a remainder of 2 when divided by 4.	4
7	$2^7 = 128$	The exponent 7 has a remainder of 3 when divided by 4.	8
8	$2^8 = 256$	**End of second cycle. The exponent 8 is a multiple of 4.**	6
9	$2^9 =$ ■	The exponent 9 has a remainder of 1 when divided by 4.	2
10	$2^{10} =$ ■	The exponent 10 has a remainder of 2 when divided by 4.	4
11	$2^{11} =$ ■	The exponent 11 has a remainder of 3 when divided by 4.	8
12	$2^{12} =$ ■	**End of third cycle. The exponent 12 is a multiple of 4.**	6
13	$2^{13} =$ ■	The exponent 13 has a remainder of 1 when divided by 4.	2
14	$2^{14} =$ ■	The exponent 14 has a remainder of 2 when divided by 4.	4
15	$2^{15} =$ ■	The exponent 15 has a remainder of 3 when divided by 4.	8
16	$2^{16} =$ ■	**End of fourth cycle. The exponent 16 is a multiple of 4.**	6
⋮	⋮	⋮	⋮
50	$2^{50} =$ ■	The exponent 50 has a remainder of 2 when divided by 4. So the ones digit is 4.	4

Note: There are more questions about patterns among the ones digits in the ACE.

Planning for the Summary

What evidence will you use in the summary to clarify and deepen understanding of the Focus Question?

What will you do if you do not have evidence?

Summarize

Orchestrating the Discussion

Ask for general patterns students found. Post these on a sheet of chart paper or add to the chart that was started in the Launch. Ask students to give reasons for the patterns. Students may not be able to explain some of the patterns until the next Problem, when the properties of exponents are developed. At this stage they may just provide examples to verify that their claims are correct. You can begin to ask them to show why it works, by having them write the numbers in expanded form.

For example,

$$3^6 = 3 \times 3 \times 3 \times 3 \times 3 \times 3$$
$$= (3 \times 3)(3 \times 3)(3 \times 3) = (3^2)^3 = 3^6$$

Or $$3^6 = (3 \times 3 \times 3)(3 \times 3 \times 3) = 3^3 \times 3^3 = 3^6$$

This summary should lead into the next Problem. The next Problem should go fairly quickly, depending on how much justification on conjectures is done in this summary.

Spend some time discussing b^{-1} and b^0. These ideas are revisited in Problem 5.2.

Note: It might be helpful to have a large poster of the completed powers table that students can refer to during this summary and for Problem 5.2.

Reflecting on Student Learning

Use the following questions to assess student understanding at the end of the lesson.

- What evidence do I have that students understand the Focus Question?
  - Where did my students get stuck?
  - What strategies did they use?
  - What breakthroughs did my students have today?
- How will I use this to plan for tomorrow? For the next time I teach this lesson?
- Where will I have the opportunity to reinforce these ideas as I continue through this Unit? The next Unit?

ACE Assignment Guide

- **Applications:** 1
- **Connections:** 67–69
- **Extensions:** 82–90

PROBLEM

5.2 Rules of Exponents

Problem Overview

Focus Question What are several rules for working with exponents and why do they work?

Problem Description

In Problem 5.2, students use patterns among exponents to formulate several important properties for operating with integral exponents:

$$a^m \times a^n = a^{m+n}$$

$$a^m \times b^m = (a \times b)^m$$

$$\frac{a^m}{a^n} = a^{m-n} \text{ for } (a \neq 0)$$

$$(a^m)^n = a^{mn}$$

They also observe that $a^0 = 1$ and that $a^{-1} = \frac{1}{a}$; $(a \neq 0)$. They use their knowledge about exponential notation and repeated factors of a number to explain why the rules work.

Problem Implementation

Students should work in groups of three or four.

Materials

- **Labsheet 5.2:** Rules for Exponents (one per group)

Vocabulary

There are no new glossary terms introduced in this Problem.

Mathematics Background

- Rules of Exponents

At a Glance and Lesson Plan

- At a Glance: Problem 5.2 Growing, Growing, Growing
- Lesson Plan: Problem 5.2 Growing, Growing, Growing

Launch

Connecting to Prior Knowledge

Refer to the completed powers table. Use the introduction to encourage students to begin noticing patterns that will lead to the rules of exponents.

Federico noticed that 16 appears twice in the powers table. It is in the column for 2^x, for $x = 4$. It is also in the column for 4^x, for $x = 2$. He said this means that $2^4 = 4^2$.

- Write 2^4 as a product of 2's. Then show that the product is equal to 4^2. ($2 \times 2 \times 2 \times 2 = (2 \times 2) \times (2 \times 2) = 4 \times 4 = 4^2$)
- Are there other numbers that appear more than once in the table? If so, write equations to show the equal exponential forms of the numbers. (Use different colors to circle these numbers. For example, 4 occurs as 2^2 and as 4^1, so $2^2 = 4^1$. Other examples are 8, 64, 9, 81, 256, and 729, 4,096, and 6,561.)

Presenting the Challenge

Tell students that in this Problem, they will look for a way to generalize these and other patterns for exponents and provide arguments for why they are true.

Depending on how rich the discussion was in the summary of Problem 5.1, the exploration of this problem may go quite quickly. If not, hand out **Labsheet 5.2: Rules for Exponents** to help students organize their work.

Explore

Providing for Individual Needs

Questions A–E are structured so that most students should be able to see the patterns. Students look at specific cases of each pattern first and are then asked to generalize the patterns.

If students have trouble explaining why a general rule works, have them connect the general rule to a specific case. For example, if students cannot explain why $a^m \times a^n = a^{m+n}$, ask them to first explain why $3^2 \times 3^4 = 3^6$. Students should be able to explain that the product of two 3's and four 3's is the product of two plus four, or six, 3's.

$$\underbrace{\underbrace{3 \times 3}_{\substack{\text{two 3s} \\ 3^2}} \times \underbrace{3 \times 3 \times 3 \times 3}_{\substack{\text{four 3s} \\ 3^4}}}_{} \; \underbrace{3 \times 3 \times 3 \times 3 \times 3 \times 3}_{\substack{\text{six 3s} \\ 3^6}}$$

Help them generalize this to $a^m \times a^n$.

$$\underbrace{(a \times a \times \ldots \times a)}_{\substack{m \text{ as} \\ a^m}} \times \underbrace{(a \times a \times \ldots \times a)}_{\substack{n \text{ as} \\ a^n}} = \underbrace{(a \times a \times \ldots \times a)}_{\substack{(m+n) \text{ as} \\ a^{m+n}}}$$

The key to understanding why the rules of exponents work is for students to visualize the structure of a^m as the product of a used m times:

$a \times a \times a \times \ldots \times a$

Planning for the Summary

What evidence will you use in the summary to clarify and deepen understanding of the Focus Question?

What will you do if you do not have evidence?

Summarize

Orchestrating the Discussion

x	1^x	2^x	3^x	4^x	5^x	6^x	7^x	8^x	9^x	10^x
1	1	2	3	4	5	6	7	8	9	10
2	1	4	9	16	25	36	49	64	81	100
3	1	8	27	64	125	216	343	512	729	1,000
4	1	16	81	256	625	1,296	2,401	4,096	6,561	10,000
5	1	32	243	1,024	3,125	7,776	16,807	32,768	59,049	100,000
6	1	64	729	4,096	15,625	46,656	117,649	262,144	531,441	1,000,000
7	1	128	2,187	16,384	78,125	279,936	823,543	2,097,152	4,782,969	10,000,000
8	1	256	6,561	65,536	390,625	1,679,616	5,764,801	16,777,216	43,046,721	100,000,000
Ones Digits of Powers	1	2, 4, 8, 6	3, 9, 7, 1	4, 6	5	6	7, 9, 3, 1	8, 4, 2, 6	9, 1	0

Ask different groups to present their reasoning for each part of the Problem. Use the completed powers table to illustrate the rules. For example, the rule $a^m \times a^n = a^{m+n}$ can be illustrated by looking at any column.

The 3^x column is highlighted in the table. Multiply two numbers in this column, for example, $9 \times 81 = 729$. The exponent for 729 is the sum of the exponents for the factors ($3^2 \times 3^4 = 3^{2+4} = 3^6$).

Ask students to give other examples. To understand the rules, it is essential that students see $3^2 \times 3^4$ as six 3's multiplied together: $3 \times 3 \times 3 \times 3 \times 3 \times 3$.

This would be a good time to ask students to explain the differences among 3^x, $3x$, and $3 + x$.

The rule $a^n \times b^n = (a \times b)^n$ is illustrated by looking at any row. The row corresponding to a^4 is highlighted in the table above. Multiply two numbers in this row, such as $16 \times 256 = 4{,}096$. In exponential form, this is $2^4 \times 4^4 = 8^4$. Students should think of a string of four 2's followed by four 4's. The factors can be rearranged to form a string of four (2×4)'s, or four 8's.

$$(2\times2\times2\times2)\times(4\times4\times4\times4)$$
$$(2\times4)\times(2\times4)\times(2\times4)\times(2\times4)$$
$$= 8\times8\times8\times8 = 8^4$$

Use the table to illustrate the other rules in a similar way.

Suggested Questions

To help students with the division rules, ask the following questions.

- Write $\frac{4^5}{4^6}$ as a single base. (4^{-1} or $\frac{1}{4}$)
- Does this fit the rules for division with exponents? (Yes. The example of $\frac{4^5}{4^6} = 4^{-1}$ illustrates that the general rule $\frac{a^m}{a^n} = a^{m-n}$ holds, even when the result has a negative exponent.)

Instead of using negative exponents, students can break the rule into two cases:

- If $m \geq n$, then $\frac{a^m}{a^n} = a^{m-n}$ for $a \neq 0$.
- If $m < n$, then $\frac{a^m}{a^n} = \frac{1}{a^{n-m}}$ for $a \neq 0$.

Be sure to check on how students are reasoning about a^0.

Check for Understanding

Have students write numeric expressions, such as the following, in simpler exponential form:

$\frac{2^5 \times 2^6}{2^9}$ $\frac{3^4 \times 2^6}{6^9}$

Depending on the goals for your course, you might also ask students to simplify algebraic expressions like these:

$(x^2)^3$ x^6x^4 $\frac{x^4x^3}{x^7}$

- Are the following equations *true* or *false*? Explain.

$2^3 \times 2^2 = 4^5$ $\qquad$ $4^2 + 4^3 = 4^5$

$5^5 \times 2^5 = 10^{25}$ $\qquad$ $18^4 = 3^4 \times 6^4$

($2^3 \times 2^2 \neq 4^5$ because $(2 \times 2 \times 2) \times (2 \times 2) = 2^5$, not 4^5.

$4^2 + 4^3 = 16 + 64$, but $4^5 = 4 \times 4 \times 4 \times 4 \times 4 = 16 \times 64$.

$$\begin{aligned} 5^5 \times 2^5 &= (5 \times 5 \times 5 \times 5 \times 5) \times (2 \times 2 \times 2 \times 2 \times 2) \\ &= (5 \times 2) \times (5 \times 2) \times (5 \times 2) \times (5 \times 2) \times (5 \times 2) \\ &= 10^5 \end{aligned}$$

$18^4 = 3^4 \times 6^4$ is true because it obeys the rule for multiplying different bases with the same exponent.)

Reflecting on Student Learning

Use the following questions to assess student understanding at the end of the lesson.

- What evidence do I have that students understand the Focus Question?
  - Where did my students get stuck?
  - What strategies did they use?
  - What breakthroughs did my students have today?
- How will I use this to plan for tomorrow? For the next time I teach this lesson?
- Where will I have the opportunity to reinforce these ideas as I continue through this Unit? The next Unit?

ACE Assignment Guide

- **Applications:** 2–25
- **Connections:** 70–71
- **Extensions:** 91

PROBLEM

5.3 Extending the Rules of Exponents

Problem Overview

Focus Question How are the rules for integral exponents related to rational exponents? How are the rules for exponents useful in writing equivalent expressions with exponents?

Problem Description

In this Problem, a graph of population growth for a certain amoeba is used to ask questions about the population of the amoeba after specific times, including times that are rational numbers. This motivates a need to explore fractional exponents by looking at graphs of population and asking questions about the population when $x = \frac{1}{2}, \frac{5}{3}$, and so on. The *n*th root is used to interpret and evaluate expressions with rational exponents.

From these explorations students observe that the rules for integral exponents apply to rational exponents. The rules for exponents are used to write and interpret equivalent expressions. In answering Question E, students use their knowledge of fractional exponents and exponential functions to solve a problem about the growth in the value of land in Alaska.

Problem Implementation

Students should work in groups of two to four.

Materials

- Teaching Aid 5.3

Vocabulary

- *n*th root

Mathematics Background

- Rules of Exponents

At a Glance and Lesson Plan

- At a Glance: Problem 5.3 Growing, Growing, Growing
- Lesson Plan: Problem 5.3 Growing, Growing, Growing

Launch

Launch Video

This animation of observing amoeba growth in one week's time motivates considering growth by smaller time intervals. This animation illustrates the story found in the Student Edition.

After showing the animation, continue with Presenting the Challenge. Visit Teacher Place at mathdashboard.com/cmp3 to see the complete video.

Connecting to Prior Knowledge

In Problem 5.2, you worked with whole-number exponents and discovered rules they obey. You saw that increasing x by one unit increases y by a factor equal to the growth factor.

Presenting the Challenge

Show the Launch Video, or have students read the example of the amoeba population in the Student Edition. Display the graph of $y = 4^x$ and pose the questions below.

Suggested Questions

- What do the variables mean in $y = 4^x$? (The growth fact is the base, 4. The number of times the initial value has increased by a factor of 4 is the exponent, x.)
- Does it make sense to write $y = 4^{\frac{1}{2}}$? (Yes; the graph makes sense. There are two amoebas after half a year.)

Students may not recognize that half of a unit time interval represents an exponent of the growth factor.

Students may point out that it makes no sense to write $y = 4^{\frac{1}{3}}$, since there is no integer value for y if x is between 0 and $\frac{1}{2}$. Remind them that in *Thinking With Mathematical Models*, they learned that a continuous graph may include points that are meaningless in the real world. In the context of continuous variation, $y = 4^{\frac{1}{3}}$ might make sense.

- What point does this correspond to on the graph?

Have students examine the graph, on which they should be able to locate the point $(\frac{1}{2}, 2)$.

Use the discussion in the introduction to propose to the class that $\sqrt{4} = 4^{\frac{1}{2}}$.

Use other examples of square roots.

Refer back to the square and cube root development that students did in *Looking for Pythagoras*. They should remember that $\sqrt{2} \times \sqrt{2} = \left(2^{\frac{1}{2}}\right)\left(2^{\frac{1}{2}}\right) = 2^1 = 2$, by connecting the area of a square to its side length. In that case the area of the square was 2, so its side length was defined as $\sqrt{2}$.

Give the class time to explore the two methods for writing equivalent expressions for $16^{\frac{2}{3}}$ (the student strategies in Question A). Then summarize their findings. At this stage, using one or the other method, they should be convinced that the rules of exponents work for rational numbers.

Then let them work on the rest of Problem 5.3.

Explore

Providing for Individual Needs

Look at students' methods of calculating. They should extend the rules for whole-number exponents by using strategies similar to those in part (1) of Question A.

Students most likely saw the equations in Question C during the discussion of Problem 1.2. At that time, students confirmed they were correct by checking the reasoning behind each equation. They now can use the rules to show that the expressions for the number of rubas are equivalent.

Planning for the Summary

What evidence will you use in the summary to clarify and deepen understanding of the Focus Question?

What will you do if you do not have evidence?

Summarize

Orchestrating the Discussion

Finish going over the answers from Questions B–E. Be sure to discuss the various ways that students may have solved individual problems.

Suggested Questions

- Do the equations for rubas in Question C make sense in light of Problem 1.2? Explain. (Some students may argue that there is no square 0 on a chessboard, or you cannot have $\frac{1}{2}$ ruba on a square. But the equation does model the context for $n = 1 - 64$.)
- Do the equations in Question D make sense in the context of Problem 4.1? Explain. (Yes. The decay factor for the area of the ballot was $\frac{1}{2}$, which can also be written as 0.5 or as 2^{-1}.)
- Can you use square roots to produce an expression equivalent to part (1) of Question E? Explain. (Yes; it is the same as $\sqrt{x}$. So $x^{\frac{1}{2}} \cdot x^{\frac{3}{2}} = \sqrt{x} \cdot \sqrt{x} \cdot x = x^2$.)
- Look back at the various situations in *Growing, Growing, Growing.* In which of these situations is it reasonable to look at fractional exponents? Explain why.
- Students may refer to problems where time is the independent variable. It is reasonable to think about $\frac{1}{2}$ year, $\frac{1}{4}$ of a month, and so on.

Reflecting on Student Learning

Use the following questions to assess student understanding at the end of the lesson.

- What evidence do I have that students understand the Focus Question?
  - Where did my students get stuck?
  - What strategies did they use?
  - What breakthroughs did my students have today?
- How will I use this to plan for tomorrow? For the next time I teach this lesson?
- Where will I have the opportunity to reinforce these ideas as I continue through this Unit? The next Unit?

ACE Assignment Guide

- **Applications:** 26–38
- **Connections:** 72–74; 77–78
- **Extensions:** 92–93

PROBLEM
5.4 Operations With Scientific Notation

Problem Overview

Focus Question How does scientific notation help to solve problems?

Problem Description

The context for Problem 5.4 is the consumption of water in the United States. The data involve large numbers that are expressed in scientific notation. This context provides an opportunity to use the rules of exponents and operations for numbers that are expressed in scientific notation.

Problem Implementation

Students should work in groups of two to four.

Materials

There are no additional materials for this Problem.

Vocabulary

There are no new glossary terms introduced in this Problem.

Mathematics Background

- Scientific Notation

At a Glance and Lesson Plan

- At a Glance: Problem 5.4 Growing, Growing, Growing
- Lesson Plan: Problem 5.4 Growing, Growing, Growing

Launch

Launch Video

This video shows the various ways that water is used. You can use this video to engage students in the context of the Problem. Show it after Connecting to Prior Knowledge.

After viewing the video, students should have an understanding of the contexts introduced in the Problem. Continue with Presenting the Challenge. Visit Teacher Place at mathdashboard.com/cmp3 to see the complete video.

Connecting to Prior Knowledge

Students were introduced to scientific notation in Investigation 1.

Suggested Questions

- How has scientific notation been used in this unit? Give an example. (Exponential functions can grow large very quickly. So when you try to find an answer to a problem using a calculator, the calculator may use scientific notation to display the answer. The answer may be an approximation of the answer.)

Presenting the Challenge

Show the Launch Video.

Connect how large numbers, like water usage, are often represented by numbers written in scientific notation. Very often numbers collected from large data sets, such as the number of people in the United States, involve very large numbers. Examples:

Irrigation uses about 1.28×10^{11} gallons of water per day.

Livestock consumes about 2.14×10^{9} gallons of water per day.

Suggested Questions

- Which is greater—the amount of water used by irrigation or the amount used by livestock? (Write both numbers with the same power of 10 and then compare them. For example, irrigation uses 128×10^{9} gallons of water per day, which is greater than 2.14×10^{9} gallons of water per day. You may make this clearer to students by noting that 10^{9} is 1 billion, so 128 billion gallons is about 60 times greater than 2.14 billion gallons of water.)

- How many gallons of water are used in a year for irrigation? (A year has 365 days.) (Multiply 365 by 1.28×10^{11}. You get 4.67×10^{13} gallons of water, which is 46.7 trillion gallons of water.)
- How might you carry out this calculation?

Students might suggest rewriting the number 1.28×10^{11} as 128,000,000,000 and then using the multiplication algorithm. This would be tedious, and even more so if the exponent were larger. It is a correct strategy, but not very efficient.

Another method would be to use the Associative Property (although students may not refer to it by name): $365 \times (1.28 \times 10^{11}) = (365 \times 1.28) \times 10^{11} = 467.2 \times 10^{11}$. Then they would convert that expression into scientific notation: $467.2 \times 10^{11} = 4.672 \times 10^{133}$.

A third method would be to rewrite 365 in scientific notation and then multiply:
$(365) \times (1.28 \times 10^{11}) = (3.65 \times 10^2)(1.28 \times 10^{11})$
$= 3.65 \times 1.28 \times 10^2 \times 10^{11} = 4.672 \times 10^{13}$.

If any of the strategies does not come up in the discussion, you might consider giving one of these as a possible strategy to solve the problem and see if students agree or disagree with it.

In Problem 5.4, you will explore water usage in the United States using scientific notation.

Before students look at Gary's and Judy's strategies in the lesson, ask the Launch question:

- How much water is used per person each day?

The two pieces of information you know are that the population of the United States in 2005 was about 301 million $= 3.01 \times 10^8$, and that about 4.10×10^{11} gallons of water was used each day in the United States.

Have students work in their groups to find a method for determining the answer to this question. Estimating could be helpful both for groups that are stuck and for groups that feel they have a satisfactory method.

Once groups have worked on the problem and have either a good estimate or a satisfactory strategy, they can move on to Question A.

Note: Students will likely have an easier time engaging with the strategies provided once they have had a chance to work through the calculations first. It is important to give them some time to try to solve the Problem first.

Explore

Providing for Individual Needs

Look for various strategies students have for carrying out the calculations. Ask students if Gary's and Judy's strategies are similar to ones they used in their groups. Make note of strategies that are close to the strategies provided or quite different. For example, students using Gary's method may have used 10^8 instead of 10^6. Students might also make connections to previous Units by scaling the ratio down to something more manageable. This is essentially what Gary was doing.

The strategies that students use in Question A will be helpful in Questions B–D. As students are working on Questions B–D, ask the groups if they are using the same strategies as they did for Question A. There may be variation across groups that stick with the same strategy, so make note of the variations for the Summarize. If groups change their strategies or shift between them, also make note of the changes for the Summarize.

Planning for the Summary

What evidence will you use in the summary to clarify and deepen understanding of the Focus Question?

What will you do if you do not have evidence?

Summarize

Orchestrating the Discussion

Go over the questions. The main purpose of the summary is to have students explore a variety of strategies for solving these problems. In some cases they may see why one strategy might work better than another.

If students have different strategies, make sure that they are correct and compare the correct strategies. What are the advantages or disadvantages of each strategy? It may be useful to have groups that stuck with the same strategy throughout share their reasoning for why they liked that strategy, and then follow it up with a different group that chose a different strategy to stick with. At the end, a group that shifted between methods may have insights about why particular problems or situations lent themselves better to one strategy or the other.

If students all choose the same strategy, you might revisit a few of the problems and see if they can make sense of how Gary's and Judy's methods (or a different strategy) might be applied to Questions B–D. This may help students see how those different methods could be used.

There are more data listed than are used in the Problem. Ask the class to design other questions they could answer with these data.

Checking for Understanding

You may want to give students some additional practice exercises at the end of the lesson. You can have students work through a few of them as a final check, or you can display one or two and have students talk with others in their group about how they would go about solving the problem.

- $(3.0 \times 10^6)(2.5 \times 10^{14})$
- $(3.5 \times 10^4)(6.0 \times 10^5)$
- $(8.4 \times 10^{12})(3.2 \times 10^2)$
- $(9.3 \times 10^{13}) \div (3.1 \times 10^9)$
- $(7.5 \times 10^8) \div (3.0 \times 10^7)$
- $(4.2 \times 10^6) \div (8.4 \times 10^4)$
- $(8.32 \times 10^{73}) \div (8.32 \times 10^{74})$

Answers:

- 7.5×10^{20}
- 2.1×10^{10}
- 2.69×10^{15}
- 3.0×10^4
- $2.5 \times 10^1 = 25$
- $5.0 \times 10^1 = 5$
- $10^{-1} = 0.1$

Reflecting on Student Learning

Use the following questions to assess student understanding at the end of the lesson.

- What evidence do I have that students understand the Focus Question?
  - Where did my students get stuck?
  - What strategies did they use?
  - What breakthroughs did my students have today?
- How will I use this to plan for tomorrow? For the next time I teach this lesson?
- Where will I have the opportunity to reinforce these ideas as I continue through this Unit? The next Unit?

ACE Assignment Guide

- **Applications:** 39–62
- **Connections:** 75–76

PROBLEM
5.5 Revisiting Exponential Functions

Problem Overview

Focus Question What are the effects of *a* and *b* on the graph of $y = a(b^x)$, $b \neq 0$?

Problem Description

This calculator-based activity will help students to generalize their understanding of how the parameters *a* and *b* in the exponential equation $y = a(b^x)$ affect the shape of the corresponding graphs. The calculator activities are similar to exponential situations involving change over time because the exponents can be nonwhole numbers. Students can trace the graphs for values of *x*, which are rational numbers.

Problem Implementation

Students should work in groups of three or four. Students who are unfamiliar with powers of 2 may benefit from working with **Labsheet 5ACE: Exercise** 15 (accessibility).

Materials

- **Labsheet 5.5A** (accessibility)
- **Labsheet 5.5B** (accessibility)
- **Labsheet 5ACE:** Exercise 15 (accessibility)
- **Self-Assessment**
- **Notebook Checklist**
- **Unit Test**

Vocabulary

There are no new glossary terms introduced in this Problem.

Mathematics Background

- Exponential Functions
- Using Graphing Calculators

At a Glance and Lesson Plan

- At a Glance: Problem 5.5 Growing, Growing, Growing
- Lesson Plan: Problem 5.5 Growing, Growing, Growing

Launch

Launch Video

This animation of the Space Junk game engages students by helping them connect their prior knowledge of the graphs of linear equations in slope-intercept form to graphing exponential equations. You can use this animation to ask students to consider how the graphs of exponential equations change in a similar way to linear equations. Visit Teacher Place at mathdashboard.com/cmp3 to see the complete video.

Connecting to Prior Knowledge

Students have sketched graphs throughout this Unit, so they should have experience with the general shape of exponential equations. Problem 5.5 builds on students' previous experience and has them use calculators to find more precise graphs. Review the effects of m and b on $y = mx + b$.

Remind students that the situations they have explored in this Unit can be modeled with equations of the form $y = a(b^x)$, where a is the initial, or starting, value and b is the growth or decay factor.

Presenting the Challenge

In this Problem students will explore the effects of a and b on the graphs of exponential functions.

Remind students that in all the examples in this unit, a has been greater than 0. It might help to recall equations for some exponential growth and exponential decay situations the class has studied.

Suggested Questions

Ask students to identify the value of a and of b in each equation. Examples:

- $y = 2^n$ ($a = 1$, $b = 2$)
- $z = 4^t$ ($a = 1$, $b = 4$)
- $Y = 25(3^d)$ ($a = 25$, $b = 3$)
- $w = 5(3^n)$ ($a = 5$, $b = 3$)

Check to see that students understand the meaning of the notation $0 \leq x \leq 5$.

Explore

Providing for Individual Needs

As you move about the class, check to see that students are discussing the effects of a and b on the graphs. In part (1) of Question A, groups should discuss the effect of increasing the value of b in the equation $y = b^x$ for values greater than 1. In part (2) of Question A, they should discuss the effect of increasing the value of b for values between 0 and 1. In Question B, the value of b in each part is fixed, allowing students to focus on the effects of varying the value of a.

The last parts of Questions A and B make excellent writing activities.

- Describe how you could predict the general shape of the graph of $y = b^x$ for a specific value of b.
- Describe how the value of a affects the graph of an equation of the form $y = a(b^x)$.

You might also ask groups to make posters illustrating their answers to these parts.

To save time in class, you may hand out **Labsheet 5.5A** (accessibility) and **Labsheet 5.B** (accessibility) to help students organize their work efficiently.

Planning for the Summary

What evidence will you use in the summary to clarify and deepen understanding of the Focus Question?

What will you do if you do not have evidence?

Summarize

Orchestrating the Discussion

If you have a calculator display, you might ask a group of students to enter the equations and window settings for part (1) of Question A. Alternatively, you could ask several groups to sketch their graphs on transparent grids or large sheets of paper. With the graphs displayed, discuss how the graphs change when $a = 1$ and b is an increasing value greater than 1.

Suggested Questions

- What similarities do you notice among the graphs? What differences do you notice? (The graphs are all increasing curves. The greater b is, the faster the y-values increase.)

Similarly, display the graphs for part (2) of Question A, and discuss how they change when $a = 1$ and b increases from 0 to 1.

- What similarities do you notice among the graphs? What differences do you notice? (The graphs are all decreasing curves. The greater b is, the more gradually the y-values decrease.)
- How could you predict the shape of the graph for the equation $y = b^x$ when given a specific value of b? (If $0 < b < 1$, the graph is a decreasing curve. If $b > 1$, the graph is an increasing curve.)
- What would the graph look like if b were equal to 1? (It would be a horizontal line.)

Follow a similar process to review Question B, displaying and discussing the graphs for each part.

- How does the value of a affect the graph of $y = a(b^x)$? (The value of a is the y-intercept. The greater the value of a, the higher the y-intercept of the graph is. And, as the value of a increases, there is a sharper increase (for a fixed value of b that is greater than 1) or decrease (for a fixed value of b that is less than 1) in the graph.

You might want to use an equation from an earlier Investigation to help students understand the role of a in a real-world context. In Problem 3.1, for example, the population of rabbits is given by the equation $P = 100(1.8)^t$. The value of a, which is 100, represents the initial population.

- How do the values of m and b affect the graph of $y = mx + b$? How do these effects compare to those for graphs of exponential equations? (They are similar. For a linear equation, if m is negative, the line is decreasing, and if m is positive, the line is increasing. For an exponential equation, if a is negative the curve slopes downward—it is exponential decay. If a is positive the curve slopes upward—it is exponential growth. The y-intercept in both situations is represented by b.)

Check for Understanding

List a few exponential equations. Without sketching a graph or using a calculator, have students describe the shape of each graph, giving as much information as they can about the *y*-intercept and patterns of change.

- $y = 4^x$
- $y = 0.25^x$
- $y = 5(3^x)$
- $y = 6x + 10$
- $y = -6x + 10$
- $y = 6x - 10$

Answers:

- $y = 4^x$ (Exponential growth, growth factor 4, *y*-intercept 1)
- $y = 0.25^x$ (Exponential decay, decay factor 0.25, *y*-intercept 1)
- $y = 5(3^x)$ (Exponential growth, growth factor 3, *y*-intercept 5)
- $y = 6x + 10$ (Linear equation, slope 6, *y*-intercept 10)
- $y = -6x + 10$ (Linear equation, slope -6, *y*-intercept 10)
- $y = 6x - 10$ (Linear equation, slope 6, *y*-intercept -10)

Reflecting on Student Learning

Use the following questions to assess student understanding at the end of the lesson.

- What evidence do I have that students understand the Focus Question?
  - Where did my students get stuck?
  - What strategies did they use?
  - What breakthroughs did my students have today?
- How will I use this to plan for tomorrow? For the next time I teach this lesson?
- Where will I have the opportunity to reinforce these ideas as I continue through this Unit? The next Unit?

ACE Assignment Guide

- **Applications:** 63–66
- **Connections:** 77–78

For students who are struggling with evaluating expressions that contain exponents, you may wish to provide hints. Optional **Labsheet 5ACE: Exercise 15** (accessibility) provides a sample of how you might support an ACE Exercise with additional hints.

Mathematical Reflections

Possible Answers to Mathematical Reflections

1. **a.** The rules include the following.
To multiply powers with the same base, keep the same base and add the exponents:

$$a^m \times a^n \ \underbrace{(a \times a \times \cdots \times a)}_{m \text{ times}} \times \underbrace{(a \times a \times \cdots \times a)}_{n \text{ times}} = \underbrace{(a \times a \times \cdots \times a)}_{m+n \text{ times}} = a^{m+n}$$

To multiply powers with the same exponent, multiply the bases and keep the exponent:

$$a^m \times b^m \ \underbrace{(a \times a \times \cdots \times a)}_{m \text{ times}} \times \underbrace{(b \times b \times \cdots \times b)}_{m \text{ times}}$$

$$= \underbrace{(ab \times ab \times \cdots \times ab)}_{m \text{ times}} = (ab)^m$$

To raise a power to a power, keep the base and multiply the exponents:

$$(a^m)^n \ \underbrace{(a^m \times a^m \times \cdots \times a^m)}_{n \text{ times}}$$

$$= \underbrace{(aa \cdots a) \times (aa \times \cdots \times a) \times \cdots \times (aa \cdots a)}_{n \text{ times}} = (ab)^{mn}$$

To divide powers of the same base, keep the base and use the numerator exponent minus the denominator exponent as the exponent:

$$\frac{a^m}{a^n} = a^{m-n} \text{ for } a \neq 0$$

If the exponent in the denominator is greater than the exponent in the numerator, this division rule results in a negative exponent.

There is a different form of the rule that always gives a positive exponent: If the exponent of the numerator is greater than the exponent of the denominator, then use the rule above. If the exponent of the denominator is greater than the exponent of the numerator, then the result is a fraction with a numerator of 1 and a base equal to the base raised to the denominator exponent minus the numerator exponent:

$$\frac{a^m}{a^n} = a^{m-n} \text{ if } m \geq n$$

$$\frac{1}{a^{n-m}} \text{ if } m < n$$

Note: Students should know why these rules work.

b. Scientific notation is a method of writing or displaying numbers in terms of a decimal number between 1 and 10, multiplied by a power of 10. Scientific notation is needed any time you need to express a number that is very big or very small. Suppose you wanted to figure out how many drops of water were in a river 12 km long, 270 m wide, and 38 m deep (assuming one drop is one ml). It's much more compact and meaningful to write the answer as about 1.23×10^{14} than 123,120,000,000,000.

2. When b is a positive number greater than 1, the graph curves upward slowly at first and then very rapidly. When b is a positive number less than 1, the graph curves downward rapidly at first and then more slowly until it is almost horizontal and very close to the x-axis. When $b = 1$, the graph is a horizontal line. When a is greater than 1, the y-intercept is greater than 1. When a is less than 1, the y-intercept is less than 1, and when a is 1, then the intercept is 1.

3. Linear functions have a constant rate of change (their slope). For exponential functions they have a constant multiplier. For example in $y = 3x$, every time x increases by 1, y increases additively by 3. In $y = 3x$, every time x increases by 1, y increases multiplicatively by three. Both functions have a single y-intercept. For simple equations of the form $y = mx$ and $y = b^x$, the y-intercept is 0 for the linear equation and 1 for the exponential. For linear equations, increasing or decreasing is dependent on the slope. (Positive slope means increasing; negative slope means decreasing.) For exponential equations, in $y = a \times b^x$ the function is increasing when $a < 0$ and $0 < b < 1$, or $a > 0$ and $b > 1$; and decreasing when $a > 0$ and $0 > b > 1$, or when $a < 0$ and $b > 1$. Linear functions are used for converting temperature (°F to °C) or representing supply and demand. Exponential functions are helpful for graphing growth, decay, or compound interest.

Possible Answers to Mathematical Practices Reflections

Students may have demonstrated all of the eight Common Core Standards for Mathematical Practice during this Investigation. During the class discussion, have students provide additional Practices that the Problem cited involved and identify the use of other Mathematical Practices in the Investigation.

One student observation is provided in the Student Edition. Here is another sample student response.

In the table of exponents for Problem 5.1, the number 64 occurred several times, as 8^2, 4^4, and 2^6. To show that they were equivalent, we found the prime factorization of each. They have the same prime factorization, $2 \times 2 \times 2 \times 2 \times 2 \times 2$. Marie grouped the 2's in different ways to show how this factorization can be written as 8^2, 4^4, and 2^6.

MP7: Look for and make use of structure.

Investigation 5

Patterns with Exponents

As you explored exponential functions in previous Investigations, you made tables of exponential growth. The table shows some values for $y = 2^n$. The y-values are given in both exponential and standard form.

$y = 2^n$

x	y
1	2^1 or 2
2	2^2 or 4
3	2^3 or 8
4	2^4 or 16
5	2^5 or 32
6	2^6 or 64
7	2^7 or 128
8	2^8 or 256

The table shows interesting patterns. For example, Roxanne noticed that in each of the products below, the sum of the exponents of all the factors is the exponent for the product.

$$2^1 \times 2^2 = 2^3$$

$$2^2 \times 2^3 = 2^5$$

- Is Roxanne correct? Explain why or why not.
- Does Roxanne's pattern hold for any number b? For instance, what is the value of the expression $b^2 \times b^3$?

Common Core State Standards

8.EE.A.1 Know and apply the properties of integer exponents to generate equivalent numerical expressions.

8.EE.A.2. Use square root and cube root symbols to represent equations of the form $x^2 = p$ and $x^3 = p$. . . .

8.EE.A.4 Perform operations with numbers expressed in scientific notation, including problems where both decimal and scientific notation are used.

Also 8.F.A.3, A-SSE.A.1a, A-SSE.A.2, A-SSE.B.3c, N-RN.A.1, N-RN.A.2, F-IF.C.7e, F-IF.C.8b, F-LE.B.5

Notes

5.1 Looking for Patterns Among Exponents

The values of a^x for a given number a are called *powers of a*. You just looked at situations involving powers of 2. In Problem 5.1, you will explore patterns with powers of 2 and other numbers.

Problem 5.1

A Copy and complete this table.

x	1^x	2^x	3^x	4^x	5^x	6^x	7^x	8^x	9^x	10^x
1	1	2	■	■	■	■	■	■	■	■
2	1	4	■	■	■	■	■	■	■	■
3	1	8	■	■	■	■	■	■	■	■
4	1	16	■	■	■	■	■	■	■	■
5	1	32	■	■	■	■	■	■	■	■
6	1	64	■	■	■	■	■	■	■	■
7	1	128	■	■	■	■	■	■	■	■
8	1	256	■	■	■	■	■	■	■	■

B 1. Describe any patterns that you see in the rows and columns.

2. Give examples for your patterns.

3. Explain why your patterns are correct.

C Delmar noticed that if you extend the pattern upwards in the table for negative values of x, you get the values shown at the right.

1. Copy the table and extend it to include columns for 3^x through 10^x.

2. Delmar claims that $a^0 = 1$ and that $a^{-1} = \frac{1}{a}$ for any positive number a. Do you agree? Explain.

-2	1	$\frac{1}{4}$
-1	$\frac{1}{1} = 1$	$\frac{1}{2}$
0	1	1
x	1^x	2^x

ACE Homework starts on page 88.

STUDENT PAGE

Notes

5.2 Rules of Exponents

In Problem 5.1, you explored patterns among the values of a^x for different values of a. For example, Federico noticed that 64 appears three times in the powers table. It is in the column for 2^x, 4^x, and 8^x. He said this means that $2^6 = 4^3 = 8^2$.

- Explain why Federico's conclusion is true.
- Are there other numbers that appear more than once in the table?
- What other patterns do you notice in the table?

In Problem 5.2, you will look at patterns that lead to some important properties of exponents.

Problem 5.2

Use your table from Problem 5.1 to help you answer these questions.

A **1.** Write each of the following in expanded form. Then, write the answer in exponential form with a single base and power.

a. $2^3 \times 2^2$ **b.** $3^4 \times 3^3$ **c.** $6^5 \times 6^5$

2. What do you notice when you multiply two powers with the same base?

3. Finish the following equation to express what you noticed. Explain why it is true.

$$a^m \times a^n = \blacksquare$$

B **1.** Rewrite each multiplication sentence as an equivalent division sentence.

a. $3^3 \times 3^2 = 3^5$ **b.** $4^6 \times 4^5 = 4^{11}$ **c.** $5^8 \times 5^4 = 5^{12}$

2. What do you notice when you divide two powers with the same base? Why do you think this happens?

3. Finish the following equation to express what you noticed. Explain your reasoning. Assume $a \neq 0$.

$$\frac{a^m}{a^n} = \blacksquare$$

Notes

Problem 5.2 continued

C 1. Write each of the following in expanded form. Then write the result in exponential form with a single base and power.

a. $2^3 \times 5^3$ b. $5^2 \times 6^2$ c. $10^4 \times 2^4$

2. What do you notice when you multiply two powers with the same exponent but different bases?

3. Finish the following equation to express what you noticed. Explain.

$$a^m \times b^m = \blacksquare$$

D 1. Mary says she can use the fact below to write a power raised to a power with a single base and power.

> I know that $(2^3)^2 = (2^3) \bullet (2^3)$.

Use that fact to write each of the following with a single base and power.

a. $(3^2)^2$ b. $(5^3)^3$ c. $(2^2)^4$

2. What do you notice when you raise a power to a power?

3. Finish the following equation to express what you know. Explain.

$$(a^m)^n = \blacksquare$$

E As he worked on Problem 5.1, Question C, Delmar made the following claim.

> $a^0 = 1$ and $a^{-1} = \frac{1}{a}$.

Use what you have learned in Questions A–D to show why each of the following is true for any nonzero value of a:

1. $a^0 = 1$
2. $a^{-1} = \frac{1}{a}$
3. Finish the following equation.

$$a^{-m} = \blacksquare$$

ACE Homework starts on page 88.

STUDENT PAGE

Notes

5.3 Extending the Rules of Exponents

In Problem 5.1 and Problem 5.2 you investigated rules for integral exponents and found the following to be true, where $x \neq 0$, $y \neq 0$, and m and n are integers.

$$x^m x^n = x^{m+n}$$

$$(x^m)^n = x^{mn}$$

$$(xy)^m = x^m y^m$$

$$\frac{x^m}{x^n} = x^{m-n}$$

$$x^{-1} = \frac{1}{x}$$

$$x^0 = 1$$

- Do these rules work for rational exponents?

Suppose a certain amoeba population quadruples every week. If you start with 1 amoeba, then the population y grows according to the relationship $y = 4^x$. The graph of this relationship appears below.

Amoeba Population Growth

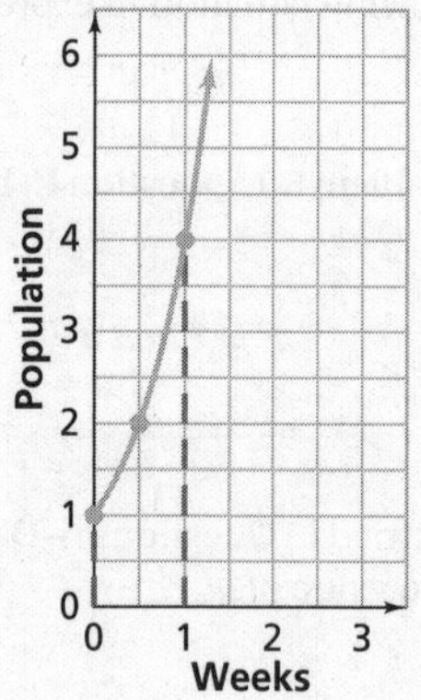

- Does it make sense to write $y = 4^{\frac{1}{2}}$?
- If so, what point does this correspond to on the graph?

Notes

The point $\left(\frac{1}{2}, 2\right)$ is the point on the graph that corresponds to an x-value of $\frac{1}{2}$. This means that $4^{\frac{1}{2}} = 2$. Chaska then reasons as follows.

Since you already know that $\sqrt{4} = 2$, it must be true that $\sqrt{4} = 4^{\frac{1}{2}}$.

- Do the rules for adding exponents apply to the exponent $\frac{1}{2}$?
  For instance, is it true that $4^{\frac{1}{2}} \cdot 4^{\frac{1}{2}} = 4^{\frac{1}{2}+\frac{1}{2}} = 4$?

Chaska then thinks about other roots.

I know that $\sqrt[3]{8} = 2$. So I conclude that the rule for the exponent $\frac{1}{2}$ can be extended to the exponent $\frac{1}{3}$.

- How can you write $\sqrt[3]{8} = 2$ using exponents?
- How can Chaska use the rules for exponents to confirm that $\sqrt[3]{8} \cdot \sqrt[3]{8} \cdot \sqrt[3]{8} = 8$?
- In general, the ***n*th root** of a number b is denoted by $\sqrt[n]{b}$ or $b^{\frac{1}{n}}$, where n is an integer greater than 1.
- Think about what Chaska found about the exponents $\frac{1}{2}$ and $\frac{1}{3}$. Is it true that $\sqrt[n]{x} = x^{\frac{1}{n}}$?

? • Do the other rules for exponents apply to exponents that are fractions?

In Problem 5.3, you will explore whether the rules for integral exponents apply for rational exponents.

STUDENT PAGE

Notes

Problem 5.3

A What does $16^{\frac{3}{2}}$ mean?

1. Mari, Latrell, and Jakayla came up with three different ways to think about $16^{\frac{3}{2}}$. Do any of these make sense? Explain.

Mari's Method	Latrell's Method	Jakayla's Method
$16^{\frac{3}{2}} = \left(16^{\frac{1}{2}}\right)^3$ $= (4)^3$ $= 64$	$16^{\frac{3}{2}} = (16^3)^{\frac{1}{2}}$ $= (4096)^{\frac{1}{2}}$ or $\sqrt{4096}$ $= 64$	$16^{\frac{3}{2}} = 16^{1+\frac{1}{2}}$ $= 16^1\left(16^{\frac{1}{2}}\right)$ or $16\sqrt{16}$ $= 16(4)$ $= 64$

2. Find the value of each of the following. Show your method.

   a. $8^{\frac{5}{3}}$

   b. $125^{\frac{4}{3}}$

B 1. Use what you learned about roots to compute each of the following.

   a. $4^{\frac{3}{2}} \cdot 4^{\frac{1}{2}}$

   b. $4^{\frac{1}{3}} \cdot 2^{\frac{1}{3}}$

   c. $\left(2^{\frac{5}{3}}\right)^3$

   d. $\dfrac{25^{\frac{3}{2}}}{25^{\frac{1}{2}}}$

2. Use the rules for integral exponents to compute the answer in a different way for each of the expressions in part (1). Do you get the same numbers? Explain why or why not.

C Suppose that in Problem 1.2, R is the number of rubas on the nth square of a chessboard. Mari and Latrell came up with the following two equations for R.

Mari	Latrell
$R = \frac{1}{2}(2^n)$	$R = 2^{n-1}$

Which equation is correct? Explain.

Notes

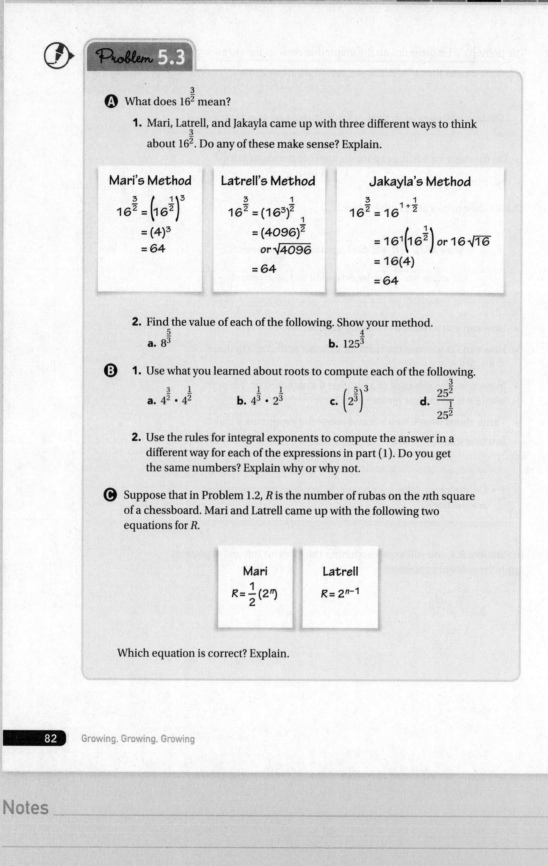

Problem 5.3 continued

D Suppose that in Problem 1.4, the number of cuts is n and the area of each piece is A. Jakayla, Mari, and Latrell came up with three ways to express the exponential relationship.

Mari	Latrell	Jakayla
$A = \frac{64}{2^n}$	$A = 64(0.5^n)$	$A = 64(2^{-n})$

Are these all correct? Explain.

E Use the rules of exponents to write an equivalent expression for each of the following.

1. $x^{\frac{1}{2}} \cdot x^{\frac{3}{2}}$ **2.** $x^{\frac{2}{3}} \div x^{\frac{7}{6}}$ **3.** $\left(2x^{\frac{1}{2}}\right)^2$ **4.** $\left(16x^{\frac{4}{3}}\right)^{\frac{1}{2}}$

ACE Homework starts on page 88.

Did You Know?

Having only a single cell, amoebas are among the simplest organisms. Even so, amoebas and humans have common features. Both have DNA and cellular structure. The life cycle of an amoeba is typically a few days.

Most amoebas have no fixed shape and are so small that they cannot be seen with the naked eye. Yet there is one species, *Gromia sphaerica*, that is the size of a grape! The plural of amoeba is *amoebas* or *amoebae*.

Notes

5.4 Operations with Scientific Notation

Gray water is a term for wastewater that is reused without any treatment. For example, some people use the water that drains from their shower, bathtub, washing machine, or dishwasher to water their gardens. Reusing water in this way helps conserve an important resource.

The United States uses a huge amount of water. To get a sense of the amounts used for various purposes, consider the following figures from a recent year.

- A total of approximately 4.10×10^{11} gallons of water is used each day in the United States.
- Water for cooling electric power plants demands 2.01×10^{11} gallons per day.
- Irrigation uses about 1.28×10^{11} gallons of water per day.
- Livestock consumes about 2.14×10^{9} gallons of water per day.

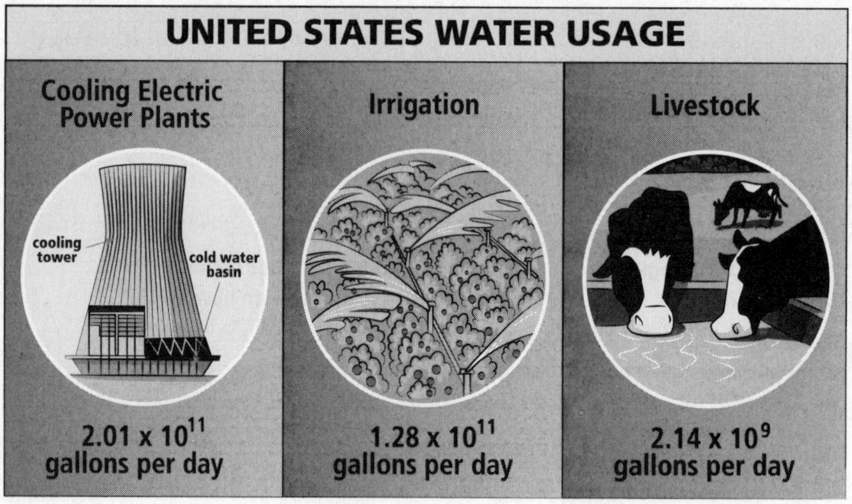

Notes

Gary and Judy are studying water use. They need to figure out how much water is used per person each day. The U.S. population in the same year was approximately 301,000,000. Assume that everyone uses the same amount of water each day.

- How much water is used per person each day?

Problem 5.4

A Gary and Judy are figuring out how much water each person uses per day. They used the following expression to find their answer: $(4.10 \times 10^{11}) \div (301{,}000{,}000)$. Each of them used a different method for carrying out the calculations. Consider their two methods for solving the problem.

Gary's Method

I thought of both numbers in millions. 10^6 is one million.
So $4.10 \times 10^{11} = 410{,}000 \times 10^6$, and $301{,}000{,}000 = 301 \times 10^6$.
Dividing gives me $410{,}000 \div 301 \approx 1{,}360$.
My result is 1,360 gallons per person per day.

Judy's Method

I converted 301,000,000 to 3.01×10^8. Then I rewrote the problem as

$$\frac{4.10 \times 10^{11}}{3.01 \times 10^8} = \frac{4.10}{3.01} \times \frac{10^{11}}{10^8} \approx 1.36 \times 10^3.$$

I know that $10^{11} \div 10^8$ equals 10^3 because $10^8 \cdot 10^3 = 10^{11}$.
So the answer is about 1.36×10^3 gallons per day for each person.

1. Which of these methods makes more sense to you? What other method could you use?
2. Do you use more than 1,000 gallons of water each day at home and at school? What might explain such a high average water use?
3. What other questions could you answer with the data given?

continued on the next page >

Notes

Problem 5.4 continued

B In Illinois, 11,600,000 people got their water from public supplies provided by cities and towns. Those people used 1.05×10^9 gallons of water each day.

1. How many gallons of water per day did each person use?
2. Compare the amount of water from public supplies to the amount used per person in all of the United States. What could account for the difference?
3. Use your answer to Question B, part (1), to find the number of gallons each person in Illinois used *per second*. (There are 86,400 seconds in a day.) Write your answer in scientific notation.

C What percent of the water used in the United States each day went to each of the following? (Total use was 4.10×10^{11} gallons of water per day.)

1. irrigation (1.28×10^{11} gallons of water per day)
2. livestock (2.14×10^9 gallons of water per day)

D Use what you know about the rules of exponents and scientific notation to solve the following. Express your answer in scientific notation.

1. $(4.0 \times 10^2) \times (3.5 \times 10^3)$
2. $(2.0 \times 10^6) \div (2.5 \times 10^2)$

ACE Homework starts on page 88.

5.5 Revisiting Exponential Functions

You have studied situations that show patterns of exponential growth or exponential decay. All of these situations represent exponential functions that are modeled with equations of the form $y = a(b^x)$. In this equation, a is the starting value and b is the growth or decay factor.

- What are the effects of *a* and *b* on the graph of the equation?

Notes

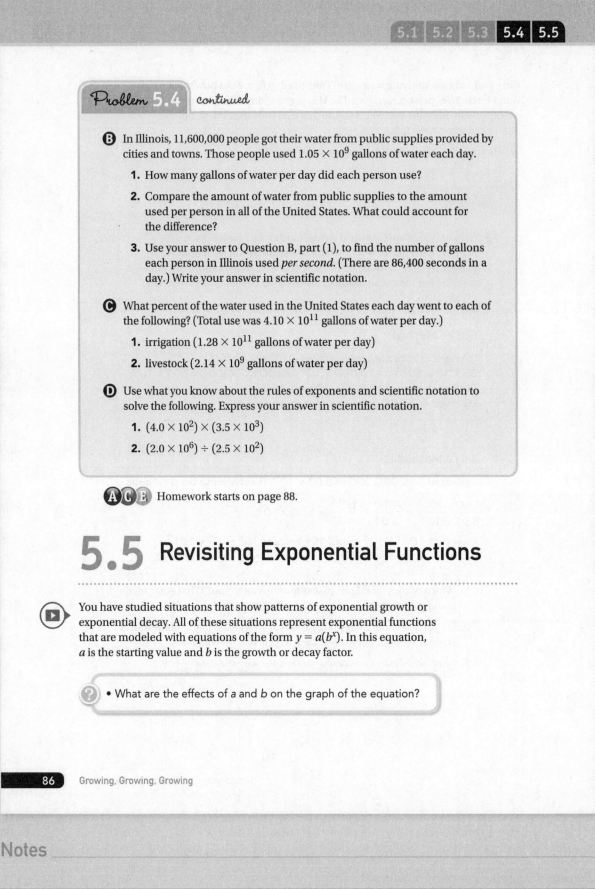

Problem 5.5

You can use your graphing calculator to explore how the values of a and b affect the graph of $y = a(b^x)$.

A 1. Let $a = 1$. Make a prediction about how the value of b affects the graph.

2. Graph the four equations below in the same window. Use window settings that show x-values from 0 to 5 and y-values from 0 to 20.

$y = 1.25^x$ $y = 1.5^x$ $y = 1.75^x$ $y = 2^x$

What are the similarities in the graphs? What are the differences? Record your observations.

3. Next, graph the three equations below in the same window. Use window settings that show $0 \le x \le 5$ and $0 \le y \le 1$.

$y = 0.25^x$ $y = 0.5^x$ $y = 0.75^x$

Record your observations.

4. Describe how you could predict the general shape of the graph of $y = b^x$ for a specific value of b.

B Next, you will explore how the value of a affects the graph of $y = a(b^x)$. You may need to adjust the window settings as you work.

1. Make a prediction about how the value of a affects the graph.

2. Graph these equations in the same window. Record your observations.

$y = 2(1.5)^x$ $y = 3(1.5^x)$ $y = 4(1.5^x)$

3. Graph these equations in the same window. Record your observations.

$y = 2(0.5^x)$ $y = 3(0.5^x)$ $y = 4(0.5)^x$

4. Describe how the value of a affects the graph of an equation of the form $y = a(b^x)$.

C You have explored the effects of a and b in the exponential equation $y = a(b^x)$. Compare those effects to the effects of m and b in the linear equation $y = mx + b$.

ACE Homework starts on page 88.

STUDENT PAGE

Notes

ACE Applications | Connections | Extensions

Applications

1. Several students were working on Question A of Problem 5.1. They wondered what would happen if they extended their table. Do you agree or disagree with each conjecture below? Explain.

Heidi's conjecture:
The 1^x column will contain only ones.

Evan's conjecture:
The bottom right corner of any table will always have the largest value.

Roger's conjecture:
So far, every number in the 2 column is even. Eventually an odd number will show up if I extend the table far enough.

Jean's conjecture:
Any odd power (an odd row) will have all odd numbers in it.

Chaska's conjecture:
To get from one row to the next in the tens column multiply the number you have by 10. For example $10^5 = 100{,}000$, so $10^6 = 100{,}000 \times 10 = 1{,}000{,}000$.

Tim's conjecture:
The row where $x = 2$ will always have square numbers in it.

2. **Multiple Choice** Which expression is equivalent to $2^9 \times 2^{10}$?

A. 2^{90} **B.** 2^{19} **C.** 4^{19} **D.** 2^{18}

Use the properties of exponents to write each expression as a single power. Check your answers.

3. $5^6 \times 8^6$
4. $(7^5)^3$
5. $\frac{8^{15}}{8^{10}}$

For Exercises 6–11, tell whether the statement is *true* or *false*. Explain.

6. $6^3 \times 6^5 = 6^8$
7. $2^3 \times 3^2 = 6^5$
8. $3^8 = 9^4$
9. $4^3 + 5^3 = 9^3$
10. $2^3 + 2^5 = 2^3(1 + 2^2)$
11. $\frac{5^{12}}{5^4} = 5^3$

Notes

12. **Multiple Choice** Which number is the ones digit of $2^{10} \times 3^{10}$?

F. 2 **G.** 4 **H.** 6 **J.** 8

For Exercises 13 and 14, find the ones digit of the product.

13. $4^{15} \times 3^{15}$

14. $7^{15} \times 4^{20}$

15. Manuela came to the following conclusion about power of 2.

> *It must be true that $2^{10} = 2^4 \cdot 2^6$, because I can group*
> $2 \cdot 2 \cdot 2 \cdot 2 \cdot 2 \cdot 2 \cdot 2 \cdot 2 \cdot 2 \cdot 2$ *as*
> $(2 \cdot 2 \cdot 2 \cdot 2) \cdot (2 \cdot 2 \cdot 2 \cdot 2 \cdot 2 \cdot 2)$

a. Verify that Manuela is correct by evaluating both sides of the equation $2^{10} = 2^4 \cdot 2^6$.

b. Use Manuela's idea of grouping factors to write three other expressions that are equivalent to 2^{10}. Evaluate each expression you find to verify that it is equivalent to 2^{10}.

c. The standard form for 2^7 is 128, and the standard form for 2^5 is 32. Use these facts to evaluate 2^{12}. Explain your work.

d. Test Manuela's idea to see if it works for exponential expressions with other bases, such as 3^8 or $(1.5)^{11}$. Test several cases. Give an argument supporting your conclusion.

For Exercises 16–21, tell whether each expression is equivalent to 1.25^{10}. Explain your reasoning.

16. $(1.25)^5 \cdot (1.25)^5$

17. $(1.25)^3 \times (1.25)^7$

18. $(1.25) \times 10$

19. $(1.25) + 10$

20. $(1.25^5)^2$

21. $(1.25)^5 \cdot (1.25)^2$

Notes

For Exercises 22–25, tell whether each expression is equivalent to $(1.5)^7$. Explain your reasoning.

22. $1.5^5 \times 1.5^2$

23. $1.5^3 \times 1.5^4$

24. 1.5×7

25. $(1.5) + 7$

26. Some students are trying to solve problems with rational exponents. Which of these solutions is correct?

Stu's Solution

$$81^{\frac{3}{4}} = \left(81^{\frac{1}{4}}\right)^3$$
$$= (3^3)$$
$$= 27$$

Carrie's Solution

$$125^{\frac{7}{3}} = 125^{\frac{6}{3} + \frac{1}{3}}$$
$$= 125^2 \cdot 125^{\frac{1}{3}}$$
$$= 15{,}625 \cdot 5$$
$$= 78{,}125$$

For Exercises 27–30, use the properties of exponents to evaluate each expression.

27. $\left(756^{\frac{1}{7}}\right)^7$

28. $342^{\frac{5}{2}} \div 342^{\frac{3}{2}}$

29. $3^{35} \cdot 3^{-35}$

30. $\left(\frac{1}{2}\right)^{40} \cdot 2^{40}$

For Exercises 31–36, decide if each statement is *always true, always false,* or *sometimes true.* Explain.

31. $2^n \cdot 2^n = 2(2^n)$

32. $2^n \cdot 2^n = (2^n)^2$

33. 2^n is less than 2^{n-1}.

34. b^n is less than b^{n-1}.

35. For the expression 3^x, when x is negative, 3^x will be smaller than 1.

36. For the expression b^x, when x is negative, b^x will be smaller than 1.

Notes

37. In 1867, the United States of America purchased the territory of Alaska from the Russian Empire. Its 586,412 square miles cost \$7.2 million. The United States paid roughly two cents per acre of land. Assume that the price of land in Alaska has increased in value by 5% a year since the purchase.

a. Write an equation that represents the price per acre in the year n.

b. What was the cost of an acre in 1900? In 2000?

c. In what year did the cost reach approximately \$1 per acre? \$100 per acre?

d. Gia calculated the cost per acre after n years on her calculator. She got the answer 2.453774647E28. For what year was she trying to find the cost?

38. Suppose n is the number of years after the United States purchased the territory of Alaska, in March of 1867. The equation $v = 7{,}200{,}000 \cdot (1.05)^n$ models the total value v of the territory. It is based on a 5% increase per year. Calculate the value of the territory during each month below. Explain what exponent you would use.

a. April 1867 **b.** May 1867 **c.** September 1867

d. June 1868 **e.** November 1868

Alaska Purchase, 1867

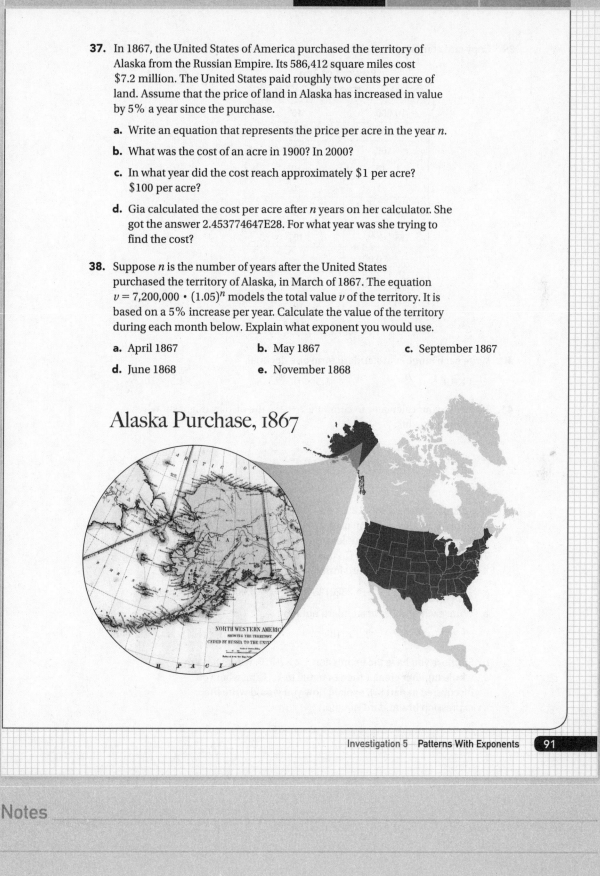

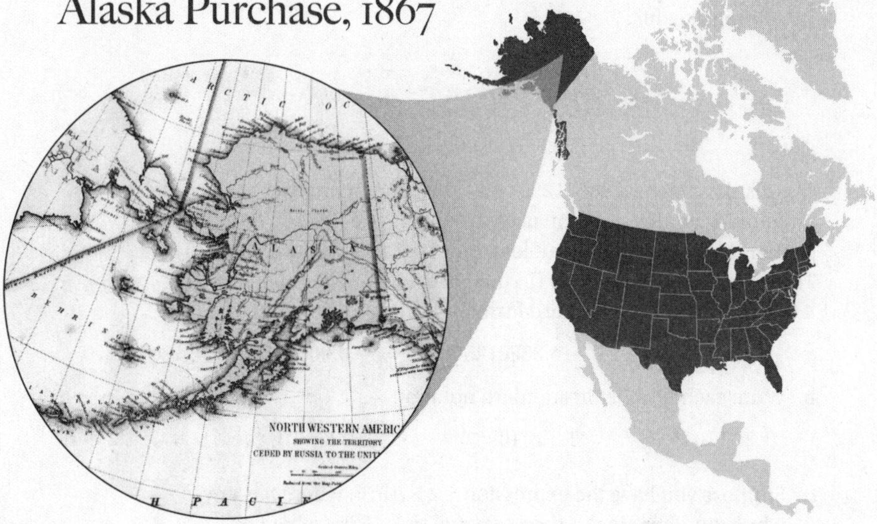

STUDENT PAGE

Notes

39. Copy and complete this table.

Powers of Ten

Standard Form	Exponential Form
10,000	10^4
1,000	10^3
100	10^2
10	10^1
1	10^0
$\frac{1}{10} = 0.1$	10^{-1}
$\frac{1}{100} = 0.01$	10^{-2}
$\frac{1}{1{,}000} = 0.001$	■
$\frac{1}{10{,}000} = 0.0001$	■
■	10^{-5}
■	10^{-6}

40. Write each number in standard form as a decimal.

3×10^{-1} $\quad$ 1.5×10^{-2} $\quad$ 1.5×10^{-3}

41. If you use your calculator to compute $2 \div 2^{12}$, the display might show something like this:

4.8828125E-4

The display means 4.8828125×10^{-4}, which is a number in scientific notation. Scientific notation uses two parts. The first is a number greater than or equal to 1 but less than 10 (in this case, 4.8828125). The second is a power of 10 (in this case, 10^{-4}). You can convert 4.8828125×10^{-4} to standard form in this way.

$$4.8828125 \times 10^{-4} = 4.8828125 \times \frac{1}{10{,}000} = 0.00048828125$$

a. Write each number in standard notation.

1.2×10^{-1} $\quad$ 1.2×10^{-2} $\quad$ 1.2×10^{-3} $\quad$ 1.2×10^{-8}

b. Suppose you have the expression 1.2×10^{-n}, where n is any whole number greater than or equal to 1. Using what you discovered in part (a), explain how you would write the expression in standard notation.

Notes

42. Write each number in scientific notation.

a. 2,000,000 **b.** 28,000,000 **c.** 19,900,000,000

d. 0.12489 **e.** 0.0058421998 **f.** 0.0010201

43. When Tia divided 0.0000015 by 1,000,000 on her calculator, she got 1.5E−12, which means 1.5×10^{-12}.

a. Write a different division problem that will give the result 1.5E−12 on your calculator.

b. Write a multiplication problem that will give the result 1.5E−12 on your calculator.

44. The radius of the moon is about 1.74×10^6 meters.

a. Express the radius of the moon in standard notation.

b. The largest circle that will fit on your textbook page has a radius of 10.795 cm. Express this radius in meters, using scientific notation.

c. Suppose a circle has the same radius as the moon. By what scale factor would you reduce the circle to fit on your textbook page?

d. Earth's moon is about the same size as Io, one of Jupiter's moons. What is the ratio of the moon's radius to the radius of Jupiter (6.99×10^7 meters)?

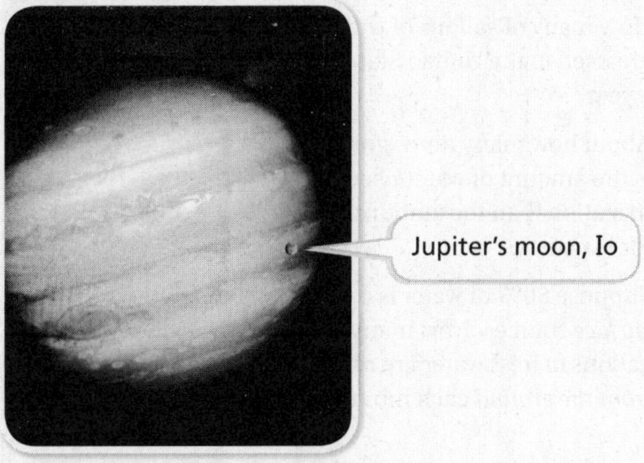

45. The number 2^7 is written in standard form as 128 and in scientific notation as 1.28×10^2. The number $\left(\frac{1}{2}\right)^7$, or $(0.5)^7$, is written in standard form as 0.0078125 and in scientific notation as 7.8125×10^{-3}. Write each number in scientific notation.

a. 2^8 **b.** $\left(\frac{1}{2}\right)^8$ **c.** 20^8 **d.** $\left(\frac{1}{20}\right)^8$

STUDENT PAGE

Notes

46. a. The boxes in the table below represent decreasing y-values. The decay factor for the y-values is $\frac{1}{3}$. Copy and complete the table.

x	0	1	2	3	4	5	6	7	8
y	30	10	■	■	■	■	■	■	■

b. For $x = 12$, a calculator gives a y-value of 5.645029269E−5. What does that mean?

c. Write the y-values for $x = 8, 9, 10$, and 11 in scientific notation.

For Exercises 47–49, use the properties of exponents to show that each statement is true.

47. $\frac{1}{2}(2^n) = 2^{n-1}$

48. $4^{n-1} = \frac{1}{4}(4^n)$

49. $25(5^{n-2}) = 5^n$

50. Use the data from Problem 5.4 to answer the following questions. Write your final answer in scientific notation.

a. How many of gallons of water are used in the United States in a year?

b. About how many times greater is the amount of water used for irrigation than the amount used for livestock?

c. Suppose 80% of water is from *surface* sources. How many gallons of freshwater are removed *from the ground* each month?

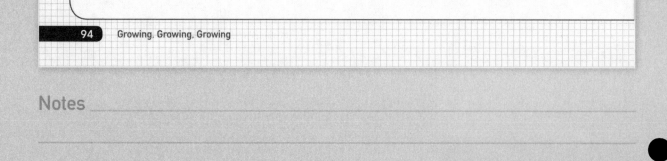

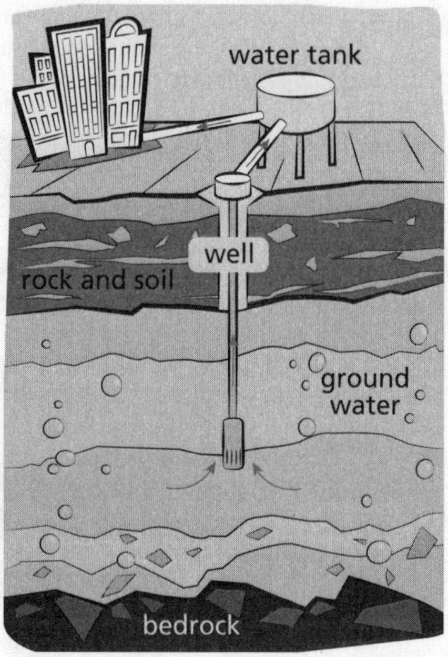

Notes

For Exercises 51–57, rewrite each expression in scientific notation.

51. $(8.2 \times 10^2) \times (2.1 \times 10^5)$

52. $(2.0 \times 10^3) \times (3.5 \times 10^6) \times (3.0 \times 10^3)$

53. $(2.0 \times 10^8) \times (1.4 \times 10^{-10})$

54. $(5.95 \times 10^8) \div (1.70 \times 10^5)$

55. $(1.28 \times 10^6) \div (5.12 \times 10^7)$

56. $(2.8 \times 10^{-4}) \div (1.4 \times 10^4)$

57. $(3.6 \times 10^2) \div (9.0 \times 10^{-3})$

For Exercises 58–62, find the missing values in each equation. Choose values such that all numbers are written in correct scientific notation.

58. $(2.4 \times 10^3) \times (g \times 10^h) = 6.0 \times 10^{12}$

59. $(j \times 10^2) \times (1.8 \times 10^k) = 9.0 \times 10^1$

60. $(m \times 10^7) \div (2.4 \times 10^n) = 5.0 \times 10^4$

61. $(6.48 \times 10^6) \div (p \times 10^q) = 2.16 \times 10^{-2}$

62. $(r \times 10^s) \times (r \times 10^s) = 1.6 \times 10^5$

63. Without actually graphing these equations, describe and compare their graphs. Be as specific as you can.

$y = 4^x$ $\quad$ $y = 0.25^x$ $\quad$ $y = 10(4^x)$ $\quad$ $y = 10(0.25^x)$

64. Explain how each of the graphs for the equations below will differ from the graph of $y = 2^x$.

a. $y = 5(2^x)$

b. $y = (5 \cdot 2)^x$

c. $y = \frac{1}{2}(2^x)$

d. $y = -1(2^x)$

e. $y = \left(\frac{1}{2}\right)^x$

STUDENT PAGE

Notes

65. Each graph below represents an exponential equation of the form $y = a(b^x)$.

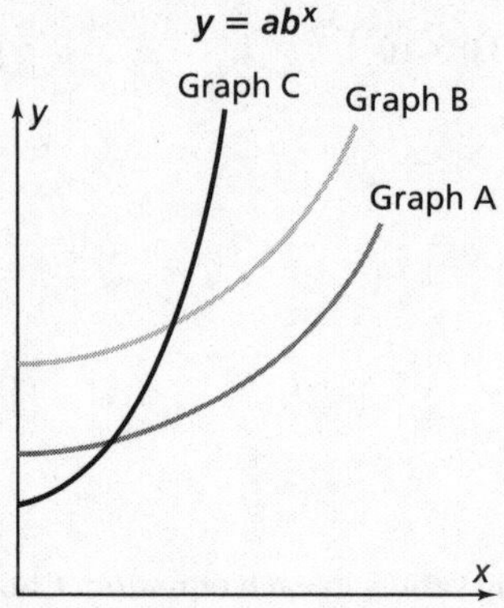

a. For which of the three functions is the value of a greatest?

b. For which of the three functions is the value of b greatest?

66. Grandville has a population of 1,000. Its population is expected to decrease by 4% a year for the next several years. Tinytown has a population of 100. Its population is expected to increase by 4% a year for the next several years. For parts (a)–(c), explain how you found each answer.

a. What is the population of each town after 5.5 years?

b. In how many years will Tinytown have a population of approximately 1,342? Explain your method.

c. Will the populations of the two towns ever be the same? Explain.

Notes

Connections

In Exercises 67–69, tell how many zeros are in the standard form of each number.

67. 10^{10}

68. 10^{50}

69. 10^{100}

In Exercises 70 and 71, find the least integer value of *x* that will make each statement true.

70. $9^6 < 10^x$

71. $3^{14} < 10^x$

In Exercises 72–74, identify the greater number in each pair.

72. 6^{10} or 7^{10}

73. 8^{10} or 10^8

74. 6^9 or 9^6

In Exercises 75 and 76, tell whether each statement is *true* or *false*. Do not do an exact calculation. Explain your reasoning.

75. $(1.56892 \times 10^5) - (2.3456 \times 10^4) < 0$

76. $\dfrac{3.96395 \times 10^5}{2.888211 \times 10^7} > 1$

77. Suppose you start with a unit cube (a cube with edges of length 1 unit). In parts (a)–(c), give the volume and surface area of the cube that results from the given transformation.

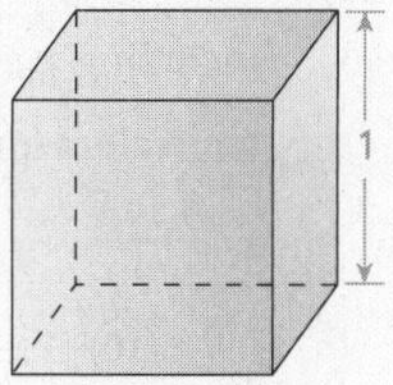

a. Each edge length is doubled.

b. Each edge length is tripled.

c. Each edge is enlarged by a scale factor of 100.

Notes

78. Suppose you start with a cylinder that has a radius of 1 unit and a height of 1 unit. In parts (a)–(c), give the volume of the cylinder that results from the given transformation.

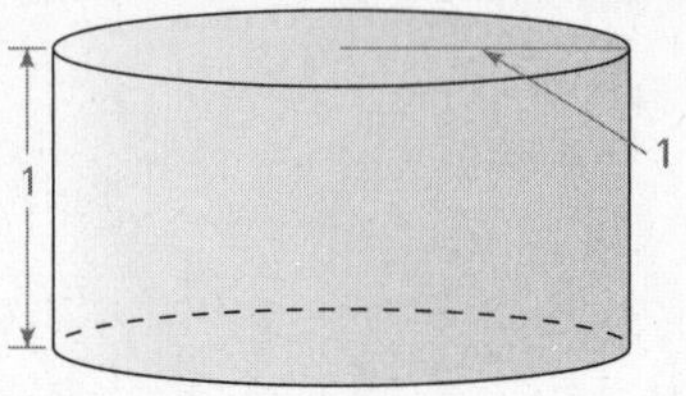

a. The radius and height are doubled.

b. The radius and height are tripled.

c. The radius and height are enlarged by a scale factor of 100.

79. a. Tell which of the following numbers are prime. (There may be more than one.)

$2^2 - 1$ $\quad$ $2^3 - 1$ $\quad$ $2^4 - 1$ $\quad$ $2^5 - 1$ $\quad$ $2^6 - 1$

b. Find another prime number that can be written in the form $2^n - 1$.

80. In parts (a)–(d), find the sum of the proper factors for each number.

a. 2^2

b. 2^3

c. 2^4

d. 2^5

e. What do you notice about the sums in parts (a)–(d)?

81. The expression $\frac{20}{10^2}$ can be written in many equivalent forms, including $\frac{2}{10}$, $\frac{1}{5}$, 0.2, and $\frac{2(10^2)}{10^3}$. In parts (a) and (b), write two equivalent forms for each expression.

a. $\frac{3(10)^5}{10^7}$

b. $\frac{5(10)^5}{25(10)^7}$

Notes

Extensions

In Exercises 82–86, predict the ones digit for the standard form of each number.

82. 7^{100}

83. 6^{200}

84. 17^{100}

85. 31^{10}

86. 12^{100}

For Exercises 87 and 88, find the value of *a* that makes each number sentence true.

87. $a^7 = 823{,}543$

88. $a^6 = 1{,}771{,}561$

89. Explain how you can use your calculator to find the ones digit of the standard form of 3^{30}.

90. **Multiple Choice** In the powers table you completed in Problem 5.1, look for patterns in the ones digit of square numbers. Which number is *not* a square number? Explain.

A. 289 **B.** 784 **C.** 1,392 **D.** 10,000

STUDENT PAGE

Notes

91. a. Find the sum for each row in the table below.

Sums of Powers of $\frac{1}{2}$

Row 1	$\frac{1}{2}$
Row 2	$\frac{1}{2} + \left(\frac{1}{2}\right)^2$
Row 3	$\frac{1}{2} + \left(\frac{1}{2}\right)^2 + \left(\frac{1}{2}\right)^3$
Row 4	$\frac{1}{2} + \left(\frac{1}{2}\right)^2 + \left(\frac{1}{2}\right)^3 + \left(\frac{1}{2}\right)^4$

b. Study the pattern. Suppose the pattern continues. Write the expression that would be in row 5 and evaluate the sum.

c. What would be the sum of the expression in row 10? What would you find if you evaluated the sum for row 20?

d. Describe the pattern of sums in words and with a symbolic expression.

e. For which row does the sum first exceed 0.9?

f. As the row number increases, the sum gets closer and closer to what number?

g. Celeste claims the pattern is related to the pattern of the areas of the ballots cut in Problem 4.1. She drew the picture below to explain her thinking.

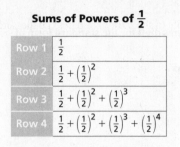

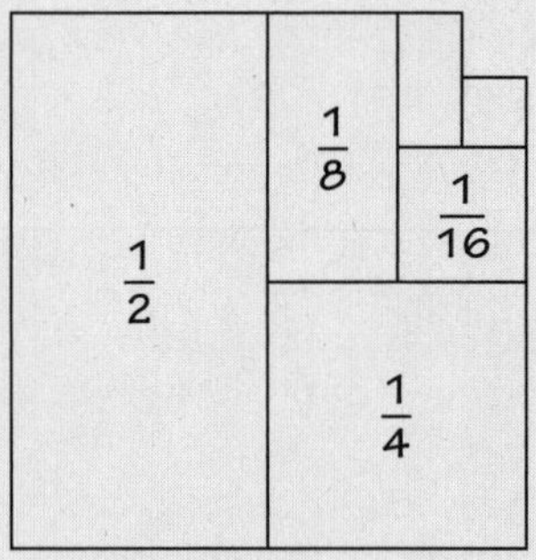

$$\text{row } 6 = \frac{1}{2} + \left(\frac{1}{2}\right)^2 + \left(\frac{1}{2}\right)^3 + \left(\frac{1}{2}\right)^4 + \left(\frac{1}{2}\right)^5 + \left(\frac{1}{2}\right)^6$$

What relationship do you think she has observed?

Notes

92. Chen, from Problem 4.1, decides to make his ballots starting with a sheet of paper with an area of 1 square foot.

a. Copy and extend this table to show the area of each ballot after each of the first 8 cuts.

Areas of Ballots

Number of Cuts	Area (ft^2)
0	1
1	$\frac{1}{2}$
2	$\frac{1}{4}$

b. Write an equation for the area A of a ballot after any cut n.

c. Use your equation to find the area of a ballot after 20 cuts. Write your answer in scientific notation.

93. In 1803, the United States bought the 828,000-square-mile Louisiana Purchase for \$15,000,000. Suppose one of your ancestors was given 1 acre of the Louisiana Purchase. Assuming an annual increase in value of 4%, what was the value of this acre in 2003? (640 acres = 1 square mile)

Notes

Mathematical Reflections 5

In this Investigation, you explored properties of exponents. You also looked at how the values of *a* and *b* affect the graph of $y = a(b^x)$. You made use of scientific notation to find relations among very large numbers. The following questions will help you summarize what you have learned.

Think about these questions. Discuss your ideas with other students and your teacher. Then write a summary of your findings in your notebook.

1. **a.** **Describe** some of the rules for operating with exponents.

   b. **What** is scientific notation? **What** are its practical applications?

2. **Describe** the effects of *a* and *b* on the graph of $y = a(b^x)$.

3. **Compare** exponential and linear functions. Include in your comparison information about their patterns of change, *y*-intercepts, whether the function is decreasing or increasing, and any other information you think is important. Include examples of how they are useful.

Notes

Common Core Mathematical Practices

As you worked on the Problems in this Investigation, you used prior knowledge to make sense of them. You also applied Mathematical Practices to solve the Problems. Think back over your work, the ways you thought about the Problems, and how you used Mathematical Practices.

Hector described his thoughts in the following way:

In Problem 5.4, we noticed that it is easy to use the rules of exponents to do multiplication when large numbers are expressed in scientific notation. Most of our group used a calculator anyway.

Since we were working with approximate data, we knew that our answers were also approximate.

We all used the graphing calculator in Problem 5.5. The calculator was faster for making the graphs so we could compare families of exponential functions.

Common Core Standards for Mathematical Practice
MP5 Use appropriate tools strategically

- What other Mathematical Practices can you identify in Hector's reasoning?
- Describe a Mathematical Practice that you and your classmates used to solve a different Problem in this Investigation.

STUDENT PAGE

Notes

Looking Back

You developed your skills in recognizing and applying exponential relationships between variables by working on Problems in this Unit.

You wrote equations of the form $y = a(b^x)$ to describe exponential growth of populations and investments and exponential decay of medicines and radioactive materials. You used equations to produce tables and graphs of the relationships. You used those tables and graphs to make predictions and solve equations.

Use Your Understanding: Algebraic Reasoning

To test your understanding and skill in finding and applying exponential models, solve these problems. These problems arise as the student council at Lincoln Middle School plans a fundraising event.

The students want to have a quiz show called *Who Wants to Be Rich?* Contestants will be asked a series of questions. A contestant will play until he or she misses a question. The total prize money will grow with each question answered correctly.

1. Lucy proposes that a contestant receive $5 for answering the first question correctly. For each additional correct answer, the total prize would increase by $10.

   a. For Lucy's proposal, what equation gives the total prize p for correctly answering n questions?

   b. How many questions would a contestant need to answer correctly to win at least $50? To win at least $75? To win at least $100?

   c. Sketch a graph of the (n, p) data for $n = 1$ to 10.

Notes

2. Armando also thinks the first question should be worth \$5. However, he thinks a contestant's winnings should double with each subsequent correct answer.

   a. For Armando's proposal, what equation gives the total prize p for correctly answering n questions?

   b. How many questions will a contestant need to answer correctly to win at least \$50? To win at least \$75? To win at least \$100?

   c. Sketch a graph of the data (n, p) for $n = 1$ to 10.

3. The council decides that contestants for *Who Wants to Be Rich?* will be chosen by a random drawing. Students and guests at the fundraiser will buy tickets like the one below.

The purchaser will keep half of the ticket and add the other half to the entries for the drawing.

   a. To make the tickets, council members will take a large piece of paper and fold it in half many times to make a grid of small rectangles. How many rectangles will there be after n folds?

   b. The initial piece of paper will be a square with sides measuring 60 centimeters. What will be the area of each rectangle after n folds?

Decide whether each statement is *true* or *false*. Explain.

4. $3^5 \times 6^5 = 9^5$

5. $8^5 \times 4^6 = 2^{27}$

6. $\frac{2^0 \times 6^7}{3^7} = 2^7$

7. $8^{\frac{3}{2}} \times 2^{\frac{1}{2}} = 32$

8. $1.39 \times 10^{-5} = 139{,}000$

9. $1.099511 \times 10^6 = 1{,}099{,}511$

END MATTER

STUDENT PAGE

Notes

Explain Your Reasoning

To answer Questions 1–3, you had to use algebraic knowledge about number patterns, graphs, and equations. You had to recognize linear and exponential patterns from verbal descriptions and represent those patterns with equations and graphs.

10. How can you decide whether a data pattern can be modeled by an exponential equation of the form $y = a(b^x)$? How will the values of a and b relate to the data pattern?

11. Describe the possible shapes for graphs of exponential relationships. How can the shape of an exponential graph be predicted from the values of a and b in the equation?

12. How are the data patterns, graphs, and equations for exponential relationships similar to those for linear relationships? How are they different?

13. Describe the rules for exponents that you used in Questions 4–9. Choose one of the rules and explain why it works.

Notes

English / Spanish Glossary

B

base The number that is raised to a power in an exponential expression. In the expression 3^5, read "3 to the fifth power", 3 is the base and 5 is the exponent.

base El número que se eleva a una potencia en una expresión exponencial. En la expresión 3^5, que se lee "3 elevado a la quinta potencia", 3 es la base y 5 es el exponente.

C

compound growth Another term for exponential growth, usually used when talking about the monetary value of an investment. The change in the balance of a savings account shows compound growth because the bank pays interest not only on the original investment, but on the interest earned.

crecimiento compuesto Otro término para crecimiento exponencial, normalmente usado para referirse al valor monetario de una inversión. El cambio en el saldo de una cuenta de ahorros muestra un crecimiento compuesto, ya que el banco paga intereses no sólo sobre la inversión original, sino sobre los intereses ganados.

D

decay factor The constant factor that each value in an exponential decay pattern is multiplied by to get the next value. The decay factor is the base in an exponential decay equation, and is a number between 0 and 1. For example, in the equation $A = 64(0.5)^n$, where A is the area of a ballot and n is the number of cuts, the decay factor is 0.5. It indicates that the area of a ballot after any number of cuts is 0.5 times the area after the previous number of cuts. In a table of (x, y) values for an exponential decay relationship (with x-values increasing by 1), the decay factor is the ratio of any y-value to the previous y-value.

factor de disminución El factor constante por el cual se multiplica cada valor en un patrón de disminución exponencial para obtener el valor siguiente. El factor de disminución es la base en una ecuación de disminución exponencial. Por ejemplo, en la ecuación $A = 64(0.5)^n$, donde A es el área de una papeleta y n es el número de cortes, el factor de disminución es 0.5. Esto indica que el área de una papeleta después de un número cualquiera de cortes es 0.5 veces el área después del número anterior de cortes. En una tabla de valores (x, y) para una relación de disminución exponencial (donde el valor x crece de a 1), el factor de disminución es la razón entre cualquier valor de y y su valor anterior.

decay rate The percent decrease in an exponential decay pattern. In general, for an exponential pattern with decay factor b, the decay rate is $1 - b$.

tasa de disminución El porcentaje de reducción en un patrón de disminución exponencial. En general, para un patrón exponencial con factor de disminución b, la tasa de disminución es $1 - b$.

Notes

decide Academic Vocabulary
To use the given information and any related facts to find a value or make a determination.

related terms *determine, find, conclude*

sample Study the pattern in the table. Decide whether the relationship is linear or exponential.

x	−1	0	1	2	3
y	−9	−7	−5	−3	−1

Each y-value Increases by 2 when each x-value Increases by 1. The relationship is linear.

decidir Vocabulario academico
Usar la información dada y los datos relacionados para hallar un valor o tomar una determinación.

terminos relacionados *decidir, hallar, calcular, concluir*

ejemplo ?Cual es una manera de determinar la descomposicion en factores primos de 27?

x	−1	0	1	2	3
y	−9	−7	−5	−3	−1

Cada valor de y aumenta en 2 cuando cada valor de x aumenta en 1. La relaclón es lineal.

describe Academic Vocabulary
To explain or tell in detail. A written description can contain facts and other information needed to communicate your answer. A diagram or a graph may also be included when you describe something.

related terms *explain, tell, present, detail*

sample Consider the following equations:

Equation 1 $y = 3x + 5$

Equation 2 $y = 5\left(3^x\right)$

Use a table to describe the change in *y*-values as the *x*-values increase in both equations.

x	0	1	2	3	4
y = 3x + 5	5	8	11	14	17
y = 5(3^x)	5	15	45	135	405

In $y = 3x + 5$, the value of y increases by 3 when x increases by 1. In $y = 5(3^x)$, the value of y increases by a factor of 3 when x increases by 1.

describir Vocabulario academico Explicar usando detalles. Puedes describir una situacion usando palabras, numeros, graficas, tablas o cualquier combinacion de estos.

terminos relacionados *explicar, decir, presentar, dar detalles*

ejemplo Considera las siguientes ecuaciones.

Ecuacion 1 $y = 3x + 5$

Ecuacion 2 $y = 5\left(3^x\right)$

Usa una tabla para describir el cambio en los valores de *y* a medida que los valores de *x* se incrementan en ambas ecuaciones.

x	0	1	2	3	4
y = 3x + 5	5	8	11	14	17
y = 5(3^x)	5	15	45	135	405

In $y = 3x + 5$, el valor de y aumenta en 3 cuando x aumenta en 1. En $y = 5(3^x)$, el valor de y aumenta por un factor de 3 cuando x aumenta en 1.

Notes

E

explain Academic Vocabulary
To give facts and details that make an idea easier to understand. Explaining can involve a written summary supported by a diagram, chart, table, or any combination of these.

related terms *describe, justify, tell*

sample Etymologists are working with a population of mosquitoes that have a growth factor of 8. After 1 month there are 6,000 mosquitoes. In two months, there are 48,000 mosquitoes.

Write an equation for the population after any number of months. Explain each part of your equation.

> I first find the initial population of mosquitoes by dividing 6,000 by 8 to get 750. I can then model the population growth with the equation $y = 750(8^m)$, where 750 represents the initial population, 8 is the growth factor, m is the number of months, and y is the population of mosquitoes after m months.

explicar Vocabulario academico
Dar hechos y detalles que hacen que una idea sea mas facil de comprender. Explicar puede implicar un resumen escrito apoyado por un diagrama, un grafica, una table o cualquier combatinacion de estos.

terminos relacionados *describir, justificar, decir*

ejemplo Los entomologos trabajan con una poblacion de mosquitos que tiene un factor de crecimiento de 8. Despues de 1 mes hay 6,000 mosquitos. En dos meses, hay 48,000 mosquitos.

Escribe una ecuacion para la poblacion despues de cualquier numero de meses. Explica cada parte de tu ecuacion.

> Primero hallo la población inicial de mosquitos dividiendo 6,000 entre 8 para obtener 750. Luego puedo modelar el crecimiento de la población con la ecuación $y = 750(8^m)$, donde 750 representa la población inicial, 8 es el factor de crecimiento, m es el número de meses y y es la población de mosquitos luego de m meses.

exponent The small raised number that tells how many times a factor is used. For example, 5^3 means $5 \times 5 \times 5$. The 3 is the exponent.

exponente El pequeño número elevado que dice cuántas veces se usa un factor. Por ejemplo, 5^3 significa $5 \times 5 \times 5$. El 3 es el exponente.

exponential decay A pattern of decrease in which each value is found by multiplying the previous value by a constant factor greater than 0 and less than 1. For example, the pattern 27, 9, 3, 1, $\frac{1}{3}$, $\frac{1}{9}$, . . . shows exponential decay in which each value is $\frac{1}{3}$ times the previous value.

disminución exponencial Un patrón de disminución en el cual cada valor se calcula multiplicando el valor anterior por un factor constante mayor que 0 y menor que 1. Por ejemplo, el patrón 27, 9, 3, 1, $\frac{1}{3}$, $\frac{1}{9}$, . . . muestra una disminución exponencial en la que cada valor es $\frac{1}{3}$ del valor anterior.

exponential form A quantity expressed as a number raised to a power. In exponential form, 32 can be written as 2^5.

forma exponencial Una cantidad que se expresa como un número elevado a una potencia. En forma exponencial, 32 puede escribirse como 2^5.

Notes

exponential functions Relationships between two variables that are exponential. For example, the function represented by $y = 4^{n-1}$ for placing 1 ruba on square one, 4 rubas on square two, 16 rubas on square three, and so on, is an exponential function.

funciones exponenciales Relaciones entre dos variables que son exponenciales. Por ejemplo, la función representada por $y = 4^{n-1}$ para poner un ruba en el cuadro uno, cuatro rubas en el cuadro dos, dieciséis rubas en el cuadro tres y así sucesivamente, es una función exponencial.

exponential growth A pattern of increase in which each value is found by multiplying the previous value by a constant factor greater than 1. For example, the doubling pattern 1, 2, 4, 8, 16, 32, . . . shows exponential growth in which each value is 2 times the previous value.

crecimiento exponencial Un patrón de crecimiento en el cual cada valor se calcula multiplicando el valor anterior por un factor constante mayor que 1. Por ejemplo, el patrón 1, 2, 4, 8, 16, 32, . . . muestra un crecimiento exponencial en el que cada valor es el doble del valor anterior.

exponential relationship A relationship that shows exponential growth or decay.

relación exponencial Una relación que muestra crecimiento o disminución exponencial.

Notes

G

growth factor The constant factor that each value in an exponential growth pattern is multiplied by to get the next value. The growth factor is the base in an exponential growth equation, and is a number greater than 1. For example, in the equation $A = 25(3)^d$, where A is the area of a patch of mold and d is the number of days, the growth factor is 3. It indicates that the area of the mold for any day is 3 times the area for the previous day. In a table of (x, y) values for an exponential growth relationship (with x-values increasing by 1), the growth factor is the ratio of any y-value to the previous y-value.

factor de crecimiento El factor constante por el cual se multiplica cada valor en un patrón de crecimiento exponencial para obtener el valor siguiente. El factor de crecimiento es la base en una ecuación de crecimiento exponencial. Por ejemplo, en la ecuación $A = 25(3)^d$, donde A es el área enmohecida y d es el número de días, el factor de crecimiento es 3. Esto indica que el área enmohecida en un día cualquiera es 3 veces el área del día anterior. En una tabla de valores (x, y) para una relación de crecimiento exponencial (donde el valor de x aumenta de 1), el factor exponencial es la razón entre cualquier valor de y y su valor anterior.

growth rate The percent increase in an exponential growth pattern. For example, in Problem 3.1, the number of rabbits increased from 100 to 180 from year 0 to year 1, an 80% increase. From year 1 to year 2, the number of rabbits increased from 180 to 324, an 80% increase. The growth rate for this rabbit population is 80%. Interest, expressed as a percent, is a growth rate. For an exponential growth pattern with a growth factor of b, the growth rate is $b - 1$.

tasa de crecimiento El porcentaje de crecimiento en un patrón de crecimiento exponencial. Por ejemplo, en el Problema 3.1, el número de conejos aumentó de 100 a 180 del año 0 al año 1, un aumento del 80%. Del año 1 al año 2, el número de conejos aumentó de 180 a 324, un aumento del 80%. La tasa de crecimiento para esta población de conejos es del 80%. El interés, expresado como porcentaje, es una tasa de crecimiento. Para un patrón de crecimiento exponencial con un factor de crecimiento b, la tasa de crecimiento es $b - 1$.

N

***n*th root** The nth root of a number b is a number r which, when raised to the power of n, is equal to b. That is, $r^n = b$ and $\sqrt[n]{b} = b^{\frac{1}{n}} = r$.

raíz enésima La raíz enésima de un número b es un número erre que, cuando se eleva a la potencia n, es igual a b. Es decir, y $r^n = b$ a un $\sqrt[n]{b} = b^{\frac{1}{n}} = r$.

Notes

P

predict Academic Vocabulary
To make an educated guess based on the analysis of real data.

related terms *estimate, expect*

sample Predict the ones digit for the expression 3^{11}.

3^1	3
3^2	9
3^3	27
3^4	81
3^5	243
3^6	729
3^7	2187
3^8	6561

The pattern for the ones digit of the powers of 3 is 3, 9, 7, 1, as the exponent increases by 1. If I continue the pattern, 3^9 will end with a 3, 3^{10} will end with a 9, and 3^{11} will end with a 7.

predecir Vocabulario academico
Hacer una conjectura informada basada en el analisis de datos reales.

terminos relacionados *estimar, esperar*

ejemplo Predice el digito de las unidades para la expresion 3^{11}.

3^1	3
3^2	9
3^3	27
3^4	81
3^5	243
3^6	729
3^7	2187
3^8	6561

El patrón para el dígito de las unidades de las potencias de 3 es 3, 9, 7, 1, a medida que el exponente aumenta en 1. Si continúo el patrón, 3^9 terminará con un 3, 3^{10} terminará con un 9, y 3^{11} terminará con un 7.

S

scientific notation A short way to write very large or very small numbers. A number is in scientific notation if it is of the form $a \times 10^n$, where n is an integer and $1 \leq a < 10$.

notación científica Una manera corta de escribir números muy grandes o muy pequeños. Un número está e notación científica si está en la forma $a \times 10^n$, donde n es un entero y $1 \leq a < 10$.

standard form The most common way we express quantities. For example, 27 is the standard form of 3^3.

forma normal La manera más común de expresar una cantidad. Por ejemplo, 27 es la forma normal de 3^3.

Notes

Index

Index

END MATTER STUDENT PAGE

Notes

Notes

Notes

Acknowledgments

Text

028 Texas Christian University Press

"Killer Weed Strikes Lake Victoria" from CHRISTIAN SCIENCE MONITOR, JANUARY 12, 1998.

Photographs

Photo locators denoted as follows: Top (T), Center (C), Bottom (B), Left (L), Right (R), Background (Bkgd)

002 Jacques Jangoux/Alamy; **003** Andy Williams/Loop Images/Alamy; **017** Scott Camazine/Science Source; **028** (CL) Ocean/Corbis, (CR) Jacques Jangoux/Alamy; **029** David Toase/Photodisc/Getty Images; **080** XUNBIN PAN/Alamy; **091** (BL) Steven Wright/Shutterstock, (BR) Ridvan EFE/Shutterstock; **093** Picture Press/Alamy.

Notes

At a Glance

Problem 1.1 Pacing $\frac{1}{2}$ Day

1.1 Making Ballots: Introducing Exponential Functions

Focus Question What are the variables in this situation and how are they related?

Launch

Describe Chen's ballot-making task. You might ask students to jot down predictions for the number of ballots that would result from three, four, or even ten cuts.

Suggested Questions

Gather a few suggestions, but let students sort the answers out as they work on the Problem.

- *How can you predict the number of ballots after 8 cuts?*
- *How can you predict how many cuts to make if we need 128 ballots?*

Key Vocabulary

There are no new glossary terms introduced in this Problem.

Materials

Accessibility Labsheets

- 1.1: Number of Ballots
- 1ACE: Exercise 3

Teaching Aid

- 1.1: Number of Ballots

- paper
- poster board
- transparencies

Explore

Encourage students to look for the multiplicative pattern in the table by asking questions like these:

- *How did you find each of the entries in your table?*
- *What is the relationship between this number of ballots and the previous number of ballots?*
- *Explain that relationship in terms of the number of cuts.*

As students work on Question C, look for interesting strategies to share during the Summarize.

Summarize

Suggested Questions

- *What does the graph look like? How could you predict this from the table?*
- *Is this a linear function? Explain.*

Display the Labsheet 1.1: Number of Ballots and ask:

- *How did you get the number of ballots for 5 cuts?*

Add a third column to the table and illustrate each calculation, showing each factor of 2. Stop after showing the calculation for 5 cuts.

- *How many times is 2 used as a factor to find the number of ballots after 1 cut? After 2 cuts? After 3 cuts? After 4 cuts? After 5 cuts?*
- *How many factors of 2 will be used to find the number of ballots after 6 cuts? After 10 cuts? After 30 cuts?*

ACE

Assignment Guide for Problem 1.1

Applications: 1–3 | Connections: 22–41

Answers to Problem 1.1

A. 1.

Number of Cuts	Number of Ballots
1	2
2	4
3	8
4	16
5	32
6	64
7	128
8	256
9	512
10	1,024

2. For each cut, the number of ballots doubles. See the table for the number of ballots for up to 10 cuts.

B. 1. The total number of ballots = $2^{(\text{the number of cuts})}$ or $T = 2^n$, where n is the number of cuts and T is the total number of ballots.

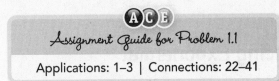

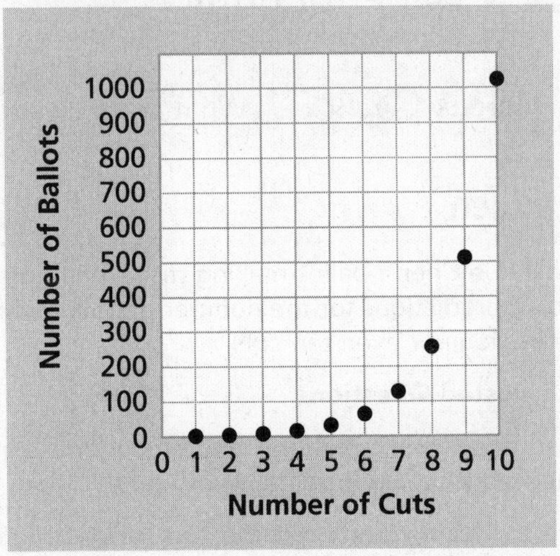

2. The number of ballots increases by the number of cuts and the number of ballots doubles from one cut to the next. After cutting 7 times, the number of ballots is over 100 and the curve of the graph is steep.

3. The relationship is not a linear function. In this relationship, as the number of cuts increases by one, the number of ballots doubles or increases by factor of 2. In linear functions, as the independent variable increases by a constant amount, the dependent variable increases by a constant amount. The graph of a linear function is a straight line and the graph of this relationship is a curve with increasing slope.

C. 1. If Chen could make 20 cuts, he would have 1,048,576 ballots. If he could make 40 cuts, he would have 1,099,511,627,776 ballots.

2. It would take 9 cuts to make at least 500 ballots.

Problem 1.2 Pacing $\frac{1}{2}$ Day

1.2 Requesting a Reward: Representing Exponential Functions

Focus Question In what ways are the relationships represented on a chessboard and in ballot-cutting situations similar? Different?

Launch

Review the terms *exponential form, exponent, base,* and *standard form.*

Suggested Questions

- *Write each expression in exponential form:* $2 \times 2 \times 2$; $5 \times 5 \times 5 \times 5$; $1.5 \cdot 1.5 \cdot 1.5 \cdot 1.5 \cdot 1.5 \cdot 1.5 \cdot 1.5$.
- *Write each expression in standard form:* 2^7, 3^3, 4.2^3.
- *Explain how the meanings of* 5^2, 2^5, *and* 5×2 *differ.*
- *Write* $1.0995111628 \times 10^{12}$ *in standard form.*
- *Write each expression in exponential form: 6,234,890,001; 20,000,033,339,999.*
- *Make a prediction as to how many rubas you think will be placed on the last square of the chessboard.*
- *If a Montarek ruba is worth 1 cent, do you think the peasant's plan is a good deal for her?*

Key Vocabulary

- base
- exponent
- exponential form
- scientific notion
- standard form

Materials

Accessibility Labsheet

- 1.2 Montarek Chessboard
- counters

Explore

Encourage students to place counters on a chessboard or Labsheet 1.2: Montarek Chessboard for at least the first five or six squares.

To help students who do not recognize the pattern immediately, ask:

- *How did the number of rubas increase from square 1 to square 2? From square 2 to square 3? From square 3 to square 4?*

Summarize

Have some students share their graphs. Ask students to describe the graph.

- *Choose points in the table and ask: Where are these points on the graph?*
- *Choose points on the graph and ask: Where are these points in the table?*
- *How does the growth pattern show up in the graph?*
- *How many rubas will be on the last square? How did you find that number?*
- *If each ruba is worth 1 cent, what is the value of the rubas on the last square in dollars?*
- *How did you find this answer?*
- *Is this plan a good deal for the peasant?*
- *In what ways are the chessboard and ballot-cutting situations similar?*

- *In what ways are the two situations different?*
- *Compare the relationships in Problems 1.1 and 1.2 to linear functions.*

ACE

Assignment Guide for Problem 1.2

Applications: 4–12 | Connections: 42–43
Extensions: 50

Materials

- square tiles or grid paper

Answers to Problem 1.2

A. 1.

Square Number	Number of Rubas
1	1
2	2
3	4
4	8
5	16
6	32
7	64
8	128
9	256
10	512

2.

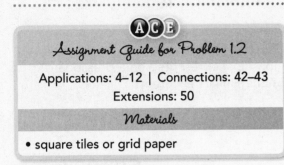

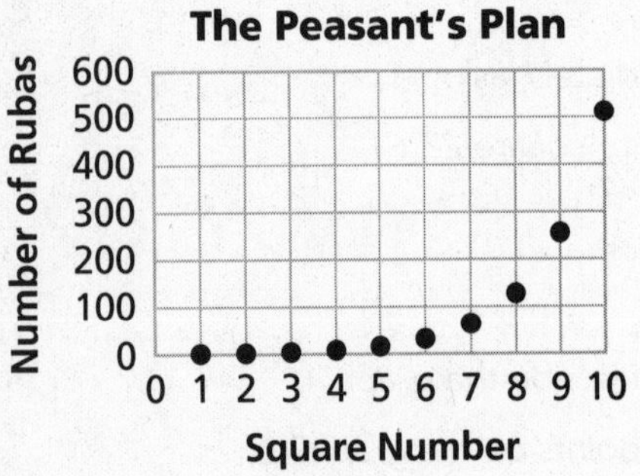

3. $r = 2^{n-1}$ or $r = \frac{1}{2}(2^n)$

B. 1. The number of rubas doubles from one square to the next.

2. In the graph, you can see the doubling pattern if you look at the *y*-values for the plotted points. The *y*-value doubles each time the number of the square increases by 1. In the equation, the base of 2 means that you are multiplying by another 2 each time the number of the square *n* increases by 1.

C. 1. The 31st square. The equation is $y = 2^{n-1}$. The exponent is always one less than the number of the square.

2. Square 21; 1,048,576 rubas. On square 20, there are $2^{20-1} = 2^{19} = 524{,}288$ rubas. On square 21, there are $2^{21-1} = 2^{20} =$ 1,048,576. So square 21 is the first square with over 1 million rubas.

D. Even though the starting points of each graph from Problem 1.1 and Problem 1.2 are different as, i.e., (1, 2) and (1, 1), both growth patterns are the doubling pattern. The *y*-value doubles each time the number of the *x*-value increases by 1.

Problem 1.3 Pacing 1 Day

1.3 Making a New Offer: Growth Factors

Focus Question How does the growth pattern for an exponential function show up in a table, graph, or equation that represents the function and how does it compare to the growth pattern in a linear function?

Launch

Check that students understand the new plans.

- *How many squares are on the board for each new plan?*
- *For each plan, how many rubas are placed on the first square?*
- *What is the rule for placing rubas on each successive square?*
- *Which plan do you think is the best for the king? For the peasant?*

Explore

You may want to have one or two pairs display their graphs. Have at least one group display all three graphs on the same set of axes.

Summarize

Begin by asking for another show of hands about which plan is best for the peasant and which is best for the king. Then discuss the answers to the Problem.

Suggested Questions

- *What are the growth factors for the relationships in Plans 1, 2, and 3?*
- *How does the growth factor show up in the table for each relationship? The equation?*
- *How does the growth factor affect the shape of the graph?*
- *Compare the growth patterns for linear and exponential functions.*

Key Vocabulary

- exponential functions
- exponential growth
- growth factor

Materials

Accessibility Labsheets

- 1.3: Different Reward Plans
- 1ACE: Exercises 17–23

Labsheet

- 1ACE: Exercise 51
- counters

ACE

Assignment Guide for Problem 1.3

Applications: 13–21 | Connections: 44–48
Extensions: 49, 51–52

Answers to Problem 1.3

A. **1.** See Figure 1.

2. a. In each plan, the number of the square is the independent variable and the number of rubas is the dependent variable.

b. All three plans start with 1 ruba on square 1. In each plan, the number of rubas for a square is found by multiplying by a fixed number. The plans are different in that the number of rubas doubles with each square in Plan 1, triples in Plan 2, and quadruples in Plan 3. There are 64 squares in Plan 1, 16 in Plan 2, and 12 in Plan 3.

3. Yes, both plans are exponential. The growth factor for Plan 2 is 3, and the growth factor for Plan 3 is 4.

B. 1. $r = 3^{n-1}$ or $r = \frac{1}{3}(3^n)$

2. The graphs of Plans 1, 2, and 3 all have a starting point of (1, 1) and all increase in a similar, curved pattern. However, the graph of Plan 3 grows at a faster rate than the graphs of Plan 1 and Plan 2.

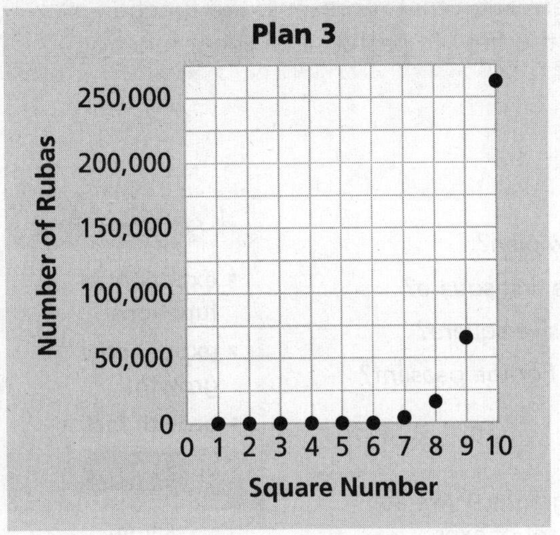

3. The growth factors for Plans 2 and 3 are represented in the equation $r = 4^{n-1}$ or $r = \frac{1}{4}(4^x)$. It is the base, which is 4 in each equation.

C. 1. See Figure 2. The growth pattern of Plans 1, 2, and 3 are exponential functions. The growth pattern of Plan 4 is not exponential because you add the constant 5 to the previous number. This pattern makes Plan 4 linear, not exponential.

2. $r = 20 + 5(n - 1)$ or $r = 15 + 5n$

D. Plan 1: 9.22×10^{18} rubas
Plan 2: 14,348,907 rubas
Plan 3: 4,194,304 rubas
Plan 4: 335 rubas
The list of rubas is listed from greatest to least.

Figure 1

Reward Plans

Square Number	Number of Rubas		
	Plan 1	Plan 2	Plan 3
1	1	1	1
2	2	3	4
3	4	9	16
4	8	27	64
5	16	81	256
6	32	243	1,024
7	64	729	4,096
8	128	2,187	16,384
9	256	6,561	65,536
10	512	19,683	262,144

Figure 2

Square Number	Number of Rubas			
	Plan 1	Plan 2	Plan 3	Plan 4
1	1	1	1	20
2	2	3	4	25
3	4	9	16	30
4	8	27	64	35
5	16	81	256	40
6	32	243	1,024	45
7	64	729	4,096	50
8	128	2187	16,384	55
9	256	6561	65,536	60
10	512	19,683	262,144	65

Problem 2.1 Pacing 1 Day

2.1 Killer Plant Strikes Lake Victoria: *y*-intercepts Other than 1

Focus Question What information do you need to write an equation that represents an exponential function?

Launch

Tell the real story about the water hyacinths taking over Lake Victoria.

- *The article says the plant doubles in size every 5 to 15 days. Does this mean the growth factor is 2?*

Now tell the class that Ghost Lake has a problem similar to the one on Lake Victoria. Discuss the first paragraph of Problem 2.1, which gives the details.

- *Is the area of the plant growing exponentially? How do you know?*
- *The initial value, 1,000 square feet, is the y-intercept for this relationship. Can anybody explain why?*

Explore

If students are having trouble writing an equation, suggest that they make a table for the first few months.

Suggested Questions

- *What is the starting value, or y-intercept?*
- *What is the growth factor?*
- *What information do you need to write an equation?*

Summarize

Call on a couple of students to display their equations and to explain what the numbers and variables mean.

Suggested Questions

- *Does it make sense to connect the dots on the graph?*
- *How would the equation change if the initial area covered was 1,500 square feet?*
- *How would the equation change if the area covered tripled every month?*
- *Use your equation to find the area of the lake that is covered with the plant after 11 months.*
- *How did you find the number of months it will take the plant to completely cover the lake?*

Let students make preliminary conjectures.

Key Vocabulary

There are no new glossary terms introduced in this Problem.

Materials

Labsheet
- 2ACE: Exercise 2

Accessibility Labsheets
- 2ACE: Exercise 3
- 2ACE: Exercise 4
- 2ACE: Exercise 33

Teaching Aid
- 2.1: Water Hyacinth Growth

- transparencies
- graph paper

ACE Assignment Guide for Problem 2.1

Applications: 1–4 | Connections: 15–23
Extensions: 33–35

Answers to Problem 2.1

A. 1. $a = 1{,}000(2^n)$ (Variable names may vary.)

2. a is the surface area of the lake covered after n months. 1,000 is the area in ft^2 covered now (at time 0). The growth factor is 2; it represents the doubling of the area each month.

3. Possible answer: All of the equations in Investigation 1 were of the form $y =$ some number raised to an exponent, such as $y = 2^n$ or $y = 3^{n-1}$, and there was no number in front of the 2 or 3. In this equation, $a = 1{,}000(2^n)$, there is a number in front of the 2. Some students will observe that this situation is more like the ballots than like the ruba situations, with a starting point at $x = 0$ instead of at $x = 1$.

B. 1.

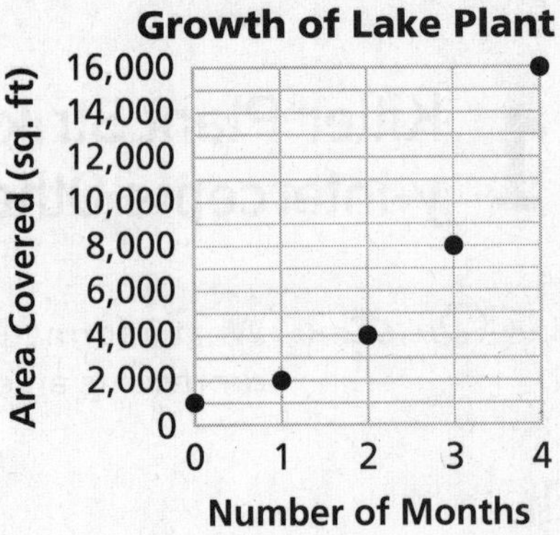

2. This graph has a y-intercept of (0, 1,000), while the ballot situation has a y-intercept of (0, 1). The ruba situations' graphs all started at (1, 1). In the ruba situations, the y-intercept had no meaning in the story because there is no such thing as square 0.

3. Yes; On the graph, two points are never plotted at different y-values for one x-value. Intuitively, this means that the area is a specific size at a single point in time. Since growth continues as time passes, this relationship is a function. **Note:** Even if growth stopped, time still passes and the relationship would be a function.

C. 1. After 12 months, $1{,}000(2^{12}) = 4{,}096{,}000\ ft^2$ will be covered.

2. It will take between 14 and 15 months for the plant to cover all 25,000,000 ft^2 because $1{,}000(2^{14}) = 16{,}384{,}000$ and $1{,}000(2^{15}) = 32{,}768{,}000$.

Problem 2.2 Pacing $\frac{1}{2}$ Day

2.2 Growing Mold: Interpreting Equations for Exponential Functions

Focus Question How is the growth factor and initial population for an exponential function represented in an equation that represents the function?

Launch

Discuss with your students the information in the student edition about moldy food. Having a piece of moldy bread or cheese on display makes a great attention grabber.

- *How much mold is there at the end of day 1? At the end of day 2? At the end of day 3?*
- *Do you see any similarities between the pattern of change in this situation and the patterns of change in some of the Problems in the last Investigation and in Problem 2.1? Explain.*

Key Vocabulary

There are no new glossary terms introduced in this Problem.

Materials

Labsheet

- 2ACE: Exercise 8

Teaching Aid

- 2.2: Mold Experiment

Explore

When students evaluate the equation for a specific *d* value, make sure they raise only the base to the exponent, and not both the base and the initial value. For example, when computing $50(3^5)$, watch for students who find 50×3 and then raise the product, 150, to the exponent of 5. This is not correct.

Remind students to follow the Order of Operations: Evaluate exponents first and then multiply. Most graphing calculators use the correct order of operations.

Summarize

To initiate a discussion, use the following.

- *How does the mold grow from one day to the next?*
- *Is the mold growth similar to other growth situations you have studied? Explain.*
- *What does each part of your equation tell you about the growth of the mold?*
- *Suppose you started with 25 mm^2 of mold and it grew in the same way that it did in the Problem. How would the equation change? How would the graph change?*

Discuss the standard form for an exponential equation introduced in Question E: $y = a(b^x)$. Help students see how this equation is similar to and different from the slope-intercept form of a linear equation.

- *In the linear equation, $y = mx + b$, which letter represents the y-intercept?*
- *In the exponential equation, which letter represents the y-intercept?*
- *Why do you think you add the y-intercept in a linear equation, but you multiply by it in an exponential equation?*

- *In the linear equation, what tells us how quickly the dependent variable is changing as the value of the independent variable increases in increments of 1?*
- *In the exponential equation, what tells us how quickly the dependent variable is changing as the value of the independent variable increases in increments of 1?*
- *What other similarities and differences do you notice between linear and exponential equations?*

Check for Understanding

Repeat the last set of questions with specific examples such as these:

$y = -3x + 4$ $\quad$ $y = 1.5x$ $\quad$ $y = 3^x$ $\quad$ $y = 10(5^x)$

ACE

Assignment Guide for Problem 2.2

Applications: 5–8 | Connections: 24, 29

Answers to Problem 2.2

A. **1.** At the first day of the experiment, the area of the mold in square millimeters is $m = 50(3^0) = 50 \times 1 = 50$; 50 mm^2.

2. The growth factor is 3. As the day increases by 1, the area covered by mold increases by a factor of 3.

3. $50(3^5) = 12{,}150$ mm^2.

4. Between day 4 and day 5; on day 4, the area was 4,050 mm^2, and on day 5, the area was 12,150 mm^2.

B. **1.** The value of *b* is 3. This represents the growth factor.

2. The value of *a* is 50. This represents the initial amount of mold, which means there was some mold at the start of the experiment.

Problem 2.3 Pacing $\frac{1}{2}$ Day

2.3 Studying Snake Populations: Interpreting Graphs of Exponential Functions

Focus Question How is the growth factor and initial population for an exponential function represented in a graph that represents the function?

Launch

Display the graph of the snake population using Teaching Aid 2.3: Garter Snake Population Growth. Briefly describe the Problem. Then challenge the students to find an equation that represents the graph of the exponential function and to use the equation to make predictions about the population of the snake.

Explore

It is difficult to read the y-intercept from the graph. To guide student thinking, ask the following:

Suggested Questions

- *Which points are easy to read?*
- *What is the growth pattern for these 3 years?*
- *If we assume this same growth pattern for years 0 to n, what is the population in year 1? What is the population in year 0?*
- *What is the y-intercept?*

Students should now be able to write the equation $p = 1(5^n)$, or just $p = 5^n$. Look for other ways students may arrive at the equation.

Summarize

Ask the class to share the ways they found their equations. Some students may have used (2, 25) as a starting point and written $p = 25(5^{n-2})$. This is also correct. You can ask students to check a few points to verify that the two equations are equivalent.

Check for Understanding

On a large sheet of paper, have each group or pair of students write an exponential equation for the growth of a population and describe the variables. As each group holds up its poster, ask the rest of the class:

- *What is the growth factor?*
- *What is the initial population?*
- *How large is the population after 4 years?*
- *How long will it take the population to reach a certain number?*
- *Compare the growth of this population to some of the previous examples we have seen.*

Key Vocabulary

There are no new glossary terms introduced in this Problem.

Materials

Labsheets
- 2ACE: Exercise 13
- 2ACE: Exercises 25–28

Accessibility Labsheet
- 2ACE: Exercise 14

Teaching Aid
- 2.3: Garter Snake Population Growth

Assessment
- Check Up

![ACE]

Assignment Guide for Problem 2.3

Applications: 9–14 | Connections: 25–28, 30–32

Answers to Problem 2.3

A. 1. The population in year 2 is 25, in year 3 is 125, and in year 4 is 625.

2. Working backward, you divide the population for each year by 5 to get the population for the previous year. So, the population for year 1 would be $25 \div 5 = 5$ snakes.

3. You can find the y-intercept by working backward and dividing the population for year 1 by 5. In this case, the *y*-intercept is (0, 1).

Note: A *y*-intercept of 1 would mean that the population started with one (presumably pregnant) snake. If students raise this issue, you may want to ask them how they would alter the graph so it makes more sense in this context. Some students may say that the snake was pregnant and giving birth at the start of the data collection.

B. The growth factor is 5 because (2, 25), (3, 125), and (4, 625) are on the graph and the *y*-value for each of these points is 5 times the previous *y*-value.

C. $p = 5^t$, or $p = 1(5^t)$, where *p* represents the snake population after *t* years.

D. Between year 4 and year 5, because $5^4 = 625$ and $5^5 = 3{,}125$.

E. Chuck is correct. The relationship is a function. Some students may also use the context to say that at any given time, the snake is only having one birth. At any point in time, the number of snakes is a specific value. The scale is a problem since it looks like the values corresponding to year 4 is a vertical line. Using a larger scale for the horizontal axis would help clarify the situation.

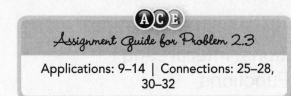

At a Glance

Problem 3.1 Pacing 1 Day

3.1 Reproducing Rabbits: Fractional Growth Patterns

Focus Question How is the growth factor in this Problem similar to that in the previous Problems? How is it different?

Launch

Discuss with students the story of the rabbits that English settlers introduced to Australia. You might tell students that one pair of rabbits can increase in 18 months to 184 rabbits, so it is difficult to completely eliminate them. Ask:

- *Does the relationship between time and rabbit population appear to be linear, exponential, or neither?*
- *By how much did the rabbit population increase in each year shown?*
- *Is that a constant rate of change?*
- *Why is this pattern exponential?*

The relationship is, in fact, exponential. However, unlike the other exponential relationships they have studied, the growth factor is not a whole number.

Key Vocabulary

There are no new glossary terms introduced in this Problem.

Materials

Accessibility Labsheet

- 3ACE: Exercise 1

Labsheet

- 3ACE: Exercise 8

Teaching Aid

- 3.1: Rabbit Population Table
- poster board

Explore

As you circulate, you might ask students questions to guide them in finding the year to year growth factors and in determining an overall growth factor.

- *How can you determine the growth factor from one year to the next?*
- *What is the growth factor from the initial year (year 0) to year 1?*
- *What is the growth factor from year 1 to year 2?*
- *Why do you think these ratios are not equal?*
- *How can you find an overall growth factor for these data?*

Summarize

Suggested Questions

- *When you look at a table of population data like this one, how can you determine whether the data represent a linear relationship? How can you determine whether the data represent an exponential relationship?*
- *How did you determine the growth factor for these data?*

Check for Understanding

- *Suppose the growth factor for a population of cats is 1.7 per year and the starting population is 50 cats. What is an equation for the population growth?*
- *When will the population double?*

ACE

Assignment Guide for Problem 3.1

Applications: 1–8 | Connections: 24–30

Answers to Problem 3.1

A. 1. About 1.80; possible explanation: I divided each population value by the previous value and then took the average. The average of $\frac{180}{100}$, $\frac{325}{180}$, $\frac{583}{325}$, and $\frac{1,050}{583}$ is approximately 1.80.

2. $p = 100(1.8)^n$; 100 represents the initial population of rabbits and 1.8 represents the growth factor.

3. After 10 years, there would have been $100(1.8)^{10} = 35,704$ rabbits. After 25 years, there would have been $100(1.8)^{25} \approx 240,886,592$ rabbits. After 50 years, there would have been about $100(1.8)^{50} \approx 5.8 \times 1014$ rabbits. **Note:** This is a good opportunity to reinforce the use of scientific notation to express large numbers. It is also an opportunity to discuss that calculators only provide approximate answers for large calculations.

4. About 16 years. Students may use a table or a graph to get a more precise answer. It takes about 15.7 years, or 15 years and 8 months.

B. 1. 1.2

2. 15 million

3. About 4 years (3.8 years)

4. About 26 million; about 4 years

5. About 93 million; about 4 years

6. The doubling times are all the same. The doubling time does not depend on the starting population.

At a Glance

Problem 3.2 Pacing 1 Day

3.2 Investing for the Future: Growth Rates

Focus Question How are the growth factor and growth rate for an exponential function related? When might you use each in an exponential growth pattern?

Launch

Discuss the story of Sam's stamp.

- *When you calculate the increase for the second year, do you base it on the original $2,500 value or on the value at the end of the first year?*
- *Why is the increase in value in the second year greater than the increase in value in the first year?*

Help the class to understand that this idea is the reason this pattern of change is called compound growth.

- *In this Problem, you will make tables to find the growth factor for the value of the stamp between successive years. How would you find the growth factor for the values between two years?*
- *Will you get the same factor between any two successive years?*

Note: Students will confirm this information during the Explore.

Key Vocabulary

- growth rate

Materials

Labsheets

- 3.2: Stamp Value Tables
- 3ACE: Exercise 9
- graphing calculators
- graph paper

Explore

Hand out Labsheet 3.2: Stamp Value Tables. As you circulate, be sure each student is calculating the value of the stamp and the growth factor correctly.

Summarize

Have groups of students share their strategies for determining the values in the tables and their answers to the questions. Display their data for the class.

- *What is the growth factor from year 1 to year 2?*
- *What is the growth factor from year 2 to year 3?*
- *What is the growth factor from year 4 to year 5?*
- *How is this relationship similar to others you have investigated in this Unit?*
- *If the growth factor is constant for consecutive values of x (or years, in this case), what kind of relationship is this?*
- *What is the growth factor for a yearly increase of 7%?*
- *What is the growth factor for a yearly increase of 70%?*
- *If you know the growth rate, or percent increase, how can you find the growth factor? Why?*
- *If you know the growth factor, how can you find the growth rate? Why?*
- *Do you think this rate of growth could continue indefinitely?*

Assignment Guide for Problem 3.2

Applications: 9–20 | Connections: 31–32
Extensions: 40–45

Answers to Problem 3.2

A. 1. **Sam's Stamp Collection at 6%**

Year	Value
0	\$2,500
1	\$2,650
2	\$2,809
3	\$2,977.54
4	\$3,156.19
5	\$3,345.56

2. Yes. This is exponential growth with a growth factor of 1.06.

3. $v = 2{,}500(1.06)^n$

4. It will take about 12 years to double the value of the investment.

B. 1. **Sam's Stamp Collection at 4%**

Year	Value
0	\$2,500
1	\$2,600
2	\$2,704
3	\$2,812.16
4	\$2,924.65
5	\$3,041.63

2. 1.04

3. $v = 2{,}500(1.04)^n$

4. It will take about 18 years to double the value of the investment.

5. The graph of the equation for 6% growth rate will increase faster than the graph of the equation for 4% growth rate.

C. 1. **a.** 1.00

b. 1.15

c. 1.3

d. 1.75

e. 2

f. 2.5

2. Possible answer: Change the growth rate to a decimal and add 1. (Be sure students know why this works.)

D. 1. **a.** 50%

b. 25%

c. 10%

d. 0%

2. Possible answer: Change the growth factor to a percent and subtract 100%. (Be sure students know why this works.)

At a Glance

Problem 3.3 Pacing 1 Day

3.3 Making a Difference: Connecting Growth Rate and Growth Factor

Focus Question How does the initial population affect the growth patterns in an exponential function?

Launch

Review the idea of compound growth. Tell the story about Mrs. Ramos and her two granddaughters' college funds.

Explore

Circulate to identify students having difficulty with growth rate.

Summarize

Discuss the Problem, paying particular attention to whether students understand how to use the given information to write an equation.

Check for Understanding

- *For a growth factor of 1.10, what is the growth rate, or percent increase?*
- *A stamp collection is worth $880 and the value will increase by 3% per year. What equation gives the value after t years? What is the growth factor?*
- *What would be the equation if the initial value were $1,760 and the projected increase were 1% per year?*

Key Vocabulary

- compound growth

Materials

Labsheet

- 3.3: College Funds Table

Assessment

- Partner Quiz
- centimeter grid paper
- graphing calculators
- graph paper

ACE

Assignment Guide for Problem 3.3

Applications: 21–23 | Connections: 33–39
Extensions: 46–47

Answers to Problem 3.3

A. 1. Cassie: $a = 1{,}250(1.04)^t$
Kaylee: $a = 2{,}500(1.04)^t$, where a is the amount in the fund and t is the time in years since the money was invested.

2. **Value of College Funds**

Year	Cassie's Fund	Kaylee's Fund
0	$1,250	$2,500
1	$1,300	$2,600
2	$1,352	$2,704
3	$1,406.08	$2,812.16
4	$1,462.32	$2,924.65
5	$1,520.82	$3,041.63
6	$1,581.65	$3,163.30
7	$1,644.91	$3,289.83
8	$1,710.71	$3,421.42
9	$1,779.14	$3,558.28
10	$1,850.31	$3,700.61

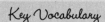

3. (See Figures 1 and 2.) Because of the difference in the initial values, Kaylee's fund graph rises more rapidly than Cassie's fund graph.

4. a. Kaylee's increase is double Cassie's increase every year. The minor discrepancies are rounding errors. This does not reflect a difference in the growth factor, but a difference in the initial value.

   b. The initial value of the fund does not affect the growth factor.

   c. The final value of Kaylee's fund will be double that of Cassie's, just as the initial investment was double.

B. 1. The initial value was $2,000, the growth factor is 1.05, the growth rate is 5%, and it is a four-year investment.

   2. In one more year, the fund will be worth $\$2{,}000(1.05)^5 = \$2{,}552.56$.

C. It depends on how long the money is left in the account. After one year, the amount in the Option 1 account is $1,030 and the amount in the Option 2 account is $848. After seven years, the amount in the Option 1 account is about $1,229.87 and the amount in the Option 2 account is about $1,202.90. After eight years, the amount in the Option 1 account is about $1,266.77 and the amount in the Option 2 account is about $1,275.08. Option 2 is better for more than 7 years.

Figure 1

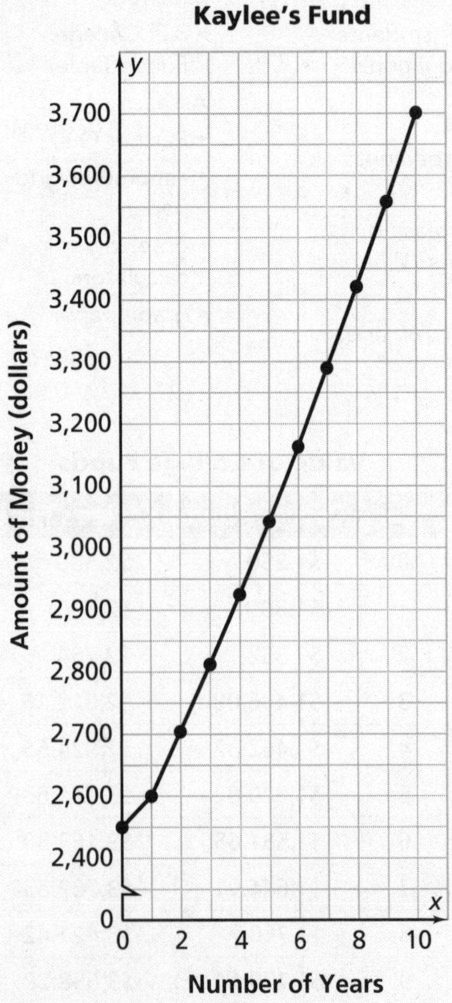

Figure 2

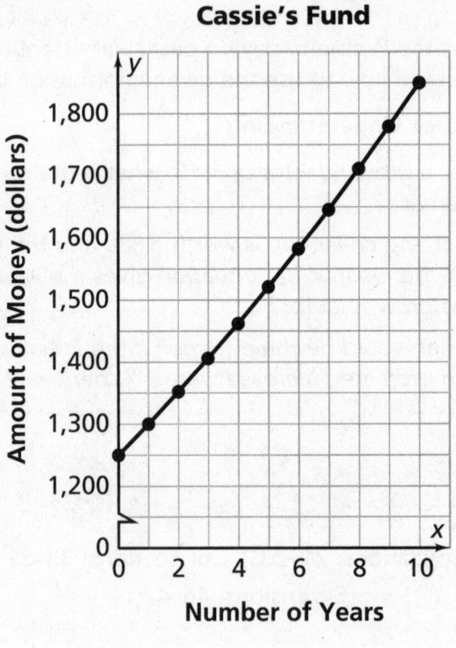

At a Glance

Problem 4.1 Pacing 1 Day

4.1 Making Smaller Ballots: Introducing Exponential Decay

Focus Question How does the pattern of change in this situation compare to the growth patterns you have studied in previous Problems? How does the difference show up in a table, graph and equation?

Launch

Hold up your square of grid paper. Then ask the following questions.

- *This sheet of paper has an area of 64 square inches. When you make the first cut, what happens to the area of a ballot?*
- *What will be the area of each ballot after the second cut?*
- *What would a ballot look like if you made 10 cuts?*
- *Do you think it would be large enough for you to write your name on it?*
- *Will you ever have a ballot with an area of 0 square inches?*

Explore

Have some students prepare their graphs to display for the Summarize.

Summarize

Have students share what they discovered in the Problem.

- *Start at the beginning and generate the table using the constant factor $\frac{1}{2}$. If you know the area of the original ballot is 64 square inches, how do you get the area of a ballot after one cut?*
- *What is the area after two cuts?*
- *How could you find the area of a ballot after 50 cuts?*
- *What is the area of a ballot after n cuts?*
- *Explain how you got your equation in Question C.*
- *What does the graph of this situation look like? How is the graph similar to and different from the graphs in the previous Problems?*

Check for Understanding

- Pick a pair of values from the table and ask students to explain what these values mean in terms of the context, the equation, and the graph.
- Have students explain how the variables and numbers in the equation relate to the context of the situation, the table, and the graph.
- Have students discuss how the pattern and features of the graph are related to the equation, situation, and table.

Then ask the following question:

- *When will the area be about 0.01 square inches? Explain your reasoning.*

Key Vocabulary

There are no new glossary terms introduced in this Problem.

Materials

Labsheets

- 4.1: Ballot Areas Table
- 4ACE: Exercise 1

Accessibility Labsheet

- 4ACE: Exercise 3
- 8-inch square of inch grid paper for demo
- inch grid paper or quarter-inch grid paper for students
- scissors

ACE

Assignment Guide for Problem 4.1

Applications: 1–3 | Connections: 19–22

Answers to Problem 4.1

A. **Areas of Ballots**

Number of Cuts	Area (in.^{2})
0	64
1	32
2	16
3	8
4	4
5	2
6	1
7	0.5
8	0.25
9	0.125
10	0.0625

B. Each cut makes the area of a ballot half the previous area.

C. $A = 64(12)^n$

D. **Area of Ballot**

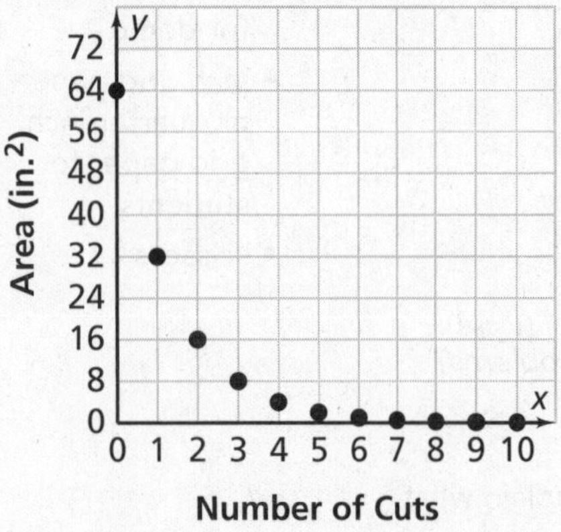

E. **1.** The pattern is different from the exponential growth patterns in that the numbers decrease instead of increase. It is similar in that you can derive each value (area) from the preceding value. Some students might notice that they can obtain each value by dividing the previous value by 2. Other students may notice that they can obtain each value by multiplying the previous value by $\frac{1}{2}$.

2. Some linear patterns of change show a decrease in the dependent variable as the independent variable increases. For example, $y = 400 - 500x$ might model a situation such as buying something for \$400 and paying that amount in \$50 increments. In this case of a linear relationship, the dependent variable decreases by a constant amount. In the case of an exponential decay relationship, the dependent variable decreases by nonconstant amounts; the decrease will be steeper to begin with and will then lessen. In the case of linear relationships, you calculate consecutive values of y by subtracting a constant amount; in the case of exponential decay relationships, you calculate consecutive values of y by multiplying by a factor less than 1.

Problem 4.2 Pacing 1 Day

4.2 Fighting Fleas: Representing Exponential Decay

Focus Question How can you recognize an exponential decay function from a contextual setting, table, graph, and equation that represents the function?

Launch

Talk with the class about the context of a flea medicine being administered to a dog and subsequently breaking down in the dog's blood. Display Teaching Aid 4.2A: Breakdown of Medicine.

Suggested Questions

- *According to the table, how much medicine was in the dog's blood initially?*
- *How much active medicine remained after 1 hour? After 2 hours?*
- *How would you describe the pattern of decline in the amount of active medicine in the dog's blood?*

Key Vocabulary

- decay factor
- exponential decay
- decay rate

Materials

Labsheet

- 4.2: Medicine Table

Teaching Aids

- 4.2A: Breakdown of Medicine
- 4.2B: Areas Versus Medicine

Explore

As you circulate, verify that students are finding a decay factor by dividing the milligrams of medicine remaining in the dog's blood in any hour by the milligrams remaining in the previous hour. Because the decay factor is less than 1, some students may be tempted to divide by the number for the next hour to get a number greater than 1.

Summarize

Have students compare the equation they wrote in this Problem to the equation for ballot area in Problem 4.1. Ask the following questions.

- *How do the equation for the ballot-area Problem,* $A = 64\left(\frac{1}{4}\right)^n$, *and the equation for this Problem,* $m = 400\left(\frac{1}{4}\right)^h$, *compare?*
- *How do these graphs compare?*
- *Why does it make sense to connect the points in the active-medicine graph but not in the ballot-area graph?*

Be sure to discuss the equation for the situation in Question B, focusing on the decay factor and its relationship to the decay rate.

- *Is the decay factor greater than 1 or less than 1?*
- *If 20% of the medicine is used each hour, what percent remains active in the blood each hour?*
- *What is the fractional equivalent of that percent?*
- *So, what is the decay factor in this situation?*

AT A GLANCE 4

ACE

Assignment Guide for Problem 4.2

Applications: 4–7 | Connections: 23–24
Extensions: 25

Answers to Problem 4.2

A. **1.** The amount of active medicine in the dog's blood each hour is one fourth the amount from the previous hour.

2. $m = 400\left(\frac{1}{4}\right)^h$

3. This graph has the same shape as the graph in Problem 4.1, but it has a greater initial value and the *y*-values decrease more quickly.

4. Both of the relationships displayed in the table and graph represent an exponential function showing exponential decay. Exponential patterns in the table and graph are similar to the pattern in Problem 4.1, in which a quantity decreases at each stage. They all show exponential decay. The decay factor in the table and graph is $\frac{1}{4}$.

B. **1.**

Breakdown of Medicine

Time Since Dose (hr)	Active Medicine in Blood (mg)
0	60
1	48
2	38.4
3	30.72
4	24.58
5	19.66
6	15.73

2.

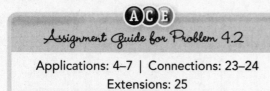

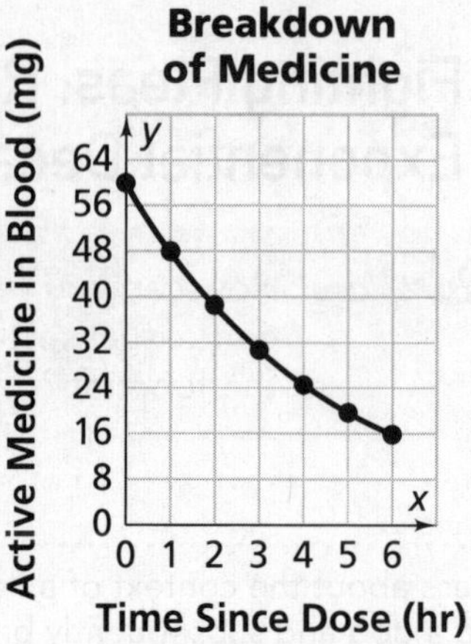

3. Janelle's equation gives the same quantities as the table. This is because when 20% of the active medicine is used, 80% remains. Therefore, the decay factor is 80%, or 0.8, and the equation is $m = 60(0.8)^h$.

4. The decay factor is the number by which you multiply one value to get the next value. With a decay rate of 20%, the medicine in the blood decreases from, for example, 60 mg to 48 mg. To get this, you have to multiply 60 by 0.8, not by 0.2. To find the amount remaining, you take away the amount that has decayed. In other words, you multiply the initial amount by 20% and then subtract the answer from the initial amount. This is the same as multiplying by 80%. For example: $60 \times 0.20 = 12$ (the amount of decay), so $60 - 12 = 48$ (the amount remaining), or $60 \times 0.8 = 48$.

5. To move from growth rate to growth factor, you add 100% to the number. For example, if the growth rate is 80%, then the growth factor is 180%. This is an example of the Distributive Property: $P + P \times 0.8 = (1 + 0.8) = 1.8P$. To move from decay rate to decay factor, you subtract the rate from 100% to get the decay factor. For example, if the decay rate is 20%, then the decay factor is 80%. This too is an example of the Distributive Property: $P - P \times 0.2 = (1 - 0.2) = P(0.8)$.

At a Glance

Problem 4.3 Pacing 1 Day

4.3 Cooling Water: Modeling Exponential Decay

Focus Question How can you find the initial population and decay factor for an exponential decay relationship?

Launch

Introduce the experiment by discussing the questions in the opening paragraph. Describe how students should conduct the experiment, emphasizing that they will need to record both the water temperature and the room temperature.

Explore

Suggested Questions

- *In Question A, in what way does the graph you have made look like or unlike other graphs of exponential decay relationships?*
- *Does the table for Question A indicate that you are working with an exponential decay relationship?*
- *Does the table in Question B indicate you are working with an exponential decay relationship? Explain.*

Summarize

As a class, compare the collected data and the graphs for each group. Ask how students found the decay factor. In the table, display for the class the ratios, which will vary. For Question B, ask the following.

- *To write an equation in the form $y = a(b)^x$, you need the values of a and b. What is the value of a in this situation?*
- *What information does a represent in this experiment?*
- *How did you find the decay factor for the cooling water?*
- *How does the decay factor affect the equation?*
- *What things might affect the cooling rate you found?*
- *If you wanted to get different cooling rates, how could you vary the experiment?*

As a class, choose one group's decay factor and starting value. Discuss the relationship of the graph of the equation to the graph of the group's experimental data. Students should notice that they are not identical. Review with the class the idea that mathematical models are a generalized view of the actual data.

Check for Understanding

- *Using the class equation, about how long will it take for the water temperature to reach room temperature?*

Key Vocabulary

There are no new glossary terms introduced in this Problem.

Materials

Labsheets
- 4.3: Water Cooling Table
- 4ACE: Exercise 15
- 4ACE: Exercise 16

- hot water
- cups for hot liquid
- watches or clocks with second hand
- graphing calculators
- graph paper
- thermometer
- CBLs

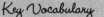

ACE

Assignment Guide for Problem 4.3

Applications: 8–18

Answers to Problem 4.3

The following answers are based on data in the Teacher's Guide, which was obtained from one class.

A. 1.

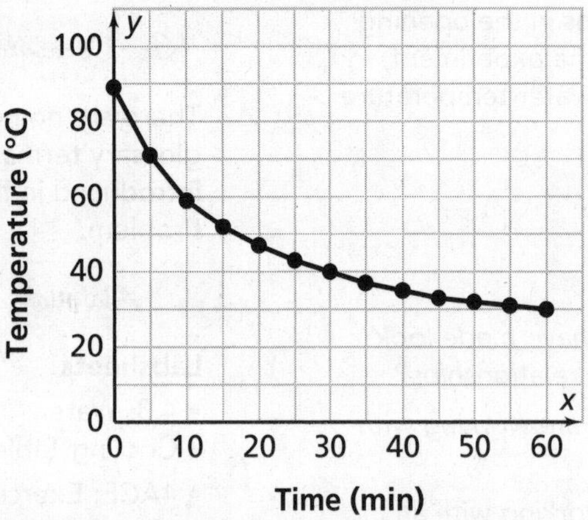

2. The temperature dropped quickly in the first 10 min; near the end of the hour, the change became minimal. The graph has the greatest change in the first 5 min and the least change at the end of the time period.

3. Students might say that the relationship is exponential because of the shape of the graph. However, if they examine the pattern of change in the table, it does not involve a decay factor. This is a good reminder of what exponential means.

B. 1. See the Teacher's Guide table.

2.

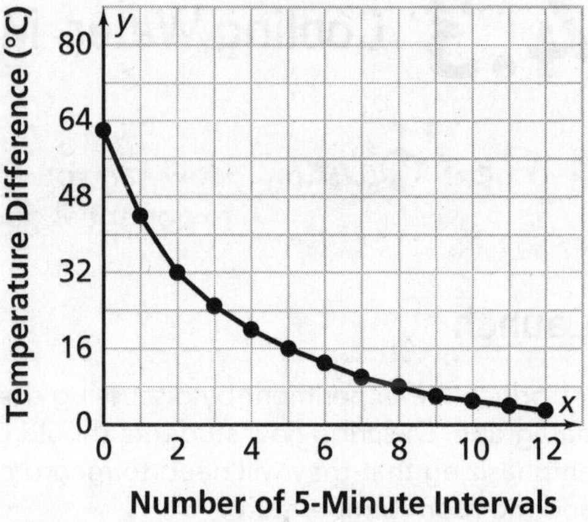

3. The time-versus-temperature-difference graph has the same pattern as the time-versus-water-temperature graph. The greatest change is in the first 5 min, and the least change is near the end of the time period.

4. You can estimate the decay factor by averaging the ratios between temperature differences: $(0.71 + 0.73 + 0.78 + 0.80 + 0.80 + 0.81 + 0.77 + 0.80 + 0.75 + 0.83 + 0.80 + 0.75) \div 12 \approx 0.78$.

5. $d = 62(0.78)^n$, where d is the temperature difference after n 5-min intervals

C. 1. The water temperature would eventually be the same as the room temperature, so the difference would become 0° C. The graph would flatten out along the x-axis.

2. Possible answers: Type of liquid; starting or room temperature; material, size, shape of the cup; movement of air across the liquid; whether the liquid was stirred.

3. Possible answers: Inaccurate timing of the readings, inaccurate reading of the thermometer, rounding.

D. The graph of A has the shape of exponential decay, but it is not an exponential decay relationship. The other graphs show exponential decay. The graphs drop quickly in the first few intervals of the x-axis and flatten out as the change becomes minimal. The rapidness of each graph is different, depending on the decay factor.

At a Glance Problem 5.1 Pacing $1\frac{1}{2}$ Days

5.1 Looking for Patterns Among Exponents

Focus Question What patterns did you observe in the table of powers?

Launch

Launch this problem by writing the values of $y = 2^x$, for whole-number x-values from 1 to 8. Write both the exponential and standard form 2^x for in the y-column.

Have students look for patterns in the table. Collect their discoveries on a large sheet of paper.

- *Does 2^4 equal $2(2^2)$? Does 2^6 equal $2(2^3)$? Explain.*

Next, introduce Problem 5.1. Make sure students understand how the table is organized.

Materials

Labsheets
- 5.1A: Table of Positive Powers
- 5.1B: Table of Negative Powers

Accessibility Labsheet
- 5.1C: Patterns in the Ones Digits

Teaching Aids
- 5.1A: Completed Table of Positive Powers
- 5.1B: Completed Table of Negative Powers
- poster of Teaching Aid 5.1A

Explore

If students are having trouble with using the patterns of the ones digits, ask the following questions.

- *What are the lengths of the cycles of repeating ones digits?*
- *Which bases have cycles of length 4? Of length 1? Of length 2?*
- *If you know the exponent, how can you use the pattern of the cycle to determine the ones digit of the power? For example, the ones digits for 2^n repeat in a cycle: 2, 4, 8, 6. How can you use this fact to find the ones digit of 2^{21}?*
- *Predict the ones digits for 31^{10}, 12^{10}, 17^{21}, and 29^{10}.*

Summarize

Ask for general patterns students found.

Spend some time discussing b^{-1} and b^0. These ideas are revisited in Problem 5.2.

ACE

Assignment Guide for Problem 5.1

Applications: 1 | Connections: 67–69
Extensions: 82–90

Answers to Problem 5.1

A. See Figure 1.

The sum of two even numbers is even. (Two rectangles with height 2 can be put together to form a larger rectangle with height 2.)

The completed table can be displayed using Teaching Aid 5.1A: Completed Table of Positive Powers.

B. Answer will vary. See the Explore notes for patterns in the ones digits for each base. The values of the digits are listed in the bottom row of Teaching Aid 5.1A: Completed Table of Positive Powers.

Here are some additional patterns students might notice.

Some numbers occur more than once in the powers chart. For example, 64 appears three times: $2^6 = 64$, $4^3 = 64$, and $8^2 = 64$.

Square numbers a^2 have ones digits 1, 4, 9, 6, 5, 6, 9, 4, 1, 0. There is symmetry around the 5. This will repeat with each 10 square numbers.

Fourth powers (1^4, 2^4, 3^4, etc.) have ones digits 0, 1, 5, and 6.

The fifth powers (1^5, 2^5, 3^5, etc.) have ones digits 1, 2, 3, 4, 5, 6, 7, 8, 9, and 0, in that order.

C. 1. Note: Students don't know the rules yet, so they look at the growth patterns in the table and work backward; multiplying by 2 produces more values going down the 2^x column, so dividing by 2 produces values going back up the 2^x column, etc. Students derive these rules in Problem 5.2.

See Figure 2.

The completed table can be displayed using Teaching Aid 5.1B: Completed Table of Negative Powers.

2. Yes. It is true that $a^0 = 1$ and that $a^{-1} = \frac{1}{a}$; for instance, $1^0 = 1$.

Figure 1

x	1^x	2^x	3^x	4^x	5^x	6^x	7^x	8^x	9^x	10^x
1	1	2	3	4	5	6	7	8	9	10
2	1	4	9	16	25	36	49	64	81	100
3	1	8	27	64	125	216	343	512	729	1,000
4	1	16	81	256	625	1,296	2,401	4,096	6,561	10,000
5	1	32	243	1,024	3,125	7,776	16,807	32,768	59,049	100,000
6	1	64	729	4,096	15,625	46,656	117,649	262,144	531,441	1,000,000
7	1	128	2,187	16,384	78,125	279,936	823,543	2,097,152	4,782,969	10,000,000
8	1	256	6,561	65,536	390,625	1,679,616	5,764,801	16,777,216	43,046,721	100,000,000
Ones Digits of Powers	1	2, 4, 8, 6	3, 9, 7, 1	4, 6	5	6	7, 9, 3, 1	8, 4, 2, 6	9, 1	0

Figure 2

−2	1	$\frac{1}{4}$	$\frac{1}{9}$	$\frac{1}{16}$	$\frac{1}{25}$	$\frac{1}{36}$	$\frac{1}{49}$	$\frac{1}{64}$	$\frac{1}{81}$	$\frac{1}{100}$
−1	$\frac{1}{1} = 1$	$\frac{1}{2}$	$\frac{1}{3}$	$\frac{1}{4}$	$\frac{1}{5}$	$\frac{1}{6}$	$\frac{1}{7}$	$\frac{1}{8}$	$\frac{1}{9}$	$\frac{1}{10}$
0	1	1	1	1	1	1	1	1	1	1
x	1^x	2^x	3^x	4^x	5^x	6^x	7^x	8^x	9^x	10^x
1	1	2	3	4	5	6	7	8	9	10
2	1	4	9	16	25	36	49	64	81	100

Problem 5.2 Pacing $1\frac{1}{2}$ Days

5.2 Rules of Exponents

Focus Question What are several rules for working with exponents and why do they work?

Launch

Tell students that in this Problem, they will look for a way to generalize these and other patterns for exponents and provide arguments for why they are true.

Materials

Labsheet
- 5.2: Rules for Exponents

Explore

If students have trouble explaining why a general rule works, have them connect the general rule to a specific case. For example, if students cannot explain why $a^m \times a^n = a^{m+n}$, ask them to first explain why $3^2 \times 3^4 = 3^6$.

Summarize

Ask different groups to present their reasoning for each part of the Problem. Use the completed powers table to illustrate the rules. For example, the rule $a^m \times a^n = a^{m+n}$ can be illustrated by looking at any column.

To help students with the division rules, ask the following questions.

- *Write $\frac{4^5}{4^6}$ as a single base.*
- *Does this fit the rules for division with exponents?*
- *How does inspecting a number tell you whether it is even or odd?*

Check for Understanding

- *Are the following equations true or false? Explain.*

$2^3 \times 2^2 = 4^5$ $\qquad$ $4^2 + 4^3 = 4^5$

$5^5 \times 2^5 = 10^{25}$ $\qquad$ $18^4 = 3^4 \times 6^4$

AT A GLANCE 5

Assignment Guide for Problem 5.2

Applications: 2–25 | Connections: 70–71
Extensions: 91

Answers to Problem 5.2

A. 1. a. $2^3 \times 2^2 = (2 \times 2 \times 2) \times (2 \times 2) = 2^5$

b. $3^4 \times 3^3 = (3 \times 3 \times 3 \times 3) \times (3 \times 3 \times 3) = 3^7$

c. $6^5 \times 6^5 = (6 \times 6 \times 6 \times 6 \times 6) \times (6 \times 6 \times 6 \times 6 \times 6) = 6^{10}$

2. If the base is same, you only need to add two exponents.

3. $a^m \times a^n = a^{m+n}$. This is true because the left side of the equality has a as a factor $m + n$ times. Or, some will write out

$$a^m \times a^n = \underbrace{(a \times a \times \ldots \times a)}_{\substack{m \text{ times} \\ a^m}} \times \underbrace{(a \times a \times \ldots \times a)}_{\substack{n \text{ times} \\ a^n}}$$

$$= \underbrace{(a \times a \times \ldots \times a)}_{\substack{(m+n) \text{ times} \\ a^{m+n}}} = a^{m+n}$$

B. 1. a. $\frac{3^5}{3^2} = 3^3$ or $\frac{3^5}{3^3} = 3^2$

b. $\frac{4^{11}}{4^5} = 4^6$ or $\frac{4^{11}}{4^6} = 4^5$

c. $\frac{5^{12}}{5^4} = 5^8$ or $\frac{5^{12}}{5^8} = 5^4$

2. If the base is the same, you only need to subtract the exponent of denominator from the exponent of numerator. Here are some examples:

$\frac{3^3}{3^2} = \frac{3 \times 3 \times 3}{3 \times 3} = 3$

$\frac{4^6}{4^5} = \frac{4 \times 4 \times 4 \times 4 \times 4 \times 4}{4 \times 4 \times 4 \times 4 \times 4} = 4^1 = 4$

$\frac{5^8}{5^4} = \frac{5 \times 5 \times 5 \times 5 \times 5 \times 5 \times 5 \times 5}{5 \times 5 \times 5 \times 5} = 5^4$

3. $\frac{a^m}{a^n} = a^{m-n}$. This is true because the left side of the equality has a as a factor $m - n$ times. Some students may claim that $\frac{a^m}{a^n} = a^{m-n}$ will lead to negative exponents if $m < n$. This is an opportunity to define a^{-n} as $\frac{1}{a^n}$.

C. 1. a. $2^3 \cdot 5^3 = (2 \times 2 \times 2) \times (5 \times 5 \times 5)$
$= (2 \times 5) \times (2 \times 5) \times (2 \times 5)$
$= 10^3$

b. $5^2 \cdot 6^2 = (5 \times 5) \times (6 \times 6)$
$= (5 \times 6) \times (5 \times 6) = 30^2$

c. $10^4 \cdot 2^4 = (10 \times 10 \times 10 \times 10) \times (2 \times 2 \times 2 \times 2)$
$= (10 \times 2) \times (10 \times 2) \times (10 \times 2) \times (10 \times 2) = 20^4$

2. If the exponent is same, you need to multiply the two bases.

3. $a^n \cdot b^n = (ab)^n$

$$a^m \times b^m = \underbrace{(a \times a \times \ldots \times a)}_{\substack{m \text{ times} \\ a^m}} \times \underbrace{(b \times b \times \ldots \times b)}_{\substack{m \text{ times} \\ b^m}}$$

$$= \underbrace{(ab \times ab \times \ldots \times ab)}_{\substack{m \text{ times} \\ ab^m}} = ab^m$$

D. 1. a. $(3^2)^2 = (3^2) \cdot (3^2) = 3^{2 \times 2} = 3^4$

b. $(5^3)^3 = (5^3) \cdot (5^3) \cdot (5^3) = 5^{3 \times 3} = 5^9$

c. $(2^2)^4 = (2^2) \cdot (2^2) \cdot (2^2) \cdot (2^2) = 2^{2 \times 4} = 2^8$

2. In raising a power to a power, you can think of $(a^m)^n$ as a^m used as a factor n times.

E. 1. $\frac{a^n}{a^n} = a^{n-n} = a^0$ but $\frac{a^n}{a^n} = 1$, so $a^0 = 1$.

Note: This is a subtle point. Some students might say that in the expression a^0, a is used as a factor 0 times, so the product should be 0. Some will use the same argument to say a^0 should be 1.

2. $\frac{1}{a}$, since $\frac{a^0}{a^1} = a^{0-1} = a^{-1}$.

3. $\frac{1}{a^m} = \frac{a^0}{a^m} = a^{0-m} = a^{-m}$

Note: Using the rules provides a logical argument that should help most students. Once a^{-n} is defined as $\frac{1}{a^n}$, the logic becomes a bit clearer.

Problem 5.3 Pacing 1 Day

5.3 Extending the Rules of Exponents

Focus Question How are the rules for integral exponents related to rational exponents? How are the rules for exponents useful in writing equivalent expressions with exponents?

Launch

Use the example of the amoeba population. Display the graph of $y = 4^x$.

Give the class time to explore the two methods for writing equivalent expressions for $16^{\frac{2}{3}}$ (the student strategies in Question A). Then summarize their findings. At this stage, using one or the other method, they should be convinced that the rules of exponents work for rational numbers.

Then let them work on the rest of Problem 5.3.

Key Vocabulary

- *n*th root

Materials

Teaching Aid

- 5.3: Graph of $y = 4^x$

Explore

Look at students' methods of calculating. They should extend the rules for whole-number exponents by using strategies similar to those in part (1) of Question A.

Summarize

Finish going over the answers from Questions B–E. Be sure to discuss the various ways that students may have solved individual problems.

Suggested Questions

- *Do the equations for rubas in Question C make sense in light of Problem 1.2? Explain.*
- *Do the equations in Question D make sense in the context of Problem 4.1? Explain.*
- *Can you use square roots to produce an expression equivalent to part (1) of Question E? Explain.*
- *Look back at the various situations in Growing, Growing, Growing. In which of these situations is it reasonable to look at fractional exponents? Explain why.*

Assignment Guide for Problem 5.3

Applications: 26–38 | Connections: 72–74; 79–81

Extensions: 92–93

Answers to Problem 5.3

A. 1. All of them are correct because

$16^{\frac{2}{3}} = 16^{\frac{1}{2}\times 3} = 16^{3\times\frac{1}{2}} = (16^1)16^{\frac{1}{2}}.$

2. Answers will vary. Possible answer:

a. Since $8 = 2^3$,

853 = ((23)13)5 = (23 × 13)5 = 25 = 32

b. Since $125 = 5^3$,

$125^{\frac{4}{3}} = \left(\left(5^3\right)^{\frac{1}{3}}\right)^4 = \left(5^{3\times\frac{1}{3}}\right)^4 = 5^4 = 625$

B. 1. Use Mari's method.

a. $4^{\frac{3}{2}} \cdot 4^{\frac{1}{2}} = \left(4^{\frac{1}{2}}\right)^3 \cdot 4^{\frac{1}{2}}$

$= 2^3 \cdot 2 = 8 \cdot 2 = 16$

b. $4^{\frac{1}{3}} \cdot 2^{\frac{1}{3}} = (4 \cdot 2)^{\frac{1}{3}} = 8^{\frac{1}{3}}$

$\left(2^3\right)^{\frac{1}{3}} = 2^{3\times\frac{1}{3}} = 2$

c. $\left(2^{\frac{5}{3}}\right)^3 = \left(2^{\frac{1}{3}}\right)^{5\times 3} = \left(2^{\frac{1}{3}}\right)^{15} = 2^5 = 32$

d. $\dfrac{25^{\frac{3}{2}}}{25^{\frac{1}{2}}} = \dfrac{\left(25^{\frac{1}{2}}\right)^3}{25^{\frac{1}{2}}} = \dfrac{5^3}{5} = 5^{3-1} = 5^2 = 25$

2. Yes.

a. $4^{\frac{3}{2}} \cdot 4^{\frac{1}{2}} = 4^{\frac{3}{2}+\frac{1}{2}} = 4^2 = 16$

b. $4^{\frac{1}{3}} \cdot 2^{\frac{1}{3}} = (4 \cdot 2)^{\frac{1}{3}} = 8^{\frac{1}{3}}$

$= (2^3)^{\frac{1}{3}} = 2^{3\times\frac{1}{3}} = 2^1 = 2$

c. $\left(2^{\frac{5}{3}}\right)^3 = 2^{\frac{5}{3}\times 3} = 2^5 = 32$

d. $\dfrac{25^{\frac{3}{2}}}{25^{\frac{1}{2}}} = \dfrac{5^{2\times\frac{3}{2}}}{5^{2\times\frac{1}{2}}} = \dfrac{5^3}{5^1} = 5^{3-1} = 5^2 = 25$ or

$25^{\frac{3}{2}-\frac{1}{2}} = 25^{\frac{2}{2}} = 25$

C. Both of them are correct, because

$\frac{1}{2}(2^n) = 2^{-1} \cdot 2^n = 2^{n-1}$

D. All three of them are correct, because

$\frac{64}{2^n} = 64 \cdot \frac{1}{2^n} = 64(2^{-n}) =$

$64(2^{-1\times n}) = 64(2^{-1})^n = 64\left(\frac{1}{2}\right)^n = 64(0.5)^n$

E. 1. $x^{\frac{1}{2}} \cdot x^{\frac{3}{2}} = x^{\frac{1}{2}+\frac{3}{2}} = x^2$

2. $x^{\frac{2}{3}} \div x^{\frac{7}{6}} = x^{\frac{2}{3}-\frac{7}{6}} = x^{-\frac{1}{2}} = \dfrac{1}{x^{\frac{1}{2}}}$

3. $\left(2x^{\frac{1}{2}}\right)^2 = 2^2 \cdot \left(x^{\frac{1}{2}}\right)^2 = 4x$

4. $\left(16x^{\frac{4}{3}}\right)^{\frac{1}{2}} = \sqrt{16} \cdot \sqrt{\left(x^{\frac{4}{3}}\right)} = 4x^{\frac{2}{3}}$

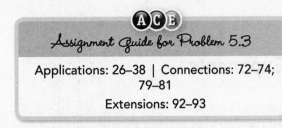

Problem 5.4 Pacing 1 Day

5.4 Operations with Scientific Notation

Focus Question How does scientific notation help to solve problems?

Launch

Suggested Questions

- *Which is greater—the amount of water used by irrigation or the amount used by livestock?*
- *How many gallons of water are used in a year for irrigation? (A year has 365 days.)*
- *How might you carry out this calculation?*

Explore

Look for various strategies students have for carrying out the calculations. Ask students if Gary's and Judy's strategies are similar to ones they did in their groups. Make note of strategies that are close to the strategies provided or quite different.

The strategies that students use in Question A will be helpful in Questions B–D. As students are working on Questions B–D, ask the groups if they are using the same strategies for as they did for Question A. There may be variation across groups that stick with the same strategy, so make note of the variations for the Summarize. If groups change their strategies or shift between them, also make note of the changes for the Summarize.

Summarize

Go over the questions. The main purpose of the summary is to have students explore a variety of strategies for solving these problems. In some cases they may see why one strategy might work better than another.

Checking for Understanding

You may want to give students some additional practice at the end of the lesson. You can have students work through a few of them as a final check, or you can display one or two and have students talk with others in their group about how they would go about solving them.

1. $(3.0 \times 10^6)(2.5 \times 10^{14})$
2. $(3.5 \times 10^4)(6.0 \times 10^5)$
3. $(8.4 \times 10^{12})(3.2 \times 10^2)$
4. $(9.3 \times 10^{13}) \div (3.1 \times 10^9)$
5. $(7.5 \times 10^8) \div (3.0 \times 10^7)$
6. $(4.2 \times 10^6) \div (8.4 \times 10^4)$
7. $(8.32 \times 10^{73}) \div (8.32 \times 10^{74})$

ACE

Assignment Guide for Problem 5.4

Applications: 39–62 | Connections: 75–76

Answers to Problem 5.4

A. 1. Answers will vary about which strategy makes the most sense to students, so make sure students justify why each strategy makes more sense. For example, Gary's strategy relates to thinking proportionally, which means the ratio of the values is the same as the ratio of the number of millions of each value. Judy's method keeps the scientific notation form throughout the problem. Any method of solution a student chooses is acceptable, as long as he or she can explain why it is equivalent to Gary's or Judy's.

2. Students may be surprised that the number of gallons water used per day per person is more than 1,000 gallons, but the data are not about personal consumption. The figure is an average for the whole country. Livestock, irrigation, and generating electricity all use huge amounts of water but go largely unnoticed. One question that students might come up with is how the water usage breaks down in their part of the country. In rural areas, it may be that the largest amount of water is used for irrigation, while in urban locations it may be that the largest amount of water is used for generating electricity.

3. Possible questions: How much more water is used for irrigation than livestock? What percent of the total water usage is used for cooling electric power plants?

B. 1. About 90.5 gallons of water is used per person per day. Students might use strategies similar to what they used for Question A. This amount is less than 7% of the average for the United States as whole.

2. Because public water supplies serve cities and towns (urban and suburban areas), there is likely a small portion of the water used for livestock and irrigation.

3. 1.05×10^{-3}

C. 1. The percent used for irrigation is $(1.28 \times 10^{11}) \div (4.10 \times 10^{11}) \approx 0.31 = 31\%$.

2. The percent used for livestock is $(2.14 \times 10^{9}) \div (4.10 \times 10^{11}) \approx 0.005 = 0.5\%$

D. 1.

$$\begin{aligned}(4.0 \times 10^2)(3.5 \times 10^3) &= (4.0 \cdot 3.5) \times (10^2 \times 10^3)\\ &= 14.0 \times 10^5\\ &= 1.4 \times 10^6\end{aligned}$$

2.

$$\begin{aligned}(2.0 \times 10^6) \div (2.5 \times 10^2) &= \frac{(2.0 \times 10^6)}{(2.5 \times 10^2)}\\ &= \frac{2.0}{2.5} \times \frac{10^6}{10^2}\\ &= 0.8 \times 10^4\\ &= 8.0 \times 10^3\end{aligned}$$

At a Glance

Problem 5.5 Pacing $1\frac{1}{2}$ Days

5.5 Revisiting Exponential Functions

Focus Question What are the effects of a and b on the graph of $y = a(b^x)$, $b \neq 0$?

Launch

Remind students that the situations they have explored in this Unit can be modeled with equations of the form $y = a(b^x)$ where a is the initial, or starting, value and b is the growth or decay factor.

Ask students to identify the value of a and of b in each equation.

- $y = 2^n$
- $z = 4^t$
- $Y = 25(3^d)$
- $w = (3^n)$

Check to see that students understand the meaning of the notation $0 \leq x \leq 5$.

Materials

Accessibility Labsheets

- 5.5A: Effects of b on $y = a(b^x)$
- 5.5B: Effects of a on $y = a(b^x)$
- 5ACE: Exercise 15

Assessments

- Self-Assessment
- Notebook Checklist
- Unit Test

Explore

Check to see that students are discussing the effects of a and b on the graphs.

Summarize

Suggested Questions

- *What similarities do you notice among the graphs? What differences do you notice?*
- *How could you predict the shape of the graph for the equation $y = b^x$ when given a specific value of b?*
- *What would the graph look like if b were equal to 1?*
- *How does the value of a affect the graph of $y = a(b^x)$?*
- *How do the values of m and b affect the graph of $y = mx + b$? How do these effects compare to those for graphs of exponential equations?*

Check for Understanding

Without sketching a graph or using a calculator, have students describe the shape of each graph, including the *y*-intercept and patterns of change.

- $y = 4^x$
- $y = 0.25^x$
- $y = 5(3^x)$
- $y = 6x + 10$
- $y = -6x + 10$
- $y = 6x - 10$

AT A GLANCE 5

Assignment Guide for Problem 5.5

Applications: 63–66 | Connections: 77–78

Answers to Problem 5.5

A. 1. Check students' work.

2. The greater b is, the faster the graph rises.

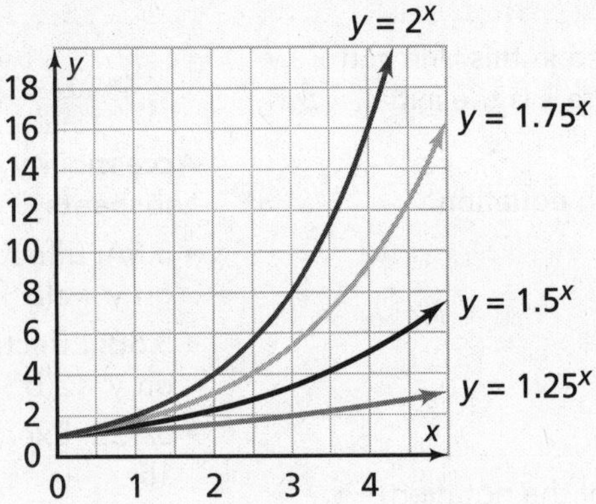

3. The smaller b is, the faster the graph falls.

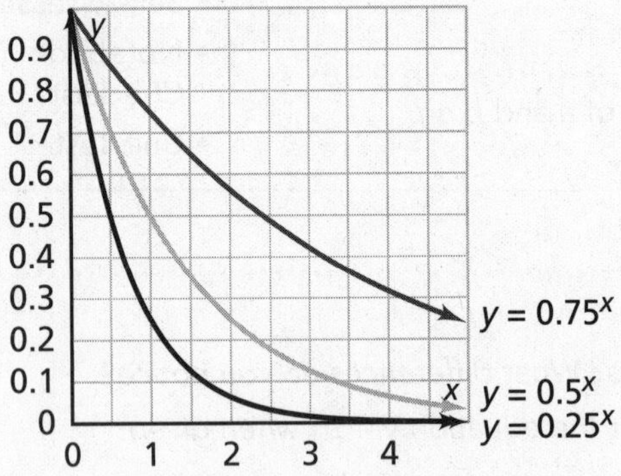

4. When b is greater than 1, the graph curves upward slowly at first and then very rapidly. When b is a positive number less than 1, the graph curves downward, rapidly at first and then more slowly until it is almost horizontal and very close to the x-axis. In both cases the y-intercept is a, because $b^0 = 1$ for all nonzero values of b.

B. 1. Answer will vary.

2.

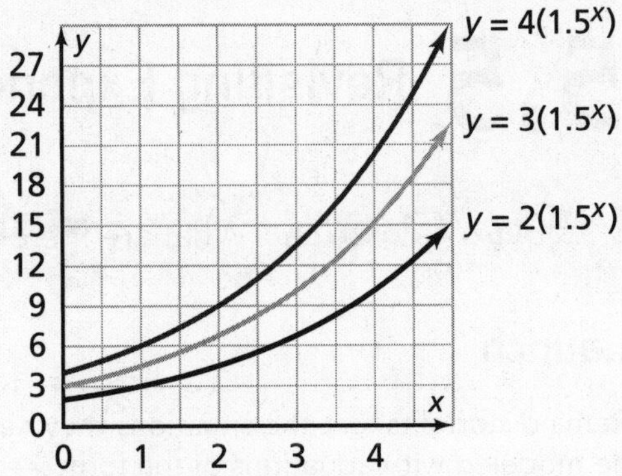

3.

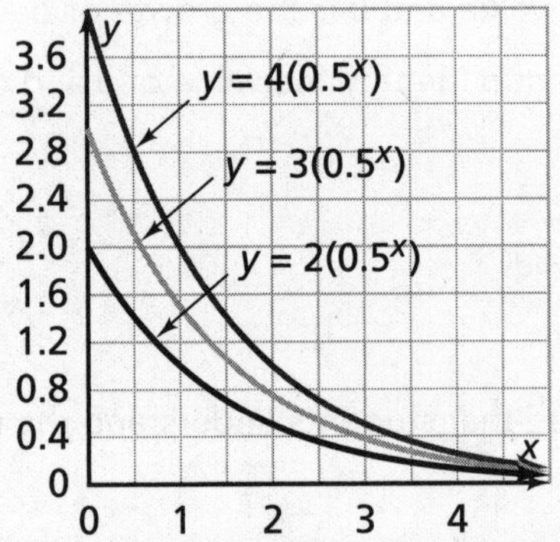

4. For an exponential function with the rule $y = a(b^x)$, the y-intercept is always equal to a. An increase in a makes the graph increase or decrease faster.

C. Linear functions have a constant rate of change (their slope, m). Exponential functions have a constant multiplier. Both functions have a single y-intercept. For linear equations, increasing or decreasing is dependent on the slope (positive slope means increasing; negative slope decreasing). For exponential equations ($y = a(b^x)$) the function increases when $a < 0$ and $0 < b < 1$, or $a > 0$ and $b > 1$. It decreases when $a > 0$ and $0 < b < 1$, or when $a < 0$ and $b > 1$.

At a Glance

Pacing ☐ Day

Mathematical Goals

Launch

Materials

Explore

Materials

Summarize

Materials

Notes

Applications

1. a.

Cutting Processes	Number of Ballots
1	3
2	9
3	27
4	81
5	243

b. $3^{10} = 59{,}049$; 3^n

c. 13. After 13 cuts, there would be $1{,}594{,}323 = 3^{13}$ ballots, which is over 1 million ballots; but 3^{12} is less than 1 million.

2. Gabriel's conjecture is correct. Because each person is cutting ballots, each person would have 8 ballots, or 32 total. The reason why Chen's conjecture is incorrect is because each person is starting with their own piece of paper. His answer would be correct if after he cut his paper in half three times he handed his pile to the next person and they continued that way.

3. a. **Angie's Ancestors**

Generation	Number of Ancestors
0	1
1	2
2	4
3	8
4	16
5	32
6	64
7	128
8	256
9	512
10	1,024
11	2,048
12	4,096

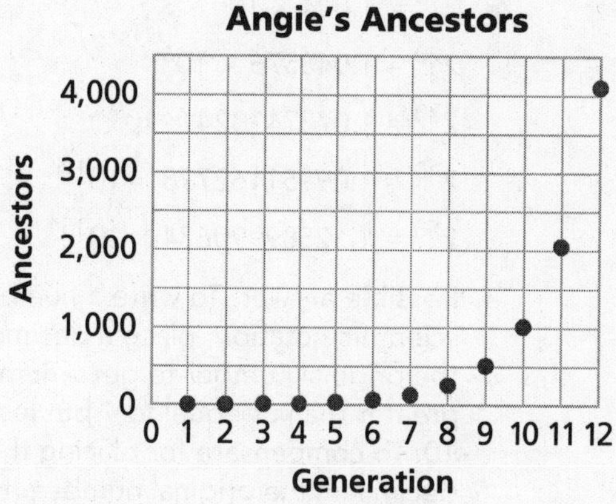

b. $a = 2^n$, where a is the number of ancestors and n is the generation number.

c. 8,190. You can find this by adding $2 + 4 + 8 + \ldots + 4{,}096$

Note: See the Math Background for a description of how to use a calculator to find the sum of a sequence. The ancestor pattern is identical to the pattern in the paper-cutting activity of Problem 1.1 and is very similar to the chessboard pattern in Problem 1.2. The only noticeable difference is that, in Problem 1.2, $n = 0$ doesn't make sense because there is not a square 0. (The graph for the rubas problem in Problem 1.2 is a translation of the graph that applies to both Problem 1.1 and the ancestor problem.) If you go back 40 generations, the number of ancestors exceeds the number of people who have ever lived!

4. a. square 33: $2^{32} = 4{,}294{,}967{,}296$

square 34: $2^{33} = 8{,}589{,}934{,}592$

square 35: $2^{34} = 17{,}179{,}869{,}184$

b. square 41; this is because it is the number of rubas on square 32 times nine more factors of 2.

c. The display probably reads 1.09951162778 E12. There is an E in the middle of the number.

d. $1.09951162778 \times 10^{12}$ (There are occasions when the calculator display will not give the last few digits exactly.)

e. $2^{10} = 1.024 \times 10^3$

$2^{20} = 1.048576 \times 10^6$

$2^{30} = 1.073741824 \times 10^9$

$2^{40} = 1.09951162778 \times 10^{12}$

$2^{50} = 1.12589990684 \times 10^{15}$

f. Possible answer: To write a number in scientific notation, place a decimal in the original number to get a number greater than or equal to 1 but less than 10. To compensate for placing the decimal in the original number, multiply the new number by a power of ten that will give you back your original number.

5. 1.0×10^8

6. $2.9678900522 \times 10^{10}$

7. 1.19505×10^{13}

8. 643,999,001

9. 889,234

10. 34,348,567,000

Values given for Exercises 11–15 are for the standard screen of the TI-83. Different calculators will give different results.

11. a. 20

b. 20

c. 9

d. 4

12. a. 10

b. 5

c. 8; **Note:** The question asks about $1{,}000(n^n)$ and not $(1{,}000n)^n$. Students often get confused by the notation $1{,}000n^n$, which means $1{,}000(n^n)$.

13. a. Amoeba Reproduction

Time (hr)	Amoebas
0	1
1	4
2	16
3	64
4	256
5	1,024
6	4,096
7	16,384
8	65,536

b. $a = 4^t$; time t is the independent variable and the number of amoebas a is the dependent variable.

c. 10 hours; at 10 hours, there will be 1,048,576 amoebas present

d. **Amoeba Reproduction**

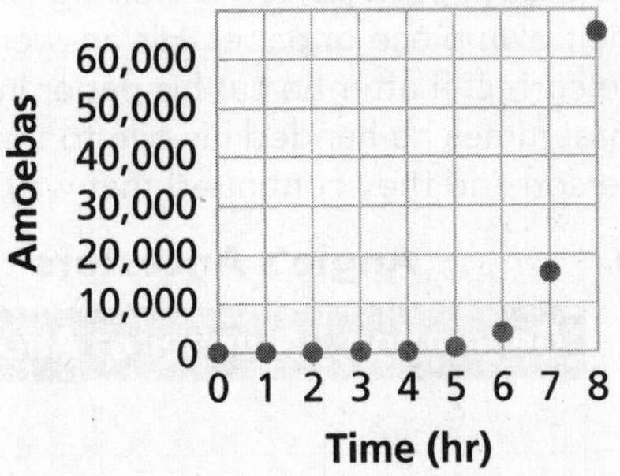

e. The pattern of change in the number of amoebas is similar to the pattern of change in the number of ancestors in ACE #2 because it is exponential. The difference between the two patterns is that the number of amoebas increases more rapidly than the number of ancestors because the number of amoebas quadruples at each stage, while the number of ancestors only doubles. This doubling pattern is also similar to the pattern of cutting a piece of paper to make ballots and to the rubas problem.

14. a. Plan 1

Day	1	2	3	4	5	6	7	8	9	10	11	12
Donation	$1	$2	$4	$8	$16	$32	$64	$128	$256	$512	$1,024	$2,048

Plan 2

Day	1	2	3	4	5	6	7	8	9	10
Donation	$1	$3	$9	$27	$81	$243	$729	$2,187	$6,561	$19,683

Plan 3

Day	1	2	3	4	5	6	7	8
Donation	$1	$4	$16	$64	$256	$1,024	$4,096	$16,384

b. Plan 1: $d = 2^n$

Plan 2: $d = 3^n$

Plan 3: $d = 4^n$

c. All three plans are exponential functions because each can be written with a growth factor.

d. Plan 2

15. a. Grandmother's and Aunt Josie's plans are linear and Uncle Sebastián's and Father's plans are exponential.

b. Grandmother: $a = 2n - 1$

Father: $a = 3^{n-1}$

Aunt Josie: $a = 1.5n + 0.5$

Uncle Sebastián: $a = 2^{n-1}$

n is the independent variable and a is the dependent variable in all four equations.

c. Grandmother: $39

Father: $1,162,261,467

Aunt Josie: $30.50

Uncle Sebastián: $524,288

16. a. Graph 1 represents $y = 2^x$ because it is a curve. Graph 2 represents $y = 2x + 1$ because it is a straight line.

b. In both graphs, the horizontal change is constant. In the graph of $y = 2x + 1$, the vertical change is also constant. In the graph of $y = 2x$, the vertical change increases.

c. Graph 1 represents an exponential function because its equation is $y = 2^x$. Graph 2 represents a linear equation because its equation is $y = 2x + 1$.

17. a. linear

b. $y = 2.5x + 10$

18. a. exponential

b. $y = 6^x$

19. neither

20. a. exponential

b. $y = 2^{x+1}$

21. neither (In fact, this is quadratic. Students will study quadratic relationships in the unit *Frogs, Fleas, and Painted Cubes*).

CONNECTIONS

22. 2^4

23. 10^7

24. $(2.5)^5$

25. 1,024

26. 100

27. 19,683

28. Because 5^2 means $5 \cdot 5$ and 5^4 means $5 \cdot 5 \cdot 5 \cdot 5$, 5^4 also equals $5^2 \cdot 5^2 = 25 \cdot 25 = 625$.

29. Because 5^{11} has one more factor of 5 than 5^{10} has, it equals $5^{10} \cdot 5 = 9{,}765{,}625 \cdot 5 = 48{,}828{,}125$.

30. A

31. 10^9

32. 9^6 is less than 1 million. Possible explanation: The product of six 9s must be less than the product of six 10s, which is 10^6 or 1 million.

33. 3^{10} is less than 1 million. Possible explanation:

$3^{10} = 3 \cdot 3 \cdot 3 \cdot 3 \cdot 3 \cdot 3 \cdot 3 \cdot 3 \cdot 3 \cdot 3 = 9 \cdot 9 \cdot 9 \cdot 9 \cdot 9 = 9^5$, which is less than 10^6.

34. 11^6 is greater than 10^6 or 1 million, because to find 11^6, you multiply 11 by itself six times. The result must be greater than if you multiply 10 by itself 6 times.

35. $5^3 = 125$

36. 2^6 or 4^3

37. 3^4

38. 5^5

39. 2^{10} or 4^5

40. 2^{12} or 4^6

41. a. After 20 cuts; $1{,}048{,}576 \div 250 \approx$ 4,194 in.; about 349.5 ft; after 30 cuts; $1{,}073{,}741{,}824 \div 250 \approx$ 4,294,967 in.; about 67.8 mi.

b. 12 cuts; a foot-high stack has $250 \times 12 = 3{,}000$ ballots. Because 11cuts gives 2,048 ballots and 12 cuts gives 4,096 ballots, Chen would have to make at least 12 cuts to get 3,000 ballots.

c. The distance to the moon, in inches, is approximately

$$240{,}000 \times 5280 \times 12 \approx 1.52 \times 10^{10}.$$

This means we need about $1.52 \times 10^{10} \times 250 \approx 3.80 \times 10^{12}$ sheets. To obtain this many sheets, we need 42 cuts, since $2^{42} \approx 4.39 \times 10^{12}$ and 41 cuts gives only half this number.

42. square 10: \$5.12; square 20: \$5,242.88; square 30: \$5,368,709.12; square 40: \$5,497,558,138.88; square 50; about $\$5.63 \times 10^{12}$; square 60: about $\$5.76 \times 10^{15}$.

43. When $n = 64$, the number of rubas is $2^{64-1} \approx 9.22 \times 10^{18}$. The stack would have been about $(9.22 \times 10^{18}) \times 0.06 = 5.53 \times 10^{17}$ in., or 4.61×10^{16} ft, or 8.73×10^{12} miles high.

44. a. $r = 100 + 25(n - 1)$ or $r = 25n + 75$

b. The graph will look linear. You might want to ask students to draw the graph.

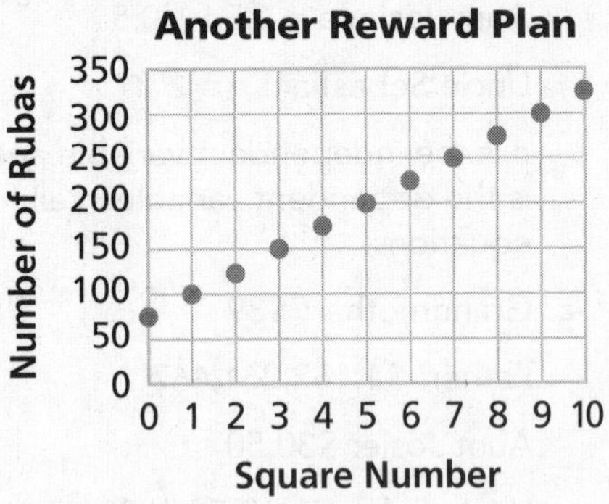

c. 2,125 rubas; 6,750 rubas

45. slope: 3; y-intercept: -10

46. slope: -5.6; y-intercept: 1.5

47. slope: $\frac{2}{5}$; y-intercept: 15

48. any equation with a coefficient of less than $\frac{2}{5}$; Possible answers: $y = \frac{1}{5}x + 3$; $y = \frac{1}{6}x + 15$

Extensions

49. a. Equation 1: $r = 3^2 - 1 = 9 - 1 = 8$

Equation 2: $r = 3^{2-1} = 3^1 = 3$

b. Equation 1: $r = 3^{10} - 1 = 59{,}048$

Equation 2: $r = 3^{10-1} = 3^9 = 19{,}683$

c. The equations give different values of r because subtraction is used differently. In one equation, 1 is subtracted from n and the result becomes the exponent of 3; in the other, n is used as the exponent of 3, and 1 is subtracted from the result.

Note: For $n \geq 0$, the result of Equation 1 will always be greater than that of Equation 2 because the exponent is greater. Subtracting from greater exponential contribution is almost insignificant.

d. The equation $r = 3^{n-1}$ represents an exponential function whose growth rate is 3. That is, as n increases by 1, r increases by a factor of 3. The equation $r = 3^n - 1$ does not represent an exponential function, because as n increases by 1, r does not increase by a constant factor.

50. a. $b = 2^n$, where b is the number of ballots made and n is the number of cuts.

b. From the table, 2^0 must equal 1. When you evaluate 2^0 with a calculator, the answer is 1.

c. The value of any non-zero number b raised to a power of 0 is 1.

Note: Talk with students about why this makes sense. Because $b^1 = b$ and because exponents tell us how many factors of the base to use, $b \times b^0 = b^{1+0}$ must equal to $1 + 0$ factors of b, which is just b; so b^0should be 1 to make all of the other ideas about exponents work out. Some students might say that for the pattern to continue backwards, 2^0 must equal 1. Explain that mathematicians decided the world of mathematics would make more sense if b^0 is defined as 1 for $b \neq 0$.

51. a.

Reward Plan 1

Square	Number of Rubas on Square	Total number of Rubas
1	1	1
2	2	3
3	4	7
4	8	15
5	16	31
6	32	63
7	64	127
8	128	255
9	256	511
10	512	1,023

b. Each entry in the total column is 1 less than the entry in the next individual square column. Another pattern is double the total rubas at a square and add 1 to get the total rubas at the next square. The relationship in the second column represents an exponential function because as the square number increases by 1, the number of rubas increases by a factor of 2. The third or last column is not an exponential function, because as the square number increases by 1, the number of rubas does not increase by a constant factor.

c. $t = 2^n - 1$

d. The total t will exceed 1,000,000 when 20 squares have been covered;

$t = 2^{20} - 1 = 1{,}048{,}575$ rubas.

e. With all 64 squares covered, the total would be $t = 2^{64} - 1 \approx 1.84 \times 10^{19}$ rubas.

52. a. Possible answer: The King would most likely pick Plan 4, since that requires him to pay the least amount of money.

b. Possible answer: The peasant would most likely pick Plan 1, since that would earn her the most money.

c. Check students' work.

ACE Answers Investigation 2

Applications

1. a. $b = 4^n$

b. $4^7 = 16{,}384$ bacteria

c. 65,536; this can be found by computing $16{,}384 \cdot 4$ because $4^8 = 4^7 \times 4$.

d. 10 hours. There will be at least 1 million bacteria in the colony after 9 hr and before 10 hr, as shown by $4^9 = 262{,}144$ and $4^{10} = 1{,}048{,}576$. (**Note:** This is essentially solving the equation $1{,}000{,}000 = 4^n$. Students can solve this problem in a variety of ways. They might guess and check values of n in 4^n. They might make a chart. They might enter the equation into a calculator and look at the table. They might trace a calculator graph, although setting an appropriate graphing window for exponential equations can be challenging.)

e. $b = 50(4^n)$

f. There will be 13,107,200 bacteria after 9 hr and 52,428,800 after 10 hr. We can find these by multiplying the number of bacteria at 8 hours by 4, and then multiplying that number by 4.

2. a. **Loon Lake Plant Growth**

Year	Area Covered (ft^2)
0	5,000
1	7,500
2	11,250
3	16,875
4	25,312.5
5	37,968.75

b. 10 yr, actually slightly more than 9 years

3. a. **Leaping Lenora's Salary**

Year	Salary
1	$20,000
2	$40,000
3	$80,000
4	$160,000
5	$320,000
6	$640,000
7	$1,280,000
8	$2,560,000
9	$5,120,000
10	$10,240,000

b. $20,460,000; **Note:** Students can find this by adding the amounts in the table or by using their calculators to find the sum of the sequence of $S = 10{,}000(2^n)$ from $n = 1$ to 10.

c. Yes, the relationship is an exponential function because the growth pattern is doubling from year to year.

d. $s = 20{,}000(2^{n-1})$ or $s = 10{,}000(2^n)$

4 a. 25 beetles; 35 beetles; 45 beetles

b. 45 beetles; 135 beetles; 405 beetles

c. $b = 5 + 10m$, where b is the number of beetles and m is the number of months

d. $b = 5(3^m)$ or $b = 15(3^{m-1})$, where b is the number of beetles and m is the number of months.

e. 19.5 months; solve $200 = 5 + 10m$.

f. Between 3 and 4 months; there are 135 beetles after 3 months and 405 beetles after 4 months. (**Note:** Students won't be able to solve the exponential equation algebraically. They can find an approximate solution by scrolling through a calculator table for the equation, using appropriate increments. Or, students might graph the equation and trace its graph.)

5. a. Yes; 60; the number of fruit flies in any generation divided by the number in the previous generation is 60.

b. 1,555,200,000;

$432{,}000 \times 60 \times 60 = 1.5552 \times 10^9$

c. $p = 2(60^g)$

d. 4

6. a. 12 mice; There were 36 mice after 1 month and the growth factor is 3. So at 0 months, there were $36 \div 3 = 12$ mice.

b. $p = 12(3^n)$. 12 is the original population, 3 is the growth factor, p is the population, n is the number of months. (Or, $p = 36(3^{n-1})$, where 36 is the population after 1 month.)

7. a. 8 fleas

b. Yes, the relationship is exponential. The growth factor is 3.

c. $8(3^{10}) = 472,392$ fleas

Note: Point out to students that this answer demonstrates that exponential growth equations have limits as models of real-life phenomena. Although something might start out increasing in a nearly exponential way, the predictive validity of the model will eventually break down.

8. a.

x	y
0	150
1	300
2	600
3	1,200
4	2,400
5	4,800

b. The starting population, or initial value, is 150, and the growth factor is 2.

9. growth factor: 3; y-intercept: 300

10. growth factor: 3; y-intercept: 300

11. growth factor: 2; y-intercept: 6,500

12. growth factor: 7; y-intercept: 2

13. a. After 2 yr, the lizard population was 40.

b. After 1 yr, the lizard population was 20.

c. between years 3 and 4

d. Divide the population for one year by the population for the previous year. For example, divide the population for year 3, which is 80, by the population for year 2, which is 40: $80 \div 40 = 2$.

14. a. The growth factor for Species X is 3 because the y-value for each point is 3 times the previous y-value.
The growth factor for Species Y is 2 because the y-value for each point is 2 times the previous y-value.

b. The y-intercept is (0, 5), so the starting population for Species X is 5.

c. The y-intercept is (0, 25), so the starting population for Species Y is 25.

d. $y = 5(3^x)$

e. $y = 25(2^x)$

f. (5, 1,215) is a solution for Species X. If we substitute 5 for x into each equation, we get 1,215 for Species X.

Connections

15. D

16. G

17. 4.88×10^7

18. Less than; 1 million is 10^6 and $3 < 10$. Therefore, $3^6 < 10^6$.

19. Less than; 1 million is 10^6 and $9 < 10$. Therefore, $9^5 < 9^6 < 10^6$.

20. Greater than; 1 million is 10^6 and $10 < 12$. Therefore, $10^6 < 12^6$.

21. $3^2 \times 5$

22. $2^4 \times 3^2$

23. $2^3 \times 11 \times 23$

24. a. The y-intercept is (0,10) for each equation.

b. If you make a table of (x, y) values for Equation 1 for consecutive x-values, you will see that the y-values decrease by 5, so the rate of change is -5. In the table for Equation 2, the values increase. If you subtract successive y-values, you get differences of 40, 200, 1,000, and so on. So the rate of change is increasing. (Students will learn in Investigation 3 that the growth rate is 400%.) (**Note:** Students may describe the pattern of change for Equation 2 multiplicatively, saying that each y-value is 5 times the previous y-value. You could ask these students to describe the change additively, which will get at the increasing rate of change described above.)

c. In Equation 1, the rate of change (the slope) is the -5 in front of the x. In the second equation the rate of change increases. Y will be growing 5 times as fast between $x = 2$ and $x = 3$ as it grew between $x = 1$ and $x = 2$. It is easier to see in a table. However, the growth factor of 5 can be seen in the equation as the number raised to the exponent. (**Note:** Students will be introduced to rate of change of exponential equations in Investigation 3, so this problem is just to get them to think about patterns of change for linear and exponential functions.)

d. Look at the vertical distance between points for each horizontal change of 1 unit. In the graph of Equation 1, the vertical distance between any two points is 5. In the graph of Equation 2, the vertical distance increases, indicating that the y-values are increasing at a faster and faster rate. Students may also describe this multiplicatively at this time. That is, each y-value is increasing 5 times the previous y-value.

25. $y = \frac{1}{4} + 4$; slope is $\frac{1}{4}$, y-intercept is (0, 4)

26. $y = 2x - 6$; slope is 2, y-intercept is $(0, -6)$

27. $y = 3$; slope is 0, y-intercept is (0, 3)

28. $y = -3x - 3$; slope is -3, y-intercept is $(0, -3)$

29. a.

Enlargement	Dimensions (cm)	Perimeter (cm)	Area (cm^2)
0 (original)	2 by 3	10	6
1	4 by 6	20	24
2	8 by 12	40	96
3	16 by 24	80	384
4	32 by 48	160	1,536
5	64 by 96	320	6,144

b. Exponential; each perimeter is multiplied by 2 to obtain the next perimeter.

c. Exponential; each area is multiplied by 4 to obtain the next area. (**Note:** Because both width and length increase by a factor of 2, area increases by a factor of 4.)

d. $P = 10(2^n)$

e. $A = 6(4^n)$ or $A = 3(2^n) \times 2(2^n)$

f. Perimeter and area would still increase exponentially, but the related equations would be $P = 10(3^n)$ and $A = 6(9^n)$.

30. Ahmad; expressed as a percent, Kele's scale factor is 200%, which is less than 250%.

31. C

32. gizmo seller, gadget inspector, widget designer

Extensions

33. a.

x	y
0	1
1	1
2	1
3	1
4	1

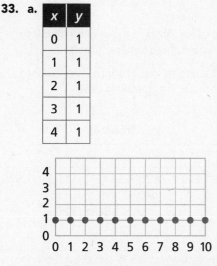

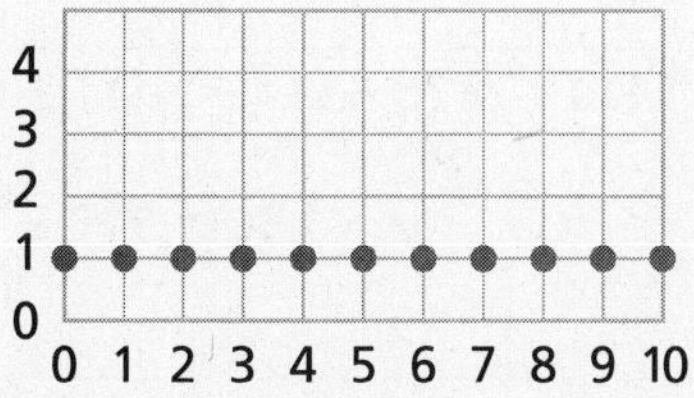

b. The equation $y = 1^x$ looks like other exponential equations, but the pattern in the table—in which every value of 1^x is 1—and in the straight-line graph looks like a linear relationship.

34. a. $y = 3(2)^x$; the growth factor can be found by dividing the y-values: $12 \div 6 = 2$. The y-intercept can be found by dividing the y-value for $x = 1$, which is 6, by the growth factor of 2. So the y-intercept is (0, 3).

b. $y = 10(3)^x$; the growth factor can be found by dividing the y-values: $270 \div 90 = 3$. The y-intercept can be found by dividing the y-value for $x = 1$, which is 30, by the growth factor of 3. So the y-intercept is (0, 10).

35. a. Liang; at the end of 20 years, Liang would have $\$1{,}000{,}000(20) = \$20{,}000{,}000$, and Dinara would have $2^{20} - 1 = \$1{,}048{,}575$. Students will probably sum up the values for each year to find Dinara's total: $\$1 + \$2 + \ldots + \$2^{19} = \$1{,}048{,}575$. **Note:** Dinara receives dollars in salary, where n is the year number, and her total for the n years is $2^n - 1$.

b. Liang will continue to have a greater salary through year 25, when Dinara will overtake her with \$33,554,431 to Liang's \$25,000,000. **Note:** You may want to discuss with students a realistic time span for players in professional basketball. It is unusual for players to remain in high demand for 20 years or more. Salaries may even decrease after time.

c. Yes, Dinara's plan is exponential because the growth factor is 2. Leaping Liang's is not exponential because the growth rate is 1 (she gets the same amount of money each year).

Applications

1. a. **Growth of Wolf Population**

Year	Wolf Population
0	20
1	24
2	29
3	35
4	41
5	50
6	60

b. $p = 20(1.2)^t$, where p is the population and t is the number of years

c. about 9 years

2. a. The growth factor for the elk population is approximately 1.9. This is because $\frac{57}{30} \approx \frac{108}{57} \approx \frac{206}{108} \approx \frac{391}{206} \approx \frac{743}{391} \approx 1.9$

b. After 10 years, there would be $30 \times (1.9)^{10} \approx 18{,}393$ elk. After 15 years, there would be $30 \times (1.9)^{15} \approx 455{,}434$ elk.

c. $p = 30 \times (1.9)^n$

d. After 16 years, the population is around 865,324 elk. After 17 years, the population is around 1,644,116 elk, so sometime between 16 and 17 years the population exceeds one million. Some industrious students might find by guess-and-check that the population exceeds one million after 16.225 years, or approximately 16 years and 3 months.

3. Between 1 and 2 years. $100(1.5) = 150$, and $100(1.5)^2 = 225$. Students may want to use a graph, a table, or guess-and-check to find a more precise answer: 1.71 years.

4. $p = 500{,}000 \times (1.6)^n$ (**Note:** This is not a good model as n gets large. In fact, in less than 500 years, it predicts there will be more squirrels than atoms in the universe.)

5. D

6. 1.3 years (**Note:** Students are likely to estimate the doubling time.)

7. 3.8 years (**Note:** Students are likely to estimate the doubling time.)

8. a.

$y = 50(2.2)^x$

x	0	1	2	3	4	5
y	50	110	242	532.4	1,171.3	2,576.8

$y = 350(1.7)^x$

x	0	1	2	3	4	5
y	350	595	1,011.5	1,719.6	2,923.2	4,969.5

b. In the first equation, the growth factor is 2.2. In the second, the growth factor is 1.7.

c. The graphs of these equations will cross because although the y-intercept of the first graph is lower, that graph is increasing at a faster rate.

d. The graphs will cross between $x = 7$ and $x = 8$. Some students might check carefully and find that the graphs cross at around $x = 7.547$.

9. a. **Maya's Savings Account**

Age	Value
0	\$100
1	\$104
2	\$108.16
3	\$112.49
4	\$116.99
5	\$121.67
6	\$126.53
7	\$131.59
8	\$136.86
9	\$142.33
10	\$148.02

b. 1.04

c. $a = 100(1.04)^n$, where a is the amount of money in the account and n is Maya's age.

10. 40%

11. 90%

12. 75%

13. 1.45

14. 1.9

15. 1.31

16. 1.25

17. **a.** 6 years; the projected population at that point is 1,340.

b. 6 years; the projected population at that time is 1,300. (**Note:** The linear equation $p = 1{,}000 + 50x$ models the problem, where p is the population in year x. Solving $1{,}300 = 1{,}000 + 50x$ shows that the population will outgrow the facilities in 6 years. You can also compare the two growth models by looking at tables for $y = 1{,}000(1.05)^x$ and $y = 1{,}000 + 50x$. This is particularly easy if you use a calculator to generate the tables. You might ask students to continue to scroll beyond the values for the first 6 years and see what they discover. Beyond that time, the exponential assumption will produce greater year-to-year growth.)

18. **a.** **Radios Sold**

Year	Number of Radios
1	1,000,000
2	1,030,000
3	1,060,900
4	1,092,727
5	1,125,509
6	1,159,274
7	1,194,052

b. **Radios Sold**

Year	Number of Radios
1	100,000
2	103,000
3	106,090
4	109,273
5	112,551
6	115,927
7	119,405

19. **a.** about \$8.72 (**Note:** The related equation is $p = 7(1.045)^t$, where p is the price of the ticket and t is the time in years; when $t = 5$, p is about \$8.72.)

b. about \$10.87 after 10 years; about \$26.22 after 30 years

c. 30 years

20. 100%

21. A. Choice A results in about 72% total growth over the 8 years. Choices B and C each give about the same total growth: 70%. Some students may find the amount at the end of each plan and compare the ending amounts.

22. **a.** initial value: \$130; growth rate: 7%, growth factor: 1.07; number of years: 5

b. \$223.36

23. Expressed as percents, the growth factors are Carlos: 114%; Mila: 125%; and Latanya: 300%.

a. Latanya's mice are reproducing most quickly.

b. Carlos's mice are reproducing most slowly.

Connections

24. $3,600

25. $300

26. $3,325

27. This pattern represents exponential growth because each value is the previous value times a growth factor of 1.1.

28. This pattern represents exponential growth because each value is the previous value times a growth factor of $\frac{5}{3}$.

29. This pattern does not represent exponential growth because there is no constant by which each value is multiplied to find the next value. The pattern is in fact linear, with an addition of $\frac{5}{3}$ for each term.

30. Answers may vary. A student could argue that the growth factor is approximately 3.2 and be correct. If this were "real world" data, most people (for most purposes) would consider this exponential growth. Another student might say that since there is variation in the growth factor between 3.18 and 3.22, this does not represent exponential growth.

31. a. 3% raise: $600; 4% raise: $800; 5% raise: $1,000

 b. 3% raise: $20,600; 4% raise: $20,800; 5% raise: $21,000

 c. Possible answer: Because 103% = 100% + 3%, 103% of $20,000 is the same as 100% of $20,000 plus 3% of $20,000. This means the same as $20,000 + (3% of $20,000). Or, since 103% = 1.03, you can reason as follows:

 103% of $20,000 = 1.03($20,000)

 = 1($20,000) + 0.03($20,000)

 = $20,000 + 0.03($20,000)

 = $20,000 + (3% of $20,000)

32. a. The bars represent the number of subscribers for each year.

 b. The implied curve represents the pattern of growth in the total number of subscribers.

 c. Answers will vary. At a glance, the pattern of change looks like exponential growth, but you cannot determine equal ratios from the graph. The 15-year growth is about 1300%, which gives an annual growth rate of about 19%. Note that the ratios of the numbers of subscribers in successive years appear to be approximately $\frac{30}{20}$, $\frac{40}{30}$, $\frac{49}{40}$, $\frac{60}{49}$, $\frac{75}{60}$, $\frac{95}{75}$, etc. These are not equal, so the pattern is not exactly an exponential function, but it can be approximated by an exponential function. It is not linear.

 d. The growth between these two years is only about 7%, a growth factor of 1.07. This is significantly less than the growth factor in the preceding years.

 e. One explanation is that many people are now using cell phones instead of landlines, and some people may have more than one subscription (for example, a business and a personal phone). Also, at some point, there may be a saturation point, when everyone has a cell phone.

33. a. The length of the diagonal is 5 cm, and the area of the shaded region is 6 cm^2.

b. For the enlargement, the length of the diagonal is 5.5 cm, and the area of the shaded region is 7.26 cm^2.

(**Note:** As each linear dimension increases by a factor of 1.1 (a 10% increase), the area increases by $(1.1)^2 = 1.21$.)

c. After five enlargements, the length of the diagonal is about 8.05 cm, and the area of the shaded region is about 15.56 cm^2.

d. Arturo is correct. For example, for the first few enlargements, the ratios are given here: $\frac{3}{4} = \frac{3.3}{4.4} = \frac{3.6}{4.84}$. The ratio is consistently $\frac{3}{4}$.

Esteban is incorrect because he is comparing a length measure to an area. Similarity requires a comparison of two length measures. If he had compared diagonal length to width, or diagonal length to length, Esteban would have been correct.

34. She is correct. If her salary the first summer is s, then under her plan, the second summer her salary will be $(1.04)s$ and $(1.03)(1.04)s$ the third summer, for a total of $s + (1.04)s + (1.03)(1.04)s$. Under the customer's plan, her total would be $s + (1.03)s + (1.04)(1.03)s$. Her earnings the third summer will be the same under both plans, but because she will make more money the second summer, her total earnings will be greater under her plan.

35. a. $\$9.00 \times 40 \times 52 = \$18{,}720$

b. $a = 360w$ (**Note:** Some students may include the paid vacation time and write the equation $a = 360w + 720$.)

c. She is trying to figure out how many weeks she needs to work in order to earn $9,000. The answer is 25 weeks.

d. **Kim's Salary**

Year	Annual Income
1	$18,720
2	$19,282
3	$19,860
4	$20,456
5	$21,070
6	$21,702
7	$22,353
8	$23,023
9	$23,714
10	$24,425

e. For the first 6 years, the $600-per-year raise plan is better. Under the $600-per-year plan, Kim would earn $21,720 in year 6 and $22,320 in year 7. In year 7, the salary for the 3% raise plan would be $22,353 and from then on would result in greater yearly salaries than the $600-per-year raise plan. The plan Kim chooses would depend on how many years she anticipates working for this company. (**Note:** Graphing the equations may not help students answer this question; for x-values from 0 to 10, both graphs look linear because the exponential growth is very slow for the first 10 years.)

36. 2.5 represents faster growth. 2.5 is greater than $25\% = \frac{1}{4}$. Note that the growth factor 2.5 represents the growth rate 1.5 or 150%. This is much faster than the growth rate 25%.

37. 130%, 1.475, $\frac{3}{2}$, 2

38. Answers may vary. Anything less than or equal to 88% (the scale factor that takes $8\frac{1}{2}$ to $7\frac{1}{2}$) will work.

39. a. Matches: 20% and 1.2; 120% and 2.2; 50% and 1.5; 400% and 5; 2% and 1.02. No match: 200%, 4, 2.

b. 2%, 20%, 50%, 120%, 200%, 400%

c. 1.02, 1.2, 1.5, 2, 2.2, 4, 5

Extensions

40. 2,500%. Because the growth factor is 26, the growth rate is 26 − 1, or 25, expressed as a percent, which is 2,500%.

41. a. According to these assumptions, in 2020, the population would be about 344.09 million.

b. about 70 years

c. The actual growth rate for this time period was less than that predicted by the model in this exercise.

42. a. Averaging the ratios gives a growth factor of

$$\left(\frac{3.02}{2.76}+\frac{3.33}{3.02}+\frac{3.69}{3.33}+\frac{4.07}{3.69}+\frac{4.43}{4.07}+\frac{4.83}{4.43}+\frac{5.26}{4.83}+\frac{5.67}{5.26}+\frac{6.07}{5.67}+\frac{6.46}{6.07}+\frac{6.84}{6.46}\right)\div 11 \approx 1.1$$

This is the growth factor for every 5 year increment, not for every 1 year.

b. $p = 2.76(1.1)^x$, where x is the number of 5-year intervals.

c. $p = 2.76(1.1)^8 \approx 5.92$ billion, so the population will double the 1955 population somewhere between 1990 and 1995 (the eighth 5-year period.)

d. When $x = 17$, $p = 2.76(1.1)^{17} \approx$ 13.95 billion, so the population will double the 2010 population somewhere between 2035 and 2040 (the seventeenth 5-year period). (**Note:** Doubling time is independent of the starting population.)

43. $p = 300(1.2)^t$, where p is the population and t is the year.

44. $p = 579(1.2)^t$, where p is the population and t is the year. Also, $p = 1{,}000(1.2)^{t-3}$ is acceptable.

45. $v = 2{,}413(1.03)^t$, where v is the value in the account and t is the year. Also, $v = 2{,}560(1.03)^{t-2}$ is acceptable.

46. a. Possible Answer: You could evaluate $(((1.5)^2)^2)^3$; in other words, multiply $1.5 \times 1.5 = 2.25$, then

$2.25 \times 2.25 = 5.0625$, and then

$5.0625 \times 5.0625 \times 5.0625 = 129.75$.

b. You have to press the × key 4 times to get the answer in the method outlined above.

47. a. $10,400

b. $10,406.04

c. $10,407.42. (**Note:** This is the exact answer using a growth factor of $1.00\overline{3} = \frac{1}{12}(0.04)$. However, students may round and use a growth factor of 1.003. This gives an answer of $10,366.00, which is significantly less. In compound growth situations, rounding leads to significantly different answers over time.)

d. He will earn more if he chooses the account for which interest is compounded monthly. The more often the interest is compounded, the faster the investment grows.

ACE Answers Investigation 4

Applications

1. **Areas of Ballots**

Number of Cuts	Area (in.^{2})
0	324
1	162
2	81
3	40.5
4	20.25
5	10.125
6	5.0625
7	2.53125
8	1.265625
9	0.6328125
10	0.31640625

a. $A = 324\left(\frac{1}{2}\right)^n$

b. 9 cuts

c. If the paper were at least 4,096 in.^{2}, he would be able to make 12 cuts: $1 \cdot 2^{12} = 4{,}096$.

2. Both arguments are correct. In an exponential function situation, an exponent of zero is defined for some value (the initial value). However, in an inverse variation situation, because *k* is chosen as some nonzero value, if $x = 0$, the equation $yx = k$ does not have a solution for *y*. The students may have made this conjecture because the general shape of the graph of an inverse variation situation can look like the graph of an exponential function. The second argument is also valid. In an exponential relationship, the two variables do not multiply together to give a constant. In an inverse variation, the two variables have a "factor-pair" relationship as seen in the equation $xy = k$, where *k* is a constant. Students might have made this conjecture since the graph of the exponential function is a curve that decreases from left to right.

3. a. **Latisha's Licorice**

Number of Friends	Licorice Remaining (in.)
1	12
2	6
3	3
4	1.5
5	0.75
6	0.375
7	0.1875
8	0.09375

b. **Latisha's Licorice**

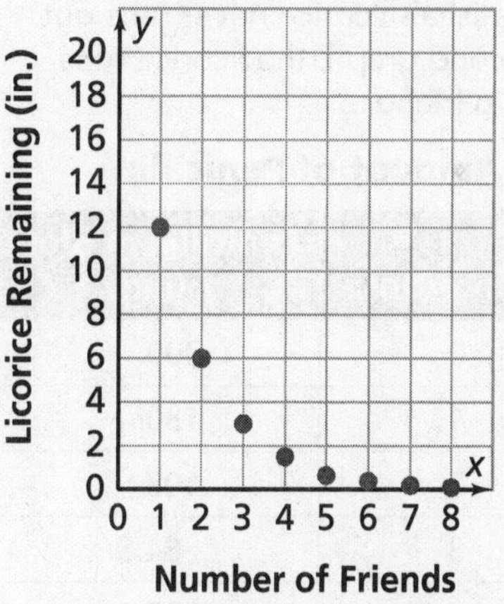

c. **Latisha's Licorice**

Number of Friends	Licorice Remaining (in.)
1	20
2	16
3	12
4	8
5	4
6	0

Latisha's Licorice

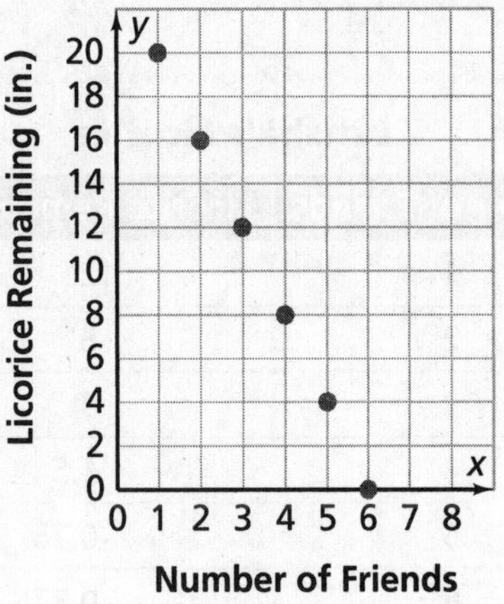

d. The first graph shows exponential decay; Latisha gave away less and less to each friend. The second graph is linear; each of the first six friends received the same amount. In the first graph, Latisha's licorice never runs out. In the second graph, the licorice runs out after 6 friends.

4. a. **Amount of Penicillin**

Days Since Dose	Penicillin in Blood (mg)
0	300
1	180
2	108
3	64.8
4	38.9
5	23.3
6	14.0
7	8.4

b. $d = 300(0.6)^m$

c. $d = 400(0.6)^m$, assuming the decay factor remains the same.

5. Exponential growth because $2.1 > 1$.

6. Exponential decay because $0.5 < 1$.

7. a. The decay factor is $\frac{1}{3}$ and the y-intercept is 300.

b. $y = 300\left(\frac{1}{3}\right)^x$

8. equation: $y = 24\left(\frac{1}{4}\right)^x$; decay factor: $\frac{1}{4}$; decay rate: $\frac{3}{4}$

9. equation: $y = 128\left(\frac{3}{4}\right)^x$; decay factor: $\frac{3}{4}$; decay rate: $\frac{1}{4}$

10. When $x = 1$, $y = 30$. Using the exponential equation $y = a(b)^x$, substitute the y-intercept 90 for a. Use the ordered pair and substitute 2 for x and 10 for y. Solve for b, the decay factor. The decay factor is $\frac{1}{3}$, so the equation is $y = 90\left(\frac{1}{3}\right)^x$. Substitute 1 for x to find y.

11. When $x = 4$, $y = \frac{5}{2}$. Using the exponential equation $y = a(b)^x$, substitute the y-intercept 40 for a. Use the ordered pair and substitute 2 for x and 10 for y. Solve for b, the decay factor. The decay factor is $\frac{1}{2}$, so the equation is $y = 40\left(\frac{1}{2}\right)^x$. Substitute 4 for x to find y.

12. When $x = -2$, $y = 1875$. Using the exponential equation $y = a(b)^x$, substitute the y-intercept 75 for a. Use the ordered pair and substitute 2 for x and 3 for y. Solve for b, the decay factor. The decay factor is $\frac{1}{5}$, so the equation is $y = 75\left(\frac{1}{5}\right)^x$. Substitute -2 for x to find y. **Note:** Students do not yet know that b^{-2} is the same as $\frac{1}{b^2}$, but they can still make sense of the negative exponent graphically.

13. When $x = 2$, $y = 0.64$. Using the exponential equation $y = a(b)^x$, substitute the y-intercept 64 for a. Use the ordered pair and substitute 3 for x and 0.064 for y. Solve for b, the decay factor. The decay factor is 0.1, so the equation is $y = 64(0.1)^x$. Substitute 2 for x to find y.

14. a. Karen thought her coupons would be used together (5% + 5% = 10% off), but that is not how coupons work. She received 5% off her original bill ($50), which made her bill $47.50. The cashier applied the next 5%-off coupon to this amount, not the original $50, so Karen's bill is $45.13.

b. $a = 50(0.95)^c$, where a represents the total amount Karen will spend and c represents the number of coupons she uses

c. $29.94

d. Students should have an answer in the 160–180 range. If Karen uses 160 coupons, her bill is $0.014. If she uses 170 coupons, her bill is $0.008. 180 coupons produces a cost of $0.00489 which would not round up to $0.01. (**Note:** You may wish to discuss with your students whether the groceries would ever really be free (with cost equal to $0).)

15. a.

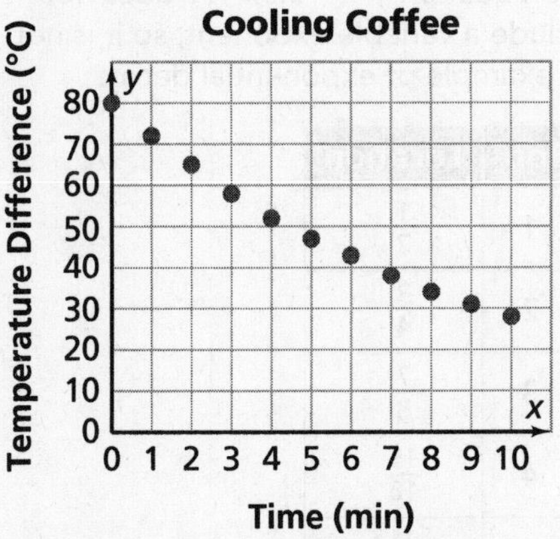

There is a slight curve in the graph, suggesting that the temperature dropped a bit more rapidly just after it was poured. The differences between the first several pairs of temperatures in the table reflect this pattern.

b. Averaging the ratios between successive temperature differences gives a decay factor of (0.90 + 0.90 + 0.89 + 0.90 + 0.90 + 0.91 + 0.88 + 0.89 + 0.91 + 0.90) ÷ 10 ≈ 0.90.

c. $d = 80(0.90)^n$, where d is temperature difference and n is time in minutes.

d. Theoretically, if the temperature decline followed an exponential pattern, the temperature would never exactly equal room temperature. However, the difference between coffee temperature and room temperature would have been less than 1°C after 42 minutes: $d = 80(0.90)^{42} = 0.96$°C

16. a. circumference $= \pi d = 5\pi \approx 15.7$ in, area $= \pi r^2 = 6.25\pi \approx 19.6$ in.^{2}

b. **Note:** Students may round answers in different ways and at different stages. This is a good opportunity to have a discussion about rounding.

Advertisement Pizza Sizes

Reduction Number	Diameter (in.)	Circumference (in.)	Area (in.^{2})
0	5.0	15.71	19.63
1	4.5	14.14	15.9
2	4.05	12.72	12.88
3	3.65	11.47	10.46
4	3.28	10.3	8.45
5	2.95	9.27	6.83

c. diameter $= 5(0.9)^n$;

circumference $= 15.7(0.9)^n$;

area $= 19.6(0.81)^n$

d. diameter $= 5(0.75)^n$;

circumference $= 15.7(0.75)^n$;

area $= 19.6(0.5625)^n$

e. $0.75 = \frac{3}{4}$; $0.5625 = \frac{9}{16}$

f. Possible answer: Yes; you can represent a 10% reduction by the expression $x - 0.10x$; you can represent 90% of original size by $0.9x$. These expressions are equivalent. (**Note:** Common language is somewhat ambiguous about the meaning of "reduction in size." If you mean reduction in dimensions, the reasoning above applies. If you mean reduction in area, it does not apply.)

17. a. 0.8; this is less than 0.9, so its product with any number will be less than the product of the same number and 0.9.

b. $\frac{2}{10}$ $\frac{2}{9}$ $(0.8)^4$ $(0.9)^4$ $(0.9)^2$ 0.84 90%

18. a. Yes, to find the growth factor of an exponential function, you divide the y-value by the previous y-value. $\frac{y_2}{y_1}$ is the growth (or decay) factor for each $(x_2 - x_1)$ unit. This is similar to defining linear growth rate, in that you need to have a change of 1 unit in x-values.

b. No, for linear relationships the growth factor is the slope, which you find by computing the change in the y-values divided by the change in the x-values.

Connections

19. molecules: 3.34×10^{22}

20. red blood cells: 2.5×10^{13}

21. Earth to sun: 9.3×10^7 mi; 1.5×10^8 km

22. size of Milky Way: 1.0×10^5 years; number of stars: 3.0×10^{11}

23. a.

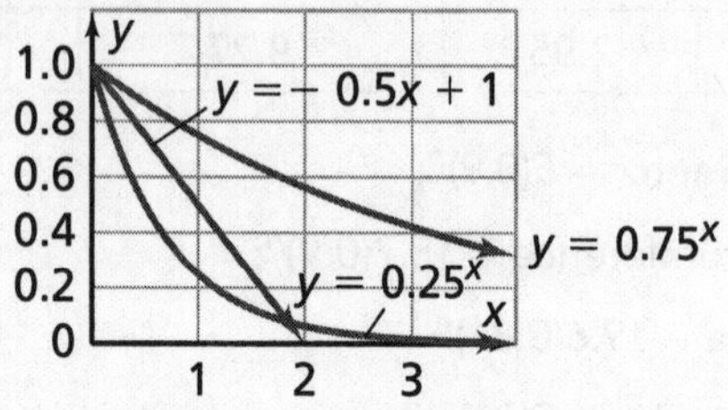

b. The three graphs intersect at the point (0, 1). The graphs of $y = -0.5x + 1$ and $y = (0.25)^x$ also intersect at about (1.85, 0.075). In Quadrant II, there is a point of intersection for $y = -0.5x + 1$ and $y = (0.75)^x$.

c. The graph of $y = (0.25)^x$ decreases faster than that of $y = -0.5x + 1$ until about $x = 0.7$. The graph of $y = -0.5x + 1$ decreases the fastest for x-values greater than 0.7.

d. Because the graph of $y = -0.5x + 1$ is a straight line, it is not an example of exponential decay.

e. The equation $y = -0.5x + 1$ does not include a variable exponent, so it is not an example of exponential decay.

24. a.

Hop	Location
1	$\frac{1}{2}$
2	$\frac{3}{4}$
3	$\frac{7}{8}$
4	$\frac{15}{16}$
5	$\frac{31}{32}$
6	$\frac{63}{64}$
7	$\frac{127}{128}$
8	$\frac{255}{256}$
9	$\frac{511}{512}$
10	$\frac{1,023}{1,024}$

b. $1 - \left(\frac{1}{2}\right)^n$ or $\frac{2^n - 1}{2^n}$

c. No, the numerator is always 1 less than the denominator. This means that the fraction approaches, but never reaches, 1.

Extensions

25. Note: A table is helpful for answering these questions. Also, this would be a good time for students to learn how to display an answer in fractional form on their calculators. The decimal form of $\left(\frac{2}{3}\right)^5$ is 0.1316872428, which is not very helpful when one is looking for patterns. To convert a displayed decimal to a fraction on a TI-73, enter the decimal and then press $F \longleftrightarrow D$ and then ENTER.

a. $\frac{32}{243}$

b. $1 - \frac{32}{243} = \frac{211}{243}$

c. $m = \left(\frac{2}{3}\right)^w$

d. $m = 1 - \left(\frac{2}{3}\right)^w$

e. The graphs are mirror images of each other across the line $y = 0.5$. One approaches the x-axis, showing that the moisture remaining approaches 0; the other approaches the line $y = 1$, showing that the moisture removed approaches 100%

Drying Lumber

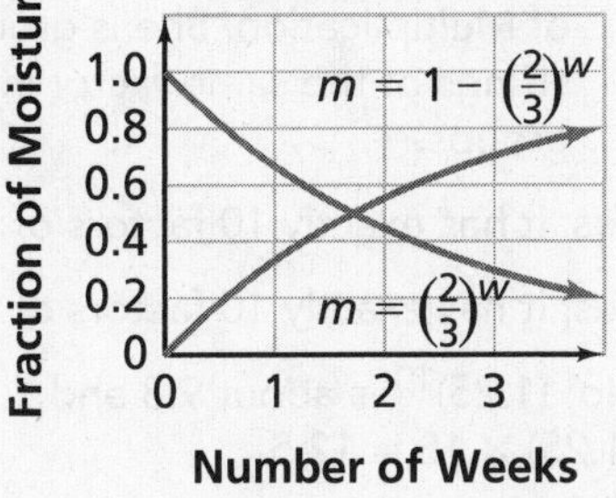

f. moisture remaining $= \left(\frac{3}{4}\right)^w$; moisture removed $= 1 - \left(\frac{3}{4}\right)^w$

g. These graphs are also mirror images across the line $y = 0.5$. They are stretched out farther to the right, which indicates that the moisture removal proceeds more slowly.

Drying Lumber

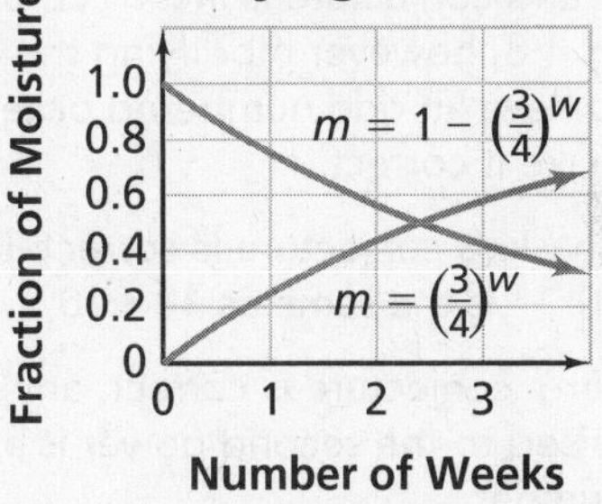

h. Possible answer: The lumber needs to go from a moisture content of 40% to one of 10%. For the first kiln, the equation is $0.1 = 0.4\left(\frac{2}{3}\right)^w$. Because $0.4\left(\frac{2}{3}\right)^3 \approx 11.9\%$ and $0.4\left(\frac{2}{3}\right)^4 \approx 7.9\%$, the first kiln would produce this loss in 3 to 4 weeks.

For the second kiln, the equation is $0.1 = 0.4\left(\frac{3}{4}\right)^w$. Since $0.4\left(\frac{3}{4}\right)^3 \approx 12.7\%$ and $0.4\left(\frac{3}{4}\right)^5 \approx 9.5\%$, the second kiln would produce this loss in 4 to 5 weeks.

Amount of Moisture

Week	Fraction of Moisture Removed	Total Fraction of Moisture Removed	Fraction of Moisture Remaining
1	$\frac{1}{3}$	$\frac{1}{3}$	$\frac{2}{3}$
2	$\frac{1}{3} \times \frac{2}{3} = \frac{2}{9}$	$\frac{1}{3} + \frac{2}{9} = \frac{5}{9}$	$\frac{4}{9}$
3	$\frac{1}{3} \times \frac{4}{9} = \frac{4}{27}$	$\frac{5}{9} + \frac{4}{27} = \frac{19}{27}$	$\frac{8}{27}$
4	$\frac{1}{3} \times \frac{8}{27} = \frac{8}{81}$	$\frac{19}{27} + \frac{8}{81} = \frac{65}{81}$	$\frac{16}{81}$
5	$\frac{1}{3} \times \frac{16}{81} = \frac{16}{243}$	$\frac{65}{81} + \frac{16}{243} = \frac{211}{243}$	$\frac{32}{243}$

ACE Answers Investigation 5

Applications

1. Heidi's conjecture is correct; any value of 1^x will always equal 1.

   Evan's conjecture is correct; students might argue that it is the largest number in its row and column, so it will be the largest overall.

   Jean's conjecture is incorrect, because $2^3 = 8$, however modifying the conjecture to have an odd numbered base would make it correct.

   Chaska's conjecture is correct, because 10^{n+1} is the same as $10 \cdot 10^n$.

   Tim's conjecture is correct; any number raised to the second power is a square number.

   Roger's conjecture is incorrect, because any number in this column has a 2 (actually many 2's) in its prime factorization, making it even.

2. B

3. 40^6

4. 7^{15}

5. 8^5

6. True; this is an example of $a^m \times a^n = a^{m+n}$ and so $6^3 \times 6^5 = 6^{3+5} = 6^8$.

7. False; $2^3 \times 3^2 = 8 \times 9 = 72$ and $72 \neq 6^5$.

8. True; $3^8 = (3 \times 3)(3 \times 3)(3 \times 3)(3 \times 3) = (3^2)^4 = 9^4$.

9. False; $4^3 + 5^3 = 64 + 125 = 189$ and $189 \neq 9^3$.

10. True; by the Distributive Property, $2^3(1 + 2^2) = (2^3 \times 1) + (2^3 \times 2^2) = 2^3 + 2^5$. Or students may evaluate both sides and find that both sides are equal to 40.

11. False; $\frac{5^{12}}{5^4} = 5^8 \neq 5^3$

12. H

13. 8; because $4^{15} \times 3^{15} = (4 \times 3)^{15} = 12^{15}$, the ones digit is the same as the units digit for $2^{15} = 32,768$.

14. 8; the ones digits for powers of 7 occur in cycles of 7, 9, 3, and 1. Because 15 divided by 4 leaves a remainder of 3, the ones digit of 7^{15} is the third digit in the cycle which is 3. The ones digits for powers of 4 occur in cycles of 4 and 6. Because 20 is evenly divisible by 2, the ones digit of 4^{20} is the second digit in the cycle, which is 6. So, the ones digit of $7^{15} \times 4^{20}$ is the ones digit of $3 \times 6 = 18$.

15. a. Manuela is correct because $2^{10} = 1,024$ and $2^4 \times 2^6 = 16 \times 64 = 1,024$.

    b. Possible answers:
    $2^2 \times 2^8 = 4 \times 256 = 1,024$
    $2^3 \times 2^7 = 8 \times 128 = 1,024$
    $2^2 \times 2^2 \times 2^6 = 4 \times 4 \times 64 = 1,024$

    c. 4096; because $2^7 = 128$ and $2^5 = 32$, 2^{12} would equal $2^7 \times 2^5 = 128 \times 32 = 4,096$.

    d. It works for other cases because you are just using the Associative Property of Multiplication. She is grouping strings of the same factor into two groups.

16. Yes; it has exactly 10 factors of 1.25.

17. Yes; it has exactly 10 factors of 1.25.

18. No; $(1.25)^{10}$ is about 9.3 and $(1.25) \times 10 = 12.5$.

19. No; $(1.25)^{10}$ is about 9.3 and $(1.25) + 10 = 11.25$.

20. Yes; $(1.25^5)^2 = 1.25^5 \times 1.25^5$ which has exactly 10 factors of 1.25.

21. No; $1.25^5 \times 1.25^5$ has exactly seven factors of 1.25, so it is equal to $(1.25)^7$, not $(1.25)^{10}$.

22. Yes; it has exactly 7 factors of 1.5

23. Yes; it has exactly 7 factors of 1.5.

24. No; $(1.5)^7$ is about 17 and $1.5 \times 7 = 10.5$.

25. No; $(1.5)^7$ is about 17 and $1.5 + 7 = 8.5$.

26. Both students are correct. For Stu, finding the fourth root might be easier first, because 81^3 is a somewhat large number. Carrie's solution is in many ways treating $\frac{7}{3}$ as if it was a mixed number, $2\frac{1}{3}$.

27. 756; the expressions simplifies to 756^1.

28. 342, because $342^{\frac{5}{2}} \div 342^{\frac{3}{2}} = 342^{\frac{5}{2}-\frac{3}{2}} = 342^{\frac{2}{2}} = 342^1$.

29. 1, because $3^{35} \cdot 3^{-35} = 3^0 = 1$.

30. 1, because $\left(\frac{1}{2}\right)^{40} = 2^{-40}$ so $\left(\frac{1}{2}\right)^{40} \cdot 2^{40} = 2^{-40} \cdot 2^{40} = 2^0 = 1$.

31. Sometimes true, for example for $n = 1$, both sides equal 4. However, for $n = 2$ the left side equals 16, and the right side equals 8.

32. Always true; any number times itself is the same as the square of the number.

33. Always false, because $2^n = 2 \cdot 2^{n-1}$.

34. Sometimes true. When $b = 2$, it is false as in Exercise 33. If $b = \frac{1}{2}$, then $\left(\frac{1}{2}\right)^n = \frac{1}{2}\left(\frac{1}{2}\right)^{n-1}$, so it is true for $b = \frac{1}{2}$.

35. Always true

36. Sometimes true; true when $b > 1$ (as in part (e)), however, if $0 < b < 1$, then for a negative value of x, $b^x > 1$.

37 a. $p = 0.02(1.05)^n$

b. 1900: $p = 0.02(1.05)^{33} = \$0.10$;
2000: $p = 0.02(1.05)^{133} = \$13.16$

c. \$1: 1947; \$100: 2041

d. 1420 years later, or in the year 3287

38. a. $n = \frac{1}{12}$, $v = \$7{,}229{,}333.69$

b. $n = \frac{1}{6}$, $v = \$7{,}258{,}786.89$

c. $n = \frac{1}{2}$, $v = \$7{,}377{,}804.55$

d. $n = \frac{5}{4}$, $v = \$7{,}652{,}778.09$

e. $n = \frac{5}{3}$, $v = \$7{,}809{,}945.35$

39.

Standard Form	Exponential Form
10,000	10^4
1,000	10^3
100	10^2
10	10^1
1	10^0
$\frac{1}{10} = 0.1$	10^{-1}
$\frac{1}{100} = 0.01$	10^{-2}
$\frac{1}{1{,}000} = 0.001$	10^{-3}
$\frac{1}{10{,}000} = 0.0001$	10^{-4}
$\frac{1}{100{,}000} = 0.00001$	10^{-5}
$\frac{1}{1{,}000{,}000} = 0.000001$	10^{-6}

40. 0.3, 0.015, 0.0015

41. a. 0.12, 0.012, 0.0012, 0.000000012

b. Because $1.2 \times 10^{-n} = 1.2 \times \frac{1}{10^n}$, the standard form is 1.2 divided by the nth power of 10. When dividing by a power of 10, the decimal point in the number moves to the left. Because 1.2 is divided by nth power of 10, the decimal place is moved to the left n places; thus

$$1.2 \times \frac{1}{10^n} = \underbrace{0.0000\ldots0000}_{n-1 \text{ zeros}}12$$

42. a. $2{,}000{,}000 = 2 \times 10^6$

b. $28{,}000{,}000 = 2.8 \times 10^7$

c. $19{,}900{,}000{,}000 = 1.99 \times 10^{10}$

d. $0.12489 = 1.2489 \times 10^{-1}$

e. $0.0058421998 = 5.8421998 \times 10^{-3}$

f. $0.0010201 = 1.0201 \times 10^{-3}$

43. a. Possible answer: $\frac{1.5 \times 10^{-4}}{10^8}$

b. Possible answer: $1.5 \times 10^{-4} \times 10^{-8}$

44. a. 1,740,000 meters

b. 1.0795×10^{-1}m = 0.10795 m.

c. The scale that would make the image fit exactly is 6.204×10^{-8}. Any scale factor smaller than this will make the image small enough to fit.

d. About 0.025 : 1

45. $2^8 = 256$, or 2.56×10^2.

b. $\left(\frac{1}{2}\right)^8 = \frac{1}{256} = 2^{-8}$,
or $0.00390625 = 3.90625 \times 10^{-3}$.

c. $20^8 = 25{,}600{,}000{,}000$, or 2.56×10^{10}

d. $\left(\frac{1}{20}\right)^8 = \frac{1}{25{,}6000{,}000{,}000} = 20^{-8}$
or 0.0000000000390625,
or 3.90625×10^{-11}

46. a. $3\frac{1}{3}, 1\frac{1}{9}, \frac{10}{27}, \frac{10}{81}, \frac{10}{243}, \frac{10}{729}, \frac{10}{2{,}187}$

b. This means $5.645029269 \times 10^{-5}$. In standard notation, it is 0.00005645029269.

c. 4.57×10^{-3}, 1.52×10^{-3}, 5.08×10^{-4}, 1.69×10^{-4}

47. $\frac{1}{2}(2)^n = 2^{-1} \cdot 2^n = 2^{n-1}$

48. $4^{n-1} = 4^n \cdot 4^{-1} = 4^{-1} \cdot 4^n = \frac{1}{4}(4)^n$

49. $25(5^{n-2}) = 5^2 \cdot 5^{n-2} = 5^{n-2+2} = 5^n$

50. a. 4.10×10^{11} gallons $\times 365 \approx$ 1.496×10^{14} gallons

b. $(1.28 \times 10^{11}) \div (2.14 \times 10^9) \approx 59.8$

c. $4.10 \times 10^{11} \times 0.80 \times 30 = 9.84 \times 10^{12}$

51. 1.722×10^8

52. 2.1×10^{13}

53. 2.8×10^{-2}

54. 3.5×10^3

55. 2.5×10^{-2}

56. 2×10^{-8}

57. 4×10^4

58. $g = 2.5$, $h = 9$

59. $j = 5$, $k = -1$

60. $m = 1.2$, $n = 2$

61. $p = 3$, $h = 8$

62. $r = 4$, $s = 2$

63. The graphs of $y = 4^x$ and $y = 10(4^x)$ have the same growth factor of 4, so they are both exponential growth patterns. The graphs $y = 0.25^x$ and $y = 10(0.25^x)$ are exponential decay patterns and have the same decay factor of 0.25. The graphs of $y = 4^x$ and $y = 0.25^x$ have a *y*-intercept of (0,1). The graphs of $y = 10(4^x)$ and $y = 10(0.25^x)$ have *y*-intercepts (0,10).

64. a. The graph is stretched vertically by a factor of 5. The *y*-values are all 5 times as far from zero (or 5 times greater than the original), though the growth factor is the same, 2.

b. This is the same as 10^x, so it should look like the graph is stretched vertically. The *y*-intercept remains the same, but the growth factor is now 5 times what it was.

c. The $\frac{1}{2}$ multiplies each *y*-value of the original graph, so it should reduce the values by a factor of $\frac{1}{2}$.

d. This graph changes the sign of all the original *y*-values resulting in a flip over the *x*-axis.

e. This graph flips the original graph over the *y*-axis.

65. a. Graph B

b. Graph C

66. a. Grandville: 799; multiply 1000 by $0.96^{5.5}$.
Tinytown: 124; multiply 100 by $1.04^{5.5}$.

b. Around 66 years; $100 \cdot 1.04^{66} \approx 1331$.

c. Yes; the two towns will have the same populations if they continue to change at the same rates. Even though Grandville has a greater starting population, its population is decreasing, while Tinytown's population is increasing. So, eventually the graphs will cross. However, it will take about 28 years for this to happen.

Connections

67. 10 zeros

68. 50 zeros

69. 100 zeros

70. 6

71. 7

Note: Students may use their calculators for Exercises 72–74, but they should be able to use the rules of exponents and some estimation or mental arithmetic. The reasoning for $6^9 > 9^6$, for example, might look like this:

$6^9 = (2 \times 3)^9 = 2^9 \times 3^9 = 2^9 \times 3^3 \times 3^6$
and
$9^6 = (3 \times 3)^6 = 3^6 \times 3^6 = 3^3 \times 3^3 \times 3^6$
Comparing these comes down to comparing 2^9 and 3^3. Because $2^9 > 3^3$, $6^9 > 9^6$.

72. 7^{10}

73. 8^{10}

74. 6^9

75. False; since $1.56892 \times 10^5 = 156{,}892$ is greater than $2.3456 \times 10^4 = 23{,}456$, the difference is greater than zero.

76. False; since $3.96395 \times 10^5 = 396{,}395$ is less than $2.888211 \times 10^7 = 28{,}882{,}110$, the quotient is less than 1.

77. a. Volume: 8 units^3; surface area: 24 units^2; the side lengths increase to 2 units. The new volume is 2^3 units^3 = $2 \times 2 \times 2$ units^3 = 8 units^3. Because there are six square faces, each with area 2^2 units^2 = 4 units^2, the total surface area is $6 \cdot 2^2$ units^3 = 24 units^3.

b. Volume: 27 units^3; surface area: 54 units^2; the side lengths increase to 3 units. The new volume is 3^3 units^3 = $3 \cdot 3 \cdot 3$ units^3 = 27 units^3, and the new surface area is $6 \cdot 3^2$ units^2 = 54 units^2.

c. Volume: 1,000,000 units^3; surface area: 60,000 units^2; the side lengths increase to 100 units each. The new volume is 100^3 units^3 = $100 \cdot 100 \cdot 100$ units^3 = 1,000,000 units^3, and the new surface area is $6 \cdot 100^2$ units^2 = 60,000 units^2.

78. a. 8π units^3; the resulting cylinder has a radius of 2 units and a height of 2 units so the volume is $\pi(2)^2 \times 2$ units^3 = 8π units^3.

b. 27π units^3; the resulting cylinder has a radius of 3 units and a height of 3 units so the volume is $\pi(3)^2 \times 3$ units^3 = 27π units^3.

c. $1{,}000{,}000\pi$ units^3; the resulting cylinder will have a radius of 100 units and a height of 100 units, so $V = \pi(100)^2 \times 100$ units^3 = $1{,}000{,}000\pi$ units^3.

79. a. The following are prime: $2^2 - 1 = 3$; $2^3 - 1 = 7$; $2^5 - 1 = 31$.

b. Other primes that fit this pattern include $2^7 - 1 = 127$ and $2^{13} - 1 = 8{,}191$.

80. a. The sum of the proper factors of 2^2 is 3.

b. The sum of the proper factors for 2^3, or 8, is $1 + 2 + 4 = 7$.

c. The sum of the proper factors for 2^4, or 16, is $1 + 2 + 4 + 8 = 15$.

d. The sum of the proper factors for 2^5, or 32, is $1 + 2 + 4 + 8 + 16 = 31$.

e. The sum of the proper factors of a power of 2 is always 1 less than the number.

81. a. Possible answer:
$\frac{3(10)^5}{10^7} = 3 \times 10^{-2} = 0.03 = \frac{3}{100}$.

b. Possible answer:
$\frac{5(10)^5}{25(10)^7} = 2 \times 10^{-3} = .002 = \frac{2}{1000} = \frac{1}{500}$.

ACE ANSWERS 5

Extensions

82. 1; the ones digits for powers of 7 cycle through 7, 9, 3, and 1. Because the exponent, 100, is a multiple of 4, the ones digit will match the fourth number in the cycle, which is 1.

83. 6; the only possibility for the units digit for a power of 6 is 6.

84. 1; the ones digits for powers of 7 cycle through 7, 9, 3, and 1. The same is true for powers of 17. Because the exponent, 100, is a multiple of 4, the ones digit will match the fourth number in the cycle, which is 1. 7^{100} and 17^{100} have the same units digit.

85. 1; to get successive powers of 31, you repeatedly multiply by 31. The ones digit is always 1 times the previous ones digit. So the ones digit is always a power of 1, or 1.

86. 6; the possibilities for the ones digit when the base is 12 are the same as when the base is 2. So the ones digits cycle through 2, 4, 8 and 6. Because the exponent, 100, is a multiple of 4, the ones digit will be the fourth number in the cycle, which is 6.

87. 7; the possibilities for a include values with ones digits 3 or 7, because the ones digit in 823,543 is 3. Since 823,543 has 6 digits and the power is 7, 3 is too small, so a must equal 7. (17 or 27 or 37 etc. is too large.)

88. 11; *a* could be any number with a ones digit equal to 1, 3, 7 or 9. Since 1,771,561 has 7 digits and $10^6 = 1{,}000{,}000$ has 7 digits, *a* must be greater than 10 but close to 10, so *a* is 11.

89. Possible answer: The ones digit is 9. The ones digits for the powers of 3 cycle through the pattern 3, 9, 7, 1, 3, 9, 7, 1 . . . So 3^{28} will end in a 1, 3^{29} will end in a 3, and 3^{30} will end in 9.

90. C; square numbers have a ones digit of 1, 4, 9, 6, 5 or 0. So 1,392 is not a square number. However, 289 and 10,000 could be square numbers since they end in 0 and 9; in fact $17^2 = 289$ and $100^2 = 10{,}000$.

91. a. Row 1: $\frac{1}{2}$, row 2: $\frac{3}{4}$, row 3: $\frac{7}{8}$, row 4: $\frac{15}{16}$

b. $\frac{1}{2} + \left(\frac{1}{2}\right)^2 + \left(\frac{1}{2}\right)^3 + \left(\frac{1}{2}\right)^4 + \left(\frac{1}{2}\right)^5 = \frac{31}{32}$

c. $\frac{1{,}023}{1{,}024}$, $\frac{1{,}048{,}575}{1{,}048{,}576}$

d. The sum of each row is a fraction with a denominator equal to 2 raised to the power of that row number, and a numerator that is 1 less than the denominator. In the *n*th row, the sum will be $\frac{2^n - 1}{2^n}$.

e. Row 4

f. 1

g. The pattern is similar to adding the areas of one of the ballots produced by each cut. It may appear that this total area will eventually equal the area of the original sheet, but the pattern demonstrates that the total of the areas of the ballots will never actually equal the area of the whole piece.

92. a.

Number of Cuts	Area (ft^2)
0	1
1	$\frac{1}{2}$
2	$\frac{1}{4}$
3	$\frac{1}{8}$
4	$\frac{1}{16}$
5	$\frac{1}{32}$
6	$\frac{1}{64}$
7	$\frac{1}{128}$
8	$\frac{1}{256}$

b. $A = \left(\frac{1}{2}\right)^n$

c. About 9.54×10^{-7} ft^2. **Note:** this doesn't make sense, because a piece of paper could not be cut this small.

93. About \$71.42 per acre; the growth factor is 1.04. The cost has been increasing for 200 years (2003 − 1803 = 200). Find the initial price per sq. mi:
\$15,000,000 ÷ 828,000 sq. mi ≈ \$18.13 per sq. mile.
To get the initial price per acre, divide this value by 640: \$18.13 per sq. mile ÷ 640 acres per sq. mile ≈ \$0.028 per acre.
Thus, the value of 1 acre of land in 2006 is $(\$.028)(1.04)^{200} = (\$.028)(2551) \approx \$71.42$.

ACE ANSWERS 5

Index

Notes